Air Transport and Regional Development Case Studies

This book is one of three inter-connected books related to a four-year European Cooperation in Science and Technology (COST) Action established in 2015. The Action, called Air Transport and Regional Development (ATARD), aimed to promote a better understanding of how the air transport related problems of core regions and remote regions should be addressed in order to enhance both economic competitiveness and social cohesion in Europe.

This book focuses on case studies in Europe related to air transport and regional development. It is divided into four geographical regions after a general chapter that compares regional air transport connectivity between remote and central areas in Europe. The first region is Northern and Western Northern Europe (case studies related specifically to Norway, Finland, the United Kingdom, and Ireland); the second is Central and Eastern Europe, (Bulgaria, Bosnia and Herzegovina, and Poland); the third is Central Western Europe (Belgium and Switzerland); and finally, the fourth is Southern Europe (Portugal, Spain, and Italy). There is no other single source publication that currently covers this topic area in such a comprehensive manner by considering so many countries.

The book aims at becoming a major reference source on the topic, drawing from experienced researchers in the field, covering the diverse experience and knowledge of the members of the COST Action. The book will appeal to academics, practitioners, and policymakers who have a particular interest in acquiring detailed comparative knowledge and understanding of air transport and regional development in many different European countries. Together with the other two books (*Air Transport and Regional Development Methodologies* and *Air Transport and Regional Development Policies*), it fills a much-needed gap in the literature.

Anne Graham is Professor of Air Transport and Tourism Management at the University of Westminster, UK. She has two main research areas: first, airport management, economics, and regulation; and second, the relationship between the tourism and aviation sectors. She has published widely with recent books including *Air Transport: A Tourism Perspective*, *Airport Finance and Investment in the Global Economy*, *Managing Airports: An International Perspective*, *The Routledge Companion to Air Transport Management*, and *Airport Marketing*. She is a previous editor-in-chief of the *Journal of Air Transport Management* and in 2016 was made a fellow of the Air Transport Research Society.

Nicole Adler is Full Professor and Head of the Department of Operations Research and Operations Management at the School of Business Administration of Hebrew University in Jerusalem. Her major research interests include game theory and productivity estimation applied to the field of transportation. Her work has analysed hub-and-spoke airline competition and mergers, public service obligation tenders, and airport productivity, and she recently has utilised game theoretic concepts in order to understand air traffic control markets. Nicole is currently an Associate Editor for *Transportation Research Part B: Methodological*.

Hans-Martin Niemeier is Director of the Institute for Transport and Development at Bremen University of Applied Sciences, Germany. He is Chairman of the German Aviation Research Society and member of the Advisory Board of the European Aviation Conference. He chaired the ATARD COST Action from 2016–2019. From 2014 through May 2019, he was member of the Performance Review Body of the Single European Sky. He has published on privatisation, regulation, and competition of airports, the reform of slot allocation, and airline and airport alliances.

Ofelia Betancor is Associate Professor of Economics in the Department of Applied Economics at the University of Las Palmas de Gran Canaria (Spain). She holds an MSc in economics from the University of London, and two doctorate degrees in economics (Institute for Transport Studies-University of Leeds and University of Las Palmas). She has participated in many research projects at the national and international level, and has also collaborated with the World Bank and the Inter-American Development Bank as specialist in air transport and the economic evaluation of projects and transport policies. The results of her works have been published in leading journals in the area of transport economics.

António Pais Antunes is Professor in the Department of Civil Engineering at the University of Coimbra (Portugal). He has been Visiting Fellow at Princeton University, Invited Professor at EPF Lausanne, Visiting Professor at MIT and a visiting researcher at the University of Bergamo. His teaching and research focus on public facility location, urban mobility (notably public transport and vehicle sharing), and air transport planning. He currently acts as Deputy Director of CITTA (Research Centre for Territory Transport and Environment) and as Coordinator of the Doctoral Programs in Spatial Planning and in Transport Systems at the University of Coimbra.

Volodymyr Bilotkach is Senior Lecturer in Economics at the Singapore Institute of Technology, Singapore. His research interests cover various issues in economics of the aviation sector including airline alliances and mergers, airport regulation, and the economics of distribution of airline tickets.

Enrique J. Calderón is a retired professor from the Department of Transport and Territorial Planning in the Polytechnic University of Madrid, Spain. He specialises in urban, regional, and environmental issues at all levels, sustainability assessment, and the integration of environmental concerns into government policies and programmes, notably in regard to transportation.

Gianmaria Martini is Full Professor of Applied Economics at the University of Bergamo, Italy. His research interests are applied econometrics and methods to estimate efficiency in the air transport sector, extended to environmental issues. Recent research activities have covered regional development and aviation, with a specific focus on African countries. He is currently Associate Editor of the *Journal of Air Transport Management* and was the chairman of the organising committee of the 2013 Air Transport Research Society Conference in Bergamo. He has been nominated as vice president for publications of the ATRS.

Air Transport and Regional Development Case Studies

Edited by Anne Graham,
Nicole Adler, Hans-Martin Niemeier,
Ofelia Betancor, António Pais Antunes,
Volodymyr Bilotkach, Enrique J.
Calderón, and Gianmaria Martini

First published 2021
by Routledge
2 Park Square, Milton Park, Abingdon, Oxon OX14 4RN

and by Routledge
52 Vanderbilt Avenue, New York, NY 10017

Routledge is an imprint of the Taylor & Francis Group, an informa business

© 2021 selection and editorial matter, Anne Graham, Nicole Adler, Hans-Martin Niemeier, Ofelia Betancor, António Pais Antunes, Volodymyr Bilotkach, Enrique J. Calderón, and Gianmaria Martini; individual chapters, the contributors

The right of Anne Graham, Nicole Adler, Hans-Martin Niemeier, Ofelia Betancor, António Pais Antunes, Volodymyr Bilotkach, Enrique J. Calderón, and Gianmaria Martini to be identified as the authors of the editorial material, and of the authors for their individual chapters, has been asserted in accordance with sections 77 and 78 of the Copyright, Designs and Patents Act 1988.

All rights reserved. No part of this book may be reprinted or reproduced or utilised in any form or by any electronic, mechanical, or other means, now known or hereafter invented, including photocopying and recording, or in any information storage or retrieval system, without permission in writing from the publishers.

Trademark notice: Product or corporate names may be trademarks or registered trademarks, and are used only for identification and explanation without intent to infringe.

British Library Cataloguing-in-Publication Data
A catalogue record for this book is available from the British Library

Library of Congress Cataloging-in-Publication Data
Names: Graham, Ann, 1956 July 22– editor. | Adler, Nicole, editor. |
    Niemeier, Hans-Martin, editor.
Title: Air transport and regional development case studies / edited by
    Anne Graham, Nicole Adler, Hans-Martin Niemeier, Ofelia Betancor,
    António Pais Antunes, Volodymyr Bilotkach, Enrique J. Calderón,
    Gianmaria Martini.
Description: New York : Routledge, 2021. | Includes bibliographical
    references and index.
Identifiers: LCCN 2020050594 (print) | LCCN 2020050595 (ebook)
Subjects: LCSH: Aeronautics, Commercial—Europe—Case studies. |
    Airports—Management—Europe—Case studies. | Regional planning—
    Europe—Case studies. | Strategic planning—Europe—Case studies.
Classification: LCC HE9842.A4 A367 2021 (print) | LCC HE9842.A4
    (ebook) | DDC 387.7094—dc23
LC record available at https://lccn.loc.gov/2020050594
LC ebook record available at https://lccn.loc.gov/2020050595

ISBN: 978-0-367-53313-7 (hbk)
ISBN: 978-1-003-09206-3 (ebk)

Typeset in Bembo
by Apex CoVantage, LLC

Contents

List of figures   vii
List of tables   x
Editors and contributors   xiii

1 Introduction   1
ANNE GRAHAM, NICOLE ADLER, HANS-MARTIN NIEMEIER, OFELIA
BETANCOR, ANTÓNIO PAIS ANTUNES, VOLODYMYR BILOTKACH,
ENRIQUE J. CALDERÓN AND GIANMARIA MARTINI

**2 The evolution of regional air transport connectivity in
Europe: a comparison between remote and core regions**   6
GIANMARIA MARTINI, FLAVIO PORTA, AND DAVIDE SCOTTI

**3 The impacts of airports in geographical peripheries:
a Norwegian case study**   26
NIGEL HALPERN

**4 The relationship between air traffic and the regional
development in Finland**   50
STAFFAN RINGBOM

5 UK regional airports: developments and challenges   64
ANNE GRAHAM

**6 Regional airport business models: Shannon Group as
a case study**   86
NOEL HINEY, MARINA EFTHYMIOU, AND EDGAR MORGENROTH

7 The air transport markets in Central and Eastern Europe   121
SONIA HUDEREK-GLAPSKA

vi *Contents*

8 **Air transport and economic growth of the regions: causality analysis in Bulgaria**   145
STELA TODOROVA AND KALOYAN HARALAMPIEV

9 **The effects of air traffic on the economic development of Bosnia and Herzegovina**   160
RAHMAN NURKOVIĆ

10 **Expenditure of inbound passengers at Wroclaw airport and the significance for the regional economy**   169
ŁUKASZ OLIPRA

11 **Intangible effects of regional airports in the aviation system: the case of Switzerland**   190
ANDREAS WITTMER AND CLAUDIO NOTO

12 **Swiss international and regional airports: an efficiency benchmarking**   203
CLAUDIO NOTO AND CAROLINA KANSIKAS

13 **A Belgian case study of the economic importance of air transport and airport activities**   223
SVEN BUYLE, FRANZISKA KUPFER, AND EVY ONGHENA

14 **The impact of Oporto Airport on the development of the Norte Region of Portugal: an econometric study**   249
SUSANA FREIRIA AND ANTÓNIO PAIS ANTUNES

15 **Spanish Transport Accounts**   264
JOSÉ MANUEL VASALLO, ARMANDO ORTUÑO, AND
OFELIA BETANCOR

16 **The spatial economic effects of airport de-hubbing: the Milan case**   289
MARCO PERCOCO

Index   300

Figures

2.1	An example of a region's connectivity	10
2.2	Map of the regions in Europe: remote, *core1*, *core2*, and intermediate	12
2.3	Average NUTS 2 air connectivity in European regions	15
2.4	Map of 2009 regional connectivity in Europe	18
2.5	Map of 2018 regional connectivity in Europe	19
3.1	Regional boundaries	30
3.2	Centrality index	32
3.3	Airports in Norway	33
3.4	Car travel time to nearest airport	34
3.5	Time saved travelling to Oslo by air versus road	37
4.1	The NUTS 3 regions and the main regional airports operated by Finavia in Finland	53
5.1	Passenger numbers at all UK airports, 2002–2018	68
5.2	Operating margin (%) at UK regional airports, 2002–2018	69
5.3	Main airlines serving all UK regional airports in 2018	70
5.4	Domestic share of total passengers (%) at all UK regional airports, 2002–2018	71
5.5	Relationship between airport size and cost per passenger at UK regional airports in 2017/2018	73
5.6	Domestic passengers at London Heathrow Airport, 2002–2018	78
6.1	Key airports operating on the island of Ireland	89
6.2	Business Model Canvas, Shannon Airport, August 2018	96
6.3	Shannon Airport's Five Forces analysis	101
6.4	Key regional airport stakeholders	111
7.1	Convergence path of CEE countries and their neighbours in 2000–2017	125
7.2	The paths of growth of air transport in CEE countries, 2004–2017	129
7.3	Air passengers by country and main European network airlines in 2017	131
8.1	Algorithm for selection of relevant causal two-variable model	151

viii *Figures*

8.2	Passengers and gross domestic product (GDP): Sofia Airport, 1995–2015	153
8.3	Passengers and gross domestic product (GDP): Burgas Airport, 1995–2015	153
8.4	Passengers and gross domestic product (GDP): Varna Airport, 1995–2015	154
9.1	Different activities at airports	162
9.2	International air routes operated from airports in Bosnia and Herzegovina in 2017	165
10.1	Number of passengers at Wroclaw airport in the period 2000–2018	176
10.2	The estimation procedure of expenditure of inbound visitors by air to the region	178
10.3	Division of passengers into categories for the expenditure estimation	179
10.4	The structure of total expenditure according to the purpose of journey, type of carrier, and destination	186
10.5	The structure of the estimated total expenditure according to the purpose of journey	186
11.1	Economic effects of regional airports, according to ACI	192
11.2	Location theories	195
13.1	Airports of Belgium	225
13.2	Passenger numbers at Belgian airports	227
13.3	Cargo traffic (in tonnes) at Belgian airports	229
13.4	Categories of activities	231
13.5	Classification of economic impacts	232
13.6	Direct, indirect, and total value added of air transport cluster and other airport-related activities, 2006–2015 (in € million, current prices)	236
13.7	Direct value added of air transport cluster and other airport-related activities, 2006–2015 (in € million, current prices)	237
13.8	Direct value added of air transport cluster 2006–2015 (in € million, current prices)	237
13.9	Direct, indirect, and total employment of air transport cluster and other airport-related activities, 2006–2015 (in FTEs)	240
13.10	Direct employment of air transport cluster and other airport-related activities, 2006–2015 (in FTEs)	240
13.11	Direct employment of air transport cluster, 2006–2015 (in FTEs)	241
13.12	Evolution of movements, area, and population impacted by >55 dB(A) L_{den} contours (index 2000)	244
14.1	Norte Region and its sub-regional areas	252
14.2	Evolution of GVA in the Norte Region between 2000 and 2016	253
14.3	Evolution of Oporto Airport activity between 2000 and 2016	255

14.4	Routes and daily flights operated from/to Oporto Airport	256
16.1	Annual supply from Malpensa airport toward non-EU destinations	292
16.2	International accessibility of Milan area	293
16.3	The labour market	296
16.4	Wage-rent curves	297

Tables

2.1	Available seats and NUTS 2 average connectivity levels from 2009 to 2018	14
2.2	Correlation between regional connectivity, FSCs seats and LCCs seats, Europe 2009–2018	16
2.3	Evolution in the number of seats, seats offered by an LCC, and air connectivity in remote regions	20
2.4	Evolution in the number of seats, seats offered by an LCC, and connectivity in core regions	21
2.5	Best-connected regions in 2016	22
3.1	Domestic connections with 1,000 or more passengers in 2017	36
3.2	Economic impact of airports in Norway in 2013	39
3.3	Direct jobs at airports in Norway in 2013	40
4.1	Unit-root tests – statistics and significances	55
4.2	Pedroni cointegration test values	56
4.3	Long-run relationships and short-run dynamics between passenger traffic and investments	58
4.4	Long-run relationships and short-run dynamics between passenger traffic and production	59
4.5	The Dumitrescu and Hurlin (2012) Granger non-causality tests with lag order 1	60
5.1	Ownership of main UK regional airports in 2019	66
5.2	Group/fund ownership of UK airports in 2019	67
5.3	Traffic and financial performance of UK regional airports, 2013–2018	73
5.4	Destination cities and Business Connectivity Index at UK regional airports in 2017	75
6.1	Total passenger numbers handled by key Irish airports in 2014–2018	90
6.2	Fastest travel time (private motor car) from main Irish cities to five largest airports	91
6.3	Shannon Group revenue analysis	98
6.4	Key financial ratios for Shannon Group	98
6.5	Shannon Airport SWOT analysis	99

6.6	Shannon Group and Glasgow Prestwick: key characteristics	104
6.7	Shannon Airport: headwinds and tailwinds	105
6.8	Overall economic impact of Shannon Group	108
6.9	Key Irish airport economic impact assessments in 2017	109
7.1	Evolution of economic performance of CEE countries, 2000–2017	125
7.2	The sources of inefficiencies in the transport sector in central planned economies	127
7.3	Air transport in CEE countries, 2004–2017	128
7.4	Main airlines in CEE countries	131
7.5	The share of LCCs in low-cost markets in CEE countries	132
7.6	Air passengers by airport in CEE countries, 2017	135
7.7	SWOT analysis of the air transport markets in CEE countries	138
8.1	Descriptive statistics of variables used in the analysis	154
8.2	IPS panel unit-root test statistics	155
8.3	Johansen Fisher panel cointegration test statistics (based on the individual intercept)	156
8.4	Results of vector error correction model for all airports	156
8.5	A summary of the causal relationships and direction between the two series	156
9.1	Critical factors influencing the development of air transport in Bosnia and Herzegovina	161
9.2	Airport passengers in Bosnia and Herzegovina, 2012–2017	164
9.3	Airport freight tonnes in Bosnia and Herzegovina, 2012–2017	166
10.1	Structure of surveyed passengers according to the type of journey (beginning, return, others)	180
10.2	Structure of surveyed passengers according to the purpose of journey	181
10.3	Average weighted length of visit and estimated average expenditure per day for different categories of passengers	183
10.4	Estimated amount of incoming air transport passengers' expenditures in Wroclaw and Lower Silesia region in 2014 (in PLN)	184
10.5	Structure of the estimated expenditures according to the purpose of journey in each of distinguished groups of passengers	185
11.1	Intangible catalytic effects of regional airports	192
11.2	Ranking of location choice criteria of production companies in the United States	196
11.3	Swiss regional airports – perspectives, stakeholders, and key aspects	197
11.4	Intangible effects of the Swiss regional airports	197
12.1	Characteristics of Swiss international and regional airports, 2015	206
12.2	Input data treatment	211

xii *Tables*

12.3	Correlations across input and output data for international and regional airports	212
13.1	Passenger numbers at Belgian airports	228
13.2	Cargo traffic (in tonnes) at Belgian airports	230
13.3	Value added of air transport cluster and other airport-related activities, 2013–2015 (in € million, current prices)	235
13.4	Employment of air transport cluster and other airport-related activities, 2013–2015 (in FTEs)	239
13.5	Aviation direct and indirect employment in Europe, 2017 (in FTEs)	242
13.6	Aviation direct and indirect value added in Europe, 2017 (in million €)	243
13.7	Evolution of the area within the L_{den} contours of Brussels Airport (ha)	245
13.8	Evolution of the population within the L_{den} contours of Brussels Airport	246
14.1	Descriptive statistics of model variables	259
14.2	Impact of aeronautical revenues on total GVA	260
14.3	Impact of aeronautical revenues on Industry GVA	260
14.4	Impact of aeronautical revenues on services GVA	261
15.1	The accounts general framework	273
15.2	Road transport aggregate account for Spain, 2013	274
15.3	Road transport disaggregate account for Spain by type of vehicle, 2013	275
15.4	Railway transport aggregate account for Spain, 2013	276
15.5	Railway transport disaggregate account for Spain by freight and passenger services, 2013	277
15.6	Railway transport disaggregate account for Spain by type of business, 2013	278
15.7	Air transport aggregate account for Spain, 2013	279
15.8	Air transport account for Spain by route origin/destination at Madrid airport, 2013	280
15.9	Air transport account for Spain by route origin/destination at Barcelona airport, 2013	281
15.10	Air transport account for Spain by route origin/destination at the smallest airports, 2013	282
15.11	Maritime transport aggregate account for Spain, 2013	283
15.12	Summary of results for aggregate accounts: coverage rates, 2013	285
16.1	Exports: baseline regression and time intervals analysis	294
16.2	Baseline regressions (OLS estimates, dependent variable: total employment)	295

Editors and contributors

Nicole Adler is Full Professor and Head of the Department of Operations Research and Operations Management at the School of Business Administration of Hebrew University in Jerusalem. Her major research interests include game theory and productivity estimation applied to the field of transportation. Her work has analysed hub-and-spoke airline competition and mergers, public service obligation tenders, and airport productivity, and she recently has utilised game theoretic concepts in order to understand air traffic control markets. Nicole is currently an Associate Editor for *Transportation Research Part B: Methodological*.

António Pais Antunes is Professor in the Department of Civil Engineering at the University of Coimbra (Portugal). He has been Visiting Fellow at Princeton University, Invited Professor at EPF Lausanne, Visiting Professor at MIT and a visiting researcher at the University of Bergamo. His teaching and research focus on public facility location, urban mobility (notably public transport and vehicle sharing), and air transport planning. He currently acts as Deputy Director of CITTA (Research Centre for Territory Transport and Environment) and as Coordinator of the Doctoral Programs in Spatial Planning and in Transport Systems at the University of Coimbra.

Ofelia Betancor is Associate Professor of Economics in the Department of Applied Economics at the University of Las Palmas de Gran Canaria (Spain). She holds an MSc in economics from the University of London, and two doctorate degrees in economics (Institute for Transport Studies-University of Leeds and University of Las Palmas). She has participated in many research projects at the national and international level, and has also collaborated with the World Bank and the Inter-American Development Bank as specialist in air transport and the economic evaluation of projects and transport policies. The results of her works have been published in leading journals in the area of transport economics.

Volodymyr Bilotkach is Senior Lecturer in Economics at the Singapore Institute of Technology, Singapore. His research interests cover various issues in economics of the aviation sector including airline alliances and mergers, airport regulation, and the economics of distribution of airline tickets.

xiv *Editors and contributors*

Sven Buyle is a Post-Doc Researcher at the Department of Transport and Regional Economics of the University of Antwerp, where he co-teaches courses on air transport and transport modeling. His research interests are within the field of air transport and airspace economics and management. His doctoral research applied industrial economics to the European air navigation service sector by using stochastic frontier analysis to assess economics of scale, cost complementarities and the impact of different business models and merger scenarios on cost efficiency.

Enrique J. Calderón is a retired professor from the Department of Transport and Territorial Planning in the Polytechnic University of Madrid, Spain. He specialises in urban, regional, and environmental issues at all levels, sustainability assessment, and the integration of environmental concerns into government policies and programmes, notably in regard to transportation.

Marina Efthymiou is Assistant Professor in Aviation Management and the Course Director of MSc Management (Aviation Leadership) at Dublin City University, Ireland. In the past, she held posts at the University of West London, UK and EUROCONTROL, the international organisation for the safety of air navigation based in Brussels. Her research interests primarily focus on aviation governance and policy, sustainable aviation, performance regulation, air navigation service providers, and air traffic management/control.

Susana Freiria is a researcher at the University of Coimbra and lecturer at the Polytechnic Institute of Coimbra, where she teaches courses such as mobility planning and land management. She has been involved in several research projects, as well as in the preparation of several spatial planning plans. In the past few years, she has developed a research interest in the impact of air transport on regional development.

Anne Graham is Professor of Air Transport and Tourism Management at the University of Westminster, UK. She has two main research areas: first, airport management, economics, and regulation; and second, the relationship between the tourism and aviation sectors. She has published widely with recent books including *Air Transport: A Tourism Perspective, Airport Finance and Investment in the Global Economy, Managing Airports: An International Perspective, The Routledge Companion to Air Transport Management,* and *Airport Marketing.* She is a previous editor-in-chief of the *Journal of Air Transport Management* and in 2016 was made a fellow of the Air Transport Research Society.

Nigel Halpern is Professor of Air Transport and Tourism Management at Kristiania University College, Norway. He has previously worked at Molde University College; London Metropolitan University; UK Department for Transport, Local Government and the Regions; UK Civil Aviation Authority; and PGL Travel. His main interests are in airport digital transformation, airport marketing and strategy, airport service quality, geographies of air transport and tourism, accessible tourism, wider impacts of air transport and tourism, and interorganisational relations in air transport and tourism. He has published books on *Airport Marketing* and the *Routledge Companion to Air Transport Management.*

Kaloyan Haralampiev has a PhD in statistics and demography. He is Associate Professor in the Department of Sociology at the Sofia University St. Kliment Ohridski, and Lecturer in Statistical Methods in Sociology and SPSS. His scientific interests are mainly in the field of probability theory, Bayesian statistics, and demographic statistics. His main publications include *Unconventional View upon Conventional Statistical Problems, Introduction to the Basic Statistical Methods for Analysis* (textbook), and *IBM SPSS – Statistical Solutions of Applied Research Tasks* (handbook).

Noel Hiney holds an MSc in management (aviation leadership) from Dublin City University and is currently part-time Lecturer in Airport Management there. His current research interest, as a PhD candidate, is European regional airports, with a specific focus the impact of stakeholder management and emerging business models on the economic relationship between such airports and their economic hinterland. In the past, Noel held roles with the Bank of Ireland, having responsibility at various times for government relations, retail strategy, and regulatory affairs.

Sonia Huderek-Glapska is Assistant Professor in the Department of Microeconomics at Poznan University of Economics and Business, Poland. Her PhD was in economics, specialising in the relationship between air transport and regional development, specifically in Central and Eastern Europe. She is the editor and co-author of a book on airport management written in Polish, and she has had international papers published in journals. She has been involved in numerous of projects at airports, including studies of airport strategic management, airport customer behaviour, and airport economic impact.

Carolina Kansikas holds a master's degree (with distinction) in economics from Aalto University, Finland, and is a MRes candidate in economics at the University of Warwick. She is interested in applied and empirical microeconomics. She has been a member of the Young Researchers Network for the ATARD COST Action and has gained previous experience both in research and institutions, including the Finnish competition authority and the Ministry for Foreign Affairs.

Franziska Kupfer used to work at the University of Antwerp as Assistant Professor and Academic Director of C-MAT (Centre for Maritime and Air Transport Management), as well as Post-Doc Researcher at the Department of Transport and Regional Economics. In her different roles at the University of Antwerp, she was responsible for (co-) teaching courses and carrying out research related to air transport economics, airport management, transport economics, and transport policy. Since 2020, Franziska is has been working at the Antwerp Transport Region, where she is part of the mobility management team. She stays connected with the University of Antwerp as a volunteer.

Gianmaria Martini is Full Professor of Applied Economics at the University of Bergamo, Italy. His research interests are applied econometrics and methods to estimate efficiency in the air transport sector, extended to environmental issues. Recent research activities have covered regional development and aviation, with a specific focus on African countries. He is currently Associate Editor of the *Journal of Air Transport Management* and was the chairman of the organising committee of the 2013 Air Transport Research Society Conference in Bergamo. He has been nominated as vice president for publications of the ATRS.

Edgar Morgenroth is full Professor of Economics in DCU Business School, Dublin City University, Dublin, Ireland. He is also an independent member of the National Economic and Social Council (NESC), a fellow of the UK Academy of Social Sciences and a fellow of the Regional Studies Association, having served as its vice-chairman and treasurer. He has held positions at the Economic and Social Research Institute (ESRI) for almost 20 years and has worked at Keele University and the Strategic Investment Board (SIB). Edgar holds a PhD in Economics from Keele University in the UK.

Hans–Martin Niemeier is Director of the Institute for Transport and Development at Bremen University of Applied Sciences, Germany. He is Chairman of the German Aviation Research Society and member of the Advisory Board of the European Aviation Conference. He chaired the ATARD COST Action from 2016–2019. From 2014 through May 2019, he was member of the Performance Review Body of the Single European Sky. He has published on privatisation, regulation, and competition of airports, the reform of slot allocation, and airline and airport alliances.

Claudio Noto is Fellow at the Center for Aviation Competence (CFAC-HSG, Switzerland). Claudio has researched the allocation of airport capacity and the economics of regional airports, supporting consulting projects and academic studies, and providing expert advice to the industry. He obtained his MA in economics at the University of Zurich in 2005 and his PhD in management at the University of St. Gallen, Switzerland, in 2016, which was awarded the annual Prize in European Aviation Economics and Management by the German Aviation Research Society (GARS). He works as an airline pilot and an air force flight instructor.

Rahman Nurković is Full Professor in the Faculty of Science at the University of Sarajevo, Bosnia and Herzegovina. He has a Doctor of Geographical

Sciences from the University of Ljubljana, Slovenia, and a Master of Geographical Sciences from the University of Zagreb, Croatia. His areas of expertise include human geography; conception and methodology in regional and spatial planning; urban and rural geography; geography; transport, regional, and spatial planning; and economics.

Łukasz Olipra is Researcher and Lecturer at Wroclaw University of Economics and Business in Wroclaw, Poland. He is a graduate of International Economic Relations programme and obtained his PhD in Economics at the same University. His research concentrates on the economic impact and importance of air transport to regional economies. He was involved in the project Air Transport and Regional Labour Markets in Poland financed by the Polish National Centre of Science, and has cooperated with Wroclaw airport in the area of market research as well as with other companies in the field of logistics.

Evy Onghena graduated as a doctor in applied economics at the University of Antwerp (UAntwerp), Belgium in 2013. Between 2013 and 2019, she continued her scientific research in the domain of air transport economics as Post-Doc Researcher in the Department of Transport and Regional Economics (TPR) of UAntwerp. Between 2013 and 2015, she was scientific director of the Flemish Policy Research Centre on Commodity and Passenger Flows. Between 2015 and 2019, she was course coordinator for various courses and was involved in the Centre of Excellence on Sustainable Transport and Logistics. As from mid-2019, Evy has been working full-time at the Antwerp Port Authority and teaching transport modelling at UAntwerp.

Armando Ortuño is Associate Professor of Spatial Planning in the Civil Engineer Department and Water and Tourism Institutes, University of Alicante, Spain. He has a PhD in civil engineering and a degree in economics, and is coordinator of the project Madrid World Construction Capital and Project Manager at INECA (Institute of Economic Research at Alicante Province). Since 2004, he has carried out many research projects and studies regarding the socio-economic and spatial planning impact on tourism and infrastructures. He has published books and papers, and taken part in many research and development projects at national and international scales.

Marco Percoco is the founding director of the GREEN (the Center for Research in Geography, Resources, Environment, Energy and Networks) at Università Bocconi in Milan, where he is also Professor of Regional and Transport Economics and Economic Geography in the Department of Social and Political Sciences. His main research interests are in the evaluation of regional and transport policies, and in the geography of energy and natural resources. He has published more than 100 papers in such fields as regional science and transport economics. Currently, he serves as an adviser in the Evaluation Unit in the Prime Minister Office and as a vice-chairman of the Bureau of the UNECE Working Party on PPP. In the past, he has

xviii *Editors and contributors*

advised the World Bank, the IADB, the Ethiopian government, and several ministries.

Flavio Porta is Post-Doc Researcher in Applied Economics at the University of Bergamo, Italy. He holds a PhD in economics and management of technology from the University of Pavia, Italy. His research interests are network analysis and applied econometrics, with a particular focus on structural models and spatial econometrics. His recent research activities cover regional development, tourism and aviation.

Staffan Ringbom is Senior Lecturer in Economics at Hanken School of Economics in Helsinki, Finland. He has a broad educational background in both statistics and economics. He obtained his PhD in international macroeconomics in 1995. In addition to international macroeconomics, Staffan's research interests are in industrial organisation covering industry studies, as well as pricing issues. Born and living in a sparsely populated country as Finland, he has a natural interest to the economic development in the rural regions.

Davide Scotti is Assistant Professor (RTD-b, tenure track) of Applied Economics at the University of Bergamo, Italy. He holds a PhD in economics and Management of technology from the University of Bergamo. His research activity is mainly focused on the aviation industry. In this regard, his main interests are airport and airline benchmarking, air transport and regional development, aviation negative externalities, and airline network structures. He has published several papers in international journals.

Stela Todorova is Professor in Economics and Management in the Faculty of Economics at the Agricultural University of Plovdiv, Bulgaria. She holds a PhD in economics and a graduate diploma in economics from the University of National and World Economy in Sofia, Bulgaria. Stela has over 70 refereed publications covering her research interests, which include problems of the regional development, land reform and CAP, regional policies, economic and social cohesion of the regions, regional sustainable development, connection between economic growth of the regions and air transport, and air transport and noise pollution.

José Manuel Vasallo is Professor in the Department of Transportation Engineering, Urban and Regional Planning at Universidad Politécnica de Madrid, Spain. He is also a member of the academic staff of the Transportation Research Centre (TRANSyT). He was Research Fellow at the Harvard Kennedy School of Government. He has worked as a consultant for the governments of Spain and Chile, and also for international organisations such as the World Bank, the Andean Corporation of Development, the International Transport Forum, and the European Investment Bank. Currently, he is member of the advisory board of the Ministry of Transportation of Spain.

Andreas Wittmer is Head of International Networks, Senior Lecturer in Management with special focus on aviation, and Head of the Center for Aviation Competence at the University of St. Gallen, Switzerland. His research focuses on network industries, such as aviation. His interests link with a better understanding of efficiencies generated by networks and the impacts on stakeholders. From this perspective, he researches consumer perception and behaviour, and service management. He serves on boards of a regional airport and aviation networks, and as a freelance aircraft accident investigator.

1 Introduction

Anne Graham, Nicole Adler, Hans-Martin Niemeier,
Ofelia Betancor, António Pais Antunes, Volodymyr
Bilotkach, Enrique J. Calderón and Gianmaria Martini

The air transport sector is a major contributor to the globalisation of the economy. Its growth has been accompanied and, to a certain extent, caused by liberalisation. The growth in traffic levels has led to congestion, at both major airports and in the airspace, and to a lack of services on thin routes, thus affecting both core and remote regions.

A four-year European Cooperation in Science and Technology (COST) Action was established in 2015, and this book is a direct product of this. The book was completed before the coronavirus pandemic in 2020, but the issues discussed remain very relevant. The Action, called Air Transport and Regional Development (ATARD), aimed to promote a better understanding of how the air transport-related problems of core regions and remote regions should be addressed in order to enhance both economic competitiveness and social cohesion in Europe. It had members with a wide variety of professions and backgrounds from 33 countries and involved conferences/workshops in various locations, PhD training schools, and short-term scientific missions of researchers to other academic institutions. The many countries that participated in different activities is a testament to the great interest that aviation research and regional development engenders among academics and practitioners.

The area of the Action, namely the relationship between transport and regional development, has been widely examined in the literature from a multiplicity of perspectives. However, most research has focused on land transport modes (especially road), whereas air transport research is far from having led to a coherent body of knowledge, despite some publications over the last two decades. Only a few methods have been used to explore the relationship, with the attention being put essentially on the economic dimensions of development. Moreover, it is clear that research on this subject is much more advanced in the United States than in Europe.

This book is one of three inter-connected books related to the most important themes that were explored during the four-year COST Action. It will focus on case studies (known here as ATARD case studies) related to air transport and regional development. The other two books will focus on methodological approaches (known here as ATARD methodologies) and policy implications (known here as ATARD policies). The three books complement each other in

2   Anne Graham, Nicole Adler, et al.

focusing on different aspects of ATARD, but are also stand-alone publications in their own right. The books fill a much-needed gap, presenting a multi-sector (airports, airlines, air navigation services, government organisations) and geographically Europe-wide coverage of both remote and core regions to fully explore all critical issues related to the linkages between air transport and regional development.

They are aimed at becoming a major reference source on the topic, within which the main findings of the Action will be condensed. There is no other single source publication that currently covers this topic area in such a comprehensive manner. The book draws from experienced researchers in the field, covering the diverse experience and knowledge of the members of the Action from 33 countries. Many of the chapters in all three books have already been presented and debated at the ATARD conferences and workshops.

The ATARD methodologies book is divided into four distinct groups of chapters; the first discussing regional economic theory, the second presenting the theory on economic impact assessment, the third describing applied economic methods covering both econometrics and game theory, and the fourth and final group debating the use of performance estimation techniques when measuring the impact of aviation on regional development.

The ATARD policies book begins with chapters that generally discuss important policy issues related to air transport and regional development in relation to connectivity and accessibility, dependency, airport governance and regulation, and air traffic control frameworks. This is followed by a number of chapters considering government studies and state aid. The final chapters then focus on other policy implications (tourism development, airport expansion, passenger taxation, and noise control).

This book (ATARD case studies) is divided into four geographical regions after a general chapter that compares regional air transport connectivity between remote and central areas in Europe. The first region is Northern and Western Northern Europe (case studies related specifically to Norway, Finland, the United Kingdom, and Ireland); the second is Central and Eastern Europe (Bulgaria, Bosnia and Herzegovina, and Poland); the third is Central Western Europe (Belgium and Switzerland); and finally, the fourth is Southern Europe (Portugal, Spain, and Italy). A summary of the different chapters of this book is provided here. The important links with the other two ATARD books are also highlighted.

In Chapter 2, Martini, Porta, and Scotti analyse air transport regional connectivity in Europe and investigate how it has recently evolved in a period of liberalisation that has shown all its effects, by potentially increasing the number of routes in European countries. This is undertaken by building a new dataset of information on intra-European Union (EU) aviation activity at the regional level for the 2009–2018 period, using the European NUTS 2 classification to identify a region. It is thus a very valid and interesting application of connectivity theory which is explored in ATARD methodologies, and of the use of connectivity metrics which are discussed in greater detail in ATARD policies.

Chapter 3, written by Halpern, focuses on geographical peripheries by considering the case of Norway which is the first chapter covering the Northern and Western Northern European region. It discusses peripheral areas and their potential impacts including economic impacts, wider impacts on regional economic and social development, and external effects on the environment, and explains that Norway is one of Europe's most peripheral countries and is highly dependent on air transport for the accessibility and social and economic development of its regions. Input-output analysis, which is critically assessed in ATARD methodologies, is used to support the discussion about economic impacts.

In Chapter 4, Ringbom investigates the relationship between air traffic and economic development, specifically in Finland. He uses a novel approach for this market, namely an econometric technique (as detailed in the ATARD methodologies) using non-stationary and cointegrated panel data with a vector error correction approach. This, he argues, yields more valid conclusions and yields deeper insights into the underlying long-run structure and short-term adjustment in the underlying variables covering real economic activity and passenger traffic.

In Chapter 5, Graham explores developments and challenges related to UK regional airports. Issues covered include ownership developments, traffic and financial performance, and regional connectivity. A number of government policies that are discussed here specifically within the UK context are privatisation, public services obligations (PSOs), and passenger taxation, with these being given more general consideration in ATARD policies.

Chapter 6 is the last chapter specially covering Northern and Northern Western Europe. Hiney, Efthymiou, and Morgenroth focus on the regional airport of Shannon, highlighting the challenges and opportunities faced by Irish airports. The innovative ownership structure of Shannon Airport is examined (an airport group incorporating tourism and property entities) as having implications for the relationship between airports and tourism authorities, which is an important aspect of regional development that is further discussed in ATARD policies.

Chapter 7, written by Huderek-Glapska, is an introductory chapter covering detailed research of the area of Central and Eastern Europe. It provides an overview of the relationship between economic performance and the air transport markets in the region, noting that they share a common history and traditional economic system. After discussing the social-economic characteristics of the countries and the air transport markets, strengths and weaknesses – as well as opportunities and threats – are presented, and conclusions are drawn regarding the relationship between regional development and air transport in this region.

Chapter 8, authored by Todorova and Haralampiev, is the first of three chapters considering individual countries within Central and Eastern Europe. This chapter aims to establish the first empirical evidence for determining causal relationships between regional aviation/airports and economic growth in Bulgaria by assessing the issues involved with isolating bidirectional short- and long-run causality between air transport and economic growth. It uses

4 *Anne Graham, Nicole Adler, et al.*

panel data econometric models which are examined in more general detail in ATARD methodologies.

In Chapter 9, Nurković then focuses on Bosnia and Herzegovina. This is a difficult country to analyse because of the lack of adequate data but nevertheless, critical factors influencing the development of air transport can be identified. Traffic trends demonstrate that Sarajevo airport has experienced substantial growth in passenger traffic in recent years, which has major implications for regional development of the surrounding area.

Chapter 10 is the final chapter covering Central and Eastern Europe, where Olipra focuses specifically on the spending of passengers at Wroclaw airport. In undertaking such research, the significance of leisure tourism to the region is assessed which has implications for airport and tourism policies which are discussed in general in ATARD policies. The main method of investigation is a passenger survey.

Chapter 11, written by Wittmer and Noto, is the first of two chapters studying Switzerland, focusing on the intangible effects of regional airports. After presenting a conceptional framework for the location choice of firms, a key part of the research is applying this is in practice using qualitative empirical data from in-depth interviews with experts and exponents of the Swiss aviation system. The chapter is closely linked to the discussion of wider economic benefits in ATARD methodologies.

Chapter 12 is the other chapter that covers Switzerland, authored by Noto and Kansikas. With their research, three international and two of the four main regional Swiss airports are benchmarked against a representative set of 112 European airports based on a stochastic frontier analysis with an input-oriented, multi-output distance function. Further explanation of the general methodology used is provided in ATARD methodologies.

In Chapter 13, Buyle, Kupfer, and Onghena also provide a case study from Central Western Europe, namely Belgium. This examines the four studies of the National Bank of Belgium that investigated the economic impact of air transport and the airport sector in Belgium. Input-output analysis is used (which is further critically assessed in ATARD methodologies), and in addition, the impact of noise pollution is evaluated.

Chapter 14, written by Freiria and Antunes, is one of the final three chapters that cover case studies from Southern Europe. This chapter uses econometric methods (which are discussed in greater detail in ATARD methodologies) to evaluate the impact of Oporto Airport on the development of the Norte Region of Portugal between 2000 and 2016, considering both industry and services sectors.

In Chapter 15, Vasallo, Ortuño, and Betancor focus on neighbouring Spain and estimate the socio-economic accounts for the four main interurban transport modes in Spain: road, rail, air, and maritime. The aim is to determine if each mode bears its costs, which includes infrastructure and the external costs to examine to what extent the 'user pays' and the 'polluter pays' principles are currently being applied.

Chapter 16 is the final case study from Southern Europe and the final chapter of the book. Percoco considers a very specific situation, namely airport de-hubbing at Milan, to explore the effects and whether they are consistent with the theory of spatial equilibrium. It views the de-hubbing development as a type of natural experiment to estimate the effect of air accessibility on local economies. Similar to a number of chapters in this book, it uses econometric models. More details about these and their general relevance to air transport and regional development is discussed in ATARD methodologies.

We would like to thank all the contributors to this book. We would also like the reviewers of the chapters for providing helpful comments and suggestions. We are especially indebted to Christian Bontemps, Frédéric Dobruszkes, Christos Evangelinos, Frank Fichert, Franziska Kupfer, Juan Carlos Martin Hernandez, Aisling Reynolds-Feighan, Sonia Huderek-Glapska, Juergen Mueller, Marco Percoco, Steve Ison, Tolga Ülkü, and Nicola Volta.

We wish you a pleasant read.

2 The evolution of regional air transport connectivity in Europe

A comparison between remote and core regions

Gianmaria Martini, Flavio Porta, and Davide Scotti

Introduction

Worldwide population demand for mobility has grown in recent years. The International Civil Aviation Organisation (ICAO) reports that in 2017, the aviation industry served a record 4.1 billion passengers, a 7.2 per cent increase over 2016 (ICAO, 2018a). Preliminary figures show that a total of 4.3 billion passengers used air transport scheduled flights in 2018. This indicates a 6.1 per cent rise over 2017 (ICAO, 2018b). Forecasts by Airbus and Boeing show that this rapid growth will generally continue (Airbus, 2018; Boeing, 2018). Airbus estimates a 2.9 per cent compound annual growth rate (CAGR) for the 2019–2036 period, while Boeing estimates a 3.2 per cent CAGR for the same period. As the importance of air transport grows, this also raises the issue of granting equitable air connectivity services to people and territories within a country or a community of countries (e.g. the European Union [EU]) to improve quality of life standards, as well as the local economy, for the population. Several contributions (Alderighi and Gaggero, 2017; Allroggen and Malina, 2014; Bilotkach, 2015; Blonigen and Cristea, 2015; Brueckner, 2003; Brugnoli et al., 2018; Percoco, 2010) have indeed shown that the aviation industry is an essential input for local economic growth and, as an extension, living standards. Air connectivity is therefore a key factor in a country's economic growth, attracting business investment, human capital, and tourist flows (Alderighi and Gaggero, 2019).

An important issue when dealing with mobility is evaluating how people and firms are served by air transport in different regions – e.g. core, intermediate, and remote regions. Remote regions are usually characterised by low connectivity (especially if they are not tourist destinations), which may be an obstacle in personal mobility and economic growth. Such areas suffer from the problem of low demand, and thus it is not convenient for airlines to offer regular flight services (Bitzan and Junkwood, 2006). As a consequence, in many countries there are policies aimed at improving remote region connectivity through a public service obligation (PSO) (Fageda et al., 2016). Conversely, core regions are usually very well connected to a global network, as their high GDP and population levels guarantee enough demand to provide frequent flights to many destinations. In many core regions, full-service carriers (FSCs) operate their hubs. Intermediate regions might be better connected than remote ones; if high heterogeneity exists in their connectivity levels, it might make such areas less well connected than remote regions with high tourist flows.

When considering air connectivity levels in different regions, it is useful to distinguish between FSCs and low-cost carriers (LCCs), since they have different network models. FSCs adopt mainly a hub-and-spoke (H&S) network, while LCCs operate point-to-point (P2P) connections. In H&S network models, there might be a 'thin' route connecting a remote region since it provides FSCs a feeder service to their central hub. However, a thin route might not be attractive in a P2P network model unless it is heavily subsidised or operated at a low cost. Hence, it is interesting to analyse how different airlines (i.e. FSCs versus LCCs) have evolved in terms of air connectivity levels to groups of regions.

The main goal of this chapter is to analyse air transport regional connectivity in Europe and investigate how it has recently evolved – i.e. in a period during which liberalisation has shown all its effects, by potentially increasing the number of routes in European countries. We analyse these issues by building a new dataset of information on intra- EU aviation activity at the regional level for the 2009–2018 period. We adopt the European nomenclature of territorial units for statistics (NUTS) 2 classification to identify a region. The chapter is organised as follows. The next section provides a literature review. Then the following section discusses the data and the methodology. The next section presents our empirical evidence, and the final section concludes the chapter.

Literature review

According to the academic literature, connectivity is defined as the degree to which vertices (or nodes) in a network are connected to each other (Burghouwt and Redondi, 2013). In the aviation context, vertices can be used to represent airports rather than cities or regions. Two main important perspectives can be distinguished in measuring connectivity – centrality and accessibility. Centrality considers the number of connection opportunities provided by a node, while accessibility refers to the ease of starting from a specific node and reaching the rest of the network (Veldhuis, 1997; Burghouwt, 2007; Malighetti et al., 2008; Redondi et al., 2011; Burghouwt and Redondi, 2013). Network indices have been extensively used in the aviation industry literature to measure connectivity (Burghouwt and Redondi, 2013; Allroggen et al., 2015; Cattaneo et al., 2018) and, in turn, centrality and accessibility.

Pure centrality measures are used generally to describe the prominence of a specific node within a network according to different definitions of relevance (i.e. degree, betweenness, eigenvector, and closeness). Degree centrality is simply the number of a node's direct ties. Betweenness centrality focuses on how many shortest paths within the network pass through the analysed node (Borgatti, 2005; Wasserman and Faust, 1994). Eigenvector centrality is greater as the number increases, as well as the importance of neighbours (Bonacich, 1972). Closeness centrality gives higher importance to nodes that are situated closer to other network nodes.

When the focus moves from the relevance of single nodes to the proximity/facility for spatial interaction, the concept of accessibility becomes central (Gutierrez, 2009). In this regard, two examples of connectivity might be measuring the so-called shortest path-length accessibility (Shaw, 1993; Shaw and Ivy, 1994; Cronrath et al., 2008) or the quickest path-length accessibility (Malighetti et al., 2008; Paleari et al., 2010). The former is based on the concept of geodesic distance and counts the average number of steps to reach any other nodes in the network, while the latter is a measure of the average travel time required to reach any other node in the network. Between pure centrality measures and accessibility indices, several further connectivity measures can be found involving temporal coordination, routing factors, and connection quality attributes.[1]

In this chapter, we rely on the concept of shortest path length (SPL) to build a connectivity index that includes direct and indirect connections. Hence, we consider the average number of steps required to reach any destination (i.e. an airport in a region) in the EU network. This measure of connectivity has been defined as a closeness centrality in the network literature (Burghouwt and Redondi, 2013; Ciliberto et al., 2019) and it is based on the geodesic distance. Our aim is to provide a simple interpretable measure of the ease with which a region is connected by air transport services to other such services. For instance, if SPL = 1, the region is directly connected to all other European regions since only one step is needed to reach them by air. SPL = 2 implies that, on average, all other European regions are reached by air in two steps.

The other key feature of this contribution is related to regional classification. The literature on development economics has classified regions according to their income and growth: differences between poor regions and rich regions might be based on GDP per capita, for example. In this contribution, we focus on a regional classification based on geographical characteristics. Some contributions (e.g. Limao and Venables, 2001) have already highlighted geographical characteristics that may have an impact on economic variables. Other contributions (e.g. Button et al., 2015) have provided some evidence that landlocked countries are less connected to the rest of the world than regions with sea ports, and aviation is essential to improve their connectivity. We focus on a specific geographical characteristic – regional remoteness – because our main goal is to investigate the different connectivity levels in Europe and their variation over the last years, especially compared with core regions. To the best of our knowledge, there have been no previous studies that have examined different connectivity levels in remote regions.

Regarding the identification of remote regions, the Organisation for Economic Co-operation and Development (OECD) has developed a geographical classification based on three categories: (1) predominantly urban; (2) intermediate; and (3) predominantly rural. This classification is mainly based on population density. In 2009, the OECD extended this classification to include the remoteness dimension along the lines proposed in Dijkstra and Poelman (2008). This expansion resulted in a different concept of remoteness and population density, implying that very peripheral regions (e.g. the Azores Islands) with high population density should no longer be considered remote.

Since our aim is to investigate regional air connectivity, we modified the OECD classification by considering islands as remote. Indeed, specific European public policies support the air connectivity of many islands. According to Fageda et al. (2018) these policies are: (1) route-based policies; (2) passenger-based policies; (3) airline-based policies; and (4) airport-based policies. All of these policies take the form of a subsidy, such as discounts and/or PSOs,[2] and they are particularly relevant for islands whose surface transport to the mainland is not available and maritime transport is an option only for short trips.

Data and methods

We built a panel dataset including all scheduled intra-European flights from 2009–2018. Since our interest is also to investigate the differential effect on regional air connectivity of LCCs and FSCs, we distinguish between these two types of airline carriers.[3] We aggregate data regarding flights to/from an airport at the regional level, taking the European NUTS 2 as a reference level. In most European countries, NUTS 2 coincides with regions;[4] however, it has two limitations: (1) the city of London is divided into 5 NUTS 2 regions, which does not make sense for our analysis and therefore we aggregate them into a single region; and (2) Germany has many more NUTS 2 regions than other large European countries (it is more densely populated), but, different from London, there is no city fragmentation. Hence, we maintain the German NUTS 2 level.

The data source is the Official Airline Guide (OAG) database. The flights have different destinations, distances, carriers (aggregated in FSCs and LCCs), frequencies, and available seats. We also collected Eurostat regional data for the NUTS 2 regions to identify core regions, using GDP as the driver. The data includes regions with no airports, and thus they are neither connected by air nor in regions where all airports operate every year. In order to exclude marginal and temporary air services, we dropped connections with fewer than 208 flights per year (i.e. at least four flights per week).

Aviation connectivity measurement

The regional connectivity level is estimated as the average number of paths to reach all other regions in a given year – i.e. an accessibility measure that takes into account the entire regional European network. The regional air connectivity index considers all flights to and from every European airport from 2009–2018 and assigns all flights departing from an airport located in a specific NUTS 2 region, which then reach an airport in another NUTS 2 region. From an arrival in a NUTS 2 region, it is then possible to take another flight to

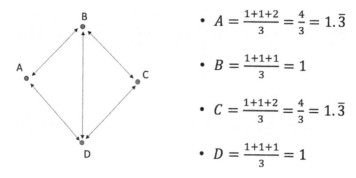

Figure 2.1 An example of a region's connectivity
Source: Devised by authors

reach another NUTS 2 region, and so forth. The first step in computing the air connectivity index consists of identifying the minimum number of paths required to travel by air from region i to reach another NUTS 2 region. The second step is to determine the value of air connectivity for each region by calculating the average number of paths required to reach all other regions. Hence high (good) levels of air connectivity are given by values close to 1, whereas low (poor) connectivity levels are expressed by higher values.

Figure 2.1 presents an example. Suppose there are only four regions: A, B, C, and D. The diagram shows that from region A, there are direct flights to regions B and D, but no direct flights to region C. However, it is possible to reach region C through connecting flights from either region B or D. Hence, regions B and D are reached in one step, region C in two steps. Simply counting these steps and dividing by the number of regions in the dataset minus the observed region (in this example, 3), we have the average number of steps to reach any other region from region A (i.e. 1.3333). In this example, regions B and D are better connected than regions A and C because they have a connectivity level equal to 1. This means that they can reach all the other regions in one step – i.e. there is no need for a connecting flight.

Identification of remote and core regions

We start with the identification of remote regions in Europe. Even if different definitions of remoteness exist (Dijkstra and Poelman, 2008), it is useful for our purposes to classify a region as remote if it is rural or an island that can be quickly connected to the mainland by air. Remote regions were identified in three steps. First, we used the 2009 OECD classification of remoteness, which is at the NUTS 3 level. More specifically, regions were defined as predominantly rural and remote by the OECD classification, as follows: (1) more than 50 per cent of the population live in rural areas; (2) less than 25 per cent of the population live in urban centres with more than 200,000 inhabitants; and (3) the driving time needed for at least 50 per cent of the population of the region to reach a populated centre (at least 50,000 inhabitants) is higher than 60 minutes.[5] However, as previously mentioned, this classification leaves some very peripheral areas (e.g. the Azores) as urban and consequently, non-remote.

In the second step, we focus on each island with an area smaller than 25,000 km[2] that is not classified as remote according to the OECD criteria. In this case, we focus on alternative modes of transport to aviation – i.e. cars (if bridges linking to the mainland are available) and ferries. We assume that the time distance using these alternative modes of transport has to be relatively short; hence, we classify an island as remote if the driving/ferry time to the closest European inland city is more than four hours. We call this modification to the OECD classification the 'island correction'. Hence, a NUTS 3 region is classified as remote if it is subject to the island correction and if the OECD has classified it as rural remote.

Third, since the OECD classification refers to the NUTS 3 level, which is too disaggregated to study air connectivity (many provinces do not have airports), we aggregate the NUTS 3 regions into NUTS 2 regions. We consider a NUTS 2 region as remote if more than 50 per cent of its population lives in a remote NUTS 3 area, according to the corrected OECD classification as previously explained.

Concerning the definition of core regions, we adopt a narrow (*core1*) and a broad (*core2*) definition. Under the former, we consider only 11 European regions: the four motors for Europe (i.e. Baden-Württemberg-Stuttgart, Catalonia, Lombardia, and Auvergne-Rhône-Alpes), the regions included in the top 30 world GDP rankings (Hawksworth et al., 2009) – i.e. London, Île de France (Paris), and Madrid – and the regions included in the top 20 European rankings both for GDP per capita and total GDP (i.e. Oberbayern, Stockholm, Zurich, and Amsterdam-Noord Holland). Since under *core1* the subset of intermediate regions (that is, those not classified as core or remote) may be considered too large and includes areas with several capital cities and/or important economic centres, we decided to enlarge the core region subset according to the broader *core2* definition.[6] Such a definition includes the 11 regions in *core1*, plus all the regions in the top 20 ranking either for total GDP or GDP per capita.[7] In this second case, we have 33 European *core2* regions.

The remaining regions are classified as intermediate. As a result, the dataset under *core1* includes 11 core regions, 262 intermediate, and 34 remote regions (307 regions in total). Under *core2*, the dataset includes 33 core regions, 240 intermediate, and 34 remote regions. Figure 2.2 shows a map of remote, intermediate, *core1*, and *core2* regions. The data do not include those European regions that belong to countries that are not currently involved in the process of EU integration – Albania, Belarus, Bosnia, Moldova, Montenegro, Serbia, Russia, and Ukraine. In these cases, the NUTS definition is not available. The dataset instead covers the countries that have applied to become members – Croatia, Macedonia, and Turkey – and those having political agreements with the EU, such as Norway.

12 *Gianmaria Martini, Flavio Porta, et al.*

Figure 2.2 Map of the regions in Europe: remote, *core1*, *core2*, and intermediate

Source: Devised by authors

Empirical evidence

We collected 3,100 observations regarding the air services provided in 310 NUTS 2 European regions in the 2009–2018 period. In this section, we present some descriptive statistics regarding the changes in air services and connectivity levels that occurred during the observed period. We then analyse the correlation between regional connectivity and aviation, taking into account the differences between FSCs and LCCs. Table 2.1 shows descriptive statistics for the different regional categories and their connectivity levels.[8] Connectivity levels were discussed previously, and *LCCseats* represents the seats offered by LCCs at the NUTS 2 level.

At the European level, regional air connectivity has slightly improved during the 2009–2018 period. In fact, the average regional connectivity level in Europe was 2.35 in 2009 and 2.26 in 2018 – a compound annual growth rate (CAGR) equal to −0.37 per cent. This improvement in air connectivity implies that the increase in traffic level (+3.39 per cent) is not only due to an increase in the number of seats on existing routes, but also to the opening of new connections. In *core1* regions (the narrow definition of most important European regions), the average air connectivity level moved from 1.75 in 2009 to 1.69 in 2018, with a CAGR equal to −0.34 per cent. Hence, the average regional connectivity level regarding intra-European flights in *core1* regions has slightly improved over the observed period. The same pattern is observed for *core2* regions (broad definition). Thus, enlarging the number of regions classified as core regions does not significantly change either the average air connectivity level or its variation over the 2009–2018 period. Considering only remote regions, connectivity was 2.59 in 2009 and 2.45 in 2018, registering a CAGR equal to −0.55 per cent. This implies the largest improvement observed in European regions.

Similar to core regions, intermediate regions also exhibit a slight improvement in air connectivity, with a CAGR close to −0.35 per cent (both *intermediate1* and *intermediate2*). Overall, we observe that remote regions are, on average, less connected than core and intermediate regions. Figure 2.3 shows the dynamic of the average NUTS 2 air connectivity levels in intra-Europe routes during the 2009–2018 period, distinguishing among the *core1*, *core2*, remote, *intermediate1*, and *intermediate2* regions.

We notice that remote regions have higher variability in air connectivity levels than other regions, and they are less connected than core and intermediate regions. Hence, mobility in a European remote region is less stable than in other regions.[9]

We observe a different trend if we consider the average seats available at the NUTS 2 level. In 2018, for example, the average number of seats at the European level was equal to 4,576,475, with a CAGR equal to 3.39 per cent in the 2009–2018 period. In *core1* regions, available seats were on average about 22 million in 2018, with a CAGR equal to about 2 per cent over the period. In *core2* regions, the average annual seats were 15,001,259 with a CAGR equal

Table 2.1 Available seats and NUTS 2 average connectivity levels from 2009 to 2018

Region type	Average seats in NUTS 2			Average LCC seats in NUTS 2			Average connectivity level in NUTS 2		
	2009	2018	CAGR	2009	2018	CAGR	2009	2018	CAGR
Europe	3,280,327	4,576,475	3.39%	969,811	2,071,825	7.89%	2.35	2.26	−0.37%
Core1	17,849,957	21,733,691	1.99%	3,555,971	7,151,971	7.24%	1.75	1.69	−0.34%
Core2	11,520,862	14,418,953	2.27%	2,686,430	5,353,527	7.14%	1.90	1.81	−0.46%
Remote	2,300,845	3,587,330	4.54%	500,053	1,621,365	12.48%	2.59	2.45	−0.55%
Intermediate1	2,569,950	3,720,623	3.77%	888,023	1,842,851	7.57%	2.34	2.26	−0.35%
Intermediate2	1,696,637	2,549,107	4.15%	656,816	1,357,233	7.53%	2.39	2.31	−0.33%

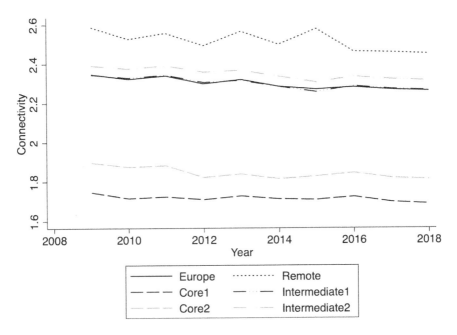

Figure 2.3 Average NUTS 2 air connectivity in European regions
Source: Devised by authors

to 2.22 per cent. In remote regions, an average of 3,587,330 seats were available on intra-Europe routes in 2018, with a CAGR equal to +4.54 per cent, while in *intermediate1* regions, the average was equal to 3,720,623 seats, with a CAGR equal to +3.77 per cent. Last, in *intermediate2* regions, the average annual seats in 2018 were equal to 2,648,168 with a CAGR of +4.08 per cent. Hence, available seats have increased in all regions in Europe, especially in remote and intermediate regions.

During the 2009–2018 period, we observe a substantial increase in the average number of seats available at the NUTS 2 level provided by LCCs. At the European level, the annual increase has been about 8 per cent, with 5.7 million LCCs seats available in *core2* regions in 2018 (CAGR +7.14 per cent), 1.6 million seats in remote regions (CAGR +12.5 per cent), and about 1.4 million LCCs seats in *intermediate2* regions, resulting in a CAGR equal to about +7.5 per cent. Hence, remote regions have experienced the largest annual increase in LCCs seats in relative terms. This is an interesting finding since remote regions are also those that have experienced the largest improvement in connectivity and it may suggest a link between the presence of LCCs and air connectivity in remote regions.

We turn now to the correlation between regional air connectivity levels and available seats. This correlation may be regarded as the first evidence on the

16 *Gianmaria Martini, Flavio Porta, et al.*

Table 2.2 Correlation between regional connectivity, FSCs seats and LCCs seats, Europe
2009–2018

	Europe			Remote regions		
	Conn.	*FSCs seats*	*LCCs seats*	*Conn.*	*FSCs seats*	*LCCs seats*
Connectivity	1.00			1.00		
FSCseats	−0.62	1.00		−0.57	1.00	
	0.00			0.00		
LCCseats	−0.63	0.52	1.00	−0.57	0.86	1.00
	0.00	0.39		0.00	0.00	
	Core1 regions			Core2 regions		
	Conn.	*FSCseats*	*LCCseats*	*Conn.*	*FSCseats*	*LCCseats*
Connectivity	1.00			1.00		
FSCseats	−0.62	1.00		−0.66	1.00	
	0.00			0.00		
LCCseats	−0.40	0.10	1.00	−0.46	−0.20	1.00
	0.00	0.30		0.00	0.00	

link between these two variables, and it may shed some light on their evolution. Table 2.2 presents the correlation matrix between air connectivity levels and seats provided by FSCs and LCCs. *FSCseats* is the volume of seats on flights operated by full-service carriers. The table also reports the *p*-value pointing out the significance level of each correlation coefficient.

At the European level, we observe that the correlation between connectivity levels and FSCs seats is negative (−0.62) and statistically significant at the 1 per cent level, which is similar to the correlation between connectivity and LCCs seats (−0.63). Hence, available seats and connectivity levels move together, which implies that in scenarios where we observe more seats (both from FSCs and LCCs), we also have better air connectivity, and vice versa. This is further evidence that the increase in available seats is not only a signal of new routes; it also implies an increase in frequency and/or in aircraft capacity on existing connections. Interestingly, the correlation between FSCs and LCCs seats is not significant.

In both *core1* and *core2* regions, we observe that connectivity is more correlated to *FSCseats* rather than to *LCCseats*. Hence, in core regions the link between FSCs seats and air connectivity is stronger than that with LCCs. In remote regions, we observe that the correlation (in absolute terms) between connectivity and FSCs seats is similar to that of LCCs seats (−0.57). Last, although not shown in Table 2.2, the correlation between FSCs seats and air connectivity is lower than that of LCCs seats (respectively, −0.55 and −0.64 with *intermediate2*), and both correlation indices are statistically significant) in intermediate regions. Hence, even if the evidence shown in Table 2.2 represents a mere correlation and not a causal link, it may suggest that both FSCs and LCCs play a role in improving regional connectivity in Europe as well as the following: (1) in core regions, air connectivity is mainly related to FSCs' activity; (2) in remote regions, air connectivity is not linked to a particular type of carrier but just to the overall air service provision, and (3) in intermediate regions, connectivity is more related to LCCs activity.

Figures 2.4 and 2.5 show the map of Europe's regional air connectivity for 2009 and 2018, respectively. We can observe that in 2009, regions with poor connectivity are concentrated in Turkey, Greece, Scandinavia, Scotland, and Wales. In 2018 (Figure 2.5), regions with poor connectivity remain in Turkey, Greece, and Scandinavia, while Wales and Scotland show a slight improvement. The comparison also allows us to identify the regions that have lost air services during the observed period (e.g. Castile-La Mancha [ES42]) or have acquired them (Umbria [ITI2]).

More details regarding the connectivity levels in remote and core regions are shown in Table 2.3 (remote regions) and Table 2.4 (core regions). In remote regions (Table 2.3), there has been an increase in air connectivity in the 2009–2018 period, with the exceptions of Extremadura (ES43) and Nord and Middle Sweden (SE31).[10] Poor performances over the observed period variations are highlighted in bold and represent negative CAGR values for seat variations and positive CAGR values for changes in air connectivity levels.

Modifications in core regions during the 2009–2018 period are presented in Table 2.4.[11] Again, poor performances over the observed period variations are highlighted in bold and represent negative CAGR values for seat variations and positive CAGR values for changes in air connectivity levels. In all core regions, air connectivity levels have improved, with the exception of Île-de-France (FR10 – Paris), Zuid-Holland (NL33 – Rotterdam), Köln (DEA2), and northeastern Scotland (Aberdeen).

The top 20 best air-connected European regions in 2018 are presented in Table 2.5. Amsterdam is first, followed by Munich, Frankfurt, Stansted, Istanbul, and Paris. All the best-connected regions are either core regions or regions with a major airport, with the exception of Düsseldorf (DEA1) and Andalucía (ES61).

Conclusion

In this chapter, we analysed air connectivity at a European regional level, focusing only on the intra-European network. Connections with an annual average frequency lower than four flights per week were not considered to avoid distortions from episodic operations. Air connectivity is measured at the NUTS 2 level. We also investigated the different connectivity levels in core, remote, and intermediate regions and considered the air-connectivity variation during the 2009–2018 period, comparing it with the variation in available seats on both FSCs and LCCs.

We find some interesting insights. First, regional air connectivity within Europe has improved in all regions, especially the remote regions. Second,

Figure 2.4 Map of 2009 regional connectivity in Europe
Devised by authors

Figure 2.5 Map of 2018 regional connectivity in Europe
Devised by authors

Table 2.3 Evolution in the number of seats, seats offered by an LCC, and air connectivity in remote regions

Region code	Name	Seats			LCC seats			Connectivity levels		
		2009	2018	CAGR	2009	2018	CAGR	2009	2018	CAGR
CY00	Cyprus	4,126,875	6,610,306	4.82%	629,445	3,435,149	18.49%	2.04	1.92	−0.62%
DK02	Sjaelland	424	1,742	15.18%	–	–	–	–	–	–
EL41	North Aegean	874,324	736,088	−1.71%	20,232	36,975	6.22%	2.89	2.79	−0.35%
EL42	South Aegean	2,581,608	6,195,908	9.15%	438,380	2,114,033	17.04%	2.30	2.02	−1.32%
EL43	Crete	2,464,341	4,931,691	7.18%	466,262	1,826,670	14.63%	2.30	1.99	−1.45%
EL53	C. Macedonia	22,554	9,120	−8.66%	–	–	–	2.91	–	–
EL54	Epirus	93,180	63,540	−3.76%	–	–	–	2.91	2.80	−0.38%
EL61	Thessaly	53,624	216,047	14.95%	2,604	32,084	28.55%	2.91	2.80	−0.38%
EL62	Ionian Islands	1,034,825	2,856,381	10.69%	209,835	1,162,218	18.67%	2.52	2.11	−1.74%
EL63	West. Greece	101,809	265,472	10.06%	32,982	118,732	13.67%	3.51	3.11	−1.21%
EL64	Central Greece	14,409	16,955	1.64%	1,302	–	–	–	2.80	–
EL65	Peloponnese	8,090	141,568	33.14%	–	26,382	–	–	3.03	–
ES43	Extremadura	59,880	40,650	−3.80%	–	–	–	**2.62**	**2.69**	**0.29%**
ES53	Illes Balears	15,700,000	23,600,000	4.16%	4,753,682	14,676,144	11.93%	1.90	1.76	−0.79%
ES70	Canarias	14,800,000	25,000,000	5.38%	2,675,171	11,747,371	15.95%	2.00	1.80	−1.06%
FI1D	Itä–Suomi	1,627,534	2,066,921	2.42%	8,136	406,886	47.88%	2.88	2.58	−1.09%
FI20	Åland	46,410	62,088	2.95%	–	–	–	2.83	2.73	−0.38%
FR83	Corse	1,757,171	2,747,571	4.57%	194,502	874,281	16.22%	2.55	2.48	−0.27%
IE01	M. & W. Ireland	737,985	526,036	−3.33%	411,381	353,997	−1.49%	2.33	2.32	−0.03%
ITG2	Sardegna	4,772,442	5,197,733	0.86%	2,017,363	2,878,770	3.62%	2.15	2.09	−0.29%
IS00	Iceland	1,439,051	4,083,458	10.99%	9,366	1,628,018	67.50%	2.24	2.07	−0.75%
MT00	Malta	1,753,919	3,922,112	8.38%	443,690	1,948,296	15.95%	2.16	2.00	−0.78%
NO02	Hedmark O. O.	16,684	1,512	−21.35%	–	–	–	2.87	–	–
NO07	Nord–Norge	4,815,638	5,630,892	1.58%	1,002,709	1,279,164	2.46%	2.80	2.79	−0.06%
PT20	R.A. dos Açores	1,330,342	1,976,848	4.04%	–	266,169	–	2.92	2.73	−0.68%
PT30	R.A. da Madeira	1,490,334	1,895,024	2.43%	268,716	747,904	10.78%	2.39	2.36	−0.14%
SE21	Småland	489,702	765,528	4.57%	19,656	58,134	11.45%	2.82	2.37	−1.73%
SE31	N.M. Swerige	152,542	114,254	−2.85%	–	5,394	–	**2.66**	**2.71**	**0.20%**
SE32	Middle Norrland	560,846	745,751	2.89%	–	7,968	–	2.82	2.72	−0.34%
TR22	Balıkesir	16,604	408,564	37.75%	–	175,173	–	–	2.59	–
TR90	Trabzon	516,522	2,144,181	15.30%	210,915	929,299	15.99%	2.74	2.55	−0.71%
UKM6	High. & Isl.	979,391	1,127,255	1.42%	186,459	284,364	4.31%	2.45	2.32	−0.56%

Table 2.4 Evolution in the number of seats, seats offered by an LCC, and connectivity in core regions

Region code	Name	Seats			LCC seats			Connectivity levels		
		2009	2018	CAGR	2009	2018	CAGR	2009	2018	CAGR
CH04	Zurich	12,000,000	15,100,000	2.32%	545,186	1,958,572	13.64%	1.76	1.71	−0.27%
DE11	Stuttgart	5,905,125	7,137,518	1.91%	2,137,042	4,747,649	8.31%	1.89	1.81	−0.45%
DE21	Oberbayern (Munich)	18,800,000	24,100,000	2.51%	1,521,738	3,635,422	9.10%	1.62	1.54	−0.49%
ES30	Comunidad de Madrid	27,100,000	25,300,000	−0.68%	5,000,733	6,855,905	3.21%	1.74	1.70	−0.20%
ES51	Cataluña	22,300,000	27,700,000	2.19%	11,165,124	21,385,057	6.71%	1.67	1.65	−0.10%
FR10	Île de France (Paris)	34,300,000	37,000,000	0.76%	5,060,668	10,362,257	7.43%	**1.61**	**1.62**	**0.06%**
FR71	Rhône-Alpes	4,897,077	5,908,827	1.90%	866,385	2,245,758	9.99%	1.91	1.88	−0.16%
ITC4	Lombardia (Milan)	20,400,000	24,200,000	1.72%	8,161,281	13,505,774	5.17%	1.74	1.65	−0.51%
NL32	Noord-Holland (Amsterdam)	16,900,000	28,100,000	5.22%	3,108,372	8,048,227	9.98%	1.63	1.51	−0.80%
SE11	Stockholm	10,400,000	17,700,000	5.46%	1,386,077	4,940,172	13.55%	1.88	1.75	−0.67%
UKI	London	23,400,000	26,800,000	1.37%	163,080	986,888	19.73%	1.77	1.73	−0.22%
AT13	Wien (with AT12)	10,300,000	14,000,000	3.12%	1,976,849	3,372,618	5.49%	1.72	1.65	−0.41%
BE10	Bruxelles (with BE24)	9,228,132	12,200,000	2.83%	1,127,398	2,719,024	9.20%	1.74	1.70	−0.20%
CZ01	Praha	6,696,289	7,803,132	1.54%	1,654,765	2,799,965	5.40%	1.78	1.75	−0.14%
DE50	Bremen	1,562,559	1,624,813	0.39%	789,210	597,038	−2.75%	2.15	2.14	−0.04%
DE60	Hamburg	7,874,205	10,500,000	2.92%	987,081	5,208,565	18.10%	1.85	1.75	−0.58%
DEA1	Düsseldorf	12,000,000	14,400,000	1.84%	2,206,552	8,370,696	14.26%	1.72	1.68	−0.22%
DEA2	Köln	6,099,632	7,518,862	2.11%	3,645,789	6,355,466	5.71%	**1.89**	**1.89**	**0.05%**
DE71	Darmstadt (Frankfurt)	20,500,000	28,100,000	3.20%	666,678	2,938,454	15.99%	1.65	1.57	−0.51%
DK01	Hovedstaden	11,700,000	17,000,000	3.81%	1,616,002	6,154,227	14.31%	1.74	1.70	−0.27%
ES61	Andalucía	11,400,000	16,000,000	3.45%	5,557,965	11,517,928	7.56%	1.91	1.70	−1.16%
FR82	Provence-Alpes-Côte d'Azur	10,400,000	12,900,000	2.18%	2,828,022	5,071,169	6.01%	1.84	1.77	−0.38%
IE02	Southern and Eastern	15,900,000	18,100,000	1.30%	8,338,995	9,022,435	0.79%	1.74	1.66	−0.46%
ITH3	Veneto	6,749,955	9,269,463	3.22%	2,453,817	5,472,192	8.35%	1.94	1.82	−0.65%
ITH5	Emilia-Romagna	3,771,399	4,579,795	1.96%	1,617,669	2,715,767	5.32%	2.07	1.89	−0.86%
ITI4	Lazio	21,600,000	23,300,000	0.76%	5,643,475	9,600,219	5.46%	1.69	1.68	−0.10%
LU00	Luxembourg	1,096,069	2,807,176	9.86%	–	529,678	–	2.11	1.93	−0.89%
NL11	Groningen (with NL13)	26,238	175,770	20.95%	17,754	49,680	10.84%	3.23	2.37	−3.03%
NL33	Zuid-Holland	575,318	1,019,042	5.88%	406,002	823,649	7.33%	**2.33**	**2.42**	**0.36%**
NO01	Oslo og Akershus	11,900,000	18,200,000	4.34%	4,337,184	8,342,932	6.76%	1.88	1.81	−0.40%
SK01	Bratislavský kraj	1,020,763	1,045,228	0.24%	850,908	767,648	−1.02%	2.29	2.29	−0.01%
UKM5	Northeastern Scotland	1,836,479	1,734,066	−0.58%	127,965	211,839	5.17%	**2.24**	**2.25**	**0.03%**

22 *Gianmaria Martini, Flavio Porta, et al.*

Table 2.5 Best-connected regions in 2016

Rank	Code	Region	Connectivity index		
			2009	*2018*	*CAGR*
1	NL32	Noord-Holland (Amsterdam)	1.63	1.51	−0.80%
2	DE21	Oberbayern (Munich)	1.62	1.54	−0.49%
3	DE71	Darmstadt (Frankfurt)	1.65	1.57	−0.51%
4	UKH3	Essex (Stansted)	1.67	1.58	−0.50%
5	TR10	Istanbul Subregion	1.76	1.61	−0.88%
6	FR10	Île de France (Paris)	1.61	1.62	0.06%
7	AT12	Niederösterreich (Wien)	1.72	1.65	−0.41%
8	ES51	Cataluña (Barcelona)	1.67	1.65	−0.10%
9	ITC4	Lombardia (Milan)	1.74	1.65	−0.51%
10	IE02	Southern and Eastern (Dublin)	1.74	1.66	−0.46%
11	UKJ2	Surrey (Gatwick)	1.70	1.67	−0.20%
12	ITI4	Lazio (Rome)	1.69	1.68	−0.10%
13	DEA1	Düsseldorf	1.72	1.68	−0.22%
14	UKD3	Greater Manchester	1.87	1.68	−1.03%
15	DK01	Hovedstaden (Copenhagen)	1.74	1.70	−0.27%
16	BE24	Prov. Vlaams-Brabant (Brussels)	1.74	1.70	−0.20%
17	ES61	Andalucía	1.91	1.70	−1.16%
18	ES30	Comunidad de Madrid	1.74	1.70	−0.20%
19	PL12	Mazowieckie (Warsaw)	1.88	1.71	−0.95%
20	CH04	Zurich	1.76	1.71	−0.27%

since the increase in available seats over the 2009–2018 period, there has been a commensurate increase in available routes (and not just in-flight frequency on existing connections). Third, if we consider only the regions with air service, the ranking is core, intermediate, and remote. Hence, remote regions are still penalised in terms of European air connectivity, as connectivity in core regions is about 30 per cent better than in remote areas. Fourth, both FSCs and LCCs have played a role in improving regional air connectivity in Europe. More specifically, in core regions, connectivity is more related to FSC activity, while in intermediate regions, it is more related to LCCs. Both carrier types have responded in the same manner to air connectivity of disadvantaged (in terms of mobility) remote European regions. The H&S model used by FFCs demonstrates the strong link to core regions air connectivity, while the P2P model used by LCCs may provide an interpretation for air connectivity in intermediate regions. In remote regions, FSCs play an important role in supplying their hubs with few connections, but they are matched in terms of relevance by LCCs. This may be due to LCCs' cost advantage (due of operating larger planes at low-flight frequencies; Calzada and Fageda, 2019), and thus, LCCs may find it convenient to operate thin routes that are not sustainable by FSCs. Hence, LCCs play an important role in developing remote regions mobility. Fifth, low air connectivity in some French, German, and UK regions may be explained by their closeness to Paris, Frankfurt and London, while in some regions in

Portugal, Spain, Greece, Turkey, and the Scandinavian peninsula, it may be explained by remoteness combined with low demand levels (these are regions with very low population density). Last, top-connected regions are those surrounding Amsterdam, Munich, Frankfurt, Essex (London Stansted), Istanbul, Paris, Wien, Barcelona, Milan (Lombardy), and Dublin.

These results do not account for some important factors such as seasonal impacts (which may be strong in islands), PSOs, and spatial effects among nearby regions. Moreover, different connectivity indices can also be considered, taking the quality of the connection (i.e., the importance of the destination and flight frequency) and the minimum connecting time into account. We leave these topics to future research.

Notes

1 See Burghouwt and Redondi (2013) for a classification of the various connectivity models.
2 For example, Calzada and Fageda (2017) argued that the EU allows member states to adopt PSOs for scheduled air services on thin routes connecting many peripheral regions with an important mainland airport to stimulate local economic and social development; see Fageda et al. (2018) for a comprehensive review.
3 LCCs are identified according to OAG carrier category (low-cost or mainline [full-service] carrier). Charters are not included. Regional airlines are always classified according to OAG. General aviation is not considered.
4 The NUTS 2 classification is a hierarchical system for dividing up the EU economic territory in order to control basic regions for the application of regional policies. We used the current NUTS 2013 classification, which is valid from 1 January 2015 and lists 98 NUTS 1 regions, 276 NUTS 2 regions, and 1,342 NUTS regions at NUTS 3 level.
5 OECD has the following regional classification: 1 – urban non remote, 2.1 – intermediate non remote, 2.2 – intermediate remote, 3.1 – rural non remote, and 3.2 – rural remote.
6 We are grateful to an anonymous referee for this suggestion.
7 We aggregate AT12 to AT13 (Wien) because Wien airport is located outside Wien and for the same reason, BE24 to BE10 (Brussels) and NL13 to NL11 (Groningen).
8 The averages are computed at the European level and do not include the regions without air service.
9 When we consider all European regions, we have 68 NUTS 2 without airports. These regions are excluded from the analysis – that is, our network is based on nodes given by regions with at least one airport.
10 Regarding the air connectivity level, certain regions do not meet our frequency threshold in some years and therefore their air connectivity cannot be computed. Moreover, we list in Table 2.3 only 32 remote regions out of 34, as Molise (ITF2) and Alentejo (PT18) have no air service at all.
11 Table 2.4 reports data only for 32 core regions out of 33 because Utrecht (NL31) does not have air service.

References

Airbus (2018). *Global market forecast 2018–2037*. Toulouse, Airbus.
Alderighi, M. and Gaggero, A. A. (2017). Fly and trade: Evidence from the Italian manufacturing industry. *Economics of Transportation*, 9, 51–60.

Alderighi, M. and Gaggero, A. A. (2019). Flight availability and international tourism flows. *Annals of Tourism Research*, 79, 102642.

Allroggen, F. and Malina, R. (2014). Do the regional growth effects of air transport differ among airports? *Journal of Air Transport Management*, 37, 1–4.

Allroggen, F., Wittman, M. D. and Malina, R. (2015). How air transport connects the world – a new metric of air connectivity and its evolution between 1990 and 2012. *Transportation Research Part E: Logistics and Transportation Review*, 80, 184–201.

Bilotkach, V. (2015). Are airports engines of economic development? A dynamic panel data approach. *Urban Studies*, 52(9), 1577–1593.

Bitzan, J. and Junkwood, C. (2006). Higher airfares to small and medium sized communities: Costly service or market power? *Journal of Transport and Economic Policy*, 40, 473–501.

Blonigen, B. A. and Cristea, A. D. (2015). Air service and urban growth: Evidence from a quasi-natural policy experiment. *Journal of Urban Economics*, 86, 128–146.

Boeing (2018). *Current market outlook 2018–2037*. Seattle, Boeing.

Bonacich, P. (1972). Factoring and weighting approaches to status scores and clique identification. *Journal of Mathematical Sociology*, 2(1), 113–120.

Borgatti, S. P. (2005). Centrality and network flow. *Social Networks*, 27(1), 55–71.

Brueckner, J. K. (2003). Airline traffic and urban economic development. *Urban Studies*, 40(8), 1455–1469.

Brugnoli, A., Dal Bianco, A., Martini, G. and Scotti, D. (2018). The impact of air transportation on trade flows: A natural experiment on causality applied to Italy. *Transportation Research Part A: Policy and Practice*, 112, 95–107.

Burghouwt, G. (2007). *Airline network development in Europe and its implications for airport planning*. Aldershot, Ashgate.

Burghouwt, G. and Redondi, R. (2013). Connectivity in air transport networks: An assessment of models and applications. *Journal of Transport Economics and Policy*, 47(1), 35–53.

Button, K., Brugnoli, A., Martini, G. and Scotti, D. (2015). Connecting African urban areas: Airline networks and intra-Sub-Saharan trade. *Journal of Transport Geography*, 42, 84–89.

Calzada, J. and Fageda, X. (2017). Competition and public service obligations in European aviation markets. *Transportation Research Part A: Policy and Practice*, 70, 104–116.

Calzada, J. and Fageda, X. (2019). Route expansion in the European air transport market. *Regional Studies*, 53(8), 1149–1160.

Cattaneo, M., Malighetti, P. and Percoco, M. (2018). The impact of intercontinental air accessibility on local economies: Evidence from the de-hubbing of Malpensa airport. *Transport Policy*, 61, 96–105.

Ciliberto, F., Cook, E. E. and Williams, J. W. (2019). Network structure and consolidation in the US airline industry, 1990–2015. *Review of Industrial Organization*, 54(1), 3–36.

Cronrath, E., Arndt, A. and Zoch, A. (2008). *Does size matter? The importance of airports in the European and German air transport network*. Presented at Air Transport Research Society Conference, Athens, July.

Dijkstra, L. and Poelman, H. (2008). *Remote rural regions: How proximity to a city influences the performance of rural regions*. Regional Focus n. 1. DG Regio, European Commission. Available at: https://ec.europa.eu/regional_policy/sources/docgener/focus/2008_01_rural.pdf.

Fageda, X., Jiménez, J. L. and Valido, J. (2016). Does an increase in subsidies lead to changes in air fares? Empirical evidence from Spain. *Transportation Research Part A*, 94, 235–242.

Fageda, X., Suárez-Alemán, A., Serebrisky, T. and Fioravanti, R. (2018). Air connectivity in remote regions: A comprehensive review of existing transport policies worldwide. *Journal of Air Transport Management*, 66, 65–75.

Gutierrez, J. (2009). Transport and accessibility. *International Encyclopedia of Human Geography*, 410–417.

Hawksworth, J., Hoehn, T. and Tiwari, A. (2009). *Global city GDP rankings 2008–2025.* London, PricewaterhouseCoopers.

ICAO (2018a). *Annual report of the council 2017.* Montreal, ICAO.

ICAO (2018b). *Preliminary figures of the annual report of the council 2018.* Montreal, ICAO.

Limao, N. and Venables, A. J. (2001). Infrastructure, geographical disadvantage, transport costs, and trade. *The World Bank Economic Review*, 15(3), 451–479.

Malighetti, P., Paleari, S. and Redondi, R. (2008). Connectivity of the European airport network: 'Self-help hubbing' and business implications. *Journal of Air Transport Management*, 14(2), 53–65.

Paleari, S., Redondi, R. and Malighetti, P. (2010). A comparative study of airport connectivity in China, Europe and US: Which network provides the best service to passengers? *Transportation Research Part E: Logistics and Transportation Review*, 46(2), 198–210.

Percoco, M. (2010). Airport activity and local development: Evidence from Italy. *Urban Studies*, 47(11), 2427–2443.

Redondi, R., Malighetti, P. and Paleari, S. (2011). New routes and airport connectivity. *Networks and Spatial Economics*, 11(4), 713–725.

Shaw, S. L. (1993). Hub structures of major US passenger airlines. *Journal of Transport Geography*, 1(1), 47–58.

Shaw, S. L. and Ivy, R. L. (1994). Airline mergers and their effect on network structure. *Journal of Transport Geography*, 2(4), 234–246.

Veldhuis, J. (1997). The competitive position of airline networks. *Journal of Air Transport Management*, 3(4), 181–188.

Wasserman, S. and Faust, K. (1994). *Social network analysis: Methods and applications*, vol. 8. Cambridge, Cambridge University Press.

3 The impacts of airports in geographical peripheries

A Norwegian case study

Nigel Halpern

Introduction

This chapter examines the impacts of airports in geographical peripheries. The chapter consists of two main parts. The first part defines geographical peripheries from a European perspective and considers different types of indicators that can be used to measure peripherality. It also provides a brief introduction to airports in Europe's peripheral areas and their potential impacts including economic impacts, wider impacts on regional economic and social development, and external effects on the environment. Geographically, Norway is one of Europe's most peripheral countries and is highly dependent on air transport for the accessibility and social and economic development of its regions. As a result, a fair amount of research has been conducted on different aspects relating to airport impacts in Norway. The second part of this chapter brings the findings of previous studies together, along with presenting some new analysis, in a case study on Norway.

Geographical peripheries, airports and their impacts

Geographical peripheries

Peripherality is a widely used term. In general, it refers to the relationship between the centre of an area and its periphery. A challenge for researchers is that peripherality can be applied to a range of contexts and situations in different ways, often depending on individual viewpoints or objectives. It can also be approached from different disciplinary perspectives (e.g. geography, economics, sociology, politics, or organisation). This chapter focuses on geographical peripheries, which helps to narrow the definition. However, geographical peripheries can also be defined in different ways, for instance, depending on the level at which areas are subdivided (e.g. global, regional, national, or local), and the criteria and measures used.

In their work on the creation of a peripherality index for Europe, Schürman and Talaat (2000) illustrate how centres and geographical peripheries can be delineated according to relative accessibility. This can be measured using simple indicators such as the length of roads, motorways, or rail tracks, the number of railway stations or airports, or travel time to the nearest network node (e.g. to a railway station or airport). Such indicators provide a good overview of a study area. However, they say little about the network effects that transport infrastructure can have on linking parts of the study area to each other, or to other areas. It is therefore important to also consider more complex indicators that include the activities reached in an area (e.g. markets, wealth, or jobs) and the effort needed to reach the area (e.g. time, distance, or cost). Different functions of activity and effort can then be used depending on the focus of the study.

Schürmann et al. (1997) and subsequent studies (e.g. Schürman and Talaat, 2000; Spiekermann and Aalbu, 2004; Spiekermann and Neubauer, 2002; Wegener et al., 2002) identify three main types of indicator: (1) travel cost, which measures the effort needed to reach a set of activities such as the distance, time, or cost associated with travelling to a capital city or cities of a certain size, based on the notion that not all activities are important to accessibility; (2) daily accessibility, which measures the activities reached such as a capital city or cities of a certain size within a day, based on the notion of a business traveller wanting to reach a certain place, conduct business there, and travel home in a day; and (3) potential accessibility, which measures the activities reached such as markets, wealth, or jobs, weighted by the effort needed to reach them, based on the notion that the attraction of an activity increases with size and decreases with the effort needed to reach it. The advantages and disadvantages of different indicators vary. In general, travel cost and daily accessibility indicators are relatively easy to compute, communicate, and understand, but their theoretical foundation is rather limited (i.e. in terms of justifying which cities to include in the analysis and why), while potential accessibility indicators are more grounded on theory but are also more difficult to compute, communicate, and understand.

Based on spatial indicators, Europe's geographical periphery tends to comprise countries or regions on the edge of Europe such as more exterior parts of the British Isles, large parts of the Nordic countries, alpine regions, and large parts of Southern/Mediterranean Europe. It also includes the outermost regions of France, Portugal, and Spain. The peripheral nature of such areas is then often associated with disparities that distinguish peripheral areas from other more centrally located areas, and potentially constrain their development. For instance, Botterill et al. (2000) suggest that peripheral areas are more likely to have a low level of economic vitality and a dependency on traditional industries, a more rural and remote setting, a declining population through out-migration and with an ageing structure, a reliance on imported technologies and ideas, a remoteness from decision-making leading to a sense of alienation and a lack of power, and poor information flows, infrastructure, and amenities. Peripheral areas may, however, also have opportunities (e.g. for agriculture, extraction, or tourism) due to an abundance of natural resources and/or a high scenic value.

Airports and their impacts

Good access to main transport networks helps to reduce peripherality. That is why air transport can play such as important role. It is often the fastest, most efficient, and cheapest mode of transport over long distances, and it is relatively unaffected by permanent geographical features such as islands and mountains. As providers of infrastructure for air services, airports are therefore often considered to be vital for peripheral areas, and several studies recognise that there is a good supply of airports in Europe's periphery (e.g. Fewings, 2010; Halpern, 2006; Halpern and Niskala, 2008; Williams et al., 2007). Despite this, many of them serve low traffic volumes and have short runway lengths that limit the type and size of aircraft they can handle. For instance, Halpern (2006) identified 217 airports in peripheral parts of Europe. Two per cent of them served five million passengers or more per year, 16 per cent served more than one million but less than five million, and 82 per cent served fewer than one million. Thirty-three per cent of them had a runway length of less than 1,800 metres, and 16 per cent had less than 1,200 metres.

In terms of airport impacts, studies tend to distinguish between direct, indirect, and induced impacts, typically on employment, income and GDP (e.g. InterVISTAS, 2015; York Aviation, 2004). Direct impacts are associated with the operation and management of airport activities, indirect impacts are associated with industries that supply and support airport activities, and induced impacts are associated with economic activity in the wider economy of employees directly or indirectly involved with airport activities. Studies also investigate wider impacts, and much of the attention has been on economic catalytic impacts (e.g. Cooper and Smith, 2005). In an airport context, economic catalytic impacts have been defined as 'employment and income generated in the economy of the study area by the wider role of the airport in improving the productivity of business and in attracting economic activities such as inward investment and inbound tourism' (York Aviation, 2004, 5). Wider impacts may include consumer welfare effects, for instance, when airports contribute to opportunities for social development (e.g. to travel, watch, and take part in sport or cultural activities, access basic local services such as hospitals and education, or influence the location and retention of residents).

Wider impacts may also include external effects such as on the environment. Airport impacts on environmental disturbance can be significant at local and global scales, resulting from the operation of the airport itself but also the operation of airlines, airport service providers such as those offering ground access, and also from any construction work taking place at or around the airport. At a local level, one of the key concerns is noise. However, there are also concerns relating to air pollution, waste management, water pollution, energy and water use, land-use planning, and biodiversity. At a global level, climate change is of great concern. In peripheral areas, there may be a high dependence on air transport, and a desire for future growth. This needs to be balanced with local community levels of tolerance and the preservation of what are often areas of outstanding natural beauty. Airports, in collaboration with other stakeholders, can play a key role in protecting the environment through initiatives that reduce their current and future impacts.

Understanding the impacts of airports is important, given the costs associated with them. Airports tend to have high fixed costs, which combined with low traffic volumes at many airports in peripheral areas means that most of them are expected to operate at a loss. In addition, maintaining adequate air service provision may not be commercially viable for airlines due to the long distances from main markets, low traffic volumes, and limited opportunities for market growth. Many national or regional governments in Europe therefore impose public service obligations (PSOs) on some routes. The obligations may require a minimum level of service, for instance regarding frequency, timing, aircraft type and number of seats, pricing and distribution, and punctuality. Airlines willing to meet those obligations can then apply to operate the route with open or restricted market access – the latter almost always being awarded with economic compensation.

Case study on Norway

Case study area and its peripherality

Norway occupies a peripheral location in Northern Europe. The country is situated on the western side of the Scandinavian peninsula and shares a border with Russia and Finland in the north and Sweden in the east. The country is divided into five regions: eastern, southern, western, central, and northern Norway (Figure 3.1). The five regions are further divided into 18 county administrations and 422 municipalities. Three of the municipalities have more than 150,000 inhabitants (SSB, 2018a): Oslo in the east (673,469 inhabitants), Bergen in the west (279,792), and Trondheim in the centre (193,501). Kristiansand is the largest municipality in the south (91,440), while Tromsø is the largest in the north (75,638). The population of 5.3 million occupies a total surface area of 323,807 km². This results in a population density of 16.4 inhabitants per km², which is the second lowest in Europe after Iceland (Eurostat, 2018).

In addition to being sparsely populated, Norway has a challenging topography and climate. It is Europe's longest country, extending almost 1,800 kilometres (km), and has the Scandinavian Mountains range running along much of the length of the country. The western part of the range forms the fjords of Norway, the longest of which is Sognefjord that extends 205 km inland. The country is generally long and thin in the north; however, it reaches 432 km at its widest point in more southern parts of the country (Great Norwegian Encyclopedia, 2018). Almost one-third of the country is located north of the Arctic Circle and most of the country experiences long periods with snow and ice during the winter. One per cent of the country's land is covered by permanent snow and glaciers (SSB, 2018c).

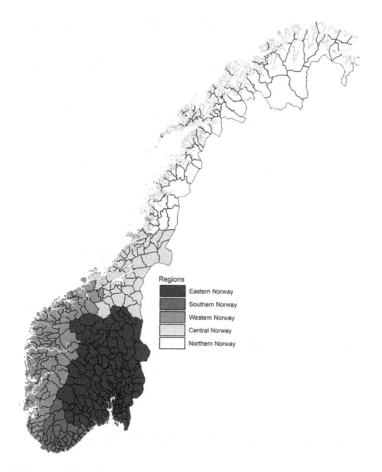

Figure 3.1 Regional boundaries
Source: Devised by author from Statistics Norway data (SSB, 2018b)

The topography and climate means that travelling around Norway by land or sea, especially over long distances, is difficult, and it is not helped by the presence of relatively limited surface transport options. The country has 95,000 km of public roads with just 750 km of motorway (SSB, 2018d). There is a conventional mainline network of long-haul rail services heading west from Oslo to Stavanger and Bergen, with respective travel times of approximately eight and seven hours, and north to Trondheim (seven hours from Oslo) and Bodø (a further ten hours after changing at Trondheim). The travel times by rail are similar to non-stop travel times by car. The only high-speed rail service is the one that connects Oslo Central Station to Oslo Airport. There is also a coastal ferry service called Hurtigruten that takes five to six days to travel from Bergen on the west coast to Kirkenes in the far north, stopping at 34 ports in each direction.

Kjærland and Mathisen (2012) classify central and northern parts of Norway as being equally or more peripheral to Europe's outermost regions, while most accessibility indicators classify the whole country as peripheral in a European context. For instance, Spiekermann and Aalbu (2004) use a potential accessibility indicator with population as the destination activity and an integrated measure of travel time by road, rail, and air as the effort. The indicator is based on data for European countries at the county level. Oslo is found to have a below average level of accessibility, while all remaining counties are peripheral, especially those in northern, central, and northwestern parts of the country that are either very or extremely peripheral. Spiekermann and Aalbu (2004) then repeat the analysis for Nordic countries only, and at the municipality level. Oslo and its surroundings are found to have above average levels of accessibility. All other municipalities (representing about 75 per cent of the population) are below average. Those that are only slightly below average include Kristiansand in the south and Stavanger and Bergen in the west. All remaining municipalities (representing about 65 per cent of the population) are peripheral, with the majority being very or extremely peripheral. Within the peripheral areas, municipalities close to an airport with good air service connections are generally less peripheral than those without.

Delineations of peripherality vary at a national level. This is shown by the results of the national centrality index that was launched in 2017 (see Høydahl, 2017). The index is composed of two parts: (1) the number of jobs that inhabitants of each area can reach by car within 90 minutes; and (2) how many different types of service features (goods and services) inhabitants of each area can reach by car within 90 minutes. Numbers are weighted so that a workplace or service function close to home counts more than one further away. Index values range from 0 (which is only theoretically possible) to 1,000. The values are grouped into six categories, with the lowest number representing the most peripheral municipalities and the highest representing the most central (Figure 3.2). As with the European and Nordic models of Spiekermann and Aalbu (2004), Oslo is the most central municipality in Norway with a value of 1,000. This is followed by several neighbouring municipalities. The country's second most populated municipality, Bergen, is in 14th place, while the third most populated, Trondheim, is in sixteenth place. Tromsø, the most populated municipality in northern Norway and Norway's 16th most populated, is in seventieth place. This shows that while some of the larger municipalities in Norway are classified as being peripheral in a European context or below average in a Nordic context, they are relatively central in a Norwegian context.

Norway's airports and their impacts on regional accessibility

Norway has relatively good infrastructure for air services. Forty-nine airports (excluding the Norwegian archipelago airport of Svalbard) provided commercial

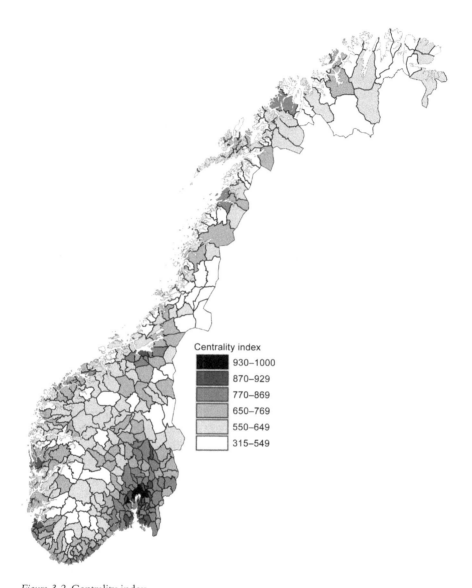

Figure 3.2 Centrality index
Source: Devised by author from Statistics Norway data (SSB, 2018e)

passenger movements in 2017 (Figure 3.3). This is equivalent to one airport per 108,074 inhabitants and 6,608 km^2 of total surface area. Forty-five of the airports in Figure 3.3 are operated by the state-owned airport operator Avinor (although operations have since stopped at Fagernes), while the remaining four (Notodden, Sandefjord, Stord, and Ørland) are independently operated.

The impacts of airports in peripheries 33

Figure 3.3 Airports in Norway
Source: Devised by author from Avinor data (Avinor, 2018a)

Collectively, the 49 airports served 53.5 million passengers in 2017 (Avinor, 2018a). Oslo is the country's largest airport. There are then eight large airports (Bergen, Trondheim, Stavanger, Tromsø, Sandefjord, Bodø, Ålesund, and Kristiansand), six medium-sized airports (Harstad/Narvik, Haugesund, Molde, Alta, Kirkenes, and Kristiansund), eight small airports (Bardufoss, Hammerfest, Florø, Leknes, Mo i Rana, Ørsta-Volda, Brønnøysund, and Stokmarknes), and 26 very small airports. The very small airports tend to be located in the most peripheral parts of the country, and many of them have a short runway length of 800–1,500 metres, which limits the types and size of aircraft, and the destinations that they can serve.

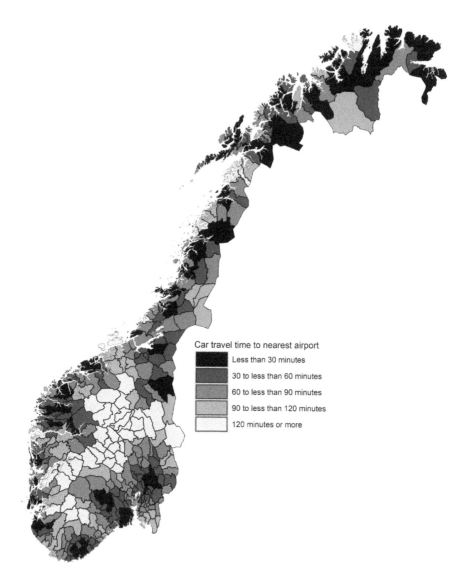

Figure 3.4 Car travel time to nearest airport
Source: Devised by author

Access to airports is good in Norway. Non-stop travel times by car are calculated from the administration centre of each of the 422 municipalities to its nearest airport (Figure 3.4). Travel time calculations are taken from Google Maps and exclude traffic disruptions. The average for all municipalities is 67 minutes. Combining the travel times and population data for each municipality, 36 per

The impacts of airports in peripheries 35

cent of the population is within 30 minutes, 75 per cent is within 60 minutes, 90 per cent is within 90 minutes, and 97 per cent is within 120 minutes. Only 3 per cent of the population is 120 minutes or more. Access is particularly good in northern and western Norway where 69 per cent and 68 per cent of the population is within a 30-minute travel time, respectively. This compares to southern, central, and eastern Norway, where 42 per cent, 18 per cent, and 15 per cent are within a 30-minute travel time, respectively.

Of course, access to a local airport is of little use unless the airport has good connections. International connections are available from Oslo, all the large airports, and several medium-sized airports. However, most of the international connections from the medium-sized airports and several larger airports are charter rather than scheduled. Domestic coverage is generally very good with direct connections from most airports, including those in the most peripheral parts of the country, to Oslo, or to other regional hubs where onward connections are available (Table 3.1).

Several studies use access to the capital city as an indicator of accessibility, especially the ability to travel there and back on the same day. Halpern and Bråthen (2010) have done this for Norway. Their study finds that over 99 per cent of the population in Norway can travel from the administration centre of their municipality to the capital city of Oslo and back with a stay of at least four hours in Oslo. Only 0.3 per cent is not able to travel to Oslo and back from their nearest airport, and would require an overnight stay. In western and central parts of the country, residents are able to save 5–10 hours when travelling to Oslo by air versus road. This figure rises to 10–15 hours in southern parts of northern Norway and to 15 hours or more in remaining parts of northern Norway (Figure 3.5). For travel by air, the calculations include the time needed to travel by car from the administration centre of the municipality to the nearest airport, the minimum check-in time for the airport, the estimated flight time to Oslo Airport (including any changes), and 45 minutes to exit Oslo Airport and travel to Oslo Central Station on the Airport Express Train. For travel by road, the calculations include a 30-minute break for every 4.5 hours of driving by car. Flight times are taken from scheduled flight timetables while drive times are taken from VisVeg, which is the travel planning tool of the Norwegian Public Roads Administration.

The study by Halpern and Bråthen (2010) is based on a daily accessibility model which measures the activities reached (in this case, the capital city of Oslo) within a day – based on the notion of a business traveller wanting to reach a certain place, conduct business there, and travel home in a day. As mentioned in the 'Geographical peripheries' section of this chapter, it is relatively easy to compute, communicate, and understand, but the theoretical foundation is rather limited; for instance, in terms of justifying why to use only Oslo. A potential accessibility model that measures the activities reached such as markets, wealth, or jobs in all parts of the country and possibly even abroad, weighted by the effort needed to reach them – not only by air, but by all potential modes of transport – would provide results that are more grounded on theory. The national centrality index mentioned in the 'Case study area

36 *Nigel Halpern*

Table 3.1 Domestic connections with 1,000 or more passengers in 2017

Passengers	Domestic connections
500,000+	Oslo–Trondheim, Oslo–Bergen, Oslo–Stavanger, Oslo–Tromsø, Oslo–Bodø, Oslo–Ålesund, Oslo–Harstad/Narvik, Bergen–Stavanger, Oslo–Kristiansand
100,000 to <500,000	Oslo–Haugesund, Bergen–Trondheim, Oslo–Molde, Trondheim–Bodø, Tromsø–Bodø, Oslo–Bardufoss, *Oslo–Kirkenes*, *Oslo–Alta*, Oslo–Kristiansund, *Tromsø–Alta*, Bergen–Sandefjord, Bergen–Kristiansand, *Tromsø–Hammerfest*, Bergen–Ålesund, Trondheim–Stavanger, Trondheim–Sandefjord, *Bodø–Leknes*
50,000 to <100,000	Oslo–Ørsta-Volda, *Bodø–Svolvær*, Bodø–Stokmarknes, Stavanger–Sandefjord, *Oslo–Førde*, *Trondheim–Brønnøysund*, Bergen–Tromsø, Trondheim–Ålesund, *Oslo–Sogndal*, *Trondheim–Mo i Rana*, Bergen–Kristiansund, *Tromsø–Lakselv*, Bergen–Florø
25,000 to <50,000	*Bodø–Mo i Rana*, Bergen–Molde, Trondheim–Kristiansand, Oslo–Florø, Bodø–Harstad-Narvik, *Trondheim–Mosjøen*, Bergen–Bodø, *Trondheim–Sandnessjøen*, Trondheim–Harstad/Narvik, *Tromsø–Kirkenes*, Tromsø–Stokmarknes, *Tromsø–Vadsø*, *Bodø–Sandnessjøen*, *Kirkenes–Vadsø*, Trondheim–Tromsø, *Tromsø–Andøya*, *Trondheim–Namsos*, *Trondheim–Røvik*, Oslo–Stord, *Tromsø–Harstad/Narvik*, *Bodø–Brønnøysund*, Oslo–Sandane, Bergen–Sogndal
10,000 to <25,000	*Oslo–Røros*, *Hammerfest–Honningsvåg*, *Bodø–Mosjøen*, *Tromsø–Sørkjosen*, *Vadsø–Vardø*, Svolvær–Andøya, *Hammerfest–Hasvik*, *Tromsø–Hasvik*, Rørvik–Namsos, *Alta–Vadsø*, *Alta–Kirkenes*, *Båtsfjord–Vardø*, *Kirkenes–Vardø*, *Bergen–Ørsta-Volda*, Oslo–Brønnøysund, Oslo–Mo i Rana, Mehamn–Honningsvåg, *Bodø–Andøya*, *Vadsø–Båtsfjord*, Stavanger–Kristiansand, *Bergen–Førde*, Tromsø–Leknes, Ørsta-Volda–Sogndal, Brønnøysund–Sandnessjøen, Leknes–Røst, Sogndal–Sandane, *Bodø–Røst*, Leknes–Stokmarknes, Molde–Kristiansund
5,000 to <10,000	Stokmarknes–Svolvær, Trondheim–Kristiansund, *Bodø–Værøy*, Oslo–Sandnessjøen, *Båtsfjord–Berlevåg*, Mo i Rana–Mosjøen, Harstad/Narvik–Andøya, Bodø–Narvik, *Hammerfest–Berlevåg*, Oslo–Mosjøen, Oslo–Lakselv, Oslo–Leknes, *Mehamn–Båtsfjord*, Oslo–Svolvær, Bodø–Bardufoss, *Alta–Lakselv*, *Hammerfest–Mehamn*, Oslo–Andøya, Molde–Stord, *Hammerfest–Sørkjosen*, Stavanger–Kristiansund, Trondheim–Molde
1,000 to <5,000	*Hammerfest–Vadsø*, Ålesund–Kristiansund, Oslo–Ørland, *Alta–Sørkjosen*, *Vadsø–Berlevåg*, *Mehamn–Berlevåg*, *Vadsø–Mehamn*, Ålesund–Florø, Tromsø–Bardufoss, Florø–Førde, Stavanger–Florø, Florø–Ørsta-Volda, Stokmarknes–Andøya, Florø–Sogndal, Mo i Rana–Rørvik, Bergen–Notodden, Kristiansund–Florø, *Alta–Hammerfest*, Mosjøen–Namsos, Molde–Florø, Kristiansand–Haugesund, Oslo–Stokmarknes, Sandnessjøen–Mosjøen, Bodø–Sandefjord, Tromsø–Honningsvåg

Source: SSB (2018f)

Notes: Routes are listed in order of traffic volume where Oslo-Trondheim is the largest with 2.1 million passengers in 2017. Routes in italics are PSOs. Two of the 56 PSOs in Norway are not listed because they served fewer than 1,000 passengers in 2017: Sandane-Ørsta-Volda (739 passengers) and Bergen-Sandane (494 passengers).

and its peripherality' section of this chapter provides a useful starting point for creating such an index.

Although the example in Figure 3.5 only uses Oslo as the destination, it helps to show that there are few alternatives available to air travel in Norway for journeys over a longer distance. However, air travel is also important in Norway for journeys over shorter distances in some areas, especially in northern

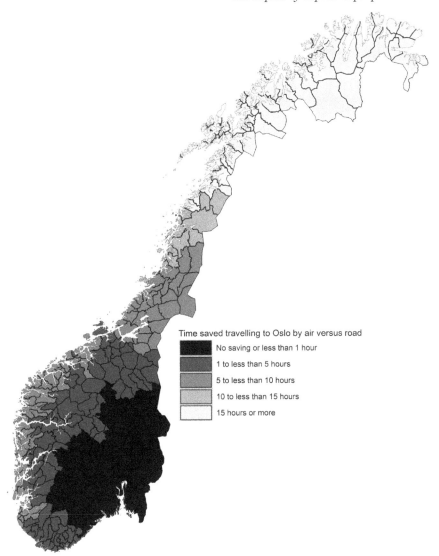

Figure 3.5 Time saved travelling to Oslo by air versus road
Source: Devised by author

and western parts of the country where islands, fjords, and mountains mean that it can take some time to travel by land or sea compared to by air.

Profitability of airports and their economic impacts

As a system, airports in Norway are profitable. Avinor's 46 airports (including Svalbard) operated at a profit of €186 million in 2017 (average operating profit of €3.5 per passenger).[1] However, profits are very much concentrated at larger airports located in less peripheral parts of the country. For instance, Oslo, Bergen, Stavanger, and Trondheim operated at a combined profit of €309 million in 2017. The four airports served 42.1 million passengers, resulting in a profit of €7.3 per passenger. Avinor's remaining 42 airports, most of which are located in more peripheral parts of the country, operated at a combined loss of €124 million. These airports served 10.8 million passengers, resulting in a loss of €11.4 per passenger. From those 42 airports, it is likely that only a few of the larger ones operate at a profit while the vast majority operate at a loss.

There is also the cost of providing air services in peripheral areas to consider. The Norwegian government imposed PSOs on 56 routes as of 2018 with a budget of €72 million (average of €13.5 per inhabitant). Also, some regions have introduced incentive schemes to stimulate direct international air services (e.g. for inbound tourism). One example is the Northern Norway Charter Fund, launched at the end of 2014 with a budget of €1 million to be allocated as aid in the form of grants that reduce the risk to tour operators establishing air services to airports in northern Norway (Halpern, 2018). Such interventions may be justified because of the importance of air access for regional social and economic development. However, the net benefit to the region is often unclear – due in part to the challenges associated with measuring the impacts.

Another issue is that many airports in Norway are reliant on one or two main carriers. They are therefore vulnerable to changes in airline strategy. This was witnessed when Ryanair closed its base at Moss Airport (a privately owned secondary airport 60 km from Oslo) at the end of 2016. Ryanair cited the introduction of a new air travel tax by the Norwegian government in 2016 as the main cause for its decision. The airport ceased civil operations when Ryanair left. Moss Airport is located in a less peripheral part of the country. However, the air travel tax is also causing increased uncertainty in more peripheral areas where the profitability of existing air services is already so marginal that regional carrier Widerøe has warned some routes will need to be reduced or withdrawn altogether (Jarvis, 2018).

Cases for airport closure exist considering that airport substitution is a common feature of the Norwegian airport system (e.g. see Halpern and Bråthen, 2010; Lian and Rønnevik, 2011; Mathisen and Solvoll, 2012). Replacing several smaller airports with a larger one in some areas is expected to reduce the reliance on state subsidies for PSO routes, minimise necessary security upgrade costs, offer passengers lower fares, increase the number of direct domestic flights, and be profitable from a welfare perspective (Mathisen and Solvoll, 2012). However, airport closure is a highly sensitive issue due to local regional politics. In addition, many of the smaller airports provide traffic feeds to larger airports in the system, thereby contributing to the profitability of those airports and to the overall airport system. Too strong a reduction in the number of smaller airports could result in a reduced service offer at the larger airports and may subsequently weaken the entire airport system.

Table 3.2 Economic impact of airports in Norway in 2013

Impacts	Jobs	Income (€ billion)	GDP (€ billion)	National GDP (%)
Direct	27,700	2.45	2.71	Not stated
Direct + indirect + induced	63,800	4.75	6.96	1.8
Total (direct + indirect + induced + catalytic)	122,600	8.74	15.29	4.0

Source: InterVistas (2015)

Several studies have estimated the economic impact of air transport in Norway (e.g. Lian et al., 2005, 2007; Oxford Economics, 2011). In addition, a more recent study by InterVISTAS (2015) focuses specifically on the impact of airports (Table 3.2). The impacts in Table 3.2 are for all airports in Norway and are therefore likely to be concentrated at Oslo and the larger airports rather than smaller airports serving more peripheral areas where the impacts are expected to be considerably less. For instance, in terms of jobs, 28 of the country's 49 airports are in the more peripheral region of northern Norway where Avinor (2014) estimated an economic impact in 2013 of 10,700 total jobs (3,200 direct, 2,900 indirect/induced, and 4,600 catalytic). The low level of employment at smaller airports is further emphasised in Table 3.3, which shows that the 25 smallest airports only supported 935 direct jobs in 2013 (average of 37 direct jobs per airport). It is interesting to note that the number of jobs per million passengers increases as airport size decreases, possibly as a result of smaller airports being less effective than larger airports in their use of resources. The figure is also higher at Oslo compared to the larger and medium-sized airports. This is likely to be due to a greater range of functions being carried out at Oslo.

Measuring direct economic impacts of airports is relatively simple. It can be done by conducting a survey of the airport operator and other companies operating at the airport. Surveys can also be used to collect data on indirect impacts. However, the ease of collecting data becomes more difficult, and the accuracy of the data becomes less certain. As a result, economic models are often used instead of surveys to estimate indirect and induced effects; for instance, using input-output models. This is the approach taken by InterVISTAS (2015) for their calculations in Table 3.2. Lian et al. (2005) also take this approach, using an input-output model called Panda to estimate indirect and induced impacts at four airports in Norway (Leknes, Molde, Bergen, and Oslo). Economic impact multipliers are derived from the models. For instance, in Table 3.2, the direct to indirect/induced multipliers are 1.30 for jobs, 0.94 for income and 1.57 for GDP. Lian et al. (2005) found similar multipliers for jobs at their airports, ranging from 1.37 for Leknes, peripherally located in the northern part of Norway, to 1.91 for Oslo, centrally located in the eastern part of Norway. Their income multipliers, which ranged from 1.39 for Leknes to 1.95 for Oslo, were however

40 *Nigel Halpern*

Table 3.3 Direct jobs at airports in Norway in 2013

Airport	Direct jobs					Million passengers	Jobs per mppa
	Airport	*Airline*	*Commercial*	*Other*	*Total*		
Oslo	1,540	6,931	3,011	841	12,323	22.957	537
8 large[1]	2,049	4,362	1,593	2,402	10,406	22.806	456
6 medium[2]	534	455	123	208	1320	2.861	461
9 small[3]	381	222	35	164	802	1.330	603
25 very small[4]	538	259	14	124	935	0.973	961
Total	5,042	12,229	4,776	3,739	25,786	50.927	506

Source: Avinor (2015)

[1] Airports serving 1 to <6 million passengers (Bergen, Stavanger, Trondheim, Tromsø, Sandefjord, Bodø, Ålesund, Kristiansand).
[2] Airports serving 250,000 to <1 million passengers (Haugesund, Harstad/Narvik, Molde, Kristiansund, Alta, Kirkenes).
[3] Airports serving 100,000 to <250,000 passengers (Bardufoss, Florø, Brønnøysund, Hammerfest, Ørsta-Volda, Mo i Rana, Leknes, Stokmarknes, Sandnessjøen).
[4] All remaining airports serving <100,000 passengers.

higher than that of InterVISTAS (2015). Lian et al. (2005) found that the multipliers increased as the size of each airport increased.

Catalytic economic impacts are even more difficult to measure. According to Lian (2010), the direction of causation is uncertain, there is often a lack of comparable areas without air services to use as control areas, and infrastructure effects tend to be long-term, meaning that most regions have benefitted from improved transport services at some time and it is therefore difficult to identify the effects. InterVISTAS (2015) estimate the catalytic economic impact of airports in European countries using econometric analysis to examine the effect of air connectivity on economic growth (GDP per capita) between 2000 and 2012. The resulting figures for Norway can be derived from Table 3.2, including 58,800 additional jobs, €3.99 billion in income, and a contribution of €8.33 billion to GDP. However, the situation regarding airports in peripheral areas is lost when considering results at the country level. When assessing the catalytic and other wider impacts of airports in peripheral areas, it is therefore useful to consider case studies from individual airports, which will be the focus of subsequent sections of this chapter, looking first at regional economic development. However, caution should be taken when interpreting the findings of case studies from individual airports because there is a potential for selection bias, as case studies often focus on the more interesting examples and in areas that have airports because they were already more prosperous than those that did not. There is also the potential for biased responses because subjects that are interviewed or surveyed may be inclined to answer strategically to defend their local airport. This is a reason why it is also useful to consider the actual use of airports and air services when attempting to shed light on their importance (Lian, 2010).

Regional economic development

Halpern and Bråthen (2012) investigate the importance of Ålesund Airport to 197 businesses in Sunnmøre in western Norway. Over 50 per cent of businesses stated that air transport supports over 60 per cent of their business trips. Air access is particularly important for attending courses and conferences, but also for contact with partners and with customers and markets. Air access is most important for the movement of people versus goods. Only 10 per cent of businesses stated that air transport supports over 60 per cent of goods value transported by the company. Eighteen per cent of businesses stated that air service provision has affected their investment decisions (56 per cent stated that they invested more in the region than they would otherwise have done so, 25 per cent invested in an alternative region, 6 per cent chose not to invest in the region, and 13 per cent selected 'other'). Proximity to an airport was selected as the fourth most important location factor for businesses after contact with customers, access to a local market for products, and general quality of life in the area. In terms of other transport, quality of the road network was ranked in sixth place, proximity to a harbour in 10th, and access to rail in 16th. Importance of proximity to an airport varies significantly by geographical structure of the company and the sector that the company is in. It is significantly more important for those with a main office abroad or a department or sister company in another part of Norway compared to those that only have offices, departments, or sister companies in the same region. It is also significantly more important for companies in hospitality and services, finance and insurance, and energy compared to other sectors.

In terms of energy, Thune-Larsen and Farstad (2018) estimate that 1.1 million trips on domestic flights in 2017 were related to oil and gas exploration. Oslo-Stavanger is the largest route, with 209,000 oil and gas-related trips, but in terms of the oil and gas share of total passengers on routes, the largest are Bergen-Kristiansand (55 per cent), Bergen-Florø (54 per cent), Bergen-Stavanger (42 per cent), Stavanger-Sandefjord (36 per cent), and Oslo-Kristiansund (20 per cent). Bråthen et al. (2014) also investigate the importance of air transport for the energy sector. In the case of major developments, they claim that air transport contributes to increased productivity and helps to avoid local cost pressures (e.g. by being able to access expertise and workers that are not available locally). It also contributes to the development and maintenance of important industrial networks within related shipyards, and allows industries to be developed further and to reach larger markets. They illustrate the importance of air transport for major developments with a case study on the construction of a natural gas field near Molde in western Norway called Ormen Lange, which commenced production in 2007 and supplies gas to the UK via one of the world's longest subsea pipelines that is approximately 1,200 km long. Their study estimates that 40,000–50,000 trips were taken via Molde Airport each year during construction. Air access made it possible to use specialised external expertise and therefore reduce local cost pressure during phase one of the development, which amounted to over €5 billion and a peak of 3,000 employees (the municipality of Molde has a total population of 26,900). Phase two of the development took place between 2014 and 2017. As of 2015, the operation had over 500 employees, including about 150 commuters by air.

In terms of their overall impact on the trade of goods, Norway's airports facilitated the movement of 206,011 tonnes of air freight in 2017 (Avinor, 2018a). Almost two-thirds (63 per cent) of air freight is exported versus imported, and almost three-quarters (74 per cent) is flown on international versus domestic air services. According to Avinor (2015), approximately 80 per cent of exports is seafood. Imports are mainly electronics, fashion, perishables, and goods with high value of time (e.g. spare parts). Oslo is the main hub for air freight in Norway, serving 82 per cent of all freight tonnes. Airports in peripheral areas therefore play a relatively small role. However, many industries along the coast of Norway – for instance, marine, oil, gas, and aquaculture – are vital for their regions and would not have a global market without good air access (Avinor, 2015). Apart from the largest four airports for air freight (Oslo, Stavanger, Bergen, and Trondheim), the ten largest are Tromsø (3,683 tonnes), Bodø (3,090 tonnes), Molde (1,696 tonnes – primarily air mail), Harstad/ Narvik Evenes (1,381 tonnes), Alta (783 tonnes), Kriatiansand (646 tonnes), Kirkenes (522 tonnes), Lakselv (502 tonnes), Hammerfest (439 tonnes), and Ålesund (313 tonnes).

Tourism is also an important export for Norway. In 2016, it directly contributed an estimated 176,000 jobs (6.6 per cent of total jobs) and €12.6 billion to GDP (4.0 per cent of total GDP) (WTTC, 2017). Over one-third (35 per cent) of all international tourist arrivals were by air in 2012 (Farstad et al., 2013), and in recent years, there has been strong growth in the number of foreign tourist arrivals on international routes to Norway. Most tourists arrive on direct international flights to Oslo and the larger regional airports. For instance, Thune-Larsen and Farstad (2018) estimate that there were 4.2 million foreign passengers at Avinor airports alone in 2017. Three-quarters of them (76 per cent) used Oslo, followed by Bergen (14 per cent), Stavanger (4 per cent), and Trondheim (3 per cent).

There has also been strong growth in the use of domestic flights by foreigners in Norway. Thune-Larsen and Farstad (2018) estimate that the number of foreign passengers has increased from one million in 2007 to two million in 2017. The largest volume of foreigners travelled on routes between Oslo and Tromsø, Oslo and Bergen, and Oslo and Trondheim. However, the highest proportion of foreigners on flights travelled on routes connecting Oslo to northern Norway including Oslo-Svalbard (53 per cent), Oslo-Kirkenes (32 per cent), Oslo-Tromsø (30 per cent), Oslo-Alta (23 per cent), and Oslo-Harstad/Narvik (20 per cent). This emphasises the importance of airports for the tourism industry in the peripheries of northern Norway. For instance, it is estimated that foreigners travelling on domestic services contributed an additional 100,000 guest nights in Tromsø alone between 2015 and 2017.

Regional social development

Norwegians took an estimated 11.8 million domestic trips in 2017, equivalent to 2.3 domestic trips per person (Thune-Larsen and Farstad, 2018). This is particularly high in northern Norway, where it is 4.8. It is also high in central (3.6) and western Norway (3.1). It is lowest in southern and eastern Norway (1.2). There is a fairly even split between travel for leisure versus business purposes (56 per cent leisure, 44 per cent business). Air transport also provides opportunities for Norwegians to travel abroad, with 7.2 million leisure trips taken by Norwegians to/from abroad in 2017.

Focusing more specifically on Norway's more peripheral areas, airports play a vital role in securing access to basic local services such as health and education. For instance, 20–25 per cent of passengers on local routes to and from Bodø and Tromsø in northern Norway are patients, which demonstrates the importance of air access to hospitals for medical treatment. In addition, approximately two-thirds of all air ambulance movements in Norway are in northern Norway (mainly at Tromsø, Bodø, Alta, Hammerfest, Kirkenes, and Brønnøysund). At many of those airports, the air ambulance service contributes over 10 per cent of all aircraft movements (e.g. 21 per cent at Alta and 17 per cent at Kirkenes) (Avinor, 2015). The service is mainly used for patients with acute illness when alternative travel is unrealistic.

In terms of attracting and retaining staff and students in higher education, and supporting staff and student mobility, Solvoll and Hanssen (2018) studied the welfare effects of aviation for 34 higher education institutions in Norway. Their study found that employees took 4.6 trips per year, which is twice as high as for all employees in Norway. The figure is particularly high in northern Norway at 6.6 trips per year. Students took 4.2 trips per year (6.9 in northern Norway). Their study estimates an annual welfare effect from aviation of €1,000 per employee and €200 per student, with total annual welfare effects being highest in western and northern Norway. Their study concludes that welfare effects are highest for higher education institutions located in more peripheral areas where distances are farthest from the capital. Maintaining good flight connections therefore plays a key role in sustaining higher education in the regions and plays a vital role for society.

Another area of interest in recent years has been the role of airports and air transport on sport and cultural activities. Bråthen et al. (2014) discuss how the sports and cultural industries are relatively small in a national economic context in Norway. However, they have the ability to engage local communities in both central and peripheral areas, enabling people to develop socially and culturally through travel, and also contributing to place identity and a sense of belonging. Airports can play a key role, providing access to air services that allow the necessary movement of artists, athletes, supporters, officials, and equipment. There are also economic benefits. For instance, Bråthen et al. (2014) estimate that air transport offers savings of up to €50 million each year for football clubs in the top divisions in Norway. Savings for teams in the top ice hockey and

44 Nigel Halpern

handball divisions are approximately one-fifth of that in football, which is still a significant amount, given the limited budgets of the clubs. Top-level organised sport in Norway would look quite different than it does today without the availability of air access.

An estimated 500–1,000 festivals are held in Norway each year, many of them in peripheral areas. They attract approximately 2.5 million attendees and €50 million in turnover (Bråthen et al., 2014). Two case studies are provided by Bråthen et al. (2014) for Molde Jazz in Molde in western Norway and Nordland Music Festival in Bodø in northern Norway. Approximately 10 per cent of attendees use air travel to access the festivals. The figure is significantly higher for artists, equipment, and officials such as the media. There is an air travel-related contribution of approximately 500–800 passengers and €200,000 for each festival. In both cases, the local airport is considered essential, especially for attracting artists to play at the festivals, although limited frequencies (e.g. for evening flights) are a constraint. Many festivals in Norway would no doubt struggle without the presence of a local airport to facilitate air access to and from the venue.

Many peripheral areas are supported by public policies that encourage their regional development with the aim of preserving areas of cultural or historical importance, or to preserve traditional settlements (Lian, 2010). Several studies have therefore investigated the relationship between distance to a local airport and population change in Norway (e.g. Halpern and Bråthen, 2010; Lian et al., 2005). The studies find that, in general, population growth declines as distance from a local airport increases. According to Lian et al. (2005), net migration also declines as distance from a local airport increases. The effects are particularly strong in the more peripheral regions of northern and western Norway. However, as mentioned earlier in this chapter, caution needs to be taken when interpreting such findings. This is emphasised by Tveter (2017) with a study on the effect of regional airports on population and employment change in Norway. His study uses a susbstantial increase in airport construction that took place in Norway in the 1970s as the source of variation. Estimates are made using an approach that compares population and employment change in municipalities that are closer to constructed airports with three sets of control municipalities. The analysis finds a positive but not significant effect. For instance, the population in municipalities closer to constructed airports increased by 5 per cent from 1970–1980. However, the overall imprecision of the estimates mean that it is not possible to reject the hypothesis that the constructed airports had no significant effect.

Similarly, Halpern and Bråthen (2011) report on a survey of 1,167 residents in Sør Helgeland in northern Norway that consider Brønnøysund Airport to be their local airport. Three-quarters of respondents strongly agree that they are more likely to continue living in the region as a result of having a local airport, primarily because of the connectivity that it provides but also because of the access it provides to health services, opportunities for holidays and contact with friends and relatives, and because they are more able to do their job.

In terms of key location factors for residents in the region, access to a local airport was ranked fourth out of ten factors – the first three being home region/near friends or relatives, nature/leisure opportunities, and opportunities for work/study. Access to a local airport ranked much higher than other transport such as access to public transport (in eighth place) and a well-developed road network (in tenth place). Such studies provide useful insights. However, as with the impact of airports on population change, caution needs to be taken when interpreting such findings due to the potential for strategic answering from respondents that wish to defend their local airport.

Climate and the environment

The national statistics office of Norway estimates that 5 per cent (2.7 million tonnes) of all greenhouse gas emissions in Norway come from jet fuel sold at its airports for civil purposes (Avinor, 2018c). Over 90 per cent of emissions in air transport are related to aircraft operations, so much of the focus in Norway is on encouraging airlines to operate a more modern and fuel-efficient fleet, making more effective use of airspace including the optimisation of take-offs and landings, the use of biofuels, and the electrification of air transport (see Avinor, 2018c for more details). See also Avinor (2008), Avinor (2015), and Lian et al. (2007) for a wider discussion on the environmental impacts of airports in Norway, scenarios for the future, and the initiatives being taken to reduce the impacts. Avinor (2014) provides a specific focus on airports in northern Norway.

Of particular relevance to smaller airports in more peripheral parts of Norway is the electrification of air transport. This is because there is a large number of airports in peripheral areas that have short runways and serve small aircraft operating short routes, which are well suited to the early stages of electrification due to the limited operating capabilities and size of new electric aircraft. For instance, the main regional airline operator in Norway is Widerøe. Seventy-four per cent of Widerøe's routes (equalling 249 city pairs) have a distance of less than 300 km and the airline operates 25 short take-off and landing (STOL)-modified Dash 100/200 aircraft serving 20 airports with approximately 800-metre-long runways (Nilsen, 2018). There are no new aircraft types available to replace the existing fleet of STOL aircraft, which is a challenge that the airline will need to resolve for the future, and at a time when environmental concerns are growing in relation to the impacts of air transport, and when future tax incentives are likely to favour newer more environmentally firendly aircraft. Electric or hybrid aircraft provide a viable solution to the challenges faced by Widerøe on their STOL network, and means that they have significant interest in the implementation of such technology – something that is also supported by the airport operator Avinor and the Norwegian government, along with other industry and community stakeholders.

Avinor, along with several partners (Widerøe, SAS, the Norwegian Association of Air Sports, and climate foundation ZERO), is wanting to be a world leader in electric aviation with the aim being for Norway to be the first country where electric flights account for a significant share of the domestic market by 2040 (Avinor, 2018b). With support from the Norwegian government, Avinor and its partners demonstrated the first electric flight on 18 June 2018. The two-seat Alpha Electro G2 aircraft took a short flight at Oslo Airport, piloted by Avinor's CEO Dag Falk-Petersen with the Minister of Transport and Communications Ketil Solvik-Olsen as the passenger. Norway's regional airline Widerøe is ambitious about the project and has reached out to aircraft manufacturers to help them to achieve the aim of replacing their entire fleet with electric aircraft by 2030. In further support of the initiative, Avinor does not intend to charge landing fees for electric aircraft, and will also allow them to recharge at their airports for free until 2025 (Avinor, 2018b).

Conclusion

Using a case study on Norway, this chapter has considered the impacts of airports in geographical peripheries. The main impact is that they offer accessibility to main transport networks. Airports can have direct, indirect, and induced economic impacts such as on jobs, income, and GDP. However, these are likely to be minimal at airports serving the most peripheral areas because of the small scale of operations at such airports. In fact, maintaining airport infrastructure and air service provision in such areas can be costly and there are questions relating to the oversupply of airport infrastructure in some parts of Norway. An interesting area for future research is linked to determining the optimal supply of airport infrastructure in peripheral areas where airport substitution occurs.

As a result of the accessibility that they provide, airports in geographical peripheries have important wider impacts; for instance, on regional economic and social development. The impacts can be modelled (i.e. using econometric analysis). However, many of the impacts have been investigated using case studies on individual airports. A problem with the case study approach is that there may be bias associated with the selection of case study areas and airports, and in the responses from any interview subjects that have an interest in defending their local airport. There is therefore often a risk that the findings become rather anecdotal. Related to this, it is not always easy to understand and quantify the net benefits of the airports in question, which is something that future studies should try to address.

Environmental impacts have received much greater attention from airport impact studies on Norway in recent years, and the focus has largely been on climate-related impacts and initiatives. Electrification is an exciting area of interest, especially for airports in peripheral areas that are well suited to the early stages of development in electric aircraft. Although there is now a much greater understanding of the environmental impacts of airports and the initiatives that airports are engaged in, there has been very little research in Norway on more local environmental impacts of airports, or on how local communities are affected by the negative impacts of airports and air transport or related

The impacts of airports in peripheries   47

activities, especially in peripheral areas where tolerance levels may vary, for instance, compared to those in more central areas. This could be an interesting avenue for future research, and would help to provide a better balance to extant literature that focuses largely on the social and economic benefits of airports.

Note

1 Figures in this and subsequent sections of the chapter have been converted from Norwegian kroner using an exchange rate of 1 NOK = €0.100202.

References

Avinor (2008). *Aviation in Norway: Sustainability and social benefit.* Oslo, Avinor.

Avinor (2014). *Avinor i Nordområdene: Muligheter og Strategier.* Oslo, Avinor.

Avinor (2015). *Luftfartens Samfunnsnytte.* Oslo, Avinor.

Avinor (2018a). *Statistics.* Available at: https://avinor.no/en/corporate/about-us/statistics/traffic-statistics (accessed 30 November 2018).

Avinor (2018b). *Norway's first electric aircraft is soon here.* Available at: https://avinor.no/en/aviation/news/first-electric-aircraft/ (accessed 30 November 2018).

Avinor (2018c). *Avinor og Norsk Luftfart 2018.* Oslo, Avinor.

Botterill, R., Owen, E., Emanuel, L., Foster, N., Gale, T., Nelson, C. and Selby, M. (2000). Perceptions from the periphery: The experience of Wales. In Brown, F. and Hall, D. (eds) *Tourism in peripheral areas: Case studies.* Clevedon, Aspects of Tourism 2, Channel View Publications.

Bråthen, S., Tveter, E., Solvoll, G. and Hanssen, T. E. S. (2014). *Luftfartens Betydning for Utvalgte Samfunnssektorer: Eksempler fra Petroleumsrelatert Virksomhet, Kultur og Sport.* Rapport 1410. Molde, Møreforsking Molde.

Cooper, A. and Smith, P. (2005). *The economic catalytic effects of air transport in Europe.* Report EEC/SEE/2005/2004. Oxford, Oxford Economics Forecasting.

Eurostat (2018). *Population density (tps00003).* Available at: https://ec.europa.eu/eurostat/web/population-demography-migration-projections/population-data/main-tables (accessed 30 November 2018).

Farstad, E., Dybedal, P. and Mata, L. (2013). *Norwegian travel survey for foreigners 2012.* Report 1295/2013. Oslo, Transport Economics Institute.

Fewings, R. (2010). Airport infrastructure in Europe's remoter regions. In Williams, G. and Bråthen, S. (eds) *Air transport provision in remoter regions.* Aldershot, Ashgate.

Great Norwegian Encyclopedia (2018). *Norway's geography.* Available at: https://snl.no/Norges_geografi (accessed 30 November 2018).

Halpern, N. (2006). *Market orientation and the performance of airports in Europe's remoter regions.* PhD Thesis, Cranfield University, Bedford.

Halpern, N. (2018). Partnerships between tourism destination stakeholders and the air transport sector. In Graham, A. and Dobruszkes, F. (eds) *Air transport: A tourism perspective.* Elsevier Series on Contemporary Issues in Air Transport. Amsterdam, Elsevier.

Halpern, N. and Bråthen, S. (2010). *Catalytic impact of airports in Norway.* Report 1008. Molde, Møreforsking Molde.

Halpern, N. and Bråthen, S. (2011). Impact of airports on regional accessibility and social development. *Journal of Transport Geography,* 19, 1145–1154.

Halpern, N. and Bråthen, S. (2012). Importance of regional airports for businesses in Norway. *Journal of Airport Management,* 6(4), 381–396.

48 *Nigel Halpern*

Halpern, N. and Niskala, J. (2008). Airport marketing and tourism in remote destinations: Exploiting the potential in Europe's northern periphery. In Graham, A., Papatheodorou, A. and Forsyth, P. (eds) *Aviation and tourism: Implications for leisure travel*. Aldershot, Ashgate.

Høydahl, E. (2017). *Ny Sentralitetsindeks for Kommunene*. Notater 2017/40. Oslo, Statistics Norway.

InterVISTAS (2015). *Economic impact of European airports: A critical catalyst to economic growth*. London, InterVISTAS.

Jarvis, H. (2018). *Widerøe CEO: New route cuts in 2019*. Available at: https://standbynordic.com/wideroe-ceo-new-route-cuts-in-2019/ (accessed 30 November 2018).

Kjærland, F. and Mathisen, T. A. (2012). Assessing the peripehral staus of local airports. *Journal of Air Transport Studies*, 3(2), 1–22.

Lian, J. I. (2010). The economic impact of air transport in remoter regions. In Williams, G. and Bråthen, S. (eds) *Air transport provision in remoter regions*. Aldershot, Ashgate.

Lian, J. I., Bråthen, S., Johansen, S. and Strand, S. (2005). *The economic impact of air transport*. Report 807/2005. Oslo, Transport Economics Institute.

Lian, J. I., Gjerdåker, A., Rønnevik, J., Jean-Hansen, V., Rypdal, K., Skeie, R. B., Berntsen, T., Fuglestvedt, J., Torvenger, A., Alfsen, K. and Thune-Larsen, H. (2007). *The economic and environmental impact of air transport*. Report 921/2007. Oslo, Transport Economics Institute.

Lian, J. I. and Rønnevik, J. (2011). Airport competition – regional airports are losing ground to main airports. *Journal of Transport Geography*, 19(1), 85–92.

Mathisen, T. A. and Solvoll, G. (2012). Reconsidering the regional airport network in Norway. *European Transport Research Review*, 4, 39–46.

Nilsen, S. (2018). *A major technology shift in the turboprop segment? Zero emission 50-seat aircraft by 2030*. Lillestrøm, Norway, ACI Airport Exchange, 28–29 November.

Oxford Economics (2011). *Economic benefits from air transport in Norway*. Oxford, Oxford Economics.

Schürmann, C., Spiekermann, K. andWegener, M. (1997). *Accessibility indicators*. Dortmund, IRPUD.

Schürmann, C. and Talaat, A. (2000). *Towards a European peripherality index: Final report*. Dortmund, IRPUD.

Solvoll, G. and Hanssen, T. E. S. (2018). Importance of aviation in higher education. *Journal of Air Transport Management*, 72, 47–55.

Spiekermann, K. and Aalbu, H. (2004). *Nordic peripherality in Europe*. Stockholm, Nordregio.

Spiekermann, K. and Neubauer, J. (2002). *European accessibility and peripherality: Concepts, models and indicators*. Nordregio Working Paper No. 2002:9. Stockholm, Nordregio.

SSB (2018a). *Population: 11342: Population and area (M) 2007–2018*. Available at: www.ssb.no/en/statbank/table/11342 (accessed 30 November 2018).

SSB (2018b). *Classification of municipalities 2018*. Available at: https://www.ssb.no/en/klass/klassifikasjoner/131 (accessed 30 November 2018).

SSB (2018c). *Land use and land cover: 09594: Classes of land use and land cover (km²) (M) 2011–2018*. Available at: www.ssb.no/en/statbank/table/09594/ (accessed 30 November 2018).

SSB (2018d). *Transport and communication in municipalities and county authorities: 11845: Roads, parking spaces, road lights, bus stops (M) 2015–2017*. Available at: www.ssb.no/statbank/table/11845/tableViewLayout1/ (accessed 30 November 2018).

SSB (2018e). *Classification of centrality 2018*. Available at: https://www.ssb.no/en/klass/klassifikasjoner/128 (accessed 30 November 2018).

SSB (2018f). *Air transport: 08509: Air transport. Passengers between Norwegian airports 2009M01-2018M06*. Available at: www.ssb.no/en/statbank/table/08509/ (accessed 30 November 2018).

Thune-Larsen, H. and Farstad, E. (2018). *The Norwegian air travel survey 2017*. Oslo, Transport Economics Institute.

Tveter, E. (2017). The effect of airports on regional development: Evidence from the construction of regional airports in Norway. *Research in Transportation Economics*, 63, 50–58.

Wegener, M., Eskelinnen, H., Fürst, F., Schürmann, C. and Spiekermann, K. (2002). *Criteria for the spatial differentiation of the EU territory: Geographical position*. Bonn, Federal Office for Building and Regional Planning.

Williams, G., Fewings, R. and Fuglum, K. (2007). Airport provision and air transport dependence in European countries. *Journal of Airport Management*, 1(4), 398–312.

WTTC (World Travel and Tourism Council) (2017). *Travel & tourism: Economic impact 2017 Norway*. London, WTTC.

York Aviation (2004). *The social and economic impact of airports in Europe*. Macclesfield, York Aviation.

4 The relationship between air traffic and the regional development in Finland

Staffan Ringbom

Introduction

For regional development, it is important to identify the strategic factors that contribute to economic growth especially in rural and peripheral regions. A critical factor for economic development is the existence of good public infrastructure and services, which also spurs economic activity in the private sector in the regions. Therefore, a good public infrastructure is a base for economic development (Martin, 1998). The interaction between public infrastructure investments and the economic activity has been the focus in the literature in development economics for a long time. For example, Romp and de Haan (2007), Melo et al. (2013), and Bom and Ligthart (2014), among others, present detailed insights and evidence that public capital investments, especially in the transport industry, contribute to regional economic development. Melo et al. (2013) and Bom and Ligthart (2014) illustrate in their research that the spillover of public investments on private economic activities is significant. By using meta regressions, they show positive spillover effects of transport industry investments on nearby regions. Also, Graham (2018) demonstrates that airports have considerable multiplier effects for the local economies. Several studies stress the same issue. The infrastructure for air transport industry as part of the broader transport industry is of particular strategic interest in Finland (Nyberg et al., 2015).

With empirical research the availability of data is an obstacle especially in relation to economic information regarding air transport. It is, in practice, impossible to separate the air transport industry from the aggregate statistics published by Statistics Finland that cover the transport industry on a more aggregated level. Therefore, it is more straightforward to study the relationship between economic activities and air transport in real terms, where good data are available at a regional level. As air transport data (passengers, landings, cargo by airport) and regional macro activities are relatively well documented, this has led to the relationship between air transport and economic activities being the focus of several papers. For example, Brueckner (2003) provides evidence for the positive link between air traffic and employment. Neal (2012) documents varying linkages between economic activity (especially labour) and air traffic during economic growth and decline. Alkaabi and Debbage (2011) study the structure of air freight shipments in the United States and its impact on different industries. Meanwhile, Percoco (2010) analyses the connection between airport activity and local development in Italy, especially with respect to the service sector employment. Bilotkach (2015) demonstrates a positive linkage between airport connectivity and economic development, where the number of direct connections from airports is crucial. Moreover, Halpern and Bråthen (2010, 2011) and Bråthen and Halpern (2012), among others, stress the importance of regional airports for the development in remote regions.

During recent years, the development of panel data econometrics has advanced significantly. Therefore, a reassessment of the previous findings in the literature is desired. The modern econometric techniques allow for analysis of vector error correction models in panel data. The advantage with these models is that they can cope with non-stationary relationships in the data as long as the variables are cointegrated. In addition, these models allow for a separation of the long-run relationship from the factors explaining the short-run dynamic relations.

In this chapter, the main findings are that: (1) air traffic has a weak impact on economic activity in the short run, but a significant impact in the long run; whereas (2) economic activity has an impact on the air traffic both in the long run and in the short run. In the short run, the economic activities cause air traffic, whereas the short run causal effect in the opposite direction cannot be verified. These findings are based on a panel vector error correction model, as well as on panel data Granger causality tests suitable for heterogenous panels. Thus, air traffic is clearly an important factor for the regional development in the long run, although less so in the short run.

Data and historical considerations

The regional classification in Finland has changed over the years. In particular, the NUTS 2 regions changed dramatically during the period 1980–2015. Therefore, it is not in practice possible to build a panel on the NUTS 2 level. In contrast to the NUTS 2 regions, the NUTS 3 regions have not altered much in Finland over the decades. It is therefore possible to construct a meaningful panel at this level. As the NUTS 3 classification is particularly well suited for the analysis of longitudinal data from Finland, it is used for the research here.

The publicly available data brings limitations to this study. The actual capital gross formation cannot be reliably separated between the air transport industry and the rest of the economy in the Finnish regional data. With respect to the transport industry, the economic activity is only available at the aggregate level 'H Transportation and Storage' (Eurostat, 2008, 76). Moreover, the industry classifications and the published data varies markedly between the industrial classifications used over the sample period, which makes the construction of a time series with respect to the entire transport industry unreliable. The situation is even worse for the air transport industry. Clearly, the data provided by

52 *Staffan Ringbom*

Finavia concerning air travel in physical terms does not suffer from changes in industry classifications over the years. As this data is reliable, it is used here.

The infrastructure measured by capacity at the Finnish airports has shown remarkably small changes over the sample period since 1980. More detailed information can be found from the local airport webpages (see www.finavia.fi/en/airports). A typical regional airport in Finland has a single runway with the length of 2,500 m. Some of the larger regional airports have second runways which are around 800 m. The smaller airports initially had shorter runways in 1980 and those have typically been extended to 2,500 m during the sample period.

The additional services at the regional airports other than those related to the handling of the air travel are of minor importance. This is due to the fact that the total number of passengers at the airports is relatively small. Typical non-aeronautical services at the regional airports include car rental, car parking, a restaurant, a cafeteria and a shop. At many airports, the commuting service to the nearby municipality is organised by taxi services.

Clearly, there have been investments in the infrastructure to ensure that the airports always fulfil at least the regulatory standards, but the information concerning investments is not available from public sources. Hence, as there are no available data on the actual investments in the airport infrastructure, and as the real changes at the airports with respect to the runway lengths have been minor or nonexistent, the incorporation of changes in the infrastructure through public investments at the airports are neglected in the statistical analysis here.

The Finnish data panel has some special features which must be taken into account. First, Åland Islands (NUTS 3 region 21) and Uusimaa (Nylandia, NUTS3 region 1 including the capital region around Helsinki) are markedly different from the rest of the regions. On Åland Islands, the air traffic has no significant impact on the economic activity, as sea transport overwhelmingly dominates the economy on the islands. Uusimaa, covering Helsinki airport, is clearly not a rural developing region in Finland and consequently of little interest for a study with focus on regional development. In addition, there are regions with no regional airports for civil traffic.[1] As the focus of this study is on regional development and air traffic, the regions Uusimaa, Åland Islands, and the regions without any air traffic were excluded from the panel. A map of the NUTS 3 regions and the airports is presented in Figure 4.1.

The macroeconomic data consists of a regional panel based on the NUTS 3 classification over the period 1980–2016. The variables collected were production, value added, labour input, and gross capital formation. Statistics Finland report the values in prices for the current year as well as for prices for the previous year. This allows for the construction of a dataset for the economic activities in real terms. The annual flight data were provided by Finavia, and cover passenger and landings information for domestic and international flights, as well as the cargo in tonnes for the period 1980–2016 at an airport level.[2]

The sample period 1980–2016 covers a long period in the recent Finnish economic history. The macroeconomic history is briefly described here,

Finnish air traffic and regional development 53

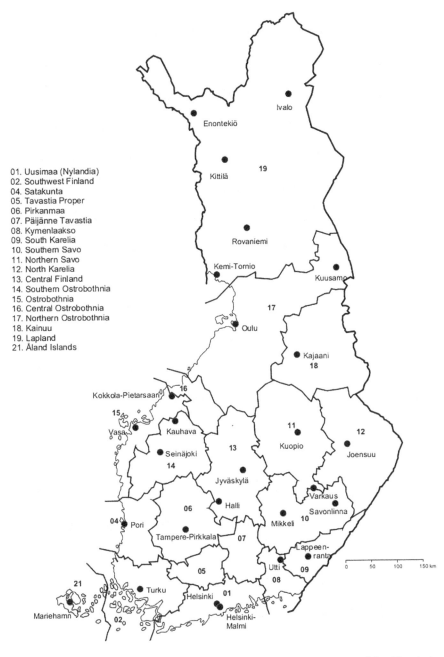

Figure 4.1 The NUTS 3 regions and the main regional airports operated by Finavia in Finland

Sources: Modified by the author from a map downloaded 19 February 2020 from www.avoindata.fi/data/en_GB/dataset/suomen-maakunnat-2021-vuoden-2018-maakuntakoodeilla; open data by National Land Survey of Finland is licensed under a Creative Commons Attribution 4.0 International License

because clearly separate regimes in the macroeconomic environment must be taken into account in the modelling. The regimes are closely linked to the Finnish exchange rates. During the period 1980–1992, the Finnish Markka was anchored to a currency basket. During the period 1990–1992, Finland suffered heavily from the collapse of the Soviet Union as it had been an important trade partner. After 7 September 1992, the Finnish Markka abandoned its target zone regime in favour of a 'dirty float' regime. The Finnish economy began its recovery from this deep recession in spring 1993. Finland joined the European Union in 1995, which also more or less coincided with the liberalisation of aviation in Europe. This liberalisation has mainly benefitted Helsinki airport, and the regional airports have indirectly been affected by this as the importance of Helsinki airport as a national hub has increased over the years. The contraction in the economy in the economic recession following the financial crisis during the period 2009–2015 was also a cause of changes in-flight activities in Finland. These macroeconomic regimes, which mostly have little to do with air traffic as such, are included in the models as dummy variables.

The statistical properties of the data

Before analysing the data with sophisticated statistical methods, the stationarity properties of the variables need to be tested. Valid inferences can be drawn from the analysis when it is assumed that the underlying relationships between the variables in the models are stationary. Therefore, models that include stationary variables are valid. Models that include non-stationary variables are sometimes valid, but not always. If, for instance, a linear combination of two non-stationary variables is stationary, then they are said to be cointegrated and a model including these variables is valid. However, this cannot be taken as granted *a priori* and it should be tested for. In the case that the variables are cointegrated, the data allows for a study of both the long-run relations and the short-run dynamics using panel vector error correction models. With the Finnish data, most of the variables are non-stationary, but stationary in time-differentiated form. Therefore, an analysis using time-differentiated variables for the economic activities and the air traffic is clearly valid. As a result, there exists interesting cointegrated relationships to be studied further. This allows for a rich study of the dynamics in the panel data.

Especially in time series and hence also in longitudinal data, it is common practice to study logarithmic values of the variables. There are several reasons for this log-transformation. For example, it transforms a geometric growth to a linear trend, and it slightly reduces problems with heteroscedasticity in the data. However, the log-transformations were not straightforward for all the underlying variables in the Finnish regional data. For instance, there exist no values in the air traffic data for passengers and cargo, as well as for landings, for some years at some airports. Clearly, the logarithms for zero and negative values must be adjusted before any log-transformation. Here, the monotone logarithmic transformation for air traffic log(passengers + 1) is chosen. On the economic activity side, investments are included with the gross capital formation as a proxy. After the economic recession following the financial crisis, there were substantial shutdowns of factories, especially paper mills. Due to these divestments, there exists negative values in the regional statistics for gross capital formation for some regions in the data. This problem with negative values is not unfamiliar in the literature. The transformation for investments in this study is done with the monotone logarithmic transformation of the gross capital formation (GCF) as follows: $inv = log(GCF + \sqrt{1 + GCF^2})$. This monotone transformation has earlier been suggested and used by Bussea and Hefeker (2007) in panel data studies of foreign direct investments (FDI). The problem here is analogous. The FDI data also covers occasional negative values, although the 'normal' case is that the values are positive.

The stationarity properties of the variables were tested with two tests. First, with the Hadri Lagrange multiplier unit-root test, where the null hypothesis is a stationary panel and the alternative hypothesis is a non-stationary panel. For this test, there are two test statistics, the $Z(\tau)$ statistics tests for stationarity with a constant and a trend, and the $Z(\mu)$ statistics tests for stationarity with a constant but without a trend (Hadri, 2000). Second, the Levin-Lin-Chu unit-root test was used. Here, the null hypothesis is a non-stationary panel and the alternative hypothesis is a stationary panel (Levin et al., 2002).

Before conducting the test unit-root test and the further analyses, the proper lag length in the time series was tested. All standard lag-order tests (AIC, BIC, and HQIC) indicate that the proper lag length is 1 in the data. The lag length one is used as the default lag length in all the analysis that follows in this chapter. The results of the stationarity test are presented in Table 4.1.

The Hadri test statistics $Z(\tau)$ tests for level and trend, $Z(\mu)$ for level without trend. The test values reported in the table are corrected for possible serial correlation in the error term. The Hadri Lagrange multiplier test rejects the stationary hypothesis in the panel for all variables. It also rejects level stationarity in Δprod but not a trend stationarity. The Levin-Lin-Chu test statistic presented in the table is the adjusted t-value, t*. This test rejects the non-stationarities for passenger traffic and investments. Thus the stationarity property remains

Table 4.1 Unit-root tests – statistics and significances

Variable	Hadri LM $Z(\tau)$, H0:stationary panel	Levin, Lin, Chu t* H0:non-stationary panel	Variable	Hadri LM $Z(\mu)$, H0:stationary panel	Hadri LM $Z(\tau)$, H0:stationary panel	Levin, Lin, Chu t* H0:non-stationary panel
Pass	11.132***	−1.95121**	Δpass	0.482	0.7914	−1.94829**
Inv	4.586***	−1.73648**	Δinv	−2.205	−0.864	−13.667***
Prod	12.048***	0.11496	Δprod	5.483***	−0.135	−10.595***
Va	6.039***	−0.35917	Δva	0.039	0.939	−11.995***
Labour	13.776***	−1.75813*	Δlabour	−0.294	1.369*	−8.6992***

Note: Significance levels: ***: $p < 0.01$; **: $p < 0.05$; *: $p < 0.1$.

56 *Staffan Ringbom*

inconclusive for these variables. The Levin-Lin-Chu test rejects the non-stationarities for all variables in time differentiated form. Thereby, it is plausible to treat all variables as I(1) variables in the statistical analysis that follows. Consequently, all variables are potential candidates for variables in a panel vector error correction model (VECM) setting.

Next, the existence of a possible cointegration relationship should be tested for before the variables are included in the model. All common cointegration tests for panel data are in the spirit of an Engel Granger two-step procedure. In the first step, the particular long run relationship of interest is fitted. The residuals from this first step are saved. In the second step, the residuals saved from the first step are tested for stationarity. If non-stationarity can be rejected in the second stage, then the variables are accepted as cointegrated; otherwise, they are not. The cointegration relationships were tested by the Pedroni panel data cointegration test (see Pedroni, 1999, 2004). The test is based on panel specific cointegration vectors and, therefore, suitable for heterogenous panels. The null hypothesis in the test is that there are no cointegration in the panel and the alternative hypothesis is that all panels are cointegrated.[3] Here cointegration relationships between passenger traffic and the economic activities are tested for. The cointegration test results are reported in Table 4.2.

Based on the panel data cointegration test, it can be concluded that:

*   The strongest and most significant long-run relationships in the data are between investments and passenger traffic, and real production and passenger traffic. The cointegration between value-added and passenger traffic is weak.
*   Labour and passenger travel are also strongly cointegrated, but here the long-run relationship between them over the decades is negative. This can be explained by the fact that the regions in the countryside have suffered from structural emigration, although the air traffic has increased over the period. This long run structural emigration reflects a shift in the production away from primary activities such as agriculture and forestry to other activities, especially in the area near Helsinki. Here, the labour force was for the entire region for all industries. A separation between the labour force in the primary and secondary sectors, and the service sector, respectively, might alter the results (see Percoco, 2010). However, this separation was not done here.
*   Cargo transport had an insignificant relationship with the economic activities in the regions over the sample period.

Table 4.2 Pedroni cointegration test values

	Va	*Prod*	*Inv*	*Labour*
Modified Phillps-Perron t	1.6256*	2.2454**	−2.9523***	2.6094***
Phillips-Perron t	1.0256	1.9877**	−3.7457***	1.9924**
ADF-t	0.7852	1.9050**	−3.3237***	2.0193**

Note: Significance levels: ***: p < 0.01; **: p < 0.05; *: p < 0.1.

Long-run relations and short-run dynamics – the vector error correction model

Modern statistical programmes such as STATA provide routines for calculating vector error correction models with panel data. The underlying vector error correction model presented here is the pooled mean-group (PMG) estimator by Blackburne and Frank (2007). It has the following autoregressive distributed lag form:

$$\Delta y_{it} = \phi_i(y_{i,t-1} - \theta_i'X_{it}) + \sum_{j=1}^{p-1}\lambda_{ij}\Delta y_{i,t-1} + \sum_{j=0}^{q-1}\delta_{ij}\Delta X_{i,t-j} + \mu_i + \sum_{j=1}^{r}\gamma_{ij}'D_{it} + \varepsilon_{it}$$

y_{it} is the dependent variable (passenger traffic or a macroeconomic indicator)

X_{it} is the k x 1 vector of explanatory variables (including dummy) for country I

$y_{i,t-1} - \theta_i'X_{it}$ is the error correction term estimated from in the first step of the regression

θ_i is the coefficient vector which determines the long run relationship between y_i and X_i

$\phi_i < 0$ captures the speed of adjustment towards the long run relationship

δ_{it} is the k × 1 coefficient vectors of explanatory variables

λ_{ij} is the scalar coefficients of lagged first-difference of dependent variable

α_i is the region-specific effect

γ_i is the r × 1 coefficient vectors for the dummy variables

ε_{it} is the disturbances that are independently distributed across regions i and time, with mean of zero and variance of $\delta^2 < 0$.

The economic indicators are strongly correlated in the data. Even though the inclusion of several economic indicators could slightly improve the model's statistics, it comes at a cost of lost intuition in the final model. The same argument applies for the flight data. Passengers and landings are highly correlated. Including both of them does not add much information of value. Including more than one macroeconomic variable into a VECM model is more problematic in a panel setting than with a single multivariate time series. This is due to the fact that a panel VECM forces exactly one cointegration vector. In contrast, in a multivariate time series, it is possible to test for the number of cointegration relationships in a rigorous manner with Johansen's cointegration tests. Such tests are not yet available for panel data. Hence, it was decided to study the relationships between only one x and one y variable in the long-run relation, provided that the cointegration test confirms the existence of a stable cointegrated relation. The choice of one x variable and one y variable is further motivated by the fact that the dependence between the economic activity and the air traffic in both directions is studied. The interpretation of the results is more transparent when there are no other variables included in the models. Choosing only one x and one y variable also allows for conclusions with respect to the causal relationships in the panel.

58 Staffan Ringbom

Table 4.3 Long-run relationships and short-run dynamics between passenger traffic and investments

	Δinv_t	Prob	$\Delta pass_t$	Prob
LR relations	0.1468908 $pass_t$ (0.0493611)	0.003***	0.2160214 inv_t (0.1115681)	0.053*
SR dynamics	−0.5224882 ec_t (0.0853207)	0.000***	−0.2352168 ec_t (0.0637064)	0.000***
	0.0890015 $\Delta pass_{t-1}$ (0.0759103)	0.241	0.1703962 Δinv_{t-1} (0.0403317)	0.000***
	0.03945 d_{8089} (0.0261086)	0.129	−0.0069203 d_{8089} (0.0312838)	0.825
	−0.1221089 d_{9092} (0.0290327)	0.000***	−0.0478098 d_{9092} (0.0217592)	0.028**
	−0.28786 d_{9394} (0.0344595)	0.000***	−0.058418 d_{9394} (0.0186812)	0.002***
	0.0154172 d_{0816} (0.0212689)	0.469	−0.0311311 d_{0816} (0.0330733)	0.347
	3.023933 cons (0.5083768)	0.000***	2.46624 cons (0.655982)	0.000***

Note: Significance levels: ***: $p < 0.01$; **: $p < 0.05$; *: $p < 0.1$.

Tables 4.3 and 4.4 present the long-run relationships and short-run dynamics between air traffic and gross investments, and air traffic and production, respectively. From Table 4.3, it can be observed that there exists a significant positive long-run relationship in both directions between passenger traffic and investments. This relationship is both significant and it spills over to a significant error correction in the short-run dynamics. A significant negative coefficient for the error correction variable indicates that there is a force to adjust deviations in the co-movement of the variables towards the long-run relationship. In addition, the lagged changes in investments positively affects the change in passenger traffic in the model.

From Table 4.4, it can be observed that there also exists a significant long-run relationship between real production in the regions and the passenger traffic. In the direction from economic activity towards passenger traffic, we observe that the long-run relationship is weak. The fact that there exists a significant long-run effect from air transport to the real economy is consistent with broader studies of the benefits from air transport in Finland (Oxford Economics, (2011) and Nyberg et al. (2015)). The short-run relationships are

Table 4.4 Long-run relationships and short-run dynamics between passenger traffic and production

	$\Delta prod_t$	Prob	$\Delta pass_t$	Prob
LR relations	0.6136413 $pass_t$ (0.0577562)	0.000★★★	0.0876356 $prod_t$ (0.1509101)	0.561
SR dynamics	−0.1098028 ec_t (0.058117)	0.059★★	−0.189211 ec_t (0.0632295)	0.003★★★
	0.0663183 $\Delta pass_{t-1}$ (0.0193579)	0.001★★★	0.843249 $\Delta prod_{t-1}$ (0.2380903)	0.000★★★
	−0.0020632 d_{8089} (0.0177907)	0.908	−0.0073067 d_{8089} (0.0265521)	0.783
	−0.0499544 d_{9092} (0.0107632)	0.000★★★	−0.0389828098 d_{9092} (0.0194518)	0.045★★
	0.0006526 d_{9394} (0.010456)	0.95	−0.098795 d_{9394} (0.0315464)	0.002★★★
	−0.0283236 d_{0816} (0.0065543)	0.000★★★		
	0.1508075 cons (0.0416337)	0.000★★★	2.142041 cons (0.7077547)	0.002★★★

Note: Significance levels: ★★★: $p < 0.01$; ★★: $p < 0.05$; ★: $p < 0.1$.

also significant in Table 4.4. The causalities in the short-run dynamics are more thoroughly investigated in the following section.

Haughwout (2001) indicates that the results at a NUTS 3 level might be diluted when the data is aggregated. Therefore, the analogous results are presented using aggregated data, where the aggregation is made on the original NUTS 3 regions included in the analysis. Due to the fact that the panel data method employed here is able to handle heterogenous panels and this heterogeneity disappears in the aggregation, it is expected that the results would be weaker in the aggregated model. Another factor contributing to weaker results is the apparent loss of degrees of freedom as a result of the aggregation. The results were indeed diluted in an aggregation of the data. As these results are of minor interest, they are not reported here.

Granger causality

The causalities in non-stationary data can partly be explained using the vector error correction models in the previous section. With the Pedroni cointegration

60   *Staffan Ringbom*

test (see Table 4.2), the value added was not significantly integrated with passenger traffic. Hence, an error correction model for value added and passenger traffic is meaningless, and at the very least, the causalities between value added and passenger traffic must be investigated in time-differentiated form. Previously, Pyyny (2011) studied the causalities between air transport and economic activities in Finland region by region with data in time-differentiated form. He concluded that a region-by-region investigation was beneficial as the panel was too heterogenous for a panel study. Here, in contrast to Pyyny (2011), a causality test presented by Dumitrescu and Hurlin (2012) which is suitable for heterogeneous panels is employed.

The passenger traffic and the variables explaining the economic activities are all difference stationary. The underlying assumption in the causality test is that the variables are stationary in the panel. Therefore, the causality tests are presented for the time differentiated data, which is verified to be stationary. The logic in the causality test is the following:

Consider a panel data model

$$y_{it} = \alpha_i + \sum_{k=1}^{K} \gamma_{ik} y_{it-k} + \sum_{k=1}^{K} \beta_{ik} x_{it-k} + \varepsilon_{it},$$

where:

x_{it} and y_{it} are the observations of two variables for region i in period t

α_i captures the region-specific effect

γ_{ik} and β_{ik} are allowed to differ across regions but assumed to be time invariant

Lag order K is assumed to be identical for all i and the panel must be balanced

Causality is found by testing for the significant effects of past values of x on the present value of y. Therefore, the null hypothesis is as follows:

$H_o : \beta_{i1} = \cdots = \beta_{ik} = 0 \qquad \forall i = 1,...,N$

The test assumes there can be causality for some individuals in the panel but not necessarily for all. Thus, the alternative hypothesis is:

$H_1 : \beta_{i1} \neq or...or \beta_{ik} \neq 0 \qquad \forall i = N_1 + 1,...,N.$

The results are presented from the Dumitrescu and Hurlin (2012) Granger non-causality tests in Table 4.5.

Table 4.5 The Dumitrescu and Hurlin (2012) Granger non-causality tests with lag order 1

	$\Delta inv \to \Delta pass$	$\Delta pass \to \Delta inv$	$\Delta va \to \Delta pass$	$\Delta pass \to \Delta va$	$\Delta prod \to \Delta pass$	$\Delta pass \to \Delta prod$
$\overline{W}$	1.0542	1.3957	2.3761	1.1502	2.1210	0.8592
$\overline{Z}$	0.1328	0.9692	3.3707***	0.3680	2.7460***	−0.3449
$\overline{\overline{Z}}$	−0.0320	0.7102	2.8415***	0.1767	2.2871**	−0.4560

Note: Significance levels: ***: p < 0.01; **: p < 0.05; *: p < 0.1.

The Wald statistics are insignificant, but the Z-statistics for heterogenous panels indicate significant causalities. In the pure short-run dynamics, it can clearly be observed that the causality goes from economic activity towards passenger traffic but it cannot be verified in the opposite direction. The results in Table 4.5 differ from those reported by Mukkula and Tervo (2013) who report a strong causality from air traffic to economic activity in peripheral regions. The results are slightly different from those presented by Button and Yuan (2013), who also observe a causal effect from air traffic to the real economy. It is worthwhile to note that only the direct short-run effects are observed in the simple causality test here. The long-run effects are observed in the VECM (presented in the previous section).

Conclusion

Earlier studies have analysed the relationship between air traffic and economic development using various types of econometric approaches. In contrast to the traditional literature, this research takes advantage of the cointegration properties in panel data. Here the non-stationary and cointegrated panel data were analysed with a vector error correction approach, which yields more valid conclusions. The approach also yields deeper insights to the underlying long-run structure and short-term adjustment in the underlying variables covering real economic activity and passenger traffic.

Regional development was analysed with the value of production value added and investment in combination with passenger traffic. The values of production and investments both have long-run and short-run positive effects on passenger traffic. The long-run positive effects are strong and significant also from passenger traffic to economic activities.

In the short run, the causality clearly goes in the direction from economic activity towards air traffic. The evidence of a short-run causality from passenger traffic to economic activities remains weak in the data. This differs from Mukkula and Tervo (2013), as well as from Button and Yuan (2013), who report clear causalities from air traffic to economic activity in the regions.

In the short run, the economic activity seems clearly to be the driver of the air traffic activity in Finland. For the long-run economic development, air traffic has a strong and significant impact, both on investments and on production as a whole. This confirms the findings in the earlier policy papers from Finland by Oxford Economics (2011) and Nyberg et al. (2015). Hence, air traffic is a strategic long-run factor in rural development.

Notes

1 Four of the regions have no regional airports with regular civil traffic, even at the borders of the regions. There are two regions with airports just on the opposite side of their borders. The flight data for these regions were assigned in equal proportions to the regions on both sides of the border. These airports were Kokkola-Pietarsaari, where the data was split between NUTS 3 regions 15 and 16, and Varkaus, where the data was split between

62 Staffan Ringbom

regions 10 and 11. In addition NUTS 3 region 9 with Lappeenrantaa airport had zero passengers in 2016. Lappenranta airport has been classified as an airport with public service obligation. The regions with zero air traffic observations were dropped from the study.

2 The macroeconomic data are available from Statistics Finland's data (http://pxnet2.stat.fi/PXWeb/pxweb/en/StatFin). The air traffic and airport data are provided by Finavia (www.finavia.fi). Although the data allows for the separation of domestic and international passengers, the benefit of this split is minor and therefore not reported here.

3 Inv = log = $(GCF + \sqrt{GCF^2 + 1})$, where GCF is gross capital formation, Prod = log(PRODUCTION), Va=log(VALUE ADDED). This transformation has been suggested by Labour=log(WORKERS+ENTREPRENEURS) where the values are collected from the regional accounts of Statistics Finland. The nominal values are deflated to real values by chain linking the current prices and the prices from the previous year in the official regional accounting statistics. The passengers are measured in the analysis with pass1=log(1+passengers).

References

Alkaabi, K. A. and Debbage, K. G. (2011). The geography of air freight: Connections to US metropolitan economies. *Journal of Transport Geography*, 19(6), 1517–1529.

Bilotkach, V. (2015). Are airports engines of economic development? A dynamic panel data approach. *Urban Studies*, 9, 1577–1593.

Blackburne, E. F. and Frank, M. W. (2007). Estimation of monstationary heterogenous panels. *Stata Journal*, 7(2), 197–208.

Bom, R. D. and Ligthart, J. E. (2014). What have we learned from three decades of research on the productivity of public capital. *Journal of Economic Surveys*, 28(5), 889–916.

Bråthen, S. and Halpern, N. (2012). Air transport service provision and management strategies to improve the economic benefits for remote regions. *Research in Transport and Business Management*, 4, 3–12.

Brueckner, J. (2003). Airline traffic and urban economic development. *Urban Studies*, 40, 1455–1469.

Bussea, M. and Hefeker, C. (2007). Political risk, institutions and foreign direct investment. *European Journal of Political Economy*, 23(2), 397–415.

Button, K. and Yuan, J. (2013). Airfreight transport and economic development: An examination of causality. *Urban Studies*, 50, 329–340.

Dumitrescu, E. I. and Hurlin, C. (2012). Testing for Granger non-causality in heterogeneous panels. *Economic Modelling*, 29(4), 1450–1460.

Eurostat (2008). *NACE Rev. 2 – Statistical classification of economic activites in the European Community*. Eurostat Methodologies and Working papers. ISSN 1977-0375. Available at: https://ec.europa.eu/eurostat/documents/3859598/5902521/KS-RA-07-015-EN.PDF.

Graham, A. (2018). *Managing airports: An international perspective*, 5th edition. Abingdon, Routledge.

Hadri, K. (2000). Testing for stationarity in heterogeneous panel data. *Econometrics Journal*, 3(2), 148–161.

Halpern, N. and Bråthen, S. (2010). *Catalytic impact of airports in Norway*. Report 1008. Molde, Møreforsking Molde.

Halpern, N. and Bråthen, S. (2011). Impact of airports on regional accessibility and social development. *Journal of Transport Geography*, 19(6), 1145–1154.

Haughwout, A. F. (2001). Infrastructure and social welfare in metropolitan America. *Economic Policy Review*, 7(3), 1–16.

Levin, A., Lin, C. F. and Chu, C. S. J. (2002). Unit root tests in panel data: Asymptotic and finite-sample properties. *Journal of Econometrics*, 108(1), 1–24.

Martin, P. (1998). Can regional policies affect growth and geography in Europe. *The World Economy*, 21(6), 757–774.

Melo, P., Graham, D. J. and Brage-Ardao, R. (2013). The productivity of transportation infrastructure investment: A meta-analysis of empircial evidence. *Regional Science and Urban Economics*, 43(5), 695–706.

Mukkula, K. and Tervo, H. (2013). Regional airports and regional growth in Europe: Which way does the causality run? *Environment and Planning A*, 45, 1508–1520.

Neal, Z. (2012). Creative employment and jet set cities: Disentangeling causal effects. *Urban Studies*, 49(42), 2693–2709.

Nyberg, M., Saari, R., Hilska, L., Ahokas, M., Sotaniemi, A. and Männistö, K. (2015). *Finland's air transport strategy 2015–2030*. Helsinki, Finnish Ministry Transport and Communications.

Oxford Economics (2011). *Economic benefits from air transport in Finland*. Oxford, Oxford Economics.

Pedroni, P. (1999). Critical values for cointegration tests in heterogeneous panels with multiple regressors. *Oxford Bulletin of Economics and Statistics*, 61(S1), 653–670.

Pedroni, P. (2004). Panel cointegration: Asymptotic and finite sample properties of pooled time series tests with an application to the PPP hypothesis. *Economic Theory*, 20(3), 597–625.

Percoco, M. (2010). Airport activity and local development: Evidence from Italy. *Urban Studies*, 47(11), 2427–2443.

Pyyny, P. (2011). *Lentoasemien vaikutukset aluetalouteen -Granger-kausaalisuus analyysin sovellus*. Jyväskylä. Available at: https://jyx.jyu.fi/handle/123456789/36914.

Romp, W. and de Haan, J. (2007). Public capital and economic growth: A critical survey. *Perspektiven der Wirtschaftspolitik*, 8, 6–52.

5 UK regional airports
Developments and challenges

Anne Graham

Introduction

The UK has a relatively large number of airports which can be primarily explained by the fact that it is an island, it has a substantial number of significant towns, and it has a relatively high per capita income. It has 30 main airports, ranging from London Heathrow with over 80 million passengers to Humberside with just under 200,000 passengers, with a significant number of even smaller airports, too. This high concentration means that catchment areas of many airports overlap. Overall UK regional airports, defined here as all airports outside the London area, handle around 40 per cent of total UK passenger traffic.

A fairly unusual feature of the UK airport industry is that most are operated, either partially or totally, by private operators. While the shift from public ownership has its origins in the 1980s, it still has repercussions today. Moreover, in recent years, UK regional airports have experienced some major changes in the traffic that they serve. Initially, many benefitted from the significant expansion of air services that was driven by the emergence of the low-cost carrier (LCC) sector. Such growth was abruptly stopped by the onset of the financial crisis and economic recession in 2008. It has subsequently returned at some airports, but for others conditions remain very challenging, particularly as LCC traffic has matured and the strategies of airlines continue to evolve and change. At the same time, the London airports, particularly Heathrow, have become more and more congested due to a lack of spare capacity.

As in other countries, these regional airports have the potential to have a major influence on economic and regional growth, but their exact role is dependent on a number of key developments and challenges that are explored in this chapter. The next section starts by looking at ownership issues. This moves onto considering traffic and financial performance, then regional connectivity. Finally, some issues related to Heathrow and other government policies are discussed, after which conclusions are drawn.

Ownership and privatisation

A pivotal development regarding government policy towards the UK airport industry was the 1986 Airports Act. This reflected the government's desire to bring privatisation to the airport sector and to reduce the burden on the public sector. Prior to this Act, a national government body, the British Airports Authority, owned seven key airports (London Heathrow, London Gatwick, London Stansted, Aberdeen, Edinburgh, Glasgow, and Prestwick) and there were a further eight small airports in the Scottish Islands and Highlands nationally owned and operated. Nearly all the other regional airports were owned by local/regional government. The Act made provision for the British Airports Authority to become a private company, BAA, through a subsequent 100 per cent share flotation in 1987. It also required all other airports with a turnover of more than £1 million in two of the previous three years to become companies. At the time, this involved 16 airports ranging from Manchester airport that had a throughput of nine million passengers to Southend airport handling just over 100,000 passengers. The shareholders at these airport companies were initially the local government owners, but the shares could then be sold off, partially or totally, to private investors if desired by the public sector owners. This was the ultimate aim of the pro-privatisation government at the time (Graham, 2008; Humphreys, 1999).

As the result of the 1986 Act, the Civil Aviation Authority (CAA) took on the role of economic regulator. Four airports (Heathrow, Gatwick, Stansted, and Manchester) were designated for price regulation to safeguard against any possible abuse of market power. They were subject to an incentive (RPI +/− price cap) type of regulation. However, in 2008, it was decided that Manchester airport did not have enough market power to warrant this regulation and so it was no longer subject to price caps (Department for Transport [DfT], 2008). A new Act and regulatory regime were introduced in 2014 (Cheong, 2015; Littlechild, 2018), replacing the previous one-size-fits-all price control regulatory policy with a more flexible licencing regime. Heathrow remains under a price control, whereas at Gatwick, a type of more light-handed approach has now been introduced for the first time (CAA, 2014a, 2014b), primarily as a result of the airport agreeing a series of commitments with its airlines on price, service conditions, and investment. At Stansted, price regulation has been dropped as it was decided that the airport no longer possessed significant market power (CAA, 2013). No regional airport is subject to any kind of price control.

As a result of these policies, all major regional airports above 200,000 passengers have experienced some degree of airport privatisation, but the ownership structures vary significantly (Table 5.1). Some airports, such as Bournemouth, Bristol, and Leeds Bradford, are fully private. Others (e.g. Birmingham, Newcastle, and Manchester) have opted for a partially privatised approach that gives them access to private finance but also enables some local public control to be maintained. Most of the very small regional airports below this size remain under local public sector ownership as does the organisation Highlands and Islands Airports Ltd that is owned by the Scottish government and receives an operating subsidy.

There are now a number of airport groups that manage more than one airport in the UK (Ison et al., 2011; Graham et al., 2014), including AGS,

66 Anne Graham

Table 5.1 Ownership of main UK regional airports in 2019

Airport	Ownership	Private interest (per cent)
Aberdeen	AGS Airports	100
Belfast City	3i Investments	100
Belfast International	Vinci Airports	100
Birmingham	Local government/Ontario Teachers' Pension Plan/Employee Share Trust	51
Bournemouth	Rigby Group	100
Bristol	Ontario Teachers' Pension Plan	100
Cardiff	Welsh government	0
Doncaster (Robin Hood)	Peel Group	100
East Midlands	MAG	35.5
Edinburgh	Global Infrastructure Partners (GIP)	100
Exeter	Rigby Group	100
Glasgow	AGS Airports	100
Humberside	Eastern Group	83
Inverness	Highlands and Islands	0
Leeds Bradford	AMP	100
Liverpool	Peel Group	100
Manchester	Manchester Airport Group (MAG): Local government/IFM Investors	35.5
Newcastle	Local government /AMP Capital	49
Newquay	Cornwall Council	0
Norwich	Rigby Group/Local government	80
Prestwick	Scottish government	0
Southampton	AGS Airports	100
Sumburgh	Highlands and Islands Airports	0

Source: Compiled by author from various sources

Note: Largest 23 airports by annual passengers (greater than around 200,000) in 2018.

MAG, Peel, Regional and City, and Stobart (Table 5.2). Such group ownership can potentially bring benefits such as economies of scale and the sharing of resources and expertise, but can also be viewed as anti-competitive, particularly when catchment areas of the airports overlap. The most notable example here is BAA. At the time of privatisation and afterwards for 20 years, there were fierce debates as to whether the airports of BAA should have been privatised as a group or separately. Eventually, in 2009, the UK's competition authority (the Competition Commission) decided that common ownership did give rise to adverse effects on competition (Competition Commission, 2009; Bush, 2010) and BAA was required to sell Gatwick, Stansted, and either Glasgow or Edinburgh (it chose Edinburgh). Heathrow Airport is now owned by a separate entity, although Aberdeen, Glasgow, and Southampton remain under the common ownership of AGS. There have also been other cases where common ownership of neighbouring regional airports has not gone ahead, for example with Bristol and Exeter airports, and also with Belfast City and Belfast International airports, because of fears of anti-competitive outcomes. Evidence

Table 5.2 Group/fund ownership of UK airports in 2019

Owner	Airport
AGS Airports★	Aberdeen, Glasgow, Southampton
AMP Capital	Leeds Bradford, Newcastle, Belfast City, Luton
Global Infrastructure Partners (GIP)	Edinburgh, Gatwick
Manchester Airports Group (MAG)	Manchester, East Midlands, Stansted
Ontario Teachers Pensions Plan	Birmingham, Bristol, London City Airport
Peel Group	Liverpool, Doncaster Robin Hood, Durham Tees Valley
Regional and City Airports (Rigby Group)	Coventry, Exeter, Norwich, Bournemouth (Also management contracts at Blackpool, City of Derry, Solent)
Stobart Group	Southend, Carlisle
Scottish government	Highlands and Islands airports, Prestwick
Vinci	Gatwick, Belfast International

Source: Compiled by author from various sources

★ Ferrovial is a major shareholder of AGS Airports and Heathrow Airport Holdings.

suggests that the splitting up of common ownership has led to improvements in terms of traffic growth, efficiency, and service quality (Competition and Markets Authority, 2016; Pagliari and Graham, 2019).

In the early stages of privatisation, a number of UK bus/rail providers such as National Express, First Group, and Stagecoach purchased regional airports in the belief that there were synergy benefits that could be exploited with their other operations. They have subsequently abandoned their involvement with such airports, and the airports have been sold onto different investors. Such secondary sales are inevitably becoming more popular in the UK as the privatisation trend becomes exhausted, and some smaller regional airports have experienced a decline in their overall financial performance (see following discussion). This has created a somewhat fluid situation as regards airport ownership, with financial investors such as investment banks and pension funds becoming the dominant players. All this raises the issue as to what is the optimum ownership and governance structure for UK regional airports. With financial investors becoming the norm, there is some concern that they focus too much on short-term financial gains that may not be compatible with long-term airport development objectives.

However, not all privatisations have been successful. Cardiff airport was sold to the Welsh government in 2013 after its traffic declined from a peak of two million passengers in 2007 to just over one million in 2012. The Welsh government viewed the airport as a critical gateway to Wales and considered its purchase vital for its long-term future. Meanwhile in Scotland, Prestwick airport – which had experienced substantial financial losses, particularly after losing much of its Ryanair traffic – was sold to the Scottish government in 2013 for just £1. A few other airports, namely Plymouth (under public ownership) and Manston (under private ownership), have permanently closed, while loss-making airports Blackpool and Coventry have experienced temporary closure and a significant scaling down of the aviation services that they provide.

Traffic and financial performance

Looking now at traffic and financial performance, Figure 5.1 shows the passenger numbers at all UK airports between 2002 and 2018. It may be seen that there was a period of strong growth from 2002–2007, followed by a more challenging era of traffic decline and stagnation from 2008–2012, and then subsequent growth again between 2013 and 2018. With the early growth, the share of regional traffic (compared to London traffic) in the UK grew from 38 per cent to a peak of 42 per cent in 2008 but has now fallen back to around 40 per cent. These traffic trends have had a major impact on the overall financial wellbeing of the airports, with operating margins being very healthy up until 2008 but subsequently reducing to a lower average level (Figure 5.2).

A key turning point as regards UK regional airports (as in many European countries) was the deregulation of European air services and the subsequent emergence of the LCC sector. LCC traffic expansion between 2002 and 2007 encouraged the strong growth at many of these regional airports and the rise in overall regional market share. However, the financial crisis and global economic recession halted this traffic growth in 2008, by dampening both business and leisure demand (Halpern and Graham, 2017; Halpern et al., 2016). At the

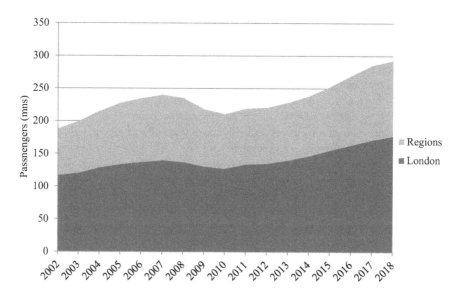

Figure 5.1 Passenger numbers at all UK airports, 2002–2018

Source: Devised by author from CAA (2003–2019) annual airport statistics

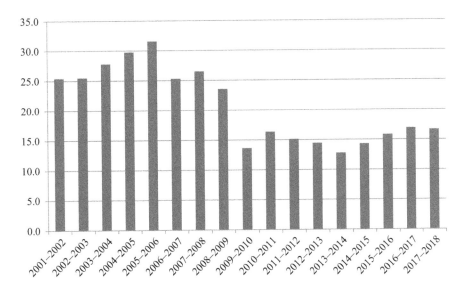

Figure 5.2 Operating margin (%) at UK regional airports, 2002–2018
Source: Devised by author from CRI (2003–2009) airport statistics/Leighfisher (2010–2019) UK airport performance indicators
Notes: The airport sample (15 in total) includes all airports shown in Table 5.1 with the exception of Belfast City, Doncaster, Exeter, Newquay, Norwich, Prestwick, and the Scottish and Islands airports for which insufficient data were available. Operating margin is defined as the operating profit divided by the operating revenue.

same time, the UK's Air Passenger Duty (APD) was increased significantly (see discussion following) and the weak pound particularly hit UK outbound tourism to the Eurozone. While growth has returned, a more volatile situation for regional airports now exists, as is reflected by the overall lower profitability figures. This has also been affected by the evolving strategies of LCCs and other airlines.

LCC traffic at a number of regional airports has become a dominant feature. In 2016 (the latest year for which separate passenger data for LCCs could be obtained) overall in the UK, 16 million passengers travelled on domestic LCC services (compared to 23 million on full service carriers [FCSs]) and 80 million travelled on LCC short-haul services (compared to 83 million on FSCs). LCC passengers represented in excess of 70 per cent of all international traffic at Belfast International, Bournemouth, Bristol, East Midlands, Leeds Bradford, Liverpool, and Prestwick airports (DfT, 2017). At the same time, charter flights, which traditionally took UK residents from the regions on international package holidays, have declined significantly. This reflects changes taking place in the outbound leisure market from the UK where passengers have been shifting to more independent and flexible travel arrangements offered by LCCs,

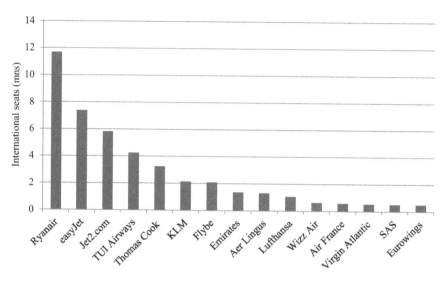

Figure 5.3 Main airlines serving all UK regional airports in 2018
Source: Devised by author from The Anker Report (2018)

including short break trips. The total number of charter passengers travelling through UK regional airports decreased from 25 million (33 per cent of total passengers) in 2002 to just nine million (8 per cent) in 2018, although these numbers are somewhat artificially reduced by certain leisure airlines reclassifying their services as 'scheduled' rather than 'charter'. However, it is still leisure routes, which would formerly have operated as charter services, which still underpin the networks of many of the lesser-sized regional airports. These cater for outbound leisure demand rather than providing much economic benefit to the locality. This is illustrated by the airlines serving international regional routes. The top three are LCCs (Ryanair, easyJet, and Jet2), followed by two 'charter' carriers (TUI and Thomas Cook – Thomas Cook actually ceased operations in 2019) (Figure 5.3). British Airways is not in the list, with KLM being the largest FSC.

Flybe was a key player in terms of domestic flights, operating from 28 UK airports in 2018. However, it struggled with profitability and was sold to the Connect Airways consortium in 2019 which was backed by Virgin Atlantic but ceased operations in March 2020. Overall, domestic passenger numbers at the regions have been growing at a much slower rate than international travel, only increasing from 27 million in 2002 to 33 million, with the domestic market share at the regions reducing from 38 per cent to 29 per cent (Figure 5.4). This development is particularly notable with services to Heathrow where capacity is being acutely squeezed (see discussion following). Other than London airport capacity constraints, this decline is also likely to be due to improved rail

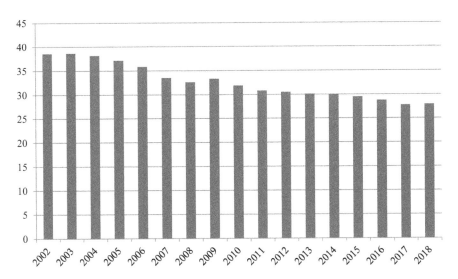

Figure 5.4 Domestic share of total passengers (%) at all UK regional airports, 2002–2018
Source: Devised by author from CAA (2003–2019) annual airport statistics

services on certain routes, the APD being much higher on domestic routes (as it is effectively charged twice for a return trip), more stringent security measures making domestic air travel more cumbersome than rail travel, and even the airline practice of charging for hold baggage. This is a worrying development for the regions, as potentially it is denying passengers from the regional airports access to other markets, particularly the important London markets, and the vital benefits of air connectivity that this can bring to UK regional economies.

As already discussed, traffic growth since 2013 has returned to the regional airports, but with some airports performing better than others (Table 5.2). As noted by Halpern et al. (2016) and Halpern and Graham (2017), it is mostly the smaller regional airports, without much natural catchment area of their own, that have fared worst (often after experiencing rapid growth from LCCs prior to 2008), as services have been consolidated onto the larger regional airports. In part, this reflects the evolution of the LCC industry. For example, in the early years, Ryanair was able to use a Boeing 737–200 aircraft with 130 seats virtually from anywhere to anywhere and fill it based on low fares, which would be sufficient to divert or stimulate enough demand. Over time, Ryanair has increased the average unit size of its fleet by using 189-seat Boeing 737–800s. This has meant greater use of larger more centrally located airports with a larger and more established local market – something that it initially avoided – and this had led to reductions in smaller nearby markets. For example, the number of Ryanair routes at Prestwick airport has declined from a peak of around 40 in 2009 to just 10 now, with LCC traffic at the larger

72 *Anne Graham*

and neighbouring airports of Glasgow and Edinburgh increasing significantly. Other LCCs, for example easyJet, have also experienced a growth in average aircraft size. At the same time, some of the major regional airports, for instance Manchester and Edinburgh, that were initially hostile to LCCs have changed their strategies and shown a greater willingness to offer incentives for new routes and traffic growth. Other LCCs seem to be reducing services at UK regional airports; for example, in 2018, Wizz Air, Norwegian, and Vueling cut their international seat capacity by around 20, 20, and 40 per cent, respectively (The Anker Report, 2018). A shift in emphasis towards serving business travel needs can also help explain the LCC movement towards larger, more traditional airports.

This increased popularity of larger regional airports is an arguably reversal of the previous trend, and it has left some regional economies more vulnerable because of loss of services at smaller airports. It has left such airports financially exposed, especially when they may have incurred capital costs to facilitate expansion and cannot cover the resultant fixed costs if traffic growth does not materialise. These changing fortunes of regional airports are very visible from their comparative profitability. Table 5.3 shows that it tends to be the larger regional airports (albeit with a few exceptions) that have larger operating margins, with all losses in 2018 being observed at airports of fewer than two million passengers. Some regional airports that seemed relatively attractive investments in the LCC boom days are now much less financially appealing. Indeed, the poor performance of Prestwick and Cardiff airport is an indication of why the airports were sold by their private owners, with the state taking over. Elsewhere, the loss-making airports of Bournemouth and Humberside were sold by MAG in order for it to concentrate on its larger airports. Doncaster Sheffield airport has consistently made large losses in most years since its opening in 2005, and the losses at Highlands and Islands airports would be much greater if the operating subsidy of £20 million is omitted. Small airports tend to be particularly vulnerable if they have to largely rely on services provided by a single airline, which is the case at some regional airports in the UK.

Clearly the profitability of these regional airports is affected by many factors. A simple plot of cost per passenger against passenger numbers in 2017/2018 indicates that the airports appear to experience considerable scale economies, with the smallest airports having the highest unit costs (Figure 5.5). This is in agreement with earlier findings of Bottasso and Conti (2012), who analysed the cost structure of the UK airport industry by estimating a variable cost function for the period 1994–2005. Their results indicated that average costs decrease until passenger traffic reaches five million, remain constant over the range between five million and 14 million passengers, and afterwards start to increase. Some other evidence (Assaf, 2009, 2010; Assaf et al., 2012; See and Li, 2015) suggests that small airports within the UK have weaker financial performance or efficiency levels, although contradictory or inconclusive research also exists (Barros, 2008; Barros and Weber, 2009) as regards the size relationship. The largest regional airport, Manchester, appears in Figure 5.5 to have

UK regional airports   73

Table 5.3 Traffic and financial performance of UK regional airports, 2013–2018

	Passengers in 2013 (000s)	Passengers in 2018 (000s)	% annual change	Operating margin in 2017/2018 (%)
Manchester	20,680	28,256	6.4	29.1
Edinburgh	9,775	14,292	7.9	42.8
Birmingham	9,114	12,455	6.4	33.7
Glasgow	7,358	9,653	5.6	34.7
Bristol	6,125	8,697	7.3	36.5
Belfast International	4,022	6,269	9.3	17.8
Newcastle	4,415	5,332	3.8	41.5
Liverpool (John Lennon)	4,186	5,042	3.8	11.0
East Midlands	4,328	4,874	2.4	11.3
Leeds Bradford	3,314	4,038	4.0	5.6
Aberdeen	3,440	3,056	−2.3	28.1
Belfast City (George Best)	2,542	2,510	−0.2	13.7
Southampton	1,722	1,991	2.9	27.1
Cardiff Wales	1,057	1,579	8.4	−31.1
Doncaster Sheffield	690	1,222	12.1	−168.0
Exeter	738	931	4.8	6.4
Inverness	607	893	8.0	−4.8★
Prestwick	1,145	681	−9.9	−32.7
Bournemouth	659	675	0.5	−36.3
Norwich	463	537	3.0	17.4
Newquay	175	457	21.2	0.3
Sumburgh	210	246	3.2	−4.8★
Humberside	235	192	−3.9	−2.0

Sources: CAA (2014c, 2019) annual airport statistics and LeighFisher (2019) UK airports performance indicators

★ Operating margin for Highlands and Islands airports.

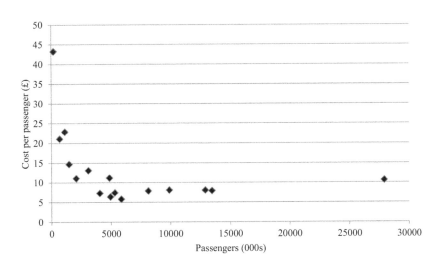

Figure 5.5 Relationship between airport size and cost per passenger at UK regional airports in 2017/2018

Source: Devised by author from LeighFisher (2019) UK airports performance indicators

Note: The sample is the same as in Figure 5.2.

slightly higher costs, very tentatively agreeing with Bottasso and Conti (2012) that unit costs may actually rise again with larger airports, and that economies of scale are exhausted at about five million passengers (Bottasso et al., 2019).

Financial performance and efficiency of UK airports is also influenced by the type of traffic, particularly LCCs. Bottasso et al. (2012) argued that productivity may increase with LCCs, as this traffic can make better use of existing capacity and costs can be lowered to ensure that the airports meet the simpler LCC operational requirements and lower fees of the LCCs. They found that LCCs have a positive impact of productivity. However as regards profitability, Lei and Pagliari (2013) concluded that most UK airports dominated by LCCs experienced below-average growth in operating profit, and Graham and Dennis (2007) observed no apparent link between LCC operations and profitability.

Somewhat more conclusive evidence exists for costs and revenues. Both Graham and Dennis (2007) and Voltes-Dorta and Lei (2013) found lower unit costs at airports with substantial LCC traffic volumes. Likewise, as regards revenues, Graham and Dennis (2007) found lower unit aeronautical revenues at airports dominated by LCC traffic, and Papatheodorou and Lei (2006) noted that other airline models made a higher contribution to aeronautical revenues. A negative relationship between LCCs and the proportion of aeronautical revenues was also observed by Halpern et al. (2016). For Graham and Dennis (2007), the situation for non-aeronautical revenues was less clear, but nevertheless overall the airports which were dominated by LCCs still had lower unit revenues. Lei and Papatheodorou (2010) observed lower non-aeronautical spend for LCC passengers, a finding that was confirmed by Lei et al. (2010), with Yokomi et al. (2017) additionally finding a negative relationship with UK LCC traffic and non-aeronautical revenue.

Other research of UK airports has found that there may be a relationship between competition and financial performance. For example, Bottasso et al. (2017) observed that more intense competition in an airport's catchment area and stronger airline countervailing power are associated with lower aeronautical charges, while Assaf et al. (2012) found that competition had a positive relationship with UK airport efficiency. Starkie (2008) went further than this by challenging popular views on scale economies at UK airports, arguing that if competition is present, then the airports can be financially viable, whatever their size.

Regional connectivity

While passenger numbers and financial data can provide some indication of the size and nature of regional airports, and the direct economic contribution from the operation of the airport itself (even though the evidence related to drivers of financial performance is not entirely conclusive), in terms of wider economic development, it is paramount to consider regional connectivity as well, and connections to major global cities. As detailed by Hackett (2014), UK regional connectivity involves consideration of a number of complex and

UK regional airports   75

Table 5.4 Destination cities and Business Connectivity Index at UK regional airports in 2017

	Destination cities directly served	Destination cities directly served at least weekly	Business Connectivity Index (direct and indirect services)
Manchester	212	115	892
Birmingham	152	71	756
Edinburgh	126	67	734
Glasgow	113	51	642
Aberdeen	42	26	598
Newcastle	81	32	567
Bristol	122	63	456
Belfast City	23	15	433
Southampton	40	21	414
Leeds Bradford	72	25	407
Cardiff Wales	50	20	338
Norwich	20	8	295
Humberside	11	3	271
Inverness	13	9	234
Exeter	35	17	139
Doncaster Sheffield	44	20	124
East Midlands	81	31	111
Liverpool	69	43	63
Belfast International	62	23	50
Newquay	19	5	27
Sumburgh	6	4	6
Prestwick	18	9	5
Bournemouth	24	8	3

Source: York Aviation (2018)

inter-related issues related to both airlines and airports regarding, for example, regulation, planning, business development, and investment practices. Moreover, there are a variety of measures of connectivity that can be used. As an example, Table 5.4 includes a simple count of all destinations served all through the year for regional airports and, arguably, a more meaningful count of destinations served at least weekly. It is also useful to assess connectivity from the perspective of the value offered to business users, these being one the main drivers of wider economic growth. This is important because while development of LCC services at regional airports has undoubtedly increased the number of destination served, many of these primarily serve outbound leisure markets (albeit some also serve economically valuable inbound tourists) that are less able to meet the demand of business travellers or provide appropriate hub connections, in spite of the increased LCC focus on the business market in recent years.

In Table 5.4, York Aviation's Business Connectivity Index (BCI) is shown that uses the research undertaken by the Globalisation and World Cities Network to value destination cities in terms of their status as world cities (York

Aviation, 2018). This data is then weighted by the level of frequency offered to these destinations, which is important to business travellers. Both direct and indirect (i.e. transferring via another airport) services are included. The picture is quite varied compared to airport size (shown in Table 5.3), with airports such as Aberdeen, Belfast City, and Southampton having relatively high BCI values compared to East Midlands, Liverpool, and Belfast International having relatively low ones. The smallest UK airports not included in Table 5.4 have very limited connectivity.

Some of the larger regional airports, such as Manchester and Edinburgh, have seen a growth in long-haul services to destinations in the United States, the Middle East, and the Far East. This development, partly driven by the inability to grow long-haul services out of the capacity-constrained Heathrow Airport, but also by new smaller and more efficient aircraft (such as the Boeing 787) becoming available, has also improved onward indirect connectivity from foreign hubs. Suau-Sanchez et al. (2016) demonstrated that overall indirect connectivity at UK regional airports has grown significantly. While this can be viewed favourably for economic development, it can also be argued that this development increases the vulnerability of the regional airports by making them reliant on foreign airports (and maybe airlines and governments) to guarantee future regional connectivity.

There are both economic and social reasons for governments to support regional air connectivity and lifeline services that connect regions. While the UK airport industry is largely under private sector control, public sector support is provided in a number of ways (Butcher, 2016), although arguably to a lesser extent than in quite a few other OECD countries (International Transport Forum [ITF], 2018). As already mentioned, the small remote 11 airports that are operated by the Scottish government-owned Highlands and Islands Airport Ltd receive an operating subsidy (£20 million in 2017/2018) and capital subsidy (£8 million in 2017/2018). This is because the airports are inherently loss-making due to handling low price-sensitive passenger numbers, and airlines with high costs and small aircraft. The subsidy allows for lower airport charges to be levied. However, air fares remain high, and so in 2006, the air discount scheme was introduced which allows for a 50 per cent discount for residents of the Highlands and Islands in Scotland (travelling for non-business reasons) to make air services more affordable, to facilitate accessibility, and to enhance social inclusion. There are also PSO routes that are operated between the Highlands and Islands and to Glasgow, which are considered to be lifeline services that without this financial support would not be financially viable.

Moreover, there is a PSO route between Cardiff and Anglesey in Wales. In addition, in 2014, the government introduced a policy to promote the use of PSOs to maintain routes from small regional airports to London that might be forced to close. Three routes are supported: Newquay-Gatwick, Dundee-Stansted and City of Derry-Stansted, the latter having been started in 2017. The government has also suggested in its recent aviation strategy consultation document (DfT, 2018a) the possibility of expanding the role of UK PSOs to support routes into airports such as Manchester or Edinburgh, where there is evidence that onward connectivity benefits open up long-haul opportunities for trade and tourism.

Funding from the current PSO London routes comes from the so-called Regional Air Connectivity Fund (RACF). In 2015, the government extended the scope of the RACF to include state start-up support for new routes and made £56 million available over the next three years. This followed a number of similar funding schemes that had been used in the early 2000s by Scotland, Wales and the northeast of England. These offered start-up aid for a limited period for new air services from airports within these areas to encourage business development and inbound tourism, and generate economic benefit for the regions by creating new links between UK regions and other UK and European cities. Beyond this start-up period, it was anticipated that the routes would be self-supporting, but their impact has been arguably limited, depending on what region is being considered (Pagliari, 2005; CAA, 2005, 2007; CAPA, 2014; Smyth et al., 2012).

For the 2015 scheme, for eligible airports of fewer than five million passengers per annum, 19 bids were received. Eventually, 11 were selected, covering domestic and international routes to four other countries, namely Ireland, Netherlands, Germany, and France. These were services from Leeds Bradford to Newquay, and Exeter to Norwich, both with Flybe, which also bid for Dundee-Amsterdam and Southampton-Lyon and -Munich routes; Newcastle and Edinburgh with Linksair services from Norwich and Oxford, respectively; a Derry–Dublin service with Citywings; and three routes with Loganair from Carlisle to Belfast City, Dublin and Southend. However, less than half of the routes that were announced have actually been launched and two of the launched routes were cancelled during the first year of operation. Now only two routes are still running (Leeds Bradford to Newquay and Exeter to Norwich), and these are not operated at the expected frequency of the initial bid (this excludes the Loganair services that did eventually start in July 2019).

This limited success led the government to state (DfT, 2018a, 91):

> 'The government is considering how the previous round of 'start up aid' has performed. Start-up aid was aimed to help address market failure by providing a limited, time-bound subsidy for routes that appear to have commercial opportunity but are not viable under current conditions. This has some benefits compared to PSOs, with a short-term financial boost providing the market with information it needs on route characteristics, and builds up passenger demand to a commercially sustainable level.
>
> An internal review of the previous start-up aid scheme found limited success. The government considers that greater success could have been achieved from a different application and assessment process.'

As a consequence, the government has not committed itself to any further start-up aid at the moment.

London Heathrow issues

One of the most high-profile issues when discussing regional air connectivity, as recognised in recent government policies such as the Aviation Policy Framework (DfT, 2013) and the Airports National Policy Statement (DfT, 2018b), is air connectivity to London, particularly Heathrow (SEO Economic Research, 2015). Figure 5.6 shows that passenger numbers on domestic routes have dropped from nearly nine million in 2002 to now just below five million. Heathrow Airport now only has nine domestic routes – Edinburgh, Glasgow, Belfast City, Manchester, Aberdeen, Newcastle, Inverness, Leeds Bradford, and Newquay. Since 1990, eight UK regional airports (Birmingham, Durham Tees Valley, East Midlands, Humberside, Inverness, Isle of Man, Liverpool, and Plymouth) have lost air service connections to Heathrow, and in some cases (e.g. Durham Tees Valley and Plymouth), this has had a dramatic impact on the viability of the airport, with in Plymouth airport's case being identified as a key reason for its closure in 2011. In addition, cities that have retained connections have in many cases seen a reduction in frequency or in the extent of competition.

Growing congestion and an increasing scarcity of take-off and landing slots from London Heathrow has meant that progressively slots have shifted from UK domestic routes to European or particularly long-haul routes, which are generally more profitable for the airlines. Hence, this is denying passengers from the regional airports access to the important London markets and the vital benefits that this can bring to regional economies. In addition, this lack of access to London from the regions means that they cannot benefit from

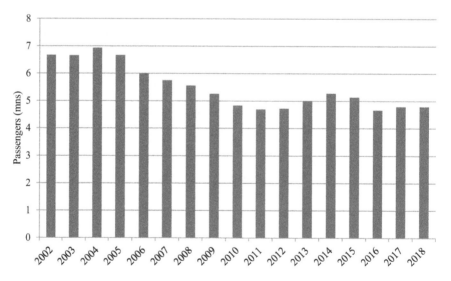

Figure 5.6 Domestic passengers at London Heathrow Airport, 2002–2018

Source: Devised by author from CAA (2003–2019) annual airport statistics

connections onwards to long-haul gateway airports, although to some degree this has been offset by the growing number of routes from regional airports to overseas hubs as previously discussed. The delayed decision over expanding airport capacity in London has compounded these problems. In response to this, Heathrow Airport introduced a £10 discount on the domestic passenger charge in 2017 – which was increased to £15 in 2018 – which the airport claims encouraged Flybe to launch new services to Edinburgh and Aberdeen. It is also establishing a £10 million start-up fund to encourage new domestic routes, which was proposed by the Airports Commission when it recommended in 2015 the development of a third runway at Heathrow (Heathrow Airport Limited, 2017; Airports Commission, 2015). EasyJet has already indicated which domestic routes it might be interested in operating from an expanded Heathrow. In its Airports National Policy Statement (DfT, 2018b, 125), the government stated that it:

> 'recognises that air routes are in the first instance a commercial decision for airlines and are not in the gift of an airport operator. But the Government is determined that new routes will be secured, and will hold Heathrow Airport to account on this. The Government requires Heathrow Airport to demonstrate it has worked constructively with its airline customers to protect and strengthen existing domestic routes, and to develop new domestic connections, including to regions currently unserved.'

However, in February 2020, plans for the third runway at Heathrow were thrown into doubt after a court ruling said that the government approval for expansion was unlawful because it had not adequately taken into account its commitments to tackle climate change. The airport operator is going to appeal the decision, and if the runway does go ahead, it could provide new opportunities to address the issue of regional connectivity, as it will be the first time that a significant number of new slots will become available at this currently severely constrained airport. The government, in its recent aviation strategy consultation document (DfT, 2018a), argued that this is a special case for intervention and has suggested ring-fencing suitable time slots through the slot allocation process to safeguard connectivity with at least 14 regional airports (e.g. with new services to Belfast International, Durham Tees Valley, Humberside, Liverpool, and Prestwick, as well as the existing ones). It has also suggested allowing more PSO domestic routes at Heathrow if such ring-fencing and commercial incentives offered by Heathrow to bring these 14 routes do not work. The government anticipated that around 15 per cent of the additional capacity brought with the new runway could be used to serve domestic connections.

Other government policies

Another key government policy affecting UK airports is the air passenger duty (APD). This tax, currently £13 for domestic/short-haul flights and £78 for long-haul flights (>2,000 miles) for economy seats (and more for business seats) has been subject to considerable and prolonged debate. As a result of this, the Northern Ireland Assembly was given powers in 2012 to set APD rates for direct long-haul flights, primarily because of the direct competition for such flights from nearby Dublin Airport. Then in 2016, the Scottish Parliament was given control over the APD in Scotland and it planned to cut the tax by 50 per cent (and abolish it completely when resources allowed). However, this reform was postponed in 2017, producing discontent amongst airlines and others, with no new date being set. The UK government has also considered devolving the APD to the Welsh Assembly but decided against this, arguing that it would create undue market distortions. There have even been calls for lower rates of the APD at English regional airports, particularly with a view to address the excess demand in London and the southeast. However, this would be difficult under EU law but, at the time of writing, could be revisited by the government after Brexit (Seely, 2019).

For domestic services, the APD can be a considerable cost, especially given that it is charged twice on a return trip, with the UK House of Commons Transport Committee (2015, 3) stating that the 'Air Passenger Duty (APD) is the principal threat to the smaller airports sector' (where smaller airports handle less than five million passengers). For this reason, flights from the Scottish Highlands and Islands airports and PSO routes are exempt from this tax. However, there has been more general industry concern of the negative impact the tax has on the feasibility of domestic services, and Heathrow Airport, among others, has called for the government to abolish it on all domestic routes once Brexit has happened (Heathrow Airport Limited, 2017). In research by Frontier Economics (2017) commissioned by the airport, it is claimed that this would produce an 8 per cent increase in domestic air travel.

There are many other factors that influence the role that the UK regional airports play in terms of economic and regional development. One important issue is the effectiveness of airport surface access strategies to ensure that the airport is well connected and easily accessible to the surrounding community in an environmentally acceptable manner (Budd et al., 2011, 2016). The current government policy recommends that airports should produce up-to-date master plans that contain airport surface access strategies (ASASs) (DfT, 2013; Humphreys and Ison, 2005; Humphreys et al., 2005). Moreover, airports with more than 1,000 annual passenger movements are advised to hold air transport forums (ATFs) to develop and monitor implementation of plans for future surface transport provision. However, it appears that over half of airport surface access strategies have not been updated in the last five years. Additional criticism is also discussed in the draft Aviation Strategy document (DfT, 2018a, 92): 'The government does not currently have a role in monitoring or enforcing the appropriateness, effectiveness, or environmental impact of airports' plans through ATFs. The industry's view is that ATFs do not have the authority to hold airports to account'.

As a result, the draft strategy recommends that the government and local bodies should play a more active role with the formalisation of the position of

ATFs, an update of the guidance should be provided, and there should be the development of an ASAS manual.

Finally, as with regional airports in other countries, the precise impact that UK regional airports have on economic development needs to be considered within the context of relevant regional, spatial, and economic development strategies. For example, it is particularly noteworthy that land surrounding certain airports has been designated as enterprise zones with simplified planning regimes and taxation support. This is the case with the Manchester Airport City project, the Newquay Aerohub, and Luton airport. Other potential developments at individual airports also need to be considered; for example, Prestwick airport is being considered as both a spaceport and as Heathrow Airport's logistics hub.

Conclusion

Evidence presented here suggests that the well-being of UK regional airports is becoming increasingly polarised, with relatively prosperous large regional airports accompanied by much more vulnerable smaller ones. In the early 2000s, many regional airports were seduced into thinking that the emergence of the LCC sector would bring long-term benefits in terms of increased direct services, which might in turn deliver broader economically beneficial connectivity. However, the hopes of quite a few of these airports were thwarted by the economic recession and changing airline strategies that have focused more on larger markets (with both business and leisure passengers) rather than on stimulating new markets with very low fares. It may well be that the LCCs have recognised that they had gone as far as they can in generating demand at some of the smaller airports. As a consequence, smaller airports, which already have some inherently economic disadvantages, have suffered disproportionately more than the larger airports and the future of some of the more fragile smaller airports seems uncertain. This is reflected in the fluid situation in terms of airport ownership, raising questions about the optimum ownership and governance situation, which clearly has serious implications for the economic well-being and development of the surrounding communities. It has also meant that the availability of onwards connections, particularly at Heathrow, has become a key issue.

At the same time, the UK aviation industry has been preoccupied with trying to find a solution to capacity shortages in the London area. The publication of the Airport National Policy Statement in 2018, that accepted in principle the case for building a third runway at Heathrow, has arguably shifted the industry closer to providing a way out to this problem. However, this outcome is still very uncertain, especially after the court ruling in 2020 declared that the government approval decision was unlawful. Regardless of the expansion outcome, the implications for regional airports are very significant. If capacity continues to be squeezed in London, domestic connectivity will continue to decline, but at the same time, more hub-bypass routes might emerge at the

82 *Anne Graham*

largest regional airports. If a third runway is built, it will not come on stream until 2028 at the earliest. Potentially, this new capacity could provide opportunities to overcome the regional connectivity problem, although some of the newer long-haul services from the regions might in turn shift to the more attractive London location when there is runway space to do this.

The domestic connectivity problem, and associated other policy challenges related to start-up aid, PSOs, the APD and airport surface access strategies, require involvement of many relevant stakeholders to determine the ultimate outcome. The instruments all have different effectiveness and have complex implications. Moreover, the relationship between the UK and the EU remains uncertain because of Brexit. If the UK leaves the single aviation market, there may well be opportunities to design new mechanisms, for example, related to slot allocation and PSOs.

Successive UK governments have generally tried to create an aviation sector with minimal state involvement or intervention, which functions on market forces as much as possible. Prime examples of this are the existence of a predominantly privately owned airport sector (with Prestwick and Cardiff airports being notable interesting exceptions) and generally a lower level of state assistance; for example, with fewer PSO routes than elsewhere at many European countries. While significantly shifting this stance is not considered realistic or favourable to address the major challenges discussed in this chapter, some key involvement of government, particularly with the special case of Heathrow because of the potentially huge increase in capacity, is arguably necessary to ensure that regional airports can play a significant role in regional connectivity and in driving economic investment and growth in the regions in the future.

References

Airports Commission (2015). *Final report*. London, Airports Commission.

The Anker Report (2018). London's airports growing faster than UK regions despite capacity problems. *The Anker Report*, 28, 1–10.

Assaf, A. (2009). Accounting for size in efficiency comparisons of airports. *Journal of Air Transport Management*, 15(5), 256–258.

Assaf, A. (2010). Bootstrapped scale efficiency measures of UK airports. *Journal of Air Transport Management*, 16(1), 42–44.

Assaf, A., Gillen, D. and Barros, C. (2012). Performance assessment of UK airports: Evidence from a Bayesian dynamic frontier model. *Transportation Research Part E*, 48(3), 603–615.

Barros, C. (2008). Technical efficiency of UK airports. *Journal of Air Transport Management*, 14(6), 175–178.

Barros, C. and Weber, W. (2009). Productivity growth and biased technological change in UK airports. *Transportation Research Part E*, 45(4), 642–653.

Bottasso, A., Bruno, M., Conti, M. and Piga, C. (2017). Competition, vertical relationship and countervailing power in the UK airport industry. *Journal of Regulatory Economics*, 52(1), 37–62.

Bottasso, A. and Conti, M. (2012). The cost structure of the UK airport industry. *Journal of Transport Economics and Policy*, 46(3), 313–332.

Bottasso, A., Conti, M. and Piga, C. (2012). Low-cost carriers and airports' performance: Empirical evidence from a panel of UK airports. *Industrial and Corporate Change*, 22(3), 745–769.

Bottasso, A., Conti, M. and Vannoni, D. (2019). Scale and (quasi) scope economies in airport technology: An application to UK airports. *Transportation Research Part A: Policy and Practice*, 125, 150–164.

Budd, L., Ison, S. and Budd, T. (2016). Improving the environmental performance of airport surface access in the UK: The role of public transport. *Research in Transportation Economics*, 59, 185–195.

Budd, T., Ison, S. and Ryley, T. (2011). Airport surface access in the UK: A management perspective. *Research in Transportation Business and Management*, 1(1), 109–117.

Bush, H. (2010). The development of competition in the UK airport market. *Journal of Airport Management*, 4(2), 114–124.

Butcher, L. (2016). *Regional airports*. Briefing Paper SN00323. London, House of Commons, 26 April.

CAA (2003–2019). *UK airport data*. Available at: https://www.caa.co.uk/Data-and-analysis/ UK-aviation-market/Airports/Datasets/UK-airport-data/ (accessed 20 April 2019).

CAA (2005). *UK regional air services*. CAP 754. London, CAA.

CAA (2007). *Air services at UK regional airports: An update on developments*. CAP 775. London, CAA.

CAA (2013). *Market power determination for passenger airlines in relation to Stansted airport – statement of reasons*. CAP 1135. London, CAA.

CAA (2014a). *Economic regulation at Heathrow from April 2014: Notice granting the licence*. CAP 1151. London, CAA.

CAA (2014b). *Economic regulation at Gatwick from April 2014: Notice granting the licence*. CAP 1152. London, CAA.

CAA (2014c). *UK airport data*. Available at: https://www.caa.co.uk/Data-and-analysis/UK-aviation-market/Airports/Datasets/UK-airport-data/ (accessed 20 April 2019).

CAA (2019). *UK airport data*. Available at: https://www.caa.co.uk/Data-and-analysis/UK-aviation-market/Airports/Datasets/UK-airport-data/ (accessed 20 April 2019).

CAPA (2014). *UK regional air connectivity fund – which airports does it help and what is a region anyway*, 25 April. Available at: https://centreforaviation.com/analysis/reports/ uk-regional-air-connectivity-fund-which-airports-does-it-help-and-what-is-a-region-anyway-160650 (accessed 20 February 2019).

Cheong, K. (2015). Aux armes, citoyens! A revolution in airport economic regulation: A regulator's perspective. *Journal of Airport Management*, 9(4), 338–346.

Competition and Markets Authority (2016). *BAA airports: Evaluation of the competition commission's 2009 market investigation remedies*. London, Competition and Markets Authority.

Competition Commission (2009). *BAA airports market investigation*. London, Competition Commission.

CRI (2003–2009). *UK Airport Statistics*. Bath, CRI.

DfT (2008). *Decision on the regulatory status of Manchester airport*. London, DfT.

DfT (2013). *Aviation policy framework*. London, DfT.

DfT (2017). *UK aviation forecasts*. London, DfT.

DfT (2018a). *Aviation 2050: The future of UK aviation – a consultation*. London, DfT.

DfT (2018b). *Airports national policy statement: New runway capacity and infrastructure at airports in the South East of England*. London, DfT.

Frontier Economics (2017). *The benefits of reducing domestic APD*. London, Frontier Economics.

84 *Anne Graham*

Graham, A. (2008). Airport planning and regulation in the UK. In Winston, C. and de Rus, G. (eds) *Aviation infrastructure performance: A study in comparative political economy*. Washington, Brookings Institution Press.

Graham, A. and Dennis, N. (2007). Airport traffic and financial performance: A UK and Ireland case study. *Journal of Transport Geography*, 15(3), 161–171.

Graham, A., Saito, S. and Nomura, M. (2014). Airport management in Japan: Any lessons learnt from the UK? *Journal of Airport Management*, 8(3), 244–263.

Hackett, P. (ed) (2014). *Making global connections: The potential of the UK's regional airports*. London, The Smith Institute.

Halpern, N. and Graham, A. (2017). Performance and prospects of smaller UK regional airports. *Journal of Airport Management*, 11(2), 180–201.

Halpern, N., Graham, A. and Dennis, N. (2016). Low cost carriers and the changing fortunes of airports in the UK. *Research in Transportation Business and Management*, 21, 33–43.

Heathrow Airport Limited (2017). *Bringing Britain closer*. London, Heathrow Airport Limited.

House of Commons Transport Committee (2015). *Smaller airports*. Ninth Report of Session 2014–15. London, The Stationery Office Limited.

Humphreys, I. (1999). Privatisation and commercialisation changes in UK airport ownership patterns. *Journal of Transport Geography*, 7(2), 121–134.

Humphreys, I. and Ison, S. (2005). Changing airport employee travel behaviour: The role of airport surface access strategies. *Transport Policy*, 12(1), 1–5.

Humphreys, I., Ison, S., Francis, G. and Aldridge, K. (2005). UK airport surface access targets. *Journal of Air Transport Management*, 11(2), 117–124.

Ison, S., Francis, G., Humphreys, C. and Page, R. (2011). UK regional airport commercialisation and privatisation: 25 years on. *Journal of Transport Geography*, 19(6), 1341–1349.

ITF (2018). *Government support measures for domestic air connectivity*. Paris, ITF.

Lei, Z. and Pagliari, R. (2013). Airport traffic growth and airport financial performance. In Forsyth, P., Gillen, D., Hüschelrath, K., Niemeier, H. M. and Wolf, W. (eds) *Liberalization in aviation*. Farnham, Ashgate.

Lei, Z. and Papatheodorou, A. (2010). Measuring the effect of low-cost carriers on regional airports' commercial revenue. *Research in Transportation Economics*, 26(1), 37–43.

Lei, Z., Papatheodorou, A. and Szivas, E. (2010). The effect of low-cost carriers on regional airports' revenue: Evidence from the UK. In Forsyth, P., Gillen, D., Muller, J. and Niemeier, H. M. (eds) *Airport competition: The European experience*. Aldershot, Ashgate, 2008.

LeighFisher (2010–2019). *UK airport performance indicators*. London, LeighFisher.

LeighFisher (2019). *UK airport performance indicators 2017/2018*. London, LeighFisher.

Littlechild, S. (2018). Economic regulation of privatised airports: Some lessons from UK experience. *Transportation Research Part A: Policy and Practice*, 114, 100–114.

Pagliari, R. (2005). Developments in the supply of direct international air services from airports in Scotland. *Journal of Air Transport Management*, 11(4), 249–257.

Pagliari, R. and Graham, A. (2019). An exploratory analysis of the effects of ownership change on airport competition. *Transport Policy*, 78, 76–85.

Papatheodorou, A. and Lei, Z. (2006). Leisure travel in Europe and airline business models: A study of regional airports in Great Britain. *Journal of Air Transport Management*, 12(1), 47–52.

See, K. F. and Li, F. (2015). Total factor productivity analysis of the UK airport industry: A Hicks-Moorsteen index method. *Journal of Air Transport Management*, 43, 1–10.

Seely, A. (2019). *Air passenger duty: Recent debates and reform*. House of Commons briefing paper CBP 5094, 14 February. Available at: https://commonslibrary.parliament.uk/research-briefings/sn05094/.

SEO Economic Research (2015). *Expanding airport capacity: Competition, connectivity and welfare discussion of options for Gatwick and Heathrow*. Paris, ITF.

Smyth, A., Christodoulou, G., Dennis, N., Al-Azzawi, M. and Campbell, J. (2012). Is air transport a necessity for social inclusion and economic development? *Journal of Air Transport Management*, 22, 53–59.

Starkie, D. (2008). *The airport industry in a competitive environment: A United Kingdom perspective*. Discussion Paper No. 2005–15. Paris, ITF.

Suau-Sanchez, P., Voltes-Dorta, A. and Rodríguez-Déniz, H. (2016). The role of London airports in providing connectivity for the UK: Regional dependence on foreign hubs. *Journal of Transport Geography*, 50, 94–104.

Voltes-Dorta, A. and Lei, Z. (2013). The impact of airline differentiation on marginal cost pricing at UK airports. *Transportation Research Part A: Policy and Practice*, 55, 72–88.

Yokomi, M., Wheat, P. and Mizutani, J. (2017). The impact of low cost carriers on non-aeronautical revenues in airport: An empirical study of UK airports. *Journal of Air Transport Management*, 64, 77–85.

York Aviation (2018). *Regional connectivity report*. Macclesfield, York Aviation.

6 Regional airport business models

Shannon Group as a case study

Noel Hiney, Marina Efthymiou, and Edgar Morgenroth

Introduction

European lawmakers regard regional aviation as a key contributor to citizens' mobility, providing better access to regions and contributing to the development of business, tourism, and related services, thereby improving the spread of economic prosperity across Europe (European Commission, 2014). Various definitions of what constitutes regional airports have been put forward. Airports Council International-Europe (ACI-Europe), a key representative body for Europe's airports, considers an airport as regional if it: (1) primarily serves short- and medium-range routes; and (2) primarily serves point-to-point destinations (ACI-Europe, 2017). An alternative, and the definition more frequently considered in this chapter, is a European Commission definition of 'regional airport', meaning an airport processing up to three million passengers per annum (European Commission, 2014).

Many regional airports in Europe feed significant passenger numbers into larger European airports, providing high levels of connectivity. In fact, such airports comprise 90 per cent of all European airports, with 209 air carriers, 14,600 routes, and 724 destinations served in 2017 (ACI-Europe, 2017). Such positioning has ensured that regional airports play a critical role as important regional economic contributors, which have a multiplier effect into local communities. This impact is achieved mostly through the provision of connectivity that provides essential links to trade and tourism activity, both within the regional catchment area and across the country. Efthymiou et al. (2016) argue that large airports provide the highest connectivity levels, but that smaller airports deliver the greatest connectivity growth. From a commercial perspective, local air access helps to stimulate direct inward investment, generating new business and triggering job creation, which in turn leads to further increases in trade. Regional airports have also become pivotal in supporting social and commercial objectives in regions and areas outside EU capitals and other large cities. As larger European airports increasingly experience capacity constraints, the increased airline use of regional airports, combined with their growth ambitions, have helped them gain additional passenger traffic.

A number of scholars (e.g. Dobruszkes et al., 2017; Graham, 2014; Adler et al., 2013; Baker and Donnet, 2012) have researched regional airports and their performance. Regional airports face increasingly robust competition from hub and other regional airports. Competition and the relatively high fixed costs associated with airport infrastructure have given rise to increasingly challenging trading conditions for the sector, with up to 76 per cent of regional airports estimated to be unprofitable (ACI-Europe, 2019). Moreover, regional airports, in particular, are more challenged than larger airports, given that adverse external shocks and volatilities can have a much higher impact on their financial performance, due to smaller economies of scale.

While regional airports are recognised as essential to the economic well-being and development of the regions they operate in, government involvement with regional airports is complicated by the 'dual dilemma' of such airports being socially and commercially beneficial to a local hinterland on the one hand, but often uneconomical to operate on the other hand. The status of a few such airports has changed due to this performance pressure. Some small regional airports have terminated operations due to low activity and profitability (e.g. Galway airport in Ireland). A small number of airports (e.g. Plymouth City airport in the UK) have terminated their operations due to low commercial traffic, but the local community has actively tried to make such airports operational again (FlyPlymouth, 2019). This indicates the strong connection of small regional airports to the local community, but also to ownership models.

This chapter outlines the case of Shannon Airport, a regional airport in Ireland which reflects some of the issues regional airports are facing. A brief history of Shannon Airport is provided and its innovative ownership structure (i.e. airport group incorporating tourism and property entities) is considered. This case study can help other airport operators identify commonalities in aspects of the contribution of airports to regional development.

Airport ownership and structures

The connection of airport ownership and structure to performance has been considered by a number of scholars (Pagliari and Graham, 2019; Adler and Liebert, 2014; Gillen, 2011; Ison et al., 2011). The diversification of airport ownership structures was identified by Graham (2014) as one of three key current airport trends, the others being privatisation and commercialisation. Almost 60 per cent of European airports were publicly owned in 2016, down from 78 per cent in 2010 (ACI-Europe, 2016). Nevertheless, corporatisation of state-owned airports does not necessarily improve performance. Cahill et al. (2017) suggest that despite a continuous process of commercialisation in Ireland's Dublin Airport Authority (DAA), total factor productivity performance declined during the 1994–2014 period mainly due to considerable long-term investment in airport infrastructure that could not be expected to generate short-term returns during the period under measurement.

Other airport ownership models include a combination of public and private shareholdings and hybrid structures, where private interests manage the activities of municipally controlled airports on a concession basis. This model is more common in the United States than in Europe. Private sector involvement is more prevalent in larger airports, where analysis shows that around 40 per cent of all airports have some private sector activity, with these airports accounting for 75 per cent of annual passenger numbers (ACI-Europe, 2016). Some publicly owned airports across Europe have many different municipal shareholders (e.g. local authorities), while another ownership model involves private or state organisations owning and managing multiple-airport organisations, such as Manchester Airports Group (UK) and Finavia (Finland).

With respect to business organisation, the majority of European airport operators are managed either on a stand-alone basis or as part of a group. They focus on core commercial activities that mostly generate aeronautical and non-aeronautical revenue. Changing airport ownership is associated with commercialisation (e.g. terminal concessions, car parking, and real estate developments outside the airport perimeter), different pricing strategies, and the provision of incentives to carriers to operate to these airports (Efthymiou et al., 2016; Graham, 2014). Airports are in favour of dual-till regulation, arguing that concessions and real estate developments do not generally possess natural monopoly characteristics (Frontier Economics, 2014), although they do from a consumer perspective, at least on airside. Airlines, on the other hand, favour the single-till approach which can be more likely to contribute to a reduction in the fees charged for aeronautical services (Efthymiou et al., 2016).

Airport operators and financial investors are increasingly joining forces to deliver airport developments through operational and financial structuring instruments, such as public-private partnerships or the concession management contract arrangements previously described. Privately owned and independent airports are perceived as more market-oriented (Halpern and Pagliari, 2007), not least because senior management is likely to be locally based and more scrutinised by local stakeholders, possibly leading to a stronger bias for action.

Regional airports have a multitude of different stakeholders whose presence and activities extend deeply into local communities. This interaction between airport and region is acknowledged as fundamentally important, with airport activity essential to local economic performance – the multiplier effect results in increased levels of trade, tourism, and travel, thereby supporting and helping to attract inward investment. In addition, airport-airline cooperation can be mutually beneficial, especially for airports with high seasonality (extreme peaks during high season and extreme lows outside these periods), notwithstanding the need for such arrangements to comply with State Aid guidelines if they involve state-owned airports (Efthymiou and Papatheodorou, 2018). This multiplier effect might also be expected to be more significant for regional airports with a business structure that incorporates a tourism entity.

The aviation industry in Ireland

Ireland has a well-established aviation industry from both a business and regulatory perspective, making a significant gross domestic product (GDP) contribution of €4.1 billion per annum, which supports 42,000 direct jobs (Department of Transport, Tourism and Sport, 2017). The aviation sector is core to Irish economic development, given the country's status as a small island nation. Ireland has three state-owned passenger airports: Dublin, Cork, and Shannon, together with a small number of mostly privately owned ones, including Ireland West (Knock), Kerry, and Donegal (Figure 6.1). However, 85.6 per cent of all Irish air travel is to and from Dublin Airport (Table 6.1).

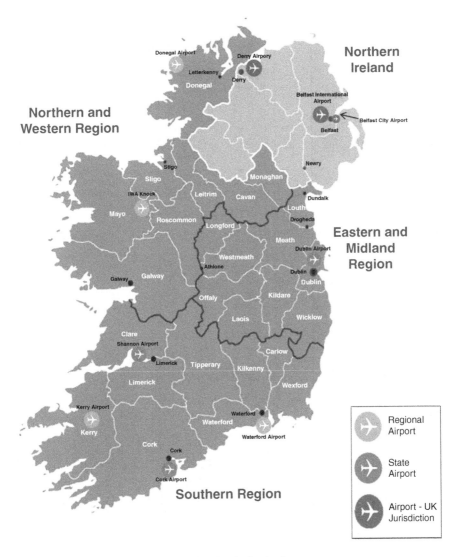

Figure 6.1 Key airports operating on the island of Ireland
Source: Department of Transport, Tourism and Sport (2019a)

Table 6.1 Total passenger numbers handled by key Irish airports in 2014–2018

Airport	2014	2015	2016	2017	2018	% change 2017–2018	% change 2014–2018
Dublin	21,694,893	24,962,518	27,778,888	29,454,474	31,319,419	+6.3	44%
Cork	2,138,057	2,065,678	2,226,233	2,301,450	2,387,806	+3.8	12%
Shannon	1,555,225	1,642,888	1,674,567	1,599,390	1,677,661	+4.9	8%
Knock	703,670	684,671	735,869	748,505	775,063	+3.5	10%
Kerry	294,955	303,039	325,670	335,480	365,339	+8.9	24%
Donegal	35,415	36,552	44,156	46,514	46,537	+0.0	31%
Waterford[1]	33,189	34,249	13,511	0	0	–	−100%
Total	**26,455,404**	**29,729,595**	**32,798,894**	**34,485,813**	**36,571,825**		

Source: Central Statistics Office (2019)

[1] No commercial flights since June 2016 from Waterford airport.

Table 6.2 Fastest travel time (private motor car) from main Irish cities to five largest airports

Airport → City ↓	Dublin	Cork	Shannon	Ireland West	Kerry	Waterford*
Dublin	21 min	2 hr 53 min	2 hr 30 min	2 hr 36 min	3 hr 27 min	2 hr 9 min
Cork	2 hr 45 min	15 min	I hr 41 min	3 hr 10 min	1 hr 31 min	1 hr 51 min
Limerick	2 hr 11 min	1 hr 40 min	26 min	1 hr 54 min	1 hr 23 min	2 hr 15 min
Galway	2 hr 17 min	2 hr 48 min	1 hr 7 min	1 hr 16 min	2hr 32 min	3 hr 22 min
Waterford	1 hr 55 min	1 hr 50 min	2 hr 25 min	3 hr 50 min	3 hr 0 min	9 mins
Sligo	2hr 36 min	3hr 49 min	2hr 12 min	38 min	3 hr 33 min	4 hr 6 min
Athlone	1 hr 20 min	2 hr 49 min	1 hr 27 min	1 hr 22 min	2 hr 49 min	2 hr 36 min
Belfast	1 hr 42 min	4 hr 23 min	4 hr 4 min	3 hr 23 min	5 hr 0 min	3 hr 39 min
Derry	3 hr 3 min	5 hr 44 min	4 hr 23 min	2 hr 48 min	5 hr 48 min	4 hr 59 min

Source: Devised by authors using Google Mapping Data, 23 September 2019 (Google Maps, 2019)

★ No current passenger traffic.

This high concentration of traffic represents a significant challenge for Ireland's regional airports, given the small geographical size of the Irish Republic and the increased ease of access to Dublin through the relatively recent completion of a motorway network providing significantly enhanced connectivity to Dublin Airport. Over 86 per cent of motorway kilometres existing in Ireland have been completed since 2002 (McCoy et al., 2018). Table 6.2 shows access times of less than 2 hours 30 minutes from most cities to the airport, with the time taken from Cork 2 hours 45 minutes.

Shannon Airport: an introduction

Shannon Airport forms a significant part of Shannon Group, a 100 per cent state-owned Irish organisation whose other companies manage significant interests in tourism and commercial property, mainly within the airport's broad hinterland. Shannon Group has also been responsible for the establishment of Ireland's largest aviation cluster, with 3,000 employees working in over 48 companies there (Shannon IASC, 2019).

Airport history

One of Europe's most westerly airports, Shannon was established in 1945 and the bilateral Ireland/US Air Services Agreement signed that year stipulated that flights to and from Ireland would route only through Shannon, resulting in its designation as Ireland's transatlantic airport. Shannon's geographical position also meant that until the mid-1950s, many European and North American airlines, who operated aircraft with limited range on transatlantic routes, used the airport as a refuelling gateway between Europe and North America. Shannon established the world's first duty-free airport shop and industrial zone during this time (Shannon Airport, 2017). The airport developed a partnership with

Aeroflot during the 1980s, involving fuel bartering and aircraft painting. This relationship led to the opening of the Soviet Union's first duty-free shop, on a joint-venture basis, in 1988. Shannon Airport established an advisory retail business (Aer Rianta International, ARI) that year which, as part of DAA, is now a major airport retailing and retail consultancy organisation (Shannon Airport, 2017a). Following an easing of restrictions in the 1990s, the requirement for traffic on air routes between Ireland and the USA to stop at Shannon in both directions was fully eliminated following the introduction of the EU-US Open Skies Agreement in 2007 (Barrett, 2009).

During 2009, the first US Customs and Border Protection (CBP) pre-clearance site outside North America and the Caribbean opened in Shannon. Due to its Atlantic location, the airport has a high proportion of transatlantic travel relative to other airports of its size, with Aer Lingus, American, Delta, and United operating routes out of Shannon using narrow-body aircraft. Norwegian and Air Canada operated routes from Shannon to the United States and Canada, respectively, using Boeing 737 Max aircraft, until the grounding of this type in March 2019. The Norwegian routes were subsequently cancelled. 2018 passenger numbers, including transit traffic, totalled 1.86 million per annum. The UK was the largest market served by Shannon, with 47 per cent of total origin and destination traffic carried. The US and European markets accounted for 26 per cent and 27 per cent of such traffic (Shannon Group, 2019).

Shannon Airport ownership

Always a state-owned entity, Shannon Airport was attached to the Irish Department of Transport before becoming part of Aer Rianta, the Irish State Airport Authority, in 1969. In 2004, the Dublin Airport Authority, DAA, replaced Aer Rianta, retaining responsibility for Cork, Dublin, and Shannon Airports, in addition to ancillary companies including ARI.

Future ownership options for Shannon were considered by the Irish government in 2012, setting in motion events, which led to the formation of Shannon Group in 2014. The then Minister for Transport commissioned a review of ownership options for Cork and Shannon airports, in advance of any decisions regarding separation of state airports (Department of Transport, Tourism and Sport, 2012). An international strategic consultancy organisation undertook this assessment, and its final report expressed concerns about prospects for Shannon, highlighting a significant drop in air traffic and passenger numbers. It suggested that demand levels were not sustainable, that niche investments might not generate required returns, and that the airport therefore faced a potential threat to its viability (Booz and Company, 2012). The alternative to Shannon remaining part of DAA was the airport's separation from this authority, addressing issues such as the impact of Shannon-identified DAA debt on future viability. The new corporate entity to be established would incorporate other companies such as Shannon Development, which changed its name to Shannon Commercial Enterprises (trading as Shannon Commercial Properties), a state-owned owner of significant commercial property interests. Shannon

Development (originally SFADCO, or Shannon Free Airport Development Company) had been established by the Irish Government in 1959, to promote the interests of Shannon Airport by driving regional economic development in the wider Shannon area in partnership with government, private companies, public bodies and the people of the region (Shannon Development, 2007).

During the stakeholder engagement process following the publication of these options, it appears that local parties were quite enthusiastic in their support for separation, with Regan (2017) highlighting the positive local reaction to the establishment of Shannon Group, his paper positioning the change in the context of previous challenges such as the arrival of the jet age and industry cycles, and emphasising Shannon's innovation DNA, as exemplified by the leadership of Dr. Brendan O'Regan over many years, for example through introduction of the world's first airport duty-free shop in 1947 and development of a free-trade zone in 1959 (O'Connell and O'Carroll, 2018).

The decision to grant Shannon Airport full independence from the Dublin Airport Authority (now daa plc) was taken in principle in May 2012, to take effect on 31 December 2012 (Department of Transport, Tourism and Sport, 2012). Shannon Group, the current corporate structure, was formally established in September 2014 and included the airport, property interests, and the Shannon Heritage tourism business (a subsidiary of Shannon Commercial Enterprises). An International Aviation Services Centre cluster, Shannon IASC, was also established. ARI, the airport retail and duty-free consultancy that started life in Shannon, was by then an integral part of daa. It has been reported that the Dublin Airport Authority retained a debt of about €110 million associated with Shannon Airport activities. This would mean that the airport started its new independent life on a debt-free basis (O'Halloran, 2018).

Ireland's Minister for Transport at that time optimistically emphasised the benefits of separation to Shannon Airport and the Shannon region, in particular: (1) a fresh approach to airport development; and (2) creation of the aviation services centre to build on a hub of aviation-related business activity. An Aviation Business Development Task Force established at this time suggested that Shannon could, within five years, be a self-sustaining, cost-efficient international airport with 2.5 million passengers per year, providing convenient short- and long-haul travel options for local businesses and travellers. It also envisaged the airport as a transit hub for passenger and cargo airlines (using its geographic position and US Customs pre-clearance advantages) and the International Aviation Services Centre (IASC) as a vibrant cluster of diverse and aviation-related businesses, providing training, education, and employment and opportunities. It contended that IASC could create and sustain 3,000–3,500 new direct jobs (Department of Transport, Tourism and Sport, 2014).

Shannon Group structure: overview

The wholly state-owned Shannon Group is 'a commercial semi-state group focused on delivering economic benefits for the West of Ireland and the wider national economy' (Shannon Group, 2017). Shannon Airport Group's mission and vision statements focus on the successful development of aviation, tourism and property assets, customer excellence, business growth and playing a pivotal role in the region it serves.

Shannon Group comprises four distinct units:

1 Shannon Airport, a regional airport with routes to the UK, Europe, and North America.
2 Shannon Commercial Properties, a company that owns and manages significant property assets, mostly in the Shannon region.
3 Shannon Heritage, a tourism company that owns and manages tourism assets across the Republic of Ireland.
4 Shannon International Aviation Services Centre (IASC), which focuses on the creation of an aerospace and aviation cluster in Shannon.

Shannon Group's structure is underpinned by a not-yet-proven hypothesis that synergies are possible for companies within the Group, through the provision of shared leadership and support for airport, tourist, and property businesses and activities within the Shannon region. In his Shannon-focused review of airport industry clusters, Zhang (2014) contends that this is a new development model supporting regional economic activity, with local enterprises and external forces as other key factors. This approach positions Shannon Airport as a key driver and enabler of regional economic development. The other companies within the Group such as Shannon Heritage, Shannon Commercial Properties, and IASC can contribute significantly by playing essential roles in attracting foreign investment and economic and tourism activity to the Shannon region and contributing to increased airport traffic. These objectives are not dissimilar to Shannon Development's original vision, as previously described.

As state-owned organisations, however, individual Shannon Group companies must operate independently and comply with State Aid regulations and requirements. Any asymmetric national regulation or state funding favouring Shannon or another airport might be likely to fall foul of such rules. However, the impact on airport competition arising out of Ireland's privately owned regional airports receiving EU-sanctioned State Aid, in the shape of operating or capital expenditure grants for safety and security matters which Shannon and other state airports cannot avail of due to a government policy not to provide such aid, should also be noted. Such anomalous arrangements have potentially disadvantaged Shannon and Cork airport performance and prospects. For example, Shannon Airport had to borrow funds to finance a recent runway overlay, while the state provided 75 per cent of financing for a similar overlay for the mostly privately owned Ireland West regional airport (O'Brien, 2019).

Analysis of Shannon Airport's strategic position

A number of academic tools have been used to describe and analyse Shannon Airport's strategic position. This activity was informed by consideration of key airport characteristics, industry trends, opportunities, challenges, and competitive threats. A broad strategic assessment of Shannon Airport was first undertaken by the authors to help assess and interpret its positioning. The following strategic models were deployed:

1   Business Model Canvas
2   Strengths, Weaknesses, Opportunities, and Threats analysis
3   Porter's Five Competitive Forces

Business Model Canvas

Osterwalder and Pigneur's Business Model Canvas (2010) outlines key components of the value model driving a company's business. This model describes how value is generated, transferred, and delivered to key stakeholders, with value deduced through three entities listed as customers and partners, core business propositions, and financial performance. A Business Model Canvas can make connections more explicit (Joyce and Paquin, 2016) and can identify opportunities for value creation (Johnson et al., 2008). Shannon Airport's Business Model Canvas reflects the airport's two distinct customer sets: passengers (business to consumer, B2C) and airlines (business to business, B2B). It suggests a focused business model for Shannon Airport, concentrating on increasing volumes of passenger and, to a lesser extent, cargo services. Strong route development activity and high levels of engagement with various companies under the umbrella of the Shannon Group, together with private and public stakeholders with interests in the Shannon region, all underpin this approach.

The airport's value proposition highlights an excellent and efficient passenger experience, enabled by ease of access, a reasonable number of destinations, speedy processing, CBP US Customs and Border pre-clearance, and a positive retail experience. Airlines receive competitive terms to operate to and from this important tourism gateway in uncongested airspace with significant terminal capacity and the longest runway in Ireland, and a potential catchment area of one million people living within 90 minutes of the airport (Anna Aero, 2019a).

Shannon customer segmentation identifies business and leisure passengers (B2C), and network and low-cost carrier airlines (B2B), operating mainly point-to-point routes to and from the UK, Europe, and the United States. Other customers include maintenance, repair, and overhaul (MRO) companies which rent hangar space at the airport. Key activities supporting Shannon's proposition include a mandate to increase aeronautical and non-aeronautical revenue and stakeholder engagement, which is concentrated on stimulating economic and tourist activity in the Shannon region. Shannon's main resources include its significant airport infrastructure, in particular a terminal with passenger capacity comfortably exceeding current traffic levels. Other Shannon Group company resources – i.e. tourism, commercial property, and aviation services – help increase economic growth and prosperity in the region. The airport continues to explore new routes and introduce innovations such as a

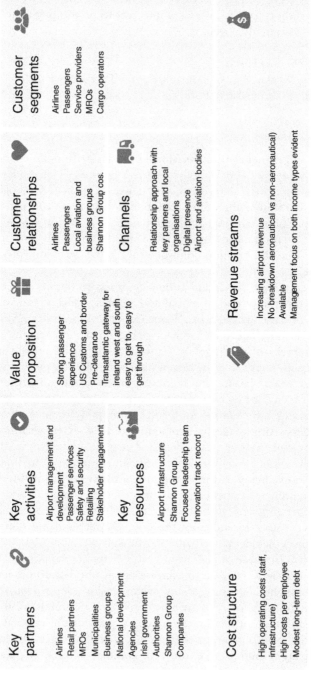

Figure 6.2 Business Model Canvas, Shannon Airport, August 2018

Source: Osterwalder and Pigneur's Business Model Canvas (2010), interpreted and applied to Shannon Airport

recently opened an autism-friendly sensory room in the airport departures area (Flynn, 2017).

Shannon's Business Model Canvas shows that major partners – including airlines, Shannon Group companies, concessionaires, and external stakeholders such as regulators and local representative bodies – are essential to the airport's business model. Municipal bodies can, through policy decisions, play a key supporting role in airport development, promoting 'win-win' policies which support advancement of the airport and the region. Papatheodorou et al. (2019) highlight this triple-win benefit of an effective stakeholder relationship triangle of airport, airline, and tourist authority partners. The relationship with principal customers, especially airlines, is fundamental to a regional airport's success. The impact of any change to an airline's network footprint will be immediately felt by the airport.

Turning to financial performance, Shannon Group's 2018 Annual Report highlights operating profit for the year of €15.7 million, an increase of almost €7 million over the previous year, with much of this the difference accounted for by the combined impact of investment revaluations and a provision for staff termination payments. This outcome presents a return on equity of just over 10 per cent. Total operating costs came to €77.6 million, this increase of 12.3 per cent from the previous year primarily accounted for by the provision for employment termination payments. Separate airport figures were not disclosed. Total revenue increased by 7.7 per cent to €77.8 million (Shannon Group, 2019).

Airport income streams were not broken down between aeronautical and non-aeronautical revenue prior to the 2018 report. This year's revenue disclosure provides a partial breakdown for 2018 and 2017, which shows specifically declared aviation revenue (Shannon Group, 2018a). Aeronautical revenue was almost identical between the two years, reflecting the challenges associated with new route development (the Max grounding occurred following year-end, and did not affect these numbers). It should be noted that a portion of Shannon Group retail and commercial revenue may be airport-related, given the fact that total airport revenue as reported was higher in previous years, but such a breakdown is not now available, and a like-for-like comparison with previous years is not therefore possible.

The absence of any material long-term debt has undoubtedly been of benefit to Shannon Group finances, the modest 2018 non-current ratio reflecting a long-term loan associated with a recent runway overlay investment. Table 6.3 shows some key financial ratios for the Group. These measures highlight a high but improving cost to income ratio of 83.2 per cent for 2018 and annual staff costs of €58,395 per employee. Both numbers appear high relative to the nature of the Group's businesses. They also provide context for the airport's staff voluntary redundancy programme and airfield re-categorisation from Category 9 to Category 9 flexible, as the number of wide-body aircraft using the airport has fallen considerably, which ultimately reduces the permanent need for the highest category of fire service. The revised categorisation seems adequate and acceptable, given Shannon's traffic volumes and aircraft types (Sheridan, 2017).

98 Noel Hiney, Marina Efthymiou, et al.

Table 6.3 Shannon Group revenue analysis

	2017 (€1,000)	2018 (€1,000)
Aeronautical and related income	**18,285**	**18,289**
Retail revenue	16,120	17,741
Tourism revenue	10,172	12,036
Commercial property revenue	10,038	10,888
Airport concession and rental revenue	**9,517**	**9,991**
Other commercial revenue	8,107	8,892
Total revenue	72,239	77,937

Source: Shannon Group (2019)

Table 6.4 Key financial ratios for Shannon Group

	2013	2014	2015	2016	2017	2018
Cost/income	99.62%	96.38%	89.87%	89.94%	88.60%	83.17%
Return on assets (ROA)	0.30%	0.42%	5.13%	4.24%	5.37%	7.22%
Return on equity (ROE)	0.44%	0.53%	6.30%	5.08%	6.92%	10.08%
Current assets/current liabilities	131.03%	178.84%	192.62%	174.74%	140.14%	101.28%
Quick assets/current liabilities	94.54%	134.02%	144.44%	135.72%	91.99%	44.81%
Gearing (non-current debt/equity %)	No non-current debt				10.10%	12.2%
Staff cost per employee in € (excl. termination payments)	No data		58,268	56,313	58,395	58,629

Sources: Calculations based on Shannon Group Annual Report and Accounts (Profit and Loss, Balance Sheet and Cash Flow Financial Statements) 2014, 2015, 2016, 2017, 2018 (Shannon Group, 2015, 2016, 2017b, 2018a, 2019)

The Business Model Canvas highlights how a change in one variable might affect others. For example, the financial impact (cost and revenue) of the provision of (say) free customer parking using available underutilised land, or subsidised public transport services, could be offset by an improved customer value proposition, higher passenger numbers, and increasing non-aeronautical revenue, achieving a local multiplier effect.

The Business Model Canvas does not, however, provide extensive insight into the macro and micro forces affecting Shannon Airport, as it is created primarily using an internal company standpoint, however, the Business Model Canvas does not provide an extensive insight into the macro and micro forces affecting Shannon Airport, These forces identify Shannon's landscape and positioning while providing reference points to where future actions may be considered. The SWOT and Five Competitive Forces models have been used to consider these factors for Shannon Airport.

Strengths, Weaknesses, Opportunities, and Threats (SWOT) analysis

The SWOT analysis examines a company's Strengths, Weaknesses, Opportunities, and Threats. The application of the SWOT analysis to Shannon Airport

Regional airport business models 99

has highlighted a small number of critical features influencing each quadrant. Main positive factors include unrestricted, cost-effective capacity for expansion and the potential for recent government planning policy announcements to improve growth prospects for the airport, enabled by strong stakeholder engagement. Key challenges identified include low population density, significant domestic airport competition, modest demand for new services and, of course, Brexit. Table 6.5 identifies these features for Shannon Airport.

Table 6.5 Shannon Airport SWOT analysis

Strengths	*Weaknesses*
• Comprehensive airport infrastructure; 24/7 availability • No delays/congestion – unrestricted capacity airside and landside • Strong passenger experience, especially westwards – ease of access, CBP pre-clearance and smooth transit to gate • Positioned between third and fourth largest Irish cities • A key part of region-based Shannon Group, focused on delivering economic benefits to its hinterland • Unique aviation brand – heritage rooted in innovation and entrepreneurship • Ideal west coast base for inbound tourism (a fundamental proposition) – Wild Atlantic Way gateway status	• Challenging route economics. Low (population)-density hinterland – impact on outbound passenger demand (expensive for carriers to operate) • Peripheral location, especially for eastbound traffic • Not ideally located for freight business • Modest route network (lack of European hub routes) and low, light frequencies • Cost base, given the scale of infrastructure, e.g. staff costs • Poor public transport connectivity (no rail, few bus services) • Group funding restrictions (airport must be self-financing; no State Aid permitted)
Opportunities	*Threats*
• Favourable public policy approach to balanced economic and tourism development (National Aviation Policy, Ireland 2040, Rural Action Plan for Jobs) • Strongly performing economy, improving business and tourism prospects • Galway now part of Shannon hinterland, following recent opening of new motorway. • Region-focused stakeholder group to pursue opportunities in a coordinated way • New funding models/partnerships – development of significant piece of local infrastructure, e.g. conference centre, aviation museum • Benefit to Shannon of holistic approach to approach to State Airport Capacity Review • New inbound markets (e.g. Asia)	• The impact of Brexit on activity and business volumes – the UK a key market (42% of passengers) • No significant change in government policy favouring Dublin and east of Ireland development (notwithstanding recent initiatives to address this) • Strong competition from Dublin, Cork, and other European airports for new airline routes • Loss of major airline customers – two airlines account for a high proportion of total traffic • Route impact of extended Boeing 737 Max grounding • Boeing 757s, heavily used in Shannon, approaching the end of their commercial life • Risk that Shannon Group structure might deflect airport focus

Source: Devised by authors

Brexit: a key threat

While the enduring economic effects of Brexit will take some time to be felt, its potential impact on Irish aviation, including airports and airlines, is likely to be significant in any no-deal scenario. Irish airports are very exposed to the UK economy, which is solely responsible for 43 per cent of total European passengers handled by Ireland's main airports in 2017 (Central Statistics Office, 2018). As Brexit is expected to have a negative impact on the UK economy at least in the short to medium term, resulting in higher unemployment and lower average income, passenger numbers are likely to be affected. From a transport and passenger transit perspective, any post-Brexit regulatory delays to aircraft and passengers departing from or arriving into Ireland would put a strain on the country's airport infrastructure.

According to a recent Irish Tourism Industry Confederation Report, receipts from visitors to Ireland from Great Britain have been declining since the fall in the value of UK currency sterling after the UK referendum vote to leave the European Union, with such visitors seeing a 12 per cent reduction in their purchasing power. (ITIC, 2019). These developments are likely to affect Shannon Heritage (tourist business) performance. In response to this challenge, Tourism Ireland, a national tourist authority, is launching a promotional campaign to increase British tourist spending by 25 per cent over the next three years (Tourism Ireland, 2019). A sustained weakening of sterling relative to the Euro, however, could see a reduction of UK traffic into Shannon, though it may make the UK a more attractive destination for outgoing passengers.

Brexit might also be likely to have an adverse impact on Shannon Commercial Properties and the International Aviation Services Centre if, for example, company decisions to invest in the region are cancelled or scaled back due to economic uncertainty. There is, however, also a possibility that Brexit might lead to some displacement of FDI away from the UK (Lawless and Morgenroth, 2016), which might benefit Shannon Commercial Properties.

The impact of Brexit on the broad activities of Shannon Airport and other Irish airports will ultimately be determined by the nature of the future relationship that will have to be negotiated. This arrangement will also define the future positioning of the UK's aviation system within EU Single European Aviation Area and Open Skies agreements.

Five Competitive Forces analysis

Michael Porter's Five Forces model (1979) specifically considers and assesses competitive threats facing an organisation. Like the business model canvas, Porter's model is a static one, representing a snapshot of the business at a given time, but not necessarily conveying industry volatility and rate of change. The model considers a company's performance under complex microeconomic conditions, capitalising on five explanatory or causal variables, described as *forces* (Grundy, 2006). Understanding the nature of these forces is essential so that the airport can prepare its response and develop/implement specific strategies to effectively deal with the issues it faces. Figure 6.3 shows that two forces

Regional airport business models 101

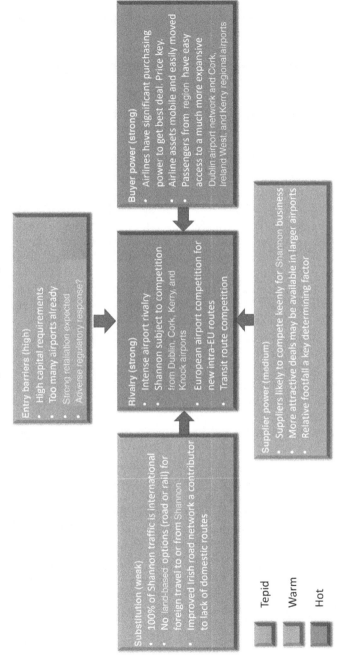

Figure 6.3 Shannon Airport's Five Forces analysis
Source: Devised by authors

have a potential adverse impact on Shannon Airport's business prospects: first, the power of buyers, both airlines and passengers; and second, an exceptionally high level of competition from other airports, particularly Dublin.

Threat of new entrants (low threat): There may already be too many airports in Ireland, evidenced by the closure of Galway airport to passenger traffic in 2013. Galway is about 1.5 hours by car from both Shannon and Knock, while Dublin is 2.5 hours away from the city. Significant capital costs would be experienced by any prospective airport entrant, given the vast infrastructure that would be required, with revenue not assured. A strong response could be expected from regulators and incumbents. Therefore, any new airport entrant is very unlikely.

Threat of substitutes (low threat): In the past, roads would have represented a significant substitute threat for domestic Shannon routes, and this is what happened some years ago. Today, 100 per cent of air traffic into and out of Shannon is international. There are no domestic or Northern Ireland air routes, perhaps because of the much-improved roads infrastructure. Other than Northern Ireland visitors, an air or sea journey is essential for international passengers travelling to and from the region. Therefore, other transport modes such as high-speed rail or roads present no substitution risk regarding such travel, although improving virtual video conference capabilities may do so for some business customers, over time.

Bargaining power – buyers (high threat): Wilkinson (2013) defines bargaining power as leverage that can be exerted on a company by customers to get the best deal possible, e.g. better slots, superior service, lower price. Airlines have significant bargaining power when dealing with Shannon Airport. Their assets (aircraft) are mobile and can be based at whichever airport offers the most favourable deal, meaning that they can extract the best possible arrangement and still transfer their business elsewhere when the contract expires (Woulfe, 2010). The incessantly commercial focus influencing this approach applies to all airlines using Shannon. Passengers equally have other airport options including Cork, Kerry, Ireland West (Knock), and Dublin airports, which have become more accessible by the much-improved motorway infrastructure. Even though airlines choose the airports to service, passengers chose the airline to fly with, and the airport to fly through. With price and convenience key differentiators, passengers have plenty of bargaining power.

Bargaining power – suppliers (medium threat): Companies supplying service, plant, and equipment to Shannon strive to win such contracts through a variety of means including price, value-added services, and discounts. However, contractors would be expected to compete more aggressively for business with more extensive facilities such as Dublin or other international airports whose scale significantly outweighs Shannon. Such contractors would be more focused on supplying 100 new information display screens in Dublin, for example, than 10 in Shannon. Dublin would benefit from higher discounts and expanded agreements. Nonetheless, most suppliers will be interested in securing such contracts, regardless of airport size.

Industry rivalry (high threat): Competition amongst airports is intense, not just from Dublin and Cork, for routes and passengers, but also other European airports which are pitching to airlines for new routes. For example, Kerry airport has 14 weekly services to Dublin on Aer Lingus Regional (Kerry Airport, 2019), which allows passengers to connect onwards, posing a high threat to Shannon. Ireland West (Knock) offered 71 weekly flights during summer 2018, of which 59 flights were UK bound (Ireland West Airport, 2019). Many airports also bid for transit routes, which use airport facilities and services en route to a final destination. Development of the Irish motorway network has significantly improved passenger access nationally to a much broader range of destinations in Dublin Airport at the expense of regional airports, including Shannon. This has led to a reduction in routes, such as the Cork and Shannon PSO services to Dublin, and connectivity at such regional airports (Vega and Reynolds-Feighan, 2016). Furthermore, intermodal passenger transport can contribute to the better airport accessibility and destination competitiveness (Efthymiou and Papatheodorou, 2015). Ireland's national bus service promotes seamless connectivity from all parts of Ireland to Dublin Airport (Bus Eireann, 2019), increasing competition from the country's dominant airport.

Peer airport comparison: Glasgow Prestwick Airport

Across Europe, there are several regional airports which previously enjoyed a busier and more prominent aviation role. Shannon is one of these, and another is Glasgow Prestwick Airport, hereafter called Prestwick, which until 1990 was a designated transatlantic airport for flights to and from Scotland, just as Shannon was for similar Irish flights until these stopovers were abolished (The Herald Scotland, 1990). Prestwick and Shannon share many characteristics, for example comprehensive infrastructure with significant capacity, airport supporting businesses, underused airspace, and 24/7 availability.

Table 6.6 compares key features of Shannon and Prestwick airports. Prestwick is currently Scotland's fifth busiest airport in terms of passenger traffic, Ryanair being the only airline operating scheduled services there. There are several dedicated charter services, while the airport operates a sizeable cargo business and supports military operations, with a number of air forces using the facility. Shannon has no military operations or base; however, the airport is regularly used for refuelling purposes by the US military, not without controversy (Lannon, 2019). Like Shannon, Prestwick has a significant commercial property portfolio of over 204,000 m^2 and an aviation cluster. The region boasts a heavy engineering presence and supports MRO operations. The airport faces

Table 6.6 Shannon Group and Glasgow Prestwick: key characteristics

	Shannon	Glasgow Prestwick
Date opened	1945 (1)	1934 (2)
Ownership	Publicly owned, corporatised (part of Shannon Group)	Publicly owned, corporatised (previously in private ownership; currently for sale)
Operations	24/7; good weather record	24/7; good weather record
Business mix	Passenger (Europe and North Atlantic), cargo, private, diversion	Cargo, passenger (Europe), military, private, diversion
Public transport access	Bus	Rail, bus
Catchment area	1m people within 90 minutes (3)	2m people within 60 minutes (4)
Direct employment (airport) 2018	271 employees (5)	315 employees (6)
Number of passengers	1.7m (7)	0.7m (8)
Volume of cargo (2018)	13,592 tonnes (9)	11,800 tonnes (10)
Number of movements (2018)	25,556 (11)	24,904 (12)
Terminal capacity	4.5m (13)	2.5m (14)
Active runway(s)	One: 3,199m (15)	Two: 2,986m and 1,905m (16)
Commercial property footprint	2m square feet of building space, 200 buildings and > 1,500 acres of development land (17)	484,376 square feet of commercial accomodation and 800 acres of land (18)
Other facilities	CBP pre-clearance, hangar rental for MROs, airline flight training	Hangar rental for MROs, airline flight training. Vying for UK Spaceport and Heathrow Logistics 'airport of choice' status
Airport revenue	N/D	€18.2m (19)

Sources:
1,13. History of Shannon Airport (Shannon Airport 2017a)
2. Glasgow Prestwick Airport History (Glasgow Prestwick Airport 2019a)
3. Anna Aero Route Shop – Shannon (Anna Aero 2019b)
4. Anna Aero Route Shop – Glasgow Prestwick (Anna Aero 2019b)
5. Shannon Group Annual Report 2017 (Shannon Group 2018a)
6,8,10,19. Glasgow Prestwick Annual Report and Financial Statements (Glasgow Prestwick Airport 2019a)
7,9,15,17. Shannon Group Annual Report 2018 (Shannon Group 2019a)
11. Shannon Group Media Release 2018 Results (Shannon Group 2019b)
12. CAA Aircraft Movements by Airport (Civil Aviation Authority 2019)
14. Glasgow Prestwick Airport: About Us (Glasgow Prestwick Airport 2020a)
16. Glasgow Prestwick Airport: Technical Information (Glasgow Prestwick Airport 2020b)
18. Glasgow Prestwick Airport: Commercial and Property (Glasgow Prestwick Airport 2020c)
N/D. Not Disclosed

Note: Differing year-ends.

Regional airport business models 105

major competition from Glasgow and Edinburgh airports and the UK rail network, which will become a more prominent competitive presence when high-speed services from southern England to Scotland are put into service. Given the proximity of Glasgow City, two million residents live within 60 minutes of the airport, versus 620,000 in Shannon. Unlike Shannon, Prestwick also has a dedicated rail terminal (Anna Aero, 2019b).

Other likely key current challenges include attracting airport investment, securing agreements with additional airlines, and developing new opportunities, such as competing for for UK Spaceport and Heathrow Logistics 'airport of choice' status.

Then Prestwick owner, British Airports Authority (BAA), was privatised in 1987. BAA sold Prestwick in 1992 and the airport underwent a series of further ownership changes before being re-nationalised by the Scottish government in 2013 (Anna Aero, 2013). The airport is currently for sale, with a process of finding a buyer including a stipulation that any purchaser must be capable of operating an airport and commit to maintaining and developing airport/aviation services (BBC News, 2019).

Strategic summary and current performance

Shannon's performance since 2014 has shown a modest increase in passenger numbers and profitability. Shannon has operational costs similar to those of bigger airports, given its comprehensive infrastructure. For example, current terminal capacity is 4.5 mppa while passenger numbers are about 1.7 mppa. Increasing these numbers (and revenue) to match this scale is a challenge, however. It will certainly be difficult to increase numbers to a targeted 2.5 mppa by 2020, with strong competition from other airports who may offer non-stop flights to a wide range of destinations one key reason for this challenge. For example, Dublin's 2018 summer schedule showed flights to 195 destinations (Dublin Airport 2018. *14 New Services And Four New Airlines This Summer At Dublin Airport* Available at https://www.dublinairport.com/latest-news/2019/05/31/14-new-services-and-four-new-airlines-this-summer-at-dublin-airport (accessed

Table 6.7 Shannon Airport: headwinds and tailwinds

Tailwinds ✓	Headwinds ✗
• Very strong airport infrastructure • Significant capacity for growth: passenger, MRO, Cargo • Positive, if modest, revenue trajectory • Strengthening regional engagement • Group structure brings opportunity (complementary activities) • Regional stakeholders broadly supportive of Group/Airport objectives	• Low population density of hinterland and relatively peripheral location • Demanding route economics for airlines • Irish economic activity concentrated around Greater Dublin area • State ownership limitations • Brexit implications • Impact of Boeing 737 Max grounding

3 March 2020)), relative to 27 destinations served by Shannon (Shannon Airport 2018. *Flights Where and When*. Available at https://web.archive.org/web/20180329141754/http://www.shannonairport.ie/gns/passengers/home.aspx (accessed 3 March 2020)). Airports in Cork (over 50 routes), Ireland West (23 routes), and Kerry (six routes) provide additional competition for Shannon.

In recent annual report updates, Shannon Group's Chairman, Rose Hynes, linked Group developments with the success of the region. She highlighted its €150-plus million investment plan to 2022 (with €85 million invested since 2014), the economic contribution of the Group to its hinterland and the key role that Shannon Group will play in enabling achievement of the government's National Planning Framework 2040, in particular the move to a more balanced national economy and society (Shannon Group, 2018a). Cost challenges for the Group were also alluded to. Steps, as previously described, have recently been taken to reduce operational and staff costs to bring them closer to those of similarly sized airports.

The National Planning Framework (NPF) policy was explicitly highlighted by the chairman as important to Shannon Group, with stakeholder engagement being vital. The NPF is the government's regional development strategy and aims to grow the scale of second-tier cities like Limerick significantly (Government of Ireland, 2018). In this context, it is noteworthy that the midwest region in which Shannon Airport is located has recorded relatively poor economic performance with above average unemployment and below average economic growth. In the 2017 report, the Group's then CEO, Mathew Thomas, highlighted 16 companies which cited Shannon Airport connectivity when announcing new or expanded operations. US connectivity – six airlines and eight destinations – was emphasised as a big plus, and transatlantic activity accounts for a more substantial proportion of total traffic than in most other airports (Shannon Group, 2018a). However, the recent grounding of the Boeing 737 Max aircraft has led to the initial suspension of three such transatlantic routes, and the subsequent cancelling of two Norwegian services (Hamilton, 2019).

The CEO also spoke of significant competition for new airline business and highlighted the airport's reliance on customer loyalty and advocacy in retaining routes, which airlines always keep under review. Other relevant areas covered included further development of the aviation cluster and the importance of, and appreciation for, a strong relationship with local stakeholders. In their paper specifically on Shannon Networking (Andreosso-O'Callaghan and Lenihan, 2008), the authors support such an approach, suggesting that within such industrial areas or innovation hubs, a networking advantage can arise because proximity brings cost efficiency and knowledge-exchange benefits to organisations.

Shannon Group is now well established, and is positioning Shannon Airport, and its sister companies collectively, as a vital economic engine for the region. Nonetheless, recent growth has come off a moderate base, and the airport faces the constant dual challenge, all too familiar to regional airports, of increasing passenger numbers and reducing costs.

The strategic models applied to Shannon Airport have highlighted company strengths and opportunities, and show the significant headwinds which the airport faces. Key recurring themes include a focus on growth and costs, opportunities arising out of national policy developments, intense competition and the challenge of operating in a peripheral, low population density location. There are no silver bullets, and local stakeholder engagement is critical.

Shannon's airport and commercial property infrastructure assets are the Group's biggest attractions. The relationship between Shannon Group and other key regional parties is also vitally important. While it may be argued that the airport's current footprint is too large and costly to maintain, and that elements of it should be right-sized, there is a danger that any such action would reduce the infrastructure advantage Shannon currently highlights when seeking new business opportunities.

Shannon Airport: broader issues

Economic impact assessment: Shannon Airport/group

A recently published company-commissioned report by W2 Consulting assessed the economic impact of Shannon Group (Shannon Group, 2018b). The economic impact report's overall methodology included an analysis of each individual Shannon Group company. An input-output model was used to produce employment, remuneration, valued-added, and economic output multipliers. This information was analysed and used to quantify the economic impact of each Shannon Group company with respect to employment, tax revenue, and gross value added (GVA), a measure broadly equivalent to gross domestic product. Direct, indirect, induced, and catalytic economic impacts were also estimated.

A total of 119 companies associated with Shannon Airport and airport activities were identified by the independent consultants and invited to participate in the research stage of this study, which was conducted between December 2016 and September 2017. Data collected and information gathered, relating to the 2016 calendar year, included nature of business, employment levels, annual payroll, expenditure on goods and services, and a profile of respondent company employment attributable to (Shannon) airport activity. Other information incorporated into the study included Shannon Group operations and planning information, data from the Central Statistics Office, tourism and employment development authorities, employer representative bodies, several regional (midwest) bodies, and aviation sources providing detail on global trends and the outlook for air transport.

Of the 119 companies approached, a response rate of 60 per cent was achieved, implying a 95 per cent confidence level. Responses were representative of the main sectors and business types associated with Shannon Airport. Various alternative sources were consulted to establish data for companies which were identified but did not participate. Further such data were inferred by applying industry averages from those companies that took part in the research. Responses received accounted for 72 per cent of overall direct employment associated with airport activities. This analysis (Table 6.8) has calculated that

108 *Noel Hiney, Marina Efthymiou, et al.*

Table 6.8 Overall economic impact of Shannon Group

Economic impact of Shannon group			
46,516 jobs €3.6 billion gross value added (GVA) €1.15 billion tax			
Shannon Airport	*Catalytic impact of airport*	*Shannon Commercial Properties*	*Shannon Heritage*
13,695 jobs €938 million GVA €318 million tax	31,900 jobs €2.6 billion GVA €821 million tax	81 jobs €12 million GVA €3.8 million tax	840 jobs €28 million GVA €8.9 million tax

Source: Shannon Group (2018b)

the airport's economic impact is just under €1 billion GVA and is responsible for 13,695 jobs in the region (the airport employs 260 staff directly).

Overall, the report contends that Shannon Group overall generates €3.6 billion in GVA in total each year, supporting over 46,500 jobs which contribute €1.15 billion in tax revenue to the Exchequer, with the Airport the most significant contributor, its direct and catalytic impact accounting for two-thirds of this total (Shannon Group, 2018b).

Table 6.9 provides a high-level comparison of the estimated economic impact of Ireland's main airports. Dublin Airport's economic impact is the highest in the list, as expected. Shannon Airport is a substantial supporter of its hinterland, providing employment and spillover effects to the region, whereas Kerry airport, the smallest airport reviewed, has a more modest but meaningful economic impact in its region. Of course, factors such as regional variability, the impact of national aviation policies, and overlapping catchment areas can affect assessment of the economic importance of airports.

Importance of regional and national planning policies to aviation

Ireland 2040 is a Government-led strategic national planning and development framework for Ireland between now and 2040 (National Planning Framework, 2017). It seeks the development of sustained, long-term, and regionally balanced physical and social infrastructure. This regional focus is vital. The Greater Dublin Area accounts for 40 per cent of the national population and 49 per cent of economic output. All roads, literally, lead to Dublin. Ireland 2040 seeks to protect the role of Dublin. However, the framework also highlights how Ireland's regional cities such as Cork, Limerick, and Galway can benefit from economic activity and employment in their regions, and recommends development of adequate infrastructure including motorway, airport, and port connectivity.

A number of other current planning initiatives, for example the *Action Plan for Rural Development*, aim to promote a more balanced regional build-up through promotion and development of an Atlantic Economic Corridor to generate jobs and investment along Ireland's western seaboard, along which

Regional airport business models 109

Table 6.9 Key Irish airport economic impact assessments in 2017

	UK market (% of total passengers)	Economic impact/gross value added	Employment	Connectivity	Information source
Shannon	UK 46%	€938 million	13,695	30 scheduled destinations served by eight airlines	Shannon Group Annual Report (2018) and Economic Impact Report (2017)
Dublin	UK 34%	€8.3 billion	117,300	176 scheduled destinations served by 41 airlines	DAA Annual Report 2017 DAA/InterVISTAS Report 2017
Cork	UK 57%	€727 million	10,710	39 scheduled destinations served by nine airlines	DAA Annual Report 2017 DAA/InterVISTAS Report 2017
Knock	UK 85%	€150 million	1,400	15 scheduled destinations served by three airlines	Ireland West Annual Review 2017 (total employment number estimated by Library & Research Service (L&R))
Kerry	UK 57%	€70 million	640	7 scheduled destinations served by two airlines	L&R, based on a similar methodology applied to similar sized airports
Total		€10.2 billion	143,745	267 scheduled routes (all airports)	

Source: Oireachtas Library and Research Service (2018)

Shannon Airport is located (Department of Arts, Heritage, Regional, Rural and Gaeltacht Affairs, 2017).

Ireland's National Aviation Policy, launched in late 2015 (Department of Transport, Tourism and Sport, 2015), focused on three key areas:

1 Enhancing Ireland's connectivity and being responsive to the needs of business, tourism, and consumers.
2 Fostering the growth of aviation enterprise to support growth creation, further helping to position Ireland as a recognised global aviation leader.
3 Maximising the contribution of aviation to Ireland's economic growth and development.

Irish state-owned Airports, including Shannon, are perceived as delivering significant strategic transport infrastructure and essential services that positively contribute in supporting state economic and social activities. They operate commercially, but their government-directed mandate requires that decisions take account of the broader national interest. Ongoing viability depends on their ability to attract inward services and passengers.

Airports are regarded as key tourism and business gateways, and continued development to this end is supported. The policy document highlighted the extensive airport coverage (Cork, Donegal, Dublin, Ireland West, and Kerry) for a small island nation with a population of 4.9 million inhabitants. It acknowledged that this presented airport operator challenges regarding traffic and performance, given the cyclical vulnerability to economic/political shocks, as well as emission targets. An abundance of airports leads to duplication of unused or inefficiently used infrastructure (European Commission, 2014). Indeed, smaller Irish airports have experienced significant difficulty in attracting passenger routes in recent times, and some of them have ceased airline operations.

The National Aviation Policy also committed to a review of airport capacity, given recent passenger increases in Dublin. However, this work is focusing on capacity constraints in Dublin, rather than taking a national, holistic perspective (Department of Transport, Tourism and Sport, 2019b), which approach might have given rise to a more balanced approach to managing future Irish airports capacity.

The Irish government contends that state ownership of the three largest Irish airports enables fulfilment of its commercial mandate, facilitating trade, tourism, and inward investment with consideration of the broader national interest, in a manner not guaranteed if the airports were privately owned. Key National Aviation Policy commitments do, however, include a review of future ownership options regarding the state-owned airports. While current policy is that Dublin, Cork, and Shannon airports will remain in public ownership, the government will formally review this approach in 2019, and every five years subsequently.

Policy impacts: Shannon Airport

Recent Irish policy initiatives, such as *Ireland 2040* (National Planning Framework), as previously described, have highlighted the potential benefit of regional economic policies to the Shannon region in general, and Shannon Group/Airport in particular, with the airport seen as having a pivotal role to play.

The nature of Irish regional policy and planning frameworks is fundamental to the development of Shannon and environs, and its tourism gateway status is a second essential factor. The potentially positive impact of Irish economic policies could facilitate development of a western business cluster in Ireland, along the lines of the tourism cluster that forms the Wild Atlantic Way. A planned new motorway linking Cork and Limerick, Ireland's second and third largest cities, should also benefit Shannon. Furthermore, two other major economic pillars for the region's development – Foynes Port and the University of Limerick – are located very close to Shannon Airport. These factors, combined with emerging capacity issues in the greater Dublin area, give rise to a potential increase in regional demand for local industrial space and activity, potentially benefiting the business of Shannon Airport and the other Group companies.

Regional airport business models   111

Stakeholder engagement

One of the most acclaimed authors on stakeholder theory, R. Edward Freeman, suggested the following stakeholder definition in 1984: 'Stakeholders are groups and individuals that have a valid interest in the activities and outcomes of a firm, and on whom the firm relies to achieve its objectives' (Freeman et al., 2004). Stakeholder engagement is described by Jeffery (2009) as a 'process whereby parties who can affect, or may be affected by, the activities of an organisation and the achievement of its goals, should have an opportunity to contribute to the development of activities and decisions that may affect them'.

The positive, enabling role of stakeholder engagement in aviation is supported by Amaeshi and Crane (2006) and Murphy and Efthymiou (2017), who identify it as a complementary mechanism to market and regulatory activities associated with airport companies. Shannon Group stakeholder activity comprises engagement with local representative groups, including local authorities in Limerick and Clare, airlines, national development agencies, chambers of commerce in counties Limerick and Clare, tourism bodies, and the Department of Transport, Tourism and Sport. Such stakeholder engagement is essential. For example, Ireland's Industrial Development Agency (IDA) continually emphasises the importance of Shannon Airport and the Group's commercial property business when marketing Shannon and Ireland's mid-west region to companies considering inward investment. These capabilities are important selling points when such investment opportunities are being pursued. Mobilisation around the Ireland 2040 National Planning Framework is another key stakeholder opportunity for the region.

Figure 6.4 highlights a broad range of regional airport stakeholders, underpinning the importance of an effective engagement approach in this area.

Figure 6.4 Key regional airport stakeholders

Source: Devised by authors

Shannon Airport: current focus

Shannon Airport's emphasis on passenger growth and route development is strongly focused on inbound tourism and business-friendly routes. Of course, airlines now seek to make money from day one on new routes. Regardless of specific introductory agreements, sustained customer demand is key. If a route fails, it is hard to win it back. This gives rise to a major challenge for peripheral airports such as Shannon, as airlines are much more likely to be interested in routes with significant population levels at both ends, something which is not one of the airport's selling points. Approximately 60 per cent of the Irish population lives within one hour of Dublin, while for Shannon the number is closer to 16 per cent. It is likely, given Ireland's much-improved motorway network, that a significant number of passengers travel from Shannon's hinterland to take a flight from Dublin Airport. It is now quite easy to do a day or overnight trip to the west of Ireland from Dublin, meaning that even if flying into Dublin, tourists can also travel to the west. In its report, *Tourism in The West: An Engine for Growth and Jobs* (Irish Tourist Industry Confederation, 2015), it was estimated that over 50 per cent of such tourists arrive into Ireland via Dublin and then travel to the west of Ireland. Even though the reverse is also true, this trend benefits the airport with the highest levels of connectivity. Indeed, Ireland's national bus company proudly advertises the fact that it provides 300 daily services to Dublin Airport from all parts of the country, including Limerick, Shannon's closest main city (Bus Eireann, 2019).

Shannon has good westward connectivity to North America, as evidenced by the number of transatlantic carriers using the airport for much of the year. This is likely to remain the case for as long as US travel operators perceive the west of Ireland as a separate tourist market. However, Shannon is not as strong an attraction for routes to the UK and, especially, Europe. Ireland is one hour behind most of Western Europe. The airport's location also means that Shannon is at least an hour away from mainland Europe in the air. Airline economics for such routes are especially challenging. Even free deals are not attractive to carriers if the seats cannot be filled. Competition for new routes will also come from the UK and mainland European airports which regularly compete to take up new airline capacity.

Given the challenging nature of airline economics for peripheral airports, as previously described, Shannon's future is more likely to involve a greater use of regional jets or turboprops (60–100 seats) on UK and European routes, which will primarily be point-to-point focused, and maximum range Boeing and Airbus narrow-bodies for transatlantic routes which is already the case, with all such connections currently operated by Boeing 757 and 737 types. It can be expected that Aer Lingus will use some of its A321neo LR aircraft, when delivered, to replace the Boeing 757s which currently operate the airline's Shannon routes on a contract basis. However, it appears that any new Aer Lingus transatlantic routes – whether launched, recently announced or contemplated – will fly out of Dublin, notwithstanding emerging capacity constraints there. This approach is consistent with the increasing use by Aer Lingus of Dublin Airport as a mini hub for North American air traffic, connecting European passengers with US destinations (and vice versa). Additionally, the use of Boeing 757s by US transatlantic operators on Shannon routes could represent a risk when these aircraft come to the end of their working life, if these carriers do not have adequate alternative aircraft available for use on routes such as Shannon in the short term. Finally, the current grounding of Boeing 737 Max has had a disproportionate effect on Shannon, with the airport's interim CEO estimating an annualised loss of 120,000 passengers (about 7 per cent of total 2018 numbers) arising from the suspension of three transatlantic Shannon routes using this type (Ryan, 2019).

These competitive factors represent a significant challenge to passenger growth at Shannon. However, given its current capacity, runway length, and CBP facility, Shannon has distinct advantages and has the potential to expand the number of transatlantic flights, particularly with low-cost long-haul carriers and US carriers. It could even develop itself into an attractive location for airlines targeting North American traffic opportunities (in the same manner that Ryanair is feeding traffic to Air Europa at Madrid, which connects passengers onwards to Latin America). Shannon has also launched a stand-alone website 'FlyShannon.ie', which enables visitors to book package holidays from Shannon, including the option to reserve a hotel room, hire a car, and arrange airport parking. This focus on non-aeronautical activity has also highlighted an opportunity for Shannon's duty-free businesses to focus on superior heritage-related products and several premium retail and hospitality outlets have recently opened.

Conclusion

European regional airports will continue to experience challenging times in increasingly volatile industry and economic conditions, and competition will remain intense. Given the critical role such airports play on the one hand, and the business challenges they face on the other hand, their financial standing and the nature and extent of external and state support will continue to weigh heavily on performance and viability. Notwithstanding high current levels of public ownership of regional airports, it is likely that many airports and governments will become more open to risk sharing models, perhaps involving greater privatisation and various hybrid partnership arrangements.

Economic and aviation-related government policies have the potential to significantly influence regional airport development, particularly in lower population density regions where stimulation of activity, for example through investment and incentives, is seen politically as necessary or desirable. There is broad agreement that neither companies nor airlines will establish operations in a specific location due to region-friendly policy positions that have no commercial basis. Such approaches could fall foul of State Aid rules and might not deliver sustainable benefits locally.

It is too early to assess the success of the Shannon Group business model. Passenger numbers have steadily increased since separation from the Dublin Airport Authority. From an airport point of view, however, Shannon faces the cost and growth challenges all such airports experience. The Group is peripherally located and faces intense competition, highlighted by the fact that about 85 per cent of Irish airport passenger growth into and out of the country from 2012–2017 was through Dublin Airport (Central Statistics Office, 2018). Furthermore, the impact of one-off events such as the Max grounding and the need to invest significantly in upgraded security screening equipment without state support, as provided to other Irish airports (Hamilton, 2018), will have a disproportionately adverse effect on airports such as Shannon.

Airport sustainability may be enhanced through group synergies, a key success factor when assessing the Shannon Group, where a cluster of vertically integrated airport assets can coalesce to improve the Group's financial performance. A similar corporate structure, i.e. one including an airport and commercial property component, is in place at Prestwick airport, suggesting that variations of the Shannon Group model are potentially applicable elsewhere in Europe, given the similarity of regional airport characteristics.

Local stakeholder engagement is also critical for European regional airports. These airports should be closely aligned with business groups, tourist bodies, local government agencies, and other networks. Airlines are likely to be react positively to the presence of such a united local front when considering the launch of new routes. Such a united coalition can also help parties maximise the potential from local business and tourism opportunities, benefiting airport passenger traffic. Strong local stakeholder relationships may result in, or happen as a result of, airport groups taking a more active role, including ownership, of related local infrastructure, as has happened in the case of Shannon Group. One risk to success is any potential dilution of focus from an airport's core business due to additional management requirements associated with a broader group company remit. It can be argued, however, that this broader focus is essential to support airport sustainability and growth.

As European aviation grows and hub airports reach capacity, there will be an opportunity for regional airports, particularly well-located ones with low costs and significant capacity. Shannon's strong transatlantic position, supported by the presence of CBP pre-clearance, provides a unique differentiator relative to other regional airports, while its location on the western edge of Europe is more likely to be able to sustain routes to the eastern corridor of North America using narrow-body aircraft types. Notwithstanding current issues, the launch into service of next generation Airbus and Boeing narrow-bodies points to new opportunities for Shannon, as the operating economics for such aircraft are substantially better than those of wide-body aircraft, making them suitable for a higher number of point-to-point routes.

It is difficult to envisage any short-term change in Shannon Airport's ownership status. The question as to whether Shannon would be best placed as a state airport or a private commercial entity remains an open one. However, any privatisation of Shannon would be likely to be politically difficult. During a 2016 address to a tourism conference in the airport's hinterland, Shannon Group Chief Executive Officer Mathew Thomas spoke about combining the best characteristics of public sector ownership, e.g. long-term vision and cautious risk profile, with private sector thinking, e.g. efficiency, creativity, and agility. These words suggest that at some future stage, the Group might consider hybrid investment models tied to specific initiatives targeting business growth (Thomas, 2016). Shannon as a group is likely to be more attractive to potential long-term investors than Shannon as an airport. Though it appears that the state has no current intention of selling down its shareholding, this position might possibly change if such a transaction was regarded as beneficial to the region as a whole. Such benefits could come through investments in a major new tourism asset or through further development of the aviation services cluster. Public-private partnership models could also be considered regarding the development of a specific piece of infrastructure; for example, a major conference centre on grounds owned by Shannon Group.

This chapter has sought to use the example of the Shannon Group to highlight the challenges and opportunities affecting regional airports, and to describe how such airports might become part of a locally based corporate entity. Shannon Group's vision and mission statements are focused on increasing airport passenger numbers by attracting more visitors and businesses to the area and delivering economic benefits to the west of Ireland. Its structure represents a strong focus on innovation and entrepreneurship, combined with a broad and more integrated regional positioning for Shannon Airport.

Consideration of similar models for other European regional airports has potential attractions, including improved performance and alignment with national and EU regional economic and airport objectives. The authors hope that these early observations from the Shannon Group experience will help readers better understand this topic.

References

ACI-Europe (2016). *The ownership of Europe's airports 2016*. Available at: www.aci-europe. org/component/downloads/downloads/5095.html (accessed 14 June 2018).

ACI-Europe (2017). *European regional airports – connecting people, places and products*. Regional Airports' Forum, April. Available at: https://blueswandaily.com/wp-content/uploads/2017/11/European-Regional-Airports-Connecting-people-places-products. pdf (accessed 12 October 2019).

ACI-Europe (2019). *Fast facts*. Available at: www.aci-europe.org/policy/fast-facts.html (accessed 20 June 2019).

Adler, N. and Liebert, V. (2014). Joint impact of competition, ownership form and economic regulation on airport performance and pricing. *Transportation Research Part A: Policy and Practice*, 64, 92–109.

Adler, N., Ülkü, T. and Yazhemsky, E. (2013). Small regional airport sustainability: Lessons from benchmarking. *Journal of Air Transport Management*, 33, 22–31.

Amaeshi, K. M. and Crane, A. (2006). Stakeholder engagement: A mechanism for sustainable aviation. *Corporate Social Responsibility and Environmental Management*, 13(5), 245–260.

Andreosso-O'Callaghan, B. and Lenihan, H. (2008). Networking: A question of firm characteristics? The case of the Shannon region in Ireland. *Entrepreneurship and Regional Development*, 20(6), 561–580.

Anna Aero (2013). *Glasgow Prestwick airport sold to Scottish government for £1*. Available at: www.anna.aero/2013/11/28/glasgow-prestwick-airport-sold-scottish-government-1-pound/ (accessed 12 November 2019).

Anna Aero (2019a). Shannon airport (SNN/EINN): Other major reasons to serve this airport. *The Route Shop*. Available at: www.therouteshop.com/profiles/shannon-airport/ (accessed 1 July 2019).

Anna Aero (2019b). *Glasgow Prestwick airport (PIK/EGPK)*. Available at: www.therouteshop.com/profiles/prestwick-airport/ (accessed 1 August 2019).

Baker, D. and Donnet, T. (2012). Regional and remote airports under stress in Australia. *Research in Transportation Business and Management*, 4, 37–43.

Barrett, S. (2009). EU/US open skies – competition and change in the world aviation market: The implications for the Irish aviation market. *Journal of Air Transport Management*, 15(2), 78–82.

BBC News (2019). *Publicly owned Prestwick airport put up for sale*. Available at: www.bbc.com/news/uk-scotland-scotland-business-48627212 (accessed 13 August 2019).

Booz and Company (2012). *Options for the future ownership and operation of Cork and Shannon Airports*. Available at: www.ennischamber.ie%2Fwp-content%2Fuploads%2F2012%2F03%2FOPTIONS_FOR_THE_FUTURE_OWNERSHIP_AND_OPERATION_OF_CORK_AND_SHANNON_AIRPORTS-0.pdf&usg=AFQjCNESvhM3reSFtMg8KXXT-mx89kf9Zg&sig2=EW7yx-bclsmjb8gOZ78RNw&bvm=bv.142059868,d.d24 (accessed 4 December 2016).

Bus Eireann (2019). *Get to the airport ready to fly*. Available at: https://youtu.be/4VqbaU62ibI (accessed 1 July 2019).

Cahill, C., Palcic, D. and Reeves, E. (2017). Commercialisation and airport performance: The case of Ireland's DAA. *Journal of Air Transport Management*, 59, 55–163.

Central Statistics Office (2018). *Aviation statistics; quarter 4 and year 2017*, 19 April. Available at: www.cso.ie/en/releasesandpublications/er/as/aviationstatisticsquarter4andyear2017/ (accessed 6 August 2019).

Central Statistics Office (2019). *Aviation statistics; quarter 4 and year 2018*. Available at: www.cso.ie/en/releasesandpublications/er/as/aviationstatisticsquarter4andyear2018/ (accessed 6 August 2019).

Civil Aviation Authority (2019). *CAA 2018 Aircraft Movements by Airport*. Available at: https://www.caa.co.uk/uploadedFiles/CAA/Content/Standard_Content/Data_and_analysis/Datasets/Airport_stats/Airport_data_2018_annual/Table_03_1_Aircraft_Movements.pdf.

Cork Airport (2019). *Cork Airport Launches 2019 Summer Schedule*. 1 April. Available at: https://www.corkairport.com/news/detail/2019/04/01/cork-airport-launches-2019-summer-schedule (accessed 30 October 2019).

Department of Arts, Heritage, Regional, Rural and Gaeltacht Affairs (2017). *Realising our rural potential: Action plan for rural development*, 23 January. Available at: www.ahrrga.gov.ie/realising-our-rural-potential-government-launches-the-action-plan-for-rural-development/ (accessed 10 June 2018).

Department of Transport, Tourism and Sport (2012). *Options for the future ownership and operation of Cork and Shannon airports*, 29 February. Available at: www.dttas.ie/aviation/

publications/english/feb-2012-options-future-ownership-and-operation-cork-and-shannon (accessed 20 August 2018).

Department of Transport, Tourism and Sport (2014). *Minister Donohoe hails new era as Shannon airport authority and Shannon development transferred to Shannon group*, 5 September. Available at: www.dttas.ie/press-releases/2014/minister-donohoe-hails-new-era-as-shannon-airport-authority-and-shannon-development (accessed 23 August 2018).

Department of Transport, Tourism and Sport (2015). *A national aviation policy for Ireland*, 20 August. Available at: www.dttas.ie/aviation/english/national-aviation-policy-ireland (accessed 15 June 2017).

Department of Transport, Tourism and Sport (2017). *Address by minister for transport, tourism and sport, Shane Ross T.D. at the national civil aviation development forum*, 20 February. Available at: www.dttas.ie/speeches/2017/address-minister-transport-tourism-and-sport-shane-ross-td-national-civil-aviation (accessed 16 May 2017).

Department of Transport, Tourism and Sport (2019a). *Regional airports public consultation programme*. Available at: www.gov.ie/en/consultation/a901a5-regional-airports-porgramme-public-consultation/ (accessed 12 September 2019).

Department of Transport, Tourism and Sport (2019b). *Independent review of capacity needs of Ireland's state airports*. Available at: www.gov.ie/en/publication/177d5f-independent-review-of-capacity-needs-of-irelands-state-airports/ (accessed 3 August 2019).

Dobruszkes, F., Givoni, M. and Vowles, T. (2017). Hello major airports, goodbye regional airports? Recent changes in European and US low-cost airline airport choice. *Journal of Air Transport Management*, 59, 50–62.

Efthymiou, M., Arvanitis, P. and Papatheodorou, A. (2016). Institutional changes and dynamics in the European aviation sector: Implications for tourism. In Pappas, N. and Bregoli, I. (eds) *Global dynamics in travel, tourism and hospitality*. Hershey, PA, IGI Global.

Efthymiou, M. and Papatheodorou, A. (2015). Intermodal passenger transport and destination competitiveness in Greece. *Anatolia*, 26(3), 459–471.

Efthymiou, M. and Papatheodorou, A. (2018). Evolving airline and airport business models. In Halpern, N. and Graham, A. (eds) *The Routledge companion to air transport management*. Abingdon, Routledge.

European Commission (2014). *Guidelines on state aid to airports and airlines*, 4 April. Available from: http://eur-lex.europa.eu/legal-content/EN/TXT/?uri=CELEX%3A52014XC0404(01) (accessed 15 July 2018).

Flynn, P. (2017). Shannon airport opens sensory room for passengers with autism. *The Irish Times*, 29 March. Available at: www.irishtimes.com/business/transport-and-tourism/shannon-airport-opens-sensory-room-for-passengers-with-autism-1.3029221 (accessed 24 May 2017).

FlyPlymouth (2019). *It's time to get Plymouth's airport flying again*. Available at: www.flyplymouth.com/ (accessed 25 August 2019).

Freeman, R. E., Wicks, A. C. and Parmar, B. (2004). Stakeholder theory and 'the corporate objective revisited'. *Organization Science*, 15(3), 364–369.

Frontier Economics (2014). *Setting airport regulated charges: The choice between single till and dual till*. London, Frontier Economics.

Gillen, D. (2011). The evolution of airport ownership and governance. *Journal of Air Transport Management*, 17(1), 3–13.

Glasgow Prestwick Airport (2019a). *Glasgow Prestwick airport history*. Available at: https://www.prestwick-airport-guide.co.uk/history.html.

Glasgow Prestwick Airport (2019b). *TS Prestwick accounts*. Available at: www.glasgowprestwick.com/wp-content/uploads/2018/12/TS-Holdco-Ltd-Accounts-Apr-17-Mar-18.pdf (accessed 23 August 2019).

118 *Noel Hiney, Marina Efthymiou, et al.*

Glasgow Prestwick Airport (2020a). *Glasgow Prestwick Airport: About Us.* Available at: https://www.glasgowprestwick.com/corporate/about-us/useful-information-2/ (accessed 4 March 2020).

Glasgow Prestwick Airport (2020b). *Glasgow Prestwick Airport: Technical information.* Available at: https://www.glasgowprestwick.com/business/commercial-and-property/ (accessed 4 March 2020).

Glasgow Prestwick Airport (2020c). *Glasgow Prestwick Airport: Business – commercial and property.* Available at: https://www.glasgowprestwick.com/business/commercial-and-property/ (accessed 4 March 2020).

Google Maps (2019). *Directions and route planner.* Available at: www.google.com/maps/dir/ (accessed 16 September 2019).

Government of Ireland (2018). *Ireland 2040: National planning framework.* Dublin, Department of Housing, Planning and Local Government.

Graham, A. (2014). *Managing airports 4th edition: An international perspective.* Routledge.

Grundy, T. (2006). Rethinking and reinventing Michael Porter's five forces model. *Strategic Change*, 15(5), 213–229.

Halpern, N. and Pagliari, R. (2007). Governance structures and the market orientation of airports in Europe's peripheral areas. *Journal of Air Transport Management,* 13(6), 376–382.

Hamilton, P. (2018). Shannon airport chief criticises lack of government support. *The Irish Times.* Available at: www.irishtimes.com/business/transport-and-tourism/shannon-airport-chief-criticises-lack-of-government-support-1.3711328 (accessed 1 June 2019).

Hamilton, P. (2019). Will Norwegian's Irish exit lead to higher transatlantic airfares? *The Irish Times.* Available at: www.irishtimes.com/business/transport-and-tourism/will-norwegian-s-irish-exit-lead-to-higher-transatlantic-airfares-1.3986002 (accessed 1 September 2019).

The Herald Scotland (1990). *Prestwick loses its monopoly: Airlines flock to Glasgow in Atlantic rush.* 7 March. Available at: https://www.heraldscotland.com/news/11936738.prestwick-loses-its-monopoly-airlines-flock-to-glasgow-in-atlantic-rush/ (accessed 16 October 2019).

Ireland West Airport (2019). *Where can I fly?* Available at: https://irelandwestairport.com/ (accessed 31 October 2019).

Irish Tourist Industry Confederation (2015). *Tourism in the West: An engine for growth and jobs,* November [Online]. Available at: www.itic.ie/wp-content/uploads/2015/11/Tourism-in-the-West-Full-Report-Nov-2015.pdf (accessed 20 June 2017).

Irish Tourist Industry Confederation (2019). *Tourism, a competitiveness report.* Available at: www.itic.ie/wp-content/uploads/2019/08/Tourism-competitiveness_ITIC-report_Aug2019.pdf (accessed 2 September 2019).

Ison, S., Francis, G., Humphreys, I. and Page, R. (2011). UK regional airport commercialisation and privatisation: 25 years on. *Journal of Transport Geography*, 19(6), 1341–1349.

Jeffery, N. (2009). *Stakeholder engagement: A road map to meaningful engagement.* Cranfield, Cranfield University.

Johnson, M., Christensen, C. and Kagermann, H. (2008). Reinventing your business model. *Harvard Business Review*, 86(12), 50–59.

Joyce, A. and Paquin, R. L. (2016). The triple layered business model canvas: A tool to design more sustainable business models. *Journal of Cleaner Production*, 135, 1474–1486.

Kerry Airport (2019). *Direct flights from Kerry airport.* Available at: https://kerryairport.ie/website/flight-info/destinations/ (accessed 30 October 2019).

Lannon (2019). A question of neutrality and Shannon airport. *RTE Brainstorm.* Available at: www.rte.ie/brainstorm/2019/0115/1023314-a-question-of-neutrality-and-shannon-airport/ (accessed 30 October 2019).

Lawless, M. and Morgenroth, E. (2016). Opportunities and risks for foreign direct investment. In Bergin, A., Morgenroth, E. and McQuinn, K. (eds) *Ireland's economic outlook: Perspectives and policy challenges*. Dublin, ESRI Forecasting Series EO1.

McCoy, D., Lyons, S., Morgenroth, E., Palcic, D. and Allen, L. (2018). The impact of local infrastructure on new business establishments. *Journal of Regional Science*, 58(3), 509–534.

Murphy, G. and Efthymiou, M. (2017). Aviation safety regulation in the multi-stakeholder environment of an airport. *Journal of Air Transport Studies*, 8(2), 1–26.

National Planning Framework (2017). *What is the national planning framework?* Available at: http://npf.ie/about/ (accessed 5 June 2017).

O'Brien, T. (2019). Knock airport to attract 1m passengers with upgraded runway. *The Irish Times*. Available at: www.irishtimes.com/news/ireland/irish-news/knock-airport-to-attract-1m-passengers-with-upgraded-runway-1.4025008 (accessed 20 September 2019).

O'Connell, B. and O'Carroll, C. (2018). *Brendan O'Regan: Irish visionary, innovator, peacemaker*. Dublin, Irish Academic Press.

O'Halloran, B. (2018). Shannon group falls short of targets set five years ago. *The Irish Times*, 17 February. Available at: www.irishtimes.com/business/transport-and-tourism/shannon-group-falls-short-of-targets-set-five-years-ago-1.3394947 (accessed 4 July 2018).

Oireachtas Library and Research Service (2018). *Ireland's main airports: An economic profile (2017)*. Available at: https://data.oireachtas.ie/ie/oireachtas/libraryResearch/2018/2018-07-05_ireland-s-main-airports-an-economic-profile_en.pdf (accessed 3 July 2019).

Osterwalder, A. and Pigneur, Y. (2010). *Business model generation: A handbook for visionaries, game changers and challengers*. London, John Wiley and Sons.

Pagliari, R. and Graham, A. (2019). An exploratory analysis of the effects of ownership change on airport competition. *Transport Policy*, 78, 76–85.

Papatheodorou, A., Vlassi, E., Gaki, D., Papadopoulou-Kelidou, L., Efthymiou, M., Pappas, D. and Paraschi, P. (2019). The airline – airport – destination authority relationship: The case of Greece. In Kozak, N. and Kozak, M. (eds) *Tourist destination management – instruments, products, and case studies*. Berlin, Springer.

Porter, M. E. (1979). How competitive forces shape strategy. *Harvard Business Review*, March. Available at: https://hbr.org/1979/03/how-competitive-forces-shape-strategy (accessed 14 June 2017).

Regan, P. (2017). Flying on course: Public-sector innovation at Shannon airport. *International Journal of Entrepreneurship and Innovation*, 18(2), 128–135.

Ryan, O. (2019). 'Looming crisis' at Shannon as passenger numbers fall and Norwegian exit. *The Clare Champion*. Available at: https://clarechampion.ie/looming-crisis-at-shannon-as-passenger-numbers-fall-and-norwegian-exit/ (accessed 1 August 2019).

Shannon Development (2007). *Shannon development – a brief profile*. Available at: https://web.archive.org/web/20071129223104/www.shannondevelopment.ie/AboutUs/Abriefprofileof ShannonDevelopment/ (accessed 30 October 2019).

Shannon Group (2015). *Shannon group plc annual report, 2014*. Available at: https://www.shannongroup.ie/getattachment/News-Media/Publications/English/Final-Shannon-Group-AR_V6-Mon-27th-April-2015-(1).pdf.aspx?lang=en-IE (accessed 20 June 2018).

Shannon Group (2016). *Shannon group plc annual report, 2015*. Available at: www.shannongroup.ie/shannon-group-plc-annual-report-2016/ (accessed 20 June 2018).

Shannon Airport (2017a). *History of Shannon airport*. Available at: www.shannonairport.ie/gns/about-us/history-of-shannon-airport.aspx (accessed 2 June 2018).

Shannon Group (2017b). *Shannon group plc annual report, 2016*. Available at: www.shannongroup.ie/shannon-group-plc-annual-report-2016/ (accessed 20 June 2018).

Shannon Group (2018a). *Shannon group plc annual report, 2017*. Available at: www.shannon-group.ie/shannon-group-annual-report-2017/ (accessed 20 August 2018).

Shannon Group (2018b). *Shannon group economic impact report*, 25 April. Available at: www.shannongroup.ie/shannon-group-economic-impact-report/ (accessed 21 August 2018).

Shannon Group (2019a). *Shannon group plc annual report, 2018*. Available at: www.shannongroup.ie/wp-content/uploads/SNN-Group-Annual-Report-2018-V5-Onscreen-FINAL-English.pdf (accessed 20 June 2019).

Shannon Group (2019b). *Shannon Group's boost to economy as its three companies record significant growth in 2018*. Available at: https://www.shannonairport.ie/passengers/news-media/latest-news/2019/shannon-group%E2%80%99s-boost-to-economy-as-its-three-comp/ (accessed 20 October 2019).

Shannon IASC (2019). *Why set up business in Shannon?* Available at: www.iasc.aero/ (accessed 10 September 2019).

Sheridan, A. (2017). Plans for Shannon airport a 'bombshell' say staff. *The Limerick Leader*, 30 March [Online]. Available at: www.limerickleader.ie/news/home/242602/measures-at-shannon-airport-are-to-reduce-costs.html (accessed 30 April 2018).

Thomas, M. (2016). *A new model for airport development*. Annual Tourism Policy Workshop, 17 November. Available at: https://tourismpolicyworkshop.files.wordpress.com/2014/10/a-new-model-for-airport-development.pdf (accessed 24 June 2018).

Tourism Ireland (2019). *Mid-year review of overseas tourism 2019*. Available at: www.tourismireland.com/Press-Releases/2019/July/Mid-year-review-of-overseas-tourism-2019 (accessed 15 August 2019).

Vega, A. and Reynolds-Feighan, A. (2016). The impact of the Great Recession on Irish air travel: An intermodal accessibility analysis. *Journal of Air Transport Management*, 51, 1–18.

Wilkinson, J. (2013). *Buyer bargaining power*, 23 July. Available at: https://strategiccfo.com/buyer-bargaining-power-one-of-porters-five-forces/ (accessed 24 June 2017).

Woulfe, J. (2010). O'Leary claims Shannon 'dying on its feet' as Ryanair cuts flights by 21%. *The Irish Examiner*, 9 September. Available at: www.irishexaminer.com/business/oleary-claims-shannon-dying-on-its-feet-as-ryanair-cuts-flights-by-21-130266.html (accessed 14 June 2017).

Zhang, M. L. (2014). Analysis on herter-organizing of airport industry cluster based on the system dynamics. *Applied Mechanics and Materials*, 556–562, 6610–6615.

7 The air transport markets in Central and Eastern Europe

Sonia Huderek-Glapska

Introduction

This chapter focuses on Central and Eastern European (CEE) countries (the Czech Republic, Poland, Slovakia, Hungary, Latvia, Lithuania, Estonia)[1] and the relationship between their economic performance and air transport markets. The countries of Central and Eastern Europe share a common history, economic system, and geographical location. This enables them to be treated as one group, and their paths of growth to be jointly investigated in terms of socio-economic development and air transport activity, with the inclusion of individual features for each country.

Over the last few decades, these countries have undergone significant political and economic changes. The process of transition began with the collapse of communism in 1989. The speed and scope of the economic reforms carried out in post-socialist countries in the early years of transformation were dependent on the power of the political system (Jóźwik, 2016). Governments representing new political forces implemented radical programmes leading to the liberalisation of the economy. The economic reforms in most countries of Central and Eastern Europe were shaped by the assumptions of neoliberal policy with programmes encompassing, among other things, the elimination of barriers to trade and foreign direct investment, privatisation of state-owned enterprises, deregulation towards a free market economy, and a guarantee of property rights (Burnewicz and Bąk, 2000).

This process of transforming the economy into a more market-oriented one was accelerated by accession to the European Union. At the time of ten new countries joining the European Union in 2004, there was a significant disproportion in the level of socio-economic development between the countries of Western and Central/Eastern Europe resulting from historical, political, and socio-economic factors. However, by the first decade of the 21st century, Central and Eastern European regions (in the vast majority of cases) had reduced their differences with Western European countries. Nevertheless, most Central European regions are still among the less developed regions of the European Union because in a relatively short period, it is difficult to catch up with well-developed European countries. In Central and Eastern Europe, the most developed are capital regions – Warsaw, Budapest, Prague, and Bratislava (Smętkowski, 2018). Despite the efforts undertaken by the European Union for socio-economic cohesion in member countries, and consequently the allocation of significant funds for the development of Central and Eastern regions, regional development is still divergent.

Before the political transition, air transport markets in the Communist Bloc countries had much in common (Janić, 1997). The supply side of the air transport market in each country was strictly regulated and the institutional foundations for agreements between the countries of the Bloc were created. The interests of national carriers, of which the biggest were LOT Polish Airlines, CSA Czech Airlines, and Malev Hungarian Airlines, were protected by bilateral agreements and their fleets consisted mainly of Soviet aircraft (Yak, Tupolev, Antonow) (Symons, 1993). Carriers from the countries of the Eastern Bloc rarely competed with airlines from Western Europe (Ivy, 1995). The airline networks of the CEE region were focused on the countries of the former Eastern Bloc. In the Baltic states, the air services were dominated by flights to the Soviet Union, which fed the Aeroflot global network in Moscow. Airlines in the Baltic countries, particularly Lithuanian Airlines in Lithuania, Latavio in Latvia, and Estonian Air in Estonia, were established after the collapse of the Soviet Union. All these carriers had previously represented the local divisions of Aeroflot Soviet Airlines.

The political and economic reforms which took place after the fall of communism brought about a gradual change in the air transport sector of CEE countries (Ivy, 1995). After 1989, many of the airports underwent a process of ownership transformation. Local authorities, who became one of the airports' shareholders, invested in infrastructure to develop the aviation business that would serve regional needs. Nevertheless, in the EU's pre-accession period, in the years 1989–2004, the air transport markets in CEE countries developed very slowly.

With the accession of Central and Eastern European countries to the European Union in 2004, an air transport revolution came about. In 2004, all CEE countries were obliged to join the common EU/EEA single aviation market and open their national markets. This was the crucial institutional change that spurred competition, encouraged more routes, and facilitated the development of smaller regional airports, making air transport services available to a larger number of people and stimulating regional economies, leading to their balanced growth.

The rapid development of civil aviation in Eastern Bloc countries to some extent copied the development model of deregulated Western markets (Graham, 1998). Since 2004, low-cost carriers have been the main driving force behind the changes (Francis et al., 2006; Fu et al., 2010). The immature market including, among other things, unused airports infrastructure and a relatively large potential demand, offered substantial growth opportunities to the new companies in Central and Eastern Europe. In particular, regional airports benefitted from the activity of low-cost carriers whose business model is focused on operating from regional airports, offering point-to-point routes and relatively low-fare air services (Hunter, 2006; Graham and Shaw, 2008; Dobruszkes, 2009).

There were changes to both the supply side and the demand side of air transport markets in CEE countries. The supply of air services increased, and the average air fare was reduced. This led to changes in the volume and structure of demand, as well as growth in the share of non-business travel (from 15 per cent in 2002 to 47 per cent in 2011 at Poznan Airport; Huderek-Glapska, 2011). Simultaneously, the changes in the demand were stimulated by external factors, including an opening of the labour market in Great Britain and Ireland, which caused large migration due to the high rate of unemployment in post-communist countries (Burrell, 2011; Dobruszkes, 2018).

Nowadays, after three decades of transformation of CEE countries into market economies, they are far from homogeneous, and both the level and growth of their economies differ across these countries. However, both the GDP growth and the increase in the air transport market in CEE countries far exceeds the EU average. According to Hamilton (2005), the internal factors such as population size and growth in income, as well as external factors such as economic openness and the ability to attract investment and tourism, affected the air traffic volume. Simultaneously, the dynamic growth in the air transport sector had an impact on the economy by creating short-term demand effects in terms of providing work places and contributing to GDP, as well as by affecting other sectors and the whole economy in the long term.

The relationships between economic development and the air transport market have been the subject of many studies (Button and Taylor, 2000; Brueckner, 2003; Green, 2007; Mukkala and Tervo, 2013; Allroggen and Malina, 2014). Their results, however, do not clearly indicate the direction and strength of these relationships, especially when applied to rapidly emerging new markets. Beyzatlar et al. (2014) argue that as long as a country does not complete the process of economic transition, the endogenous relationship between its GDP and transport sector activities is not observed. The lack of clear results regarding the impact of air transport activity on regional development in terms of the impact on employment growth and on incomes was observed in case studies on Poland (Cieslik, 2017) and Bulgaria (Todorova, 2017).

The aim of the chapter is to provide a brief overview of the relationship between economic performance and the situation in the air transport markets in the two groups within Central and Eastern European countries – namely the Visegard Group of Poland, the Czech Republic, Slovakia, and Hungary, and the Baltic states of Estonia, Latvia, and Lithuania – after the three decades of market transition. These groups of countries were chosen for analysis because of their long-term participation in one political-economic bloc, their geographical location, and most importantly, the simultaneous opening of their air transport markets when joining the European Union. The chapter is organised as follows: the socio-economic background of the CEE countries is presented in the next section; the air transport markets are described in the following section; then

124 *Sonia Huderek-Glapska*

the strengths and weaknesses, as well as opportunities and threats, of the CEE aviation markets are presented; and the conclusions regarding the relationship between regional development and aviation are drawn in the final section.

The economic performance of Central and Eastern European countries in 1990–2017

Compared to other developing economies, such as in Latin America, Africa, and parts of Asia, the macro region of post-socialist countries stands out mainly due to being located relatively close to highly developed economies (Germany, the United Kingdom, and France), a factor which stimulates the flow of people, goods and capital (Jankiewicz and Huderek-Glapska, 2016). This localisation creates possibilities regarding the movement of people for migration, work, and tourism (VF&R travel) purposes, facilitates the export and import of goods, and contributes to the inflow of direct investment.

The reforms implemented in the first years of market transformation in the Visegard Group of countries (Poland, the Czech Republic, Slovakia, and Hungary) were focused on cooperation and economic integration with Western Europe. The results of GDP dynamic analysis indicate four characteristic stages in the economic development of this group of Central and Eastern European countries (Jóźwik, 2016). The first stage covers the years 1989–1994, in which a recession caused by the transformation was observed. The second stage is the years 1994–2007, defined in the literature as a period of new economic growth in transformation countries. This growth was facilitated by the accession of CEE countries to the European Union. In 2004, all seven investigated Central and Eastern European countries, together with Slovenia, Malta, and Cyprus, joined the European Union and entered the single aviation market. Among them, Baltic countries and Slovakia joined the Eurozone between 2009 to 2015.

In the third stage of 2008–2009, an economic downturn returned, but this time resulting from a global economic crisis. Up until 2008, the process of European integration and rapid development in CEE countries continued and was implemented without inflationary pressures and with increasing employment levels. The global crisis, which reached its peak in 2008–2009, restrained the current impetus of international trade and forced individual countries into budget difficulties, particular with regards to the fiscal situation. The countries of Central and Eastern Europe, due to their strong trade and production integration with the Eurozone, were very much affected by these turbulences (Marczewski, 2018). The only European country that did not suffer a recession during the financial crisis was Poland, called a 'green island'. One of the main reasons for this was high foreign demand. International trade allowed the maintenance of positive GDP dynamics in Poland during the period 2008–2009 (Polanski, 2014). After the economic crisis, the fourth period of moderate economic growth arrived; however, there are warning signals that another recession is approaching.

Despite the difficulties as previously listed, the countries of the CEE region followed a path of growth in the years 2000–2017. Table 7.1 presents the

Table 7.1 Evolution of economic performance of CEE countries, 2000–2017

	GDP per capita (1,000s) (€)			FDI stock per capita ($)			Export (EUR) (mns)		
	2000	2010	2017	2000	2010	2017	2002	2010	2017
Czech Republic	6.5	15.0	18.2	2,103	12,196	14,453	40,706	100.311	161,214
Estonia	4.4	11.0	17.9	1,891	11,674	17,675	3,642	8,743	12,861
Latvia	3.6	8.4	13.8	709	5,161	8,839	2,417	7,191	12,371
Lithuania	3.6	8.9	14.8	667	4,291	6,081	5,537	15,651	26,411
Hungary	5.0	9.9	12.7	2,238	9,151	9,601	36,503	72,024	100,752
Poland	4.9	9.5	12.3	868	4,895	6,142	43,499	120,483	207,385
Slovakia	5.9	12.5	15.6	1,291	9,313	9,551	15,234	48,777	74,726

Sources: UNCTAD (2018)

Notes: GDP at current prices per capita; foreign direct investments: inward, at current prices per capita.

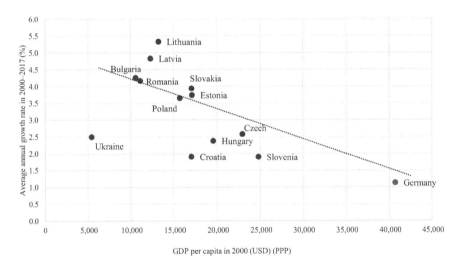

Figure 7.1 Convergence path of CEE countries and their neighbours in 2000–2017
Source: The Conference Board Total Economy Database (2018); Marczewski (2018)

macroeconomic overview of the economic situation of CEE countries in the years 2000–2017. Within the first two decades of the 21st century, the economies of Baltic states, measured by the GDP per capita, grew almost four times; and the Visegard Group of countries more than doubled their GDP per capita. However, compared with the developed economies of Western European regions, Central and Eastern European countries still lag behind them in terms of the level of GDP per capita. The most developed countries in Europe have a GDP per capita almost two times higher than countries in the CEE region.

The convergence process in CEE countries, expressed in the evolution of the level of GDP per capita in the years 2000–2017 (Figure 7.1), is characterised by

126   *Sonia Huderek-Glapska*

an inverse relationship between the level of GDP per capita and its growth rate. This situation can be explained by the theory of beta-convergence according to which the higher the initial level of GDP per capita in a given country, the lower the average long-term growth rate. Matkowski and Próchniak (2007) argue that economic convergence is closely related to international cooperation, including trade and capital flows, technology transfer, labour movements, increased competition, economies of scale, and policy coordination.

Apart from international trade, the level of foreign direct investments (FDIs) plays an important role in the growth of CEE countries (Smętkowski, 2018). The processes of transition into a market economy and integration with global markets have stimulated the growth of Western European and US outward direct investment in CEE countries. This growth was associated with the elimination of the barriers to FDIs, with the market potential and comparative advantages (i.e. low relative unit labour costs, corporate tax rates, skilled workforce) of CEE regions. Countries that have market potential and sound legal and economic environments (Poland, the Czech Republic, Hungary, Slovakia) have been successful in attracting FDIs, even though they have relatively high unit labour cost. However, in the cases of Bulgaria and Romania, the transition process was relatively slow, and combined with a risky economic environment, constituted obstacles for foreign investors.

Changes in privatisation policies into more foreign-oriented ones created a more favourable environment for FDIs. The stated findings from the work of Carstensen and Toubal (2004) were extended by the conclusion that integration with the European Union increases the market potential of CEE countries due to, inter alia, a reduction in the economically relevant distance to the EU that results in changes in transport costs. Smętkowski (2018) claims that accessibility, which either enables or facilitates the influx of inward capital and drives the export of local enterprises, plays an important role in achieving a high level of development in the post-socialist countries. Transport infrastructure and particular international airports give advantages to regions which, in effect, are more easily accessible from the better developed neighbouring countries and have an enhanced access to Western European markets.

Air transport as both the subject and driver of the process of transformation and integration of CEE countries

The evolution of the air transport markets in CEE countries was carried out within the framework shaped by the changes in their economic systems as a whole and by changes of a specific character in the air transport sector. The transformation that occurred in CEE countries economic systems were of a structural, functional, technical, technological, fiscal, economic, organisational, social, and spatial nature. These changes influenced the air transport sector and have impacted its efficiency. Before the market transition, the airports, airlines, and other entities operating in the air transport market were state owned, had a monopoly position, and enjoyed the right to budget subsidies. The airport

Table 7.2 The sources of inefficiencies in the transport sector in central planned economies

Guaranteed monopoly position
Preference for state ownership
Discrimination against private ownership
Regulation of transport activity by the administration
The use of fixed prices for services
Fixed asset expenditures being incorporated in the state budget
Central planning of infrastructure investments and transport rolling stock
The treatment of mass transport as a 'public service'
The granting of discriminatory subsidies to unprofitable transport services
The commitment of companies and transport users to use the services of national carriers
A ban on foreign capital having access to transport infrastructure

Source: Burnewicz and Bąk (2000)

infrastructure was centrally planned, and expenditures on fixed assets were incorporated in the state budget. There were no democratic procedures, the managers being appointed by the state authorities. The aim of the companies was to fulfil the plan instead of generating a profit. The trade unions were very strong, with their main goal being to provide the employees preferred level of employment instead of undertaking activities that would lead to a growth in productivity. The air transport market was strictly regulated, which caused high access barriers. There were supply shortages in the market, along with a low quality of services. The prices of those services were not shaped by market mechanism, and therefore there were no favourable conditions for the demand to increase. The sources of these inefficiencies are summarised in Table 7.2.

For the air transport sector in CEE countries, an inheritance from the past was its relatively well-developed airport infrastructure and state-owned national carriers having a market monopoly. In the 1990s, after introducing political and economic changes in the CEE region, the ownership, structural, and capital transformations of airports began. Almost all CEE airports were nationalised and fully publicly owned. However, the changes on the supply side of the air transport market were not enough to provide for its significant development. In the years 1990–2004, the air services developed slowly in CEE countries. The main obstacle was market regulation that prevented the appearance of competition. It was accession to the European Union and the resultant liberalisation of the air transport sector that brought about dynamic changes in the air transport markets of CEE countries. The fundamental source of development of air services was the activity of low-cost carriers, which broke the monopoly established by national carriers, thereby increasing competition on the air transport market (Dobruszkes, 2009; Gabor, 2010; Bjelicic, 2013; Pijet-Migoń, 2017; Červinka, 2017). The immature markets of CEE countries offered substantial potential for new companies to grow. The catalysts for the development of low-cost carriers included, among other factors, large potential demand, the increasing wealth of the countries, and unused airport infrastructure. The main features of the new air travel business model were operating from regional

128   Sonia Huderek-Glapska

Table 7.3 Air transport in CEE countries, 2004–2017

	Number of passengers (mns)			Air cargo (1,000s tonnes)			PAX per capita
	2004	2010	2017	2004	2010	2017	2017
Czech	10.15	12.43	16.36	57.47	65.53	89.33	1.5
Estonia	0.99	1.38	2.64	5.00	11.89	11.23	2.0
Latvia	1.06	4.67	6.10	8.33	11.27	21.20	3.1
Lithuania	1.45[a]	2.33	5.25	9.54[a]	9.76	20.29	1.8
Hungary	6.38	8.17	13.38	61.27	65.30	87.28	1.4
Poland	6.09	18.43	37.73	30.23	61.39	117.30	1.0
Slovakia	1.12	1.89	2.43	8.19	17.83	27.19	0.4
Total CEE_7	27.25	49.31	83.89	180.03	242.97	373.83	1.2
Total EUROPE[b]	944.44	1,141.99	1,595.36	12,378.12	15 133.92	18,571.73	3.0
Share of CEE_7	2.9%	4.3%	5.3%	1.5%	1.6%	2.0%	–

Source: EUROSTAT (2018)

[a] Data for 2005.
[b] Europe including: EU28, Iceland, Switzerland and Norway.

airports, point-to-point routes, and relatively low fares for air services (Hunter, 2006; Graham and Shaw, 2008; Dobruszkes, 2009), which led to very significant changes in the air transport sector of post-communist countries.

Among the analysed CEE countries, the largest ones in terms of area and population are Poland, Hungary, and the Czech Republic. These countries experienced the greatest increase in the number of passengers handled (Table 7.3), which confirms the view that the potential of a country is an important factor determining the air transport volume (Hamilton, 2005). Regarding income, CEE countries up until now have not reached the level of development of Western Europe, and their GDP per capita is much below the EU average – with Poland and Hungary having the lowest GDP per capita of all CEE countries (Table 7.1). Smyth and Pearce (2008) claim that the income elasticity in developing countries on short- and medium-haul routes is 2.0, as compared to a 1.4 for developed markets. This could be interpreted that in the first group of countries income growth stimulates the development of air traffic volume much more than in the second group. Indeed, the large potential of the economies in CEE countries and the low initial volume of air traffic led to substantial growth in aviation markets. As a result of LCC expansion and the increased activity of network carriers, the number of passengers carried in CEE countries tripled between 2004 and 2017, from 27 million to 84 million (Table 7.3). After accession to the European Union, the air traffic growth rate in CEE countries was the highest in the world. Until 2008, all the air transport markets of CEE countries continued their paths of growth (Figure 7.2).

In 2009, aviation experienced a breakdown in the trend of growth due to the global economic crisis. Latvia was the only country which, despite the slowdown in the economy, reported an increase in air traffic. The reason for

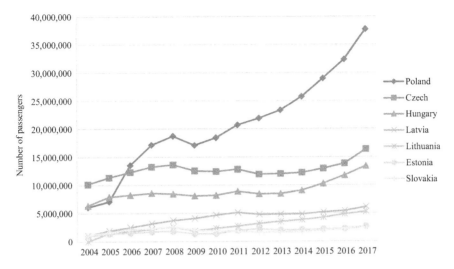

Figure 7.2 The paths of growth of air transport in CEE countries, 2004–2017
Source: EUROSTAT (2018)

this was the activities of airBaltic, the flag carrier of the Latvian state (80 per cent shareholding in 2017) with its hub in Riga. The hub strategy of airBaltic was successful and absorbed the impact of the economic crisis for Latvia. Riga airport dynamics became less related to the local economic situation and more related to the economies of the regions and cities connected through the hub (Dobruszkes and Van Hamme, 2011). However, in 2010, airBaltic struggled with ownership, management, and financial problems and, as a result, cancelled flights and temporarily dismissed nearly half of its employees. After receiving financial support from the Latvian state, making changes in management, and having implemented a cost-cutting strategy, airBaltic returned to profitability in 2014. Since then the airline – and, as a result, Riga airport and the air transport market in Latvia – has followed a path of steady growth.

The situation in the air transport market is, to some extent, related to the performance of the flag carrier. The downturn in air traffic development in Hungary in 2012 was the result of the collapse of its national carrier Malev. The Hungarian airline ceased operations in 2012 due to its financial problems caused by, among other things, years of ineffective management and state ownership (Akbar et al., 2014). Although low-cost carriers, namely Wizz Air and Ryanair, replaced key routes offered by Malev, Budapest Airport was not able to recover its transfer market. The fierce competition from low-cost carriers, as well as financial problems, led to the collapse of two other flag carriers in CEE countries. Slovak Airlines, the national carrier of Slovakia, ceased operations in 2007; and Lithuanian Airlines went bankrupt in 2009. Estonian Air, the former flag carrier of Estonia, entered a process of liquidation in 2015 after an announcement by the European Union that the government funding received by the airline was illegal. At the same time, the Estonian government established the Nordic Aviation Group and new airline Nordica.

In 2016, the Polish flag carrier LOT, owned by the Polish state, bought 49 per cent of Nordica shares. Earlier, in 2014, LOT had been supported with €200 million of financial aid provided by the Polish government. In this case, the European Commission approved a government bailout under the condition that LOT would give up routes and slots at certain airports to ensure that competition in the market was not disturbed. LOT expanded rapidly from the moment when the EU lifted restrictions on the carrier's network growth. In 2017, LOT carried 8.5 million passengers, compared with 5.8 million passengers carried in 2014. The good condition of Poland's national airline was the reason for the Polish government to establish Polish Aviation Group. In the autumn of 2018, LOT Polish Airlines, the flag carrier of Poland; LOTAMS and LS Technics, aircraft maintenance services providers; and LSAS, the ground-handling agency, were integrated into the state-controlled company created to consolidate state assets of the aviation market and to strengthen the Polish position as a regional leader in the sector.

Re-evaluations of the aviation value chain, changes in the structure of the air transport market, and increased competition between carriers led to national airlines reshaping their strategies. Airlines are looking for strategies that will allow them to operate in conditions of uncertainty and growing competition. One of these strategies is the integration of market cooperation. Effective consolidation by enterprises fosters the development and improvement of cooperation, sharing markets while operating in a competitive environment.

Western Europe is basically divided between three large airline groups (IAG, Air France/KLM, Lufthansa), but the CEE aviation market remains very fragmented (Figure 7.3). The biggest airline in the CEE region is Wizz Air, a privately owned low-cost carrier operating a fleet of around 100 Airbus aircraft and serving more than 550 routes. In 2017, Wizz Air transported on board its aircraft about 23.8 million passengers and made a profit of €246 million (Table 7.4). The strategy of Wizz Air is not only focused on its home market in Hungary, as the carrier is expanding its network and connectivity between Eastern and Western Europe rather than developing connectivity within CEE region countries. The largest country pairs in the CEE region in terms of capacity in numbers of one-way seats offered in 2016 were: Poland-UK (3.9 million seats), Poland-Germany (2.7 million seats), Poland-Norway (1.2 million seats), Hungary-Germany (1.1 million seats), Hungary-UK (1.1 million seats), Czech Republic-UK (1.1 million seats), Poland-Italy (1 million seats) and Czech Republic-Germany (0.8 million seats) (Anna Aero, 2016). The distribution of air routes in CEE countries is dominated by the connections between Eastern and Western Europe.

LOT Polish Airlines is focused on expanding its network in the CEE region. Poland, with a considerable and increasing domestic market, has created an

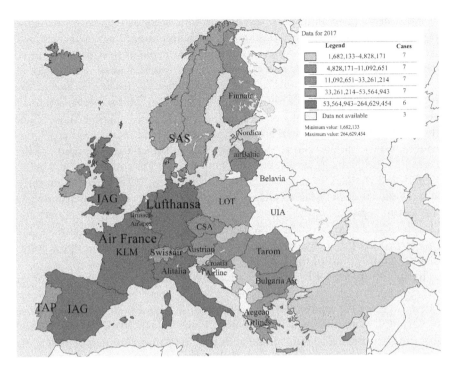

Figure 7.3 Air passengers by country and main European network airlines in 2017
Source: EUROSTAT (2018)

Table 7.4 Main airlines in CEE countries

Airline (alliance)	Country of origin	Year of establishing	Fleet in services (orders)	Passengers (mn) (2017)	Revenues (mn €) (2017)	Net profit (mn €) (2017)
LOT (Star Alliance)	Poland	1929	72 (13)	8.5	1,123	83
CSA (Sky Team)	Czech Republic	1923	17 (13)	2.9	n.a.	9 (2016)
Wizz Air	Hungary	2003	104 (265)	23.8	1,571	246
airBaltic	Latvia	1995	36 (30)	3.5	348	4.6
Nordica (Star Alliance)	Estonia	2015	13 (9)	0.6	83	0.9

Source: airBaltic (2018), CSA (2018), LOT (2018), Nordica (2018), Wizz Air (2018)

opportunity for the airline to grow. Warsaw, like Prague and Budapest, is favourably located to become a hub for a medium-sized carrier. However, Prague and Budapest would need a strong network airline in order to develop its transfer market. The Czech flag carrier CSA has about 18 per cent share of seats at Prague Airport, compared with 40 per cent LOT market share at Warsaw airport and almost 50 per cent airBaltic share at Riga airport. As the third carrier in the CEE region in terms of the number of passengers carried, airBaltic has very ambitious plans to develop and triple its fleet despite limited demand from Baltic states and the northern geographical location of Riga.

In the period of 2016–2017, LOT was the fastest-growing airline in the region, mainly due to the lifting of the EU restrictions and air services renewals after network limitations related to the EU financial support rules. Since that time, LOT expanded its network and introduced, among others, long-haul flights to Asia and North America which enhanced the integration of the region to the global aviation industry. Due to capacity constraints at Warsaw airport and the lack of national carrier in Hungary, LOT started to develop and rebuild, after the Malev collapse, the transfer market in Budapest, offering services to regional capitals (Warsaw, Prague, Belgrade, Sofia, Bucharest) and long-haul flights to Seoul and New York. Apart from the high business and tourist potential in point-to-point traffic, European routes also supply long-distance connections to the United States and South Korea.

In the future, the CEE network airline market needs to consolidate in order to face the competition from low-cost carriers. Currently the biggest low-cost carrier in the CEE region is Ryanair, having the largest low-cost market share in Poland, Latvia, Lithuania and Slovakia (Table 7.5). In 2013, Ryanair for the first time became the leading airline in Poland in terms of number of passengers carried. The substantial potential of CEE countries has also been recognised by Western network carriers. Lufthansa has been present in the CEE region for decades and is gradually increasing its share in CEE air transport markets, thus feeding its hubs in Frankfurt and Munich. KLM, Air France and SAS are progressively interested in operating at CEE aviation market and are thus gradually opening new routes from CEE airports.

The year 2017 was very successful for all air transport markets in CEE countries. The growth rate in air traffic expressed in the number of passengers was twice as high in CEE countries (14 per cent) compared to Western Europe (7 per cent) in the period 2016/2017. The highest increases were registered in Estonia and the Czech Republic (19 per cent), ahead of Poland (17 per cent)

Table 7.5 The share of LCCs in low-cost markets in CEE countries

Country	LCC number 1 (%)		LCC number 2 (%)		LCC number 3 (%)	
Poland	Ryanair	51.6	Wizz Air	39.5	easyjet	4.1
Czech Republic	easyjet	28.0	Ryanair	19.5	Wizz Air	12.2
Hungary	Wizz Air	49.3	Ryanair	25.8	easyjet	8.5
Latvia	Ryanair	57.1	Wizz Air	29.3	Norwegian	13.4
Lithuania	Ryanair	53.2	Wizz Air	42.3	Norwegian	4.2
Slovakia	Ryanair	75.3	Wizz Air	20.9	Flydubai	3.7

Source: Wizz Air Holdings Plc (2017)

Air transport in Central/Eastern Europe 133

and Hungary (15 per cent) (Eurostat, 2018). Nevertheless, the air travel mobility indicator (passengers per capita) in CEE countries is still low (Table 7.3). This means that there is still a large potential for air traffic growth in CEE countries, and it could be expected that within a few decades, the number of passengers carried by air will reach 200 million in the CEE region. As for now, the share of CEE countries in the European passenger air transport market is 5.3 per cent.

The share of air cargo in CEE countries, in relation to the total volume of goods and mail transported by air in Europe, is even lower than the share of CEE countries in the European passenger market and is only 2 per cent. There are factors in both the demand and supply side of CEE economies that affects this situation. On the demand side, there is the structure of economies and export possibilities in CEE countries. Although the goods exported in the years 2000–2017 increased significantly in CEE countries (Table 7.1), this is still below the EU average and includes products of a type and value that do not require air transport. Currently, CEE countries are not specialised in the export of high-value or time-sensitive commodities. International trade is driven mainly by large companies with a dominant role of foreign capital (NBP, 2014). In CEE countries, the share of exports is significantly higher among companies from the industrial sector than those from the service or agriculture sectors. The exports of CEE countries are, to a large extent, focused on EU markets, while in Western Europe, the important cargo markets are the United States and Asia, which require long-haul flights. On the supply side of the air transport market, the factor that hinders the development of air cargo is the dominance of low-cost carriers which offer limited or no cargo capacity. Furthermore, Slovakia and the Baltic states suffer from not enough interest of network carriers in developing air cargo services. However, Estonia and Latvia are trying to benefit from their favourable location near the East and are trying to attract air freight services in order to increase cargo flows from the East.

The largest airports in CEE countries (Warsaw, Prague, and Budapest) have wide catchment areas and may serve as cargo hubs for the whole region. Warsaw airport is extending its cargo infrastructure further and is implementing a long-term cargo development strategy in order to retain existing customers and capture new ones from mainly road feeder services. The main partner in implementing this strategy is LOT, which has introduced new long-haul routes with wide-body aircraft to North America and Asia, thus significantly enhancing belly hold cargo capacity. However, Warsaw airport suffers from restrictions in its night-time operations which could hinder the development of air cargo. Budapest Airport is recovering with plans of cargo development after the collapse of Malev. Turkish Cargo and Emirates are offering cargo services from Budapest to the East, and modern infrastructure offers new possibilities in the shipment of goods. Freighters such as DHL have been given incentives in order to use Budapest as their Central and Eastern Europe parcel hub. Prague is increasing its accessibility through improving highway links with southern Germany and eastern Czech Republic. Czech Airlines cargo services are developing steadily. Considering the significant dynamics of cargo movements in recent years, plans for cargo development at airports, the strengthening of LOT's position in cargo transport, and improvements in the macroeconomic situation of CEE regions, it could be expected that cargo movements will increase at airports. However, CEE airports are subject to fierce competition from western cargo hubs located in Germany (i.e. Leipzig/Halle) and Austria (Vienna).

Analysing the changes in the performance of air transport markets (Figure 7.2), CEE countries can be divided into three groups. The first group includes small countries: Latvia, Lithuania, Estonia, and Slovakia. The second group encompasses the Czech Republic and Hungary. Poland, in the third group, clearly stands out and is the leader in terms of passenger volume. The high level of air traffic in Poland results from various factors related to the potential of the country. One of them is the size of the market. The airport system in Poland is relatively well developed. Poland had 15 active airports in 2017 that handle international civil air traffic with scheduled passenger services compared to the Czech Republic (five active airports in 2017), Hungary (two), Slovakia (three), Lithuania (four), Estonia (one), and Latvia (one) (Table 7.6). The high level of airport density in Poland results from the wide area they serve, as Poland is more than three times larger than Hungary in terms of land coverage. The second reason for high air traffic is the size of the population, and particularly the high demand generated by work migration. The opening of job markets in the UK, Ireland, Scandinavia, and Germany for workers from Eastern Europe, together with relatively low income and a high unemployment rate, stimulated the movement of people. Low-cost carriers took advantage of this situation and by offering low fares together with a dense air network generated high demand for air services.

Compared with Western Europe, Central and Eastern European airports have few long-haul connections. At Prague and Budapest, long-haul connectivity is mainly provided by foreign carriers from Asia and North America. China Eastern Airlines, Hainan, Korean Air Lines, and Sichuan Airlines offer direct flights from Asia to Prague. This is mainly the result of the increasing importance of Prague as a tourism destination. The potential for Asian direct flights in other CEE countries is gradually being exploited by LOT that has offered new routes to the Far East from Warsaw and Budapest. Long-haul transatlantic regular routes are provided by LOT and American Airlines, accompanied by United Airlines and Air Canada with seasonal traffic.

Regional airports in CEE countries are dynamically increasing their output due to the expansion of low-cost carriers. However, the geographical distribution of low-cost traffic between airports is uneven. Low-cost traffic is concentrated in central airports and in major regional airports that are located in economically strong regions with high potential demand for air services (Huderek-Glapska and Nowak, 2016). According to Barbot (2006), the ability of a low-cost carrier to generate high passenger traffic at an airport strengthens the bargaining power of airlines and causes an imbalance in airport-airline

Air transport in Central/Eastern Europe 135

Table 7.6 Air passengers by airport in CEE countries, 2017

Country	Airport[a]	Number of passengers	Average growth rate[b] (2013–2017)	Revenue per pax (EUR)
Poland	Warsaw	15,757,010	0.10	14.1
Czech	Prague	15,434,019	0.09	18.1
Hungary	Budapest	13,061,494	0.12	20.3
Latvia	Riga	6,097,556	0.06	8.7
Poland	Krakow	5,830,002	0.13	10.0
Poland	Gdansk	4,602,012	0.13	8.7
Poland	Katowice	3,899,831	0.11	8.9
Lithuania	Vilnius	3,763,103	0.09	6.3
Poland	Modlin	2,931,503	0.71	5.3
Poland	Wroclaw	2,817,347	0.10	15.7
Estonia	Tallinn	2,636,856	0.08	11.4
Slovakia	Bratislava	1,950,240	0.10	14.6
Poland	Poznan	1,842,496	0.09	9.4
Lithuania	Kaunas	1,184,022	0.14	6.3
Poland	Rzeszow	691,706	0.04	20.8
Poland	Szczecin	578,442	0.16	6.2
Slovakia	Kosice	505,472	0.21	22.6
Czech	Brno	476,357	−0.01	16.4
Poland	Lublin	428,902	0.23	13.7
Czech	Ostrava	336,298	0.04	27.4
Poland	Bydgoszcz	328,533	−0.01	16.5
Hungary	Debrecen	318,342	0.25	16.7
Lithuania	Palanga	302,672	0.24	6.3
Poland	Lodz	207,377	−0.12	18.3
Poland	Olsztyn	101,306	–	n.a.
Czech	Pardubice	87,741	−0.17	n.a.
Slovakia	Poprad	80,605	0.35	n.a.
Czech	Karlovy Vary	21,258	−0.33	n.a.
Poland	Zielona Góra	17,128	0.21	n.a.
Poland	Radom	9,903	–	n.a.
Lithuania	Siauliai	712	–	n.a.

Sources: Eurostat (2018), Civil Aviation Authority in Poland (2018), Airports financial statements.

[a] International civil airports with scheduled traffic in 2017.
[b] Growth rate is measured by the changes in the number of passangers handled.

relations. This has an impact on the financial situation of airports. Airports that serve fewer than one million passengers per year – arguably the average threshold for an airport's ability to cover its operational costs – are in a difficult situation. Network carriers may not be interested in operating from small airports; therefore, there is a need to search for other strategies like establishing contracts with low-cost carriers, even at the cost of providing them with financial support in offering air services (Červinka, 2017). According to Kazda et al. (2017), small airports may have problems in becoming profitable not only due to low passenger volumes, but also because other sources of income from non-aeronautical services are limited. The small international airports in Slovakia

(Sliac, Zilina, Piestany), Hungary (Heviz-Balaton, Gyor-Per, Pecs-Pogany), Poland (Radom, Zielona Góra), Latvia (Liepaja, Ventspils), and Estonia (Tartu, Kuressaare, Kardla, Parnu) struggle with a lack of regular flights. Unsuccessful attempts to generate air traffic are continually being carried out by both scheduled and charter airlines; however, the results are that the routes are being discontinued due to low demand.

Table 7.6 presents the airports in CEE countries that handled scheduled passenger traffic in 2017. The largest in terms of the number of passengers are Warsaw and Prague (15 million passengers each), Budapest (13 million passengers), and Riga (6 million passengers). Half of the active airports in CEE countries served more than one million passengers in 2017. This group of airports had stable development with an average annual growth rate of 15 per cent in the period 2013–2017. More volatile development was observed among a group of small airports. Some of them experienced substantial growth and more than doubled the number of passengers they served during 2013–2017 (Kosice, Lublin, Debrecen, Planga, Poprad), while others (Lodz, Pardubice, Karlovy Vary) lost traffic due to route closures.

During the period 2013–2017, a significant number of route openings and closures in CEE countries was observed. There are a number of reasons for such disruptions in air routes: variability of demand, structural changes in the low-cost carrier network (i.e. focusing on primary rather than secondary airports by Ryanair), the characteristics of the low-cost business model related to maximising route-related profits (de Wit and Zuidberg, 2016), and the impact of increasing competition between airports. Lodz is located in the catchment area of Warsaw airport, while Pardubice and Karlovy Vary are near Prague, so their location may be an advantage in terms of being close to a densely populated and wealthy agglomeration. However, airlines may prefer to operate from central airports due to greater demand, among other things (Dobruszkes et al., 2017).

The largest airports in CEE countries in terms of the number of passengers handled, namely Prague, Warsaw, and Budapest, have relatively high revenue per passenger ratios. The level of revenues at the airport depends on different factors such as the level of airport charges, the structure of air traffic and the range of non-aviation services. The financial situation of an airport is also influenced by the phase of the investment life cycle. The vast majority of airports in CEE countries have carried out infrastructure investments in order to meet the needs of airlines and ground-handling agencies, and to respond to the increasing demand for air services. The accession to the EU enabled airport owners and managers to apply for EU funds in order to co-fund their infrastructural projects. In particular, growing air traffic has led to problems with capacity at various airports. According to Augustyniak et al. (2015), the series of investment carried out in Polish airports doubled or tripled technical efficiency. Moreover, the EU subsidies positively influenced the financial situation by both decreasing capital costs and by increasing other revenues.

Despite ongoing investment in infrastructure, the growing traffic has led to development constraints at airports. Prague and Budapest are struggling with passenger terminal capacity limits. In addition, Warsaw is operating close to its runway and terminal capacity, with almost no possibility to significantly develop its infrastructure due to environmental constraints. This lack of potential for future growth may hinder not only the development of Warsaw airport, but also the Polish flag carrier LOT. Therefore, there are plans to build a new central airport in close proximity to Warsaw that can serve as a hub for Central and Eastern Europe.

Analysis of air transport markets in CEE countries

Close proximity to developed economies constitutes an advantage for CEE countries in terms of stimulating the flow of people, goods, and capital, but on the other hand may cause fierce competition between air transport markets. Airports located in Berlin, Vienna, and Frankfurt will compete for passengers and cargo with Polish, Czech Republic, Slovak, and Hungarian airports. That is why Poles fly from Berlin Airports; Czechs from Frankfurt Airport; and Slovaks from Vienna Airport; the result being the so-called neighbourhood effect at a national scale (Jankiewicz and Huderek-Glapska, 2016). As a consequence of integration of countries, the national character of the airport has become less important. Passengers consider the total time and cost of travel in their decision of airport choice. Therefore, increasing accessibility of an airport is an essential step in the process of enhancing growth at the airport.

Public ownership is a favourable factor that can enhance the decision about opening an airport and attracting air carriers. All CEE airports, except for Budapest, are publicly owned. The development and adaptation of airport infrastructure to accommodate growing air traffic has been accelerated by the funding possibilities from EU funds. However, some aviation development projects did not have the required economic justification due to insufficient demographic and economic potential, or the threat of distortion of competition in the market. The tightening by the EU of the criteria for receiving funds for aviation infrastructure development made it possible to reduce uncertainty in economic investments. Some airports which received financial assistance face the threat of having to return it due to their failure to achieve the assumed operational volume. The issue of constructing reliable forecasts for developing air traffic in an uncertain and dynamically changing environment is difficult; however, it is important for funding purposes and for the process of building strategy of an airport.

The starting point for the process of building a strategy for the development of air transport markets in CEE countries is the recognition of internal and external factors affecting the activities in the air transport market. One of the techniques used to identify these factors is strengths, weakness, opportunities, and threats (SWOT) analysis. Despite the heterogeneity of air transport in CEE countries, an attempt has been made to gather both internal and external factors, discussed previously, that are favourable and unfavourable for the development of aviation in the CEE region within the framework of a SWOT analysis (Table 7.7).

138 *Sonia Huderek-Glapska*

Table 7.7 SWOT analysis of the air transport markets in CEE countries

Strengths	Weakness
• Well-developed modern airport infrastructure • Low production costs (labour, capital) compared to Western Europe • Favourable location – between Western Europe, Asia, and the Middle East; close to well-developed markets (Western Europe) and close to markets with good potential (Middle East, Asia) • Growing strengths of air carriers (LOT, airBaltic, Travel Services) • Plans for the construction of a central airport in Poland which is to become a transfer hub for CEE	• Further expansion of low-cost carriers (Ryanair, Wizz Air, easyJet) and the growth of their bargaining power in relations with airports; the increase in competition in the CEE aviation market • Publicly owned airports and potential for low operational efficiency • Polarisation in the development of airports • Fragmented air services market • Lack of feeder airline at airports in Budapest and Bratislava • Competition from Western Europe carriers (mainly Lufthansa) and airports (Berlin, Frankfurt) • Air network focused on routes between CEE and Western Europe • Increasing environmental costs that constrain air transport development
Opportunities	Threats
• Very high potential of CEE countries for the growth of air services • Growing role of CEE countries as tourism destinations and the phenomena of 'overtourism' in well-developed countries which may led to shifts in trips to less crowded attractive places in CEE countries • Growing demand in new, neighbouring markets – Ukraine and Belarus • Changes in consumer trends in terms of mobility, frequency of using transport services, and the method of organising the journey and stay • Changes in passenger structure – a growing share of passengers flying for non-business reasons • Growing ease in air travel (mainly due to expansion of low-cost carriers) • Changes in the value chain of aviation, more intense cooperation between airports, airlines, ground-handling agents, and other companies operating in the air transport market • New fuel options	• Signs of world economic recession and unfavourable macroeconomic indicators (exchange rate, inflation, increasing labour cost) both globally and in CEE countries • Brexit – threats of decreases in the number of passengers carried by air due to high passenger flows from CEE to UK resulting from work migration • Growing social unrest which makes it necessary to incur additional costs related to strengthening security • Decreasing source of financial possibilities from European Union funds • Changes in aviation fuel prices

Source: Author assessment

In the coming decades, it can be expected that there will be further development of air transport markets in the CEE region, mainly due to the high economic potential of CEE countries and the immature aviation markets. This potential can be exploited to some extent by CEE airlines if they gain competitive advantage alone or through strategic partnerships. Airports, in order to handle the increased number of passengers, will need to invest in their infrastructure. The development of each airport should be planned within the whole airport system at national and international levels with the consideration of social costs. Likewise, the challenge is also to provide appropriate airspace capacity to accommodate growing demand from airspace users.

Conclusion

The transformation of CEE economies from centrally managed to market-driven, initiated at the end of the 20th century, led to gradual changes in air transport markets at the beginning of this process. The political transformation of countries in their initial phase did not introduce a competition mechanism and did not establish rules allowing for a free pricing system. Therefore, it did not contribute to improvements in the quality and availability of air services. The most visible change at this period was the commercialisation of regional airports.

It was only the institutional change, namely the political and legal factors resulting from the accession of CEE countries to the European Union in 2004, that determined the profound changes and directions of the air transport markets. The liberalisation process opened up aviation markets in CEE countries and stimulated the internationalisation of air transport activities. The potential of CEE countries in terms of population and growing economies has been released, the supply of air services has been boosted with substantial energy, demand has responded to the increased offer, the average fare has dropped, and the quality and availability of air services have improved. Airports have diversified their sources of revenue from their activities and expanded their product portfolios. As a result, changes in the behaviour of consumers and companies have occurred, complementary markets have been developed, and technical and technological progress has been accelerated. The transformation of the air transport market has been conducted bi-directionally through internal changes involving launching a market-based mechanism and stabilising its functionality, and external changes that aim to establish an institutional framework for cooperation on a regional, national and international scale.

In line with liberalisation processes, public authorities have withdrawn from many pre-existing rules and practices in the field of air transport and have instead introduced rules based on market principles. However, the public sector is still present in the air transport market in CEE countries. As a result of the commercialisation of airports, regional and local authorities have become shareholders in regional airports. Local government authorities have supported initiatives for infrastructure development in the region, being aware of the interdependencies between regional development and air transport activities. Apart from the involvement of local government authorities in financing or co-financing of investments in airport infrastructure, they have also supported the development of air transport networks through the use of marketing fees for air carriers, or promoting the airport and the region internationally. At the national level, state authorities have supported activities focused on the development of a national airport and carrier resulting from their ownership (except for Budapest Airport and Wizz Air in the CEE region).

After a decade of liberalisation, a polarisation in the development of airports has emerged. Airports located in economically strong regions are intensifying their activities, while other small ones are operating on the edge of profitability. In this area, the role of government should be visible. It is necessary to strengthen the role of the state in strategic airport infrastructure planning. Designing a strategy for the development of the air transport market and the airport system requires an analysis of the entire system's dynamics in terms of assessing the efficiency of the airport network at the national and international level, including the current and future transport needs of the country. The airport network development model should take into account the balanced and sustainable development of regions and the equal accessibility to air transport services for the whole society, as well as the compatibility of airport infrastructure with the existing and planned networks of road and rail. National strategies for the development of the airport infrastructure network should be coordinated at the international level in the case of the analysed countries, not only within the CEE region but also with neighbouring countries.

Air transport liberalisation accelerated the transformation and integration processes of CEE countries, not only in the field of air transport markets, but also through the development of whole economies. The air transport sector can stimulate the process of transformation and integration of CEE countries. The growth in aviation led to the increase in mobility of people, had an impact on tourism traffic, and affected the inflow of goods. In the first decade of the 21st century, the growth of economies in CEE countries was driven by the external consumption. Now the challenge is to shift towards endogenous factors – growth driven by investment and productivity improvement – so as to ensure sustainable growth and convergence with EU income and productivity in their economies (Radosevic and Ciampi Stancova, 2018). In the catching-up process, firm actions are of crucial importance. Regardless of a country's level of economic development or its progress along the transition path, the decisions of individual firms have a profound impact on the efficiency and productivity not only of the business they run, but of the whole economy (EBRD, 2014). In this sense, the aviation sector can stimulate the endogenous factors growth. In the long run, the development of the air transport market will have an impact on investments, location decision of enterprises, and technology transfer, and an impact on labour supply and on productivity by increasing the mobility of production resources and more efficient allocation.

While generalising the issues discussed in this chapter, it should be emphasised that they constitute a basis for further analysis of the functioning and development of air transport markets in CEE countries by taking into account the diversity of the individual air transport markets and the economies in which they operate.

Note

1 The definitions of Central and Eastern European countries are heterogeneous in various studies. The reasons for this are the differences in terms of geographical, historical, political, socio-cultural, and economic factors. Among Central and Eastern European countries, one can distinguish the Baltic States (Estonia, Lithuania, and Latvia); the Visegard Group countries (the Czech Republic, Poland, Slovakia, and Hungary); the Balkan States (Bulgaria, Croatia, Romania, and Slovenia); Balkan countries that are not members of the European Union (Albania, Bosnia and Herzegovina, Montenegro, Kosovo, Macedonia, and Serbia); and former republics of the Soviet Union that are not members of the European Union (Belarus, Moldova, Russia, and Ukraine) (Jóźwik, 2016).

References

airBaltic (2018). *Basic company information* [Online]. Available at: https://www.airbaltic.com/en/basic-company-information (accessed 4 November 2018).

Akbar, Y., Nemeth, A. and Niemeier, H. (2014). Here we go again . . . the permanently failing organization: An application to the airline industry in Eastern Europe. *Journal of Air Transport Management*, 35, 1–11.

Allroggen, F. and Malina, R. (2014). Do the regional growth effects of air transport differ among airports? *Journal of Air Transport Management*, 37(1), 1–4.

Anna Aero (2016). *Wizz Air and Ryanair are the biggest and fastest-growing airlines in Central Europe; Poland-UK remains biggest country pair*. Available at: www.anna.aero/2016/11/23/wizz-air-and-ryanair-dominate-in-central-europe/ (accessed 23 November 2018).

Augustyniak, W., López-Torres, L. and Kalinowski, S. (2015). Performance of Polish regional airports after accessing the European Union: Does liberalisation impact on airports' efficiency? *Journal of Air Transport Management*, 43, 11–19.

Barbot, C. (2006). Low-cost airlines, secondary airports, and state aid: An economic assessment of the Ryanair – Charleroi airport agreement. *Journal of Air Transport Management*, 12(4), 197–203.

Beyzatlar, M., Karacal, M. and Yetkiner, H. (2014). Granger-causality between transportation and GDP: A panel data approach. *Transportation Research Part A*, 63(1), 43–55.

Bjelicic, B. (2013). Low cost carriers in Eastern Europe. In Gross, S. and Luck, S. (eds) *The low cost carrier worldwide*. Farnham, Ashgate.

Brueckner, J. (2003). Airline traffic and urban economic development. *Urban Studies*, 40(8), 1455–1469.

Burnewicz, J. and Bąk, M. (2000). Transport in economies in transition. In Polak, J. B. and Heertje, A. (eds) *Analytical transport economics*. Cheltenham, Edward Elgar Publishing.

Burrell, K. (2011). Going steerage on Ryanair: Cultures of migrant air travel between Poland and the UK. *Journal of Transport Geography*, 19(5), 1023–1030.

Button, K. and Taylor, S. (2000). International air transportation and economic development. *Journal of Air Transport Management*, 6(4), 209–222.

Carstensen, K. and Toubal, F. (2004). Foreign direct investment in Central and Eastern European countries: A dynamic panel analysis. *Journal of Comparative Economics*, 32(1), 3–22.

Červinka, M. (2017). Small regional airport performance and low cost carrier operations. *Transportation Research Procedia*, 28, 51–58.

Cieslik, A. (2017). *The role of airports for regional economic development: Evidence from Poland.* 21st Air Transport Research Society World Conference, University of Antwerp, Antwerp.

Civil Aviation Authority in Poland (2018). *Statistics and analysis of Air transport market* [Online]. Available at: https://www.ulc.gov.pl/en/market-regulation/statictics-and-analysis-of-air-transport-market (accessed 2 November 2018).

The Conference Board Total Economy Database (2018). *Data* [Online]. Available at: https://www.conference-board.org/data/economydatabase/total-economy-database-productivity (accessed 15 July 2018).

CSA (2018). *About us* [Online]. Available at: https://www.csa.cz/pl-en/about-us/ (accessed 4 November 2018).

de Wit, J. G. and Zuidberg, J. (2016). Route churn: An analysis of low-cost carrier route continuity in Europe. *Journal of Transport Geography*, 50, 57–67.

Dobruszkes, F. (2009). New Europe, new low-cost air services. *Journal of Transport Geography*, 17(6), 423–432.

Dobruszkes, F. (2018). Air services at risk: The threat of a hard Brexit at the airport level. *Environment and Planning A: Economy and Space*, 51(1), 3–7.

Dobruszkes, F., Givoni, M. and Vowles, T. (2017). Hello major airports, goodbye regional airports? Recent changes in European and US low-cost airline airport choice. *Journal of Air Transport Management*, 59, 50–62.

Dobruszkes, F. and Van Hamme, G. (2011). The impact of the current economic crisis on the geography of air traffic volumes: An empirical analysis. *Journal of Transport Geography*, 19(6), 1387–1398.

EBRD (2014). *Transition report: Innovation in transition* [Online]. Available at: www.ebrd.com/news/publications/transition-report/transition-report-2014.html (accessed 14 October 2018).

EUROSTAT (2018). *Air transport* [Online]. Available at: https://ec.europa.eu/eurostat/databrowser/view/ttr00012/default/table?lang=en (accessed 10 October 2018).

Francis, G., Dennis, N., Ison, S., Humphreys, I. and Aicken, M. (2006). Where next for low cost airlines? A spatial and temporal comparative study. *Journal of Transport Geography*, 14(2), 83–94.

Fu, X., Oum, T. and Zhang, A. (2010). Air transport liberalization and its impacts on airline competition and air passenger traffic. *Transportation Journal,* 49(4), 24–41.

Gabor, D. (2010). Low-cost airlines in Europe: Network structures after the enlargement of the European Union. *Geographica Pannonica*, 14(2), 49–58.

Graham, B. (1998). Liberalization, regional economic development and the geography of demand for air transport in the European Union. *Journal of Transport Geography*, 6(2), 87–104.

Graham, B. and Shaw, J. (2008). Low-cost airlines in Europe: Reconciling liberalization and sustainability. *Geoforum*, 39(3), 1439–1451.

Green, R. (2007). Airports and economic development. *Real Estate Economics*, 35, 91–112.

Hamilton, F. (2005). The external forces: Towards globalization and European integration. In Hamilton, F., Dmitrovska Andrews, K. and Pichler-Milanović, N. (eds) *Transformation of cities in Central and Eastern Europe: Towards globalization*. New York, United Nations University Press.

Huderek-Glapska, S. (2011). Charakterystyka pasażerów portów regionalnych. In Rekowski, M. (ed) *Regionalne Porty Lotnicze w Polsce – Charakterystyka i Tendencje Rozwojowe*. Poznań, Poland, Wydawnictwo Uniwersytetu Ekonomicznego.

Huderek-Glapska, S. and Nowak, H. (2016). Airport and low-cost carrier business relationship management as a key factor for airport continuity: The evidence from Poland. *Research in Transportation Business and Management*, 21, 44–53.

Hunter, L. (2006). Low cost airlines: Business model and employment relations. *European Management Journal*, 24(5), 315–321.

Ivy, R. (1995). The restructuring of air transport linkages in the new Europe. *Professional Geographer*, 47, 280–288.

Janić, M. (1997). Comparison of the quality of rail and air networks in West, Central and Eastern Europe. *Transport Policy*, 4(2), 85–93.

Jankiewicz, J. and Huderek-Glapska, S. (2016). The air transport market in Central and Eastern Europe after a decade of liberalisation – different paths of growth. *Journal of Transport Geography*, 50, 45–56.

Jóźwik, B. (2016). Transformacja i rozwój gospodarczy w państwach Europy Środkowej. *Rocznik Instytutu Europy Środkowo-Wschodniej*, 14(5), 49–66.

Kazda, A., Hromádka, M. and Mrekaj, B. (2017). Small regional airports operation: Unnecessary burdens or key to regional development. *Transportation Research Procedia*, 28, 59–68.

LOT (2018). *About us* [Online]. Available at: https://corporate.lot.com/pl/en/about-us (accessed 4 November 2018).

Marczewski, K. (2018). Wprowadzenie. In Srojny, M. (ed) *Wyzwania Ekonomiczne dla Europy Środkowo-Wschodniej*. Warszawa, Oficyna Wydawnicza SGH.

Matkowski, Z. and Próchniak, M. (2007). Economic convergence between the CEE-8 and the European Union. *Eastern European Economics*, 45(1), 59–76.

Mukkala, K. and Tervo, H. (2013). Air transportation and regional growth: Which way does the causality run? *Environment and Planning A*, 45(6), 1508–1520.

NBP (Narodowy Bank Polski) (2014). *Sytuacja Gospodarcza w Krajach Europy Środkowej i Wschodniej*. Warszawa, Instytut Ekonomiczny Warszawa, 1.

Nordica (2018). *Nordica* [Online]. Available at: https://www.nordica.ee/en/home/ (accessed 4 November 2018).

Pijet-Migoń, E. (2017). The geopolitics of low-cost carriers in Central and Eastern Europe. In Hall, D. (ed) *Tourism and geopolitics: Issues and concepts from Central and Eastern Europe*. Wallingford, CABI, 307–321.

Polanski, Z. (2014). Poland during the crisis: A 'Green Island' approaching the Euro area? In Hölscher, J. (ed) *Poland and the Eurozone: Studies in economic transition*. London, Palgrave Macmillan.

Radosevic, S. and Ciampi Stancova, K. (2018). Internationalising smart specialisation: Assessment and issues in the case of EU new member states. *Journal of the Knowledge Economy*, 9(1), 263–293.

Smętkowski, M. (2018). The role of exogenous and endogenous factors in the growth of regions in Central and Eastern Europe: The metropolitan/non-metropolitan divide in the pre- and post-crisis era. *European Planning Studies*, 26(2), 256–278.

Smyth, M. and Pearce B. (2008). *Air travel demand: IATA economics briefing no. 9* [Online]. IATA. Available at: http://www.travelready.org/PDF%20Files/Travel%20-%20IATA%20-%20Air%20Travel%20Demand.pdf (accessed 30 September 2018).

Symons, L. (1993). Airlines in transition to the market economy. In Hall, D. H. (ed) *Transport and economic development in the New Central and Eastern Europe*. London, Belhaven Press.

144 *Sonia Huderek-Glapska*

Todorova, S. (2017). *Influence of air traffic on the dynamics of economic growth in the Republic of Bulgaria*. Presented at COST Workshop on Air Transport and Regional Development: Case Studies on Core Regions, Dublin City University, Dublin, November.

UNCTAD (2018). *Data center* [Online]. Available at: https://unctadstat.unctad.org/wds/ReportFolders/reportFolders.aspx?sCS_ChosenLang=en (accessed 7 October 2018).

Wizz Air Holdings Plc (2017). *Results for the 12 months to 31 March 2017*. Available at: https://corporate.wizzair.com/en-GB/investor_relations/results_presentations (accessed 28 October 2018).

Wizz Air (2018). *Company information* [Online]. Available at: https://wizzair.com/en-gb/information-and-services/about-us/company-information (accessed 4 November 2018).

8 Air transport and economic growth of the regions

Causality analysis in Bulgaria

Stela Todorova and Kaloyan Haralampiev

Introduction

Infrastructure is often considered to be critical as a factor for the growth and development of countries and regions (Percoco, 2010). Air transport is an important structure in the connection of regions. This is significant in the context of globalisation because air transport is one of the most important means of linking modern industrialised societies (Feldhoff, 2002). Anecdotal evidence suggests that air transport improves business operations by providing rapid access to input supplies, stimulates interaction by enabling face-to-face meetings, and provides critical input for 'just-in-time' industries (Oxford Economic Forecasting, 2006). Air travel not only connects people, but it also connects economies to further develop the global economy. Therefore, airport development is linked with economic development. Much of the discussion on the relationship between airport and economic development focuses on four key sub-topics: public finance, economic development, transportation and agglomerate economics, and airports in general. Airports can be considered impure public goods; therefore, in order to completely understand their worth, it is necessary to determine each individual's marginal utility that results from the presence of a runway (Green, 2007).

There is considerable literature on airports and economic development. In their book *Aerotropolis*, Kasarda and Lindsay (2011) argue that airports represent a new model of regional economic development. Airports are among the largest investments a city and region can make. However, airports play a key role in connecting the places they serve to the global economy. The connection between airports and regional development has also been noted in several studies. A statistical study by Green (2007) found correlation between airport passengers and both metro population and employment growth. A study by Brueckner (2003) also notes the close connection between airline passengers and regional employment growth, finding that a 10 per cent increase in passengers in a metro generates a 1 per cent increase in regional employment. Brueckner finds, however, that airports and air transport contribute more to knowledge- and service-based businesses than to industrial manufacturing. Rosenthal and Strange (2004) note that airports play a role in spurring regional productivity due to the positive externalities that stem from the agglomeration economies that develop around these locations. Bel and Fageda (2008) find the availability of non-stop, direct international flights is a key factor in how corporate headquarters select locations in Europe.

Blonigen and Cristea (2012) examine the role of airports over two decades and the role of the 1978 US Airline Deregulation Act. They concluded that airline traffic has a significant effect on regional population, income, and employment growth, but that the effects differ depending on regional size and industry structure. Airports can help create 'favoured positions' in the global economy, which provide, 'superior access to global flows of people, goods, money and information' (Bowen, 2002, 425). Airports move two kinds of objects: people and goods. A significant amount of the literature on airports and economic development is focused on moving goods. For example, the benefits that an airport provides to a region and companies have also been demonstrated to influence exporters in locational decisions, specifically on where to locate their business (Lovely et al., 2005). In today's knowledge and creative economy, the ability to move people may matter even more than moving goods.

While considerable research has been undertaken to examine this outcome for major cities, there has been less attention to the contribution of air services to regional development outcomes (Blonigen and Cristea, 2012). There is a lack of research in this area. One of the reasons is a difficult (econometric) simultaneity issue (Green, 2007). Another reason is that in order to find a causal link between airport services and economic growth, it is important to have panel datasets on both dimensions for a long period of time. It is certainly reasonable to posit the general observation that airports generally lead to economic growth (Zhang and Zhang, 2001), but it is also reasonable to posit that economic development leads to increased airport traffic.

Airports have been associated with four main types of economic impact: (1) direct impacts – employment and income generated by the direct construction and operation of the airport; (2) indirect impacts – employment and income generated by the chain of suppliers of goods and services; (3) induced impact – the employment and income generated by the spending of incomes by employees create the direct and indirect effects; and (4) catalytic impacts – the employment and income generated by the role of the airport as a driver of productivity growth, and then as an attractor of new firms (Percoco, 2010). To illustrate the magnitude of the impacts, Oxford Economics and ATAG (2014) estimated that aviation contributes approximately US$2.4 trillion to the global economy. A study using panel data from 19 airports in Germany found positive GDP effects of air services provided by large and medium-sized airports (Allroggen and Malina, 2014). A negative effect is reported for small-sized airports.

The economic impact of Bulgarian airports has rarely been studied in the literature. Petkov et al. (2015) reported that the air industry represents 1.66 per cent of the country's GDP for 2012 based on the economic results of the activity of the Bulgarian aviation industry.

This chapter aims to provide an assessment of the issues involved here by isolating bidirectional short- and long-run causality between regional air transport activity and economic growth in their relevant regions. This will be done by linking the passenger traffic data at three international airports (Sofia, Burgas, and Varna) in Bulgaria with economic growth data (GDP) of the regions that surround those airports.

Overview of airports in Bulgaria

The construction and maintenance of Bulgaria's transport infrastructure is based on the following strategic documents: *The Integrated Transportation Strategy 2030*; *The Strategy for Development of the Transport Infrastructure of the Republic of Bulgaria until 2015*; and *The Operational Program 'Transport' and General Plan for Transport (Master Plan)*. A well-developed airport infrastructure is of substantial importance for the development of tourism in the country. The country's geographic location predetermines it to be the point of departure and the destination, mostly of flights from and to Western Europe. For the period 2007–2017, a gradual increase in the number of passengers passing through the Sofia, Burgas, Varna, and Plovdiv airports was observed.

For the period between 2005–2014, the total passenger flow through airports in the country increased from 5,035,900 to 7,795,400; i.e. it grew by 1.55 times (Petkov et al., 2015). According to Stoyanov's research, the increase in passenger flows of 116.13 per cent in Bulgaria over the period between 2007–2012 was mainly due to the increase in short-haul flights (116.4 per cent). The domination of short-haul transport in the Bulgarian aviation market means that 95.5 per cent and 95.2 per cent of flights, respectively, in 2012 and 2007 were with a duration of less than three flight hours (Stoyanov, 2014). Therefore, only five of every 100 performed passenger flights that had a destination which is farther than three hours of flight distance away. This confirms that the profile of the national consumer preferences for the usage of air transport is formed under the conditions defined by its convenience, speed of transport, focus of local business, and independent tourism.

The Bulgarian passenger civil aviation market is relatively small, with a size of 6.89 million consumers[1] and an annual volume of commercial transport of 7.26 million passengers[2] on international and national scheduled and charter airlines, with numerous opportunities for further development. Bulgaria's major airports are Sofia, Varna, Burgas, Plovdiv, and Gorna Oryahovitsa. This research includes only the first three airports as they have scheduled flights, while Plovdiv has only charters and Gorna Oryahovitsa is not functioning in practice.

Sofia Airport is the main international airport in the country, with the largest passenger flows. Its 80th anniversary was celebrated in 2017. The airport has an asphalt-paved runway of 3,600 × 45 m. The runway is fully equipped and has ICAO Category IIIB status, which means there are navigational aids installed that enable landing operations under low visibility conditions, allowing the use of instrument climbing with a horizontal visibility of 150 m and a vertical visibility of 15 m. It has two passenger terminals, the second of which is built on an area of 56,500 m². It is equipped with seven passenger boarding bridges and was commissioned at the end of 2006. The planned annual traffic is 2.6 million passengers. It has a capacity of 2,000 peak hour passengers and it complies with modern standards for passenger (category 'C' in IATA) and airline servicing. Terminal 1 was built in the first half of the 20th century and has been extensively expanded and upgraded, receiving an overhaul in 2000. Its total area is 9,800 m². Its declared operating capacity is 1.8 million passengers per annum. The economic outcomes of the operation of Sofia Airport provide significant revenue for the airport (revenue from financing, ground handling, and other commercial activities), as well as for the Ministry of Transport (revenue from airport taxes). Sofia Airport provides jobs for more than 2,000 employees. It also provides opportunities for tourism, business, and other trips, for a significant number of citizens and foreigners, and offers connections between Bulgaria and other countries.

Burgas Airport is public state property awarded to Fraport Twin Star Airport Management AD for a 35-year-long concession. It has a concrete runway which is 3,200 m long and 45 m wide. The airport has two passenger terminals. Terminal 2 has a total area of 21 000 m². Its annual capacity is 2.7 million passengers, and it can provide 1,263 departures and 1,220 arrivals at peak load. The passenger service class of the airport is IATA Class C. Burgas Airport has an acute summer seasonality problem. Most of the passenger service activities at the airport take place between June and September, with 92 per cent of the airport's annual traffic during this period. The busiest months in the peak season are July and August, with approximately 57–60 per cent of passenger traffic.

Varna Airport is also a state-owned public property awarded to Fraport Twin Star Airport Management AD for a 35-year-long concession. The airport has an asphalt-paved runway of 2550 × 55m. The airport's operations are again markedly seasonal in nature, connected with tourist services during the summer season. Summer charter programmes begin in the middle of March and finish at the end of October, with the peak months, similar to Burgas, occurring in July and August. From August 2013, all passengers at the Varna Airport were serviced in the newly constructed Terminal 2. The new terminal is situated on an area of about 20,000 m². With the commissioning of Terminal 2, Terminal 1 (initially built in 1972) was closed. The annual airport capacity is 2.4 million passengers, with 1,037 departing and 1,043 arriving passengers in peak hours. Its service category under IATA codes is C.

Plovdiv Airport is located 10 km southeast of the city, on the main Plovdiv-Asenovgrad road. The airport boasts a 2,500 m runway. As of 2009, there was a new passenger terminal with an area of 5,000 m², providing service level C under IATA codes. It is thus capable of servicing 1,000 passengers per hour in its peak. In March 2016, the government of the country adopted a decision to open a service concession procedure for Plovdiv Airport for a period of 35 years. The winning concessionaire has not yet been announced.

Gorna Oryahovitsa Airport was built in 1925 and has had international status since 1995. It is located 4 km northeast of the town of Gorna Oryahovitsa. The asphalt-paved runway is 2,450 m long and 45 m wide. It has a taxiway and five aircraft stands. The passenger terminal is in relatively good condition, but is equipped to serve only domestic flights. The passenger terminal has an area of 2209 m². There are no regular scheduled flights from Gorna Oryahovitsa Airport, and charter flights are performed only when necessary. In 2016, the Consortium 'Gorna Oryahovitsa Civil Airport' was awarded a 35-year-long concession of Gorna Oryahovitsa. For a period of 35 years, the concessionaire has to invest over BGN32 million for the development of the airport, with BGN22.4 million being required to be invested in the first four years of the concession.

Data and methods

Data

The empirical analysis was conducted using annual data on total airport passenger movements (PAX), and GDP by regions for the period 1995–2015 for Bulgaria. The former was used to represent the level of airport activities, whereas the latter was used to derive the economic growth.

Airport passenger data

Panel data on scheduled regular public transport (RPT) services of the three Bulgarian international airports was obtained from the Directorate General Civil Aviation Administration (CAA, 2019). The time series of the dataset covered 21 fiscal years ranging from 1995–2015. The datasets included all international airports in Bulgaria per year. Consequently, charter or other non-scheduled air services were not included in the datasets. Total passenger numbers were calculated by summing both inbound and outbound traffic for international and domestic services. The national carrier (Bulgaria Air) runs RPT services between the capital and regional centres (major tourist centres – Burgas and Varna).

Economic growth data

The economic growth data was gathered from the National Statistical Institute (NSI, 2019) of Bulgaria and the Eurostat database (EUROSTAT, 2019). Economic growth is usually understood as growth of output, growth of output per worker, or growth of output per capita. Here, GDP per region – whereby an airport is located for the previously mentioned time period – was used. The

Organisation for Economic Co-operation and Development (OECD) defines GDP as

> an aggregate measure of production equal to the sum of the gross value added for all resident and institutional units engaged in production (plus any taxes, and minus any subsidies, on products not included in the value of their outputs).
>
> (OECD, 2019)

There are different indicators for economic growth. For example, the World Bank[3] uses the growth in gross national income (GNI), net national income (NNI), value added by economic sectors, exports and imports, final consumption expenditures, gross capital formation, and GDP. However, value added by economic sectors, exports and imports, final consumption expenditures, and gross capital formation are components of GDP. The decision here was also driven by the data that was available from the NSI and Eurostat database and its robustness in terms of cross-regional comparison, since NSI provides regional data only for GDP but not for GNI and NNI. Therefore, GDP was used as an appropriate indicator as there was data for it by region where the airports were located.

Causality models

Works of Granger (1969, 2003) and Baker et al. (2015) led to the following algorithm:

1 If the time series are stationary, then we use Granger's simple causal two-variable model (Granger, 1969, 431) with the time series in level form. If the time series are non-stationary, then we work with the first differences.
2 If the time series are cointegrated, then we use the error correction term.

Almost the same algorithm is suggested by Petkov (2007).

Choice of method for panel unit-root testing

The tests for stationarity are known as unit-root tests. Since we work with panel data, we have to choose the panel unit-root test. Barbieri made a comprehensive overview of the panel unit-root tests and a comparison between them. Unfortunately, she does not make a clear recommendation which test is the best (Barbieri, 2006a). Our own literature review (Anagnostou et al., 2013; Bidirici and Bohur, 2015; Hlouskova and Vagner, 2005) led us to the choice of the IPS for the panel unit-root testing. According to the IPS test, the null hypothesis is that all individual time series have no unit root; i.e. they are non-stationary. The alternative hypothesis is that 'some (but not all) of the individual series have unit roots' (Barbieri, 2006a, 9); i.e. some (but not all) of them are stationary.

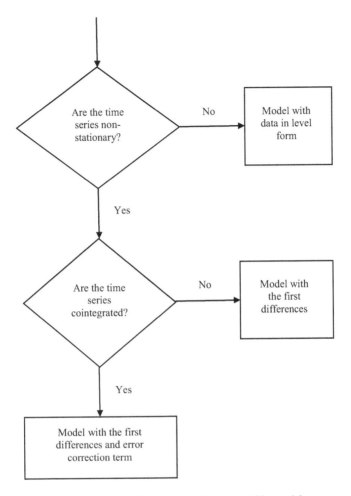

Figure 8.1 Algorithm for selection of relevant causal two-variable model
Source: Devised by authors

For each time series, we perform the IPS test four times:

- Test for unit root in the time series in level form with individual intercept included in the test equation.
- Test for unit root in the time series of the first differences with individual intercept included in the test equation.
- Test for unit root in the time series in level form with individual intercept and trend included in the test equation.
- Test for unit root in the time series of the first differences with individual intercept and trend included in the test equation.

Simultaneously with each of these four tests, we perform the Schwarz information criterion for automatic selection of the observations-based maximum lag length. Depending on the results of these four tests, we apply the panel cointegration test in the appropriate way.

Choice of method for panel cointegration testing

Since we work with panel data, we have to choose the panel cointegration test. Similar to the case of the panel unit-root tests, Barbieri (2006b) has also made a comprehensive overview of the panel cointegration tests and a comparison between them. Unfortunately, again she does not make a clear recommendation which test is the best. Our own literature review (Anagnostou et al., 2013; Baker et al., 2015; Hakim and Merkert, 2016) led us to the choice of the Fisher test for the panel cointegration testing. We chose the form of the Fisher test according to the results of the IPS test:

- In the case of individual intercept and trend in the test equation, if the time series in level form are non-stationary but the time series of the first differences are stationary, then we perform the Fisher test with intercept and trend.
- In the case of individual intercept only in the test equation, if at least one of the previously mentioned conditions is not satisfied and at the same time the time series in level form are non-stationary, but the time series of the first differences are stationary, then we perform Fisher test with intercept only.

Results and discussion

Empirical results

Description of the time series and correlation between them

The strongest correlation between GDP and the number of passengers is obtained for Sofia Airport – 0.973 (Figure 8.2). The correlation for Burgas Airport is almost the same – 0.932 (Figure 8.3). The weakest correlation is obtained for Varna Airport – 0.781 (Figure 8.4).

Generally, the dynamics of both time series for the three airports are upwards. The larger correlation corresponds to larger parallelism between the two time series. It can be observed that the dynamics of the GDP and PAX for Sofia Airport are almost identical, while the dynamics of the GDP and PAX for Varna Airport are different.

The results show that according to GDP, the variation between regions is larger than the variation within regions (Table 8.1). Relating this to the number of passengers, the situation is opposite – the variation within airports is larger than the variation between airports. The main reason is that the southwestern region of Bulgaria (where Sofia Airport is located) is the most developed.

Air transport and regional economic growth 153

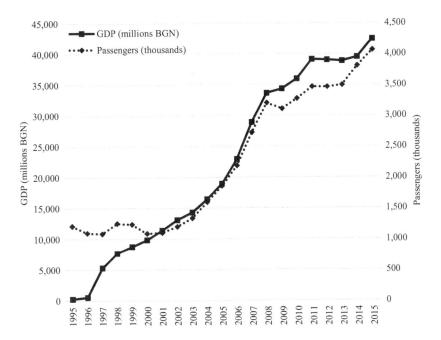

Figure 8.2 Passengers and gross domestic product (GDP): Sofia Airport, 1995–2015

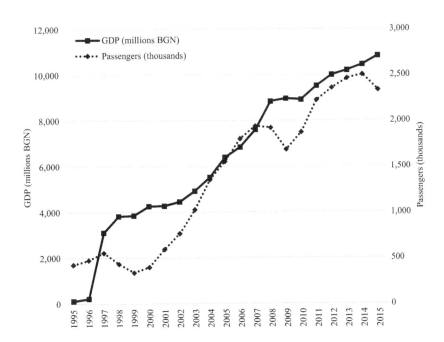

Figure 8.3 Passengers and gross domestic product (GDP): Burgas Airport, 1995–2015

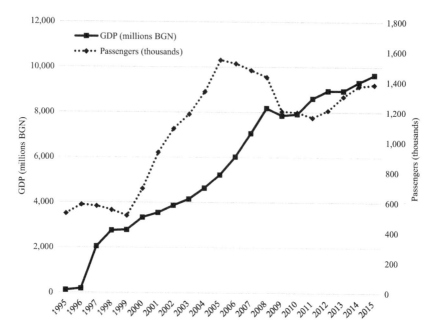

Figure 8.4 Passengers and gross domestic product (GDP): Varna Airport, 1995–2015

Table 8.1 Descriptive statistics of variables used in the analysis

Variable		All airports		
		Mean	SD	Observation
GDP (millions BGN)	Overall	11,261.24	11,380.68	63
	Between		7,574.50	3
	Within		6,711.83	21
Passengers (thousands)	Overall	1,566.28	927.82	63
	Between		485.42	3
	Within		699.69	21

Therefore, the difference in GDP between the southwestern region and the two other regions is very large, and hence, the variation between regions is also substantial.

Panel unit-root test

According to the previously mentioned consideration we used the test for individual root of Im, Pesaran and Shin (IPS). The IPS unit-root test hypotheses are:

H_0: The time series are non-stationary.
H_1: The time series are stationary.

Air transport and regional economic growth 155

Table 8.2 IPS panel unit-root test statistics

Variables	Deterministic	Level form		First-difference	
		Statistics[a]	Probability	Statistics[a]	Probability
GDP (millions BGN)	Individual intercept	0.42 (1)	0.661	−4.28 (0)	0.000
	Individual intercept and trend	−0.86 (3)	0.194	−3.72 (0)	0.000
Passengers (thousands)	Individual intercept	1.12 (1)	0.868	−1.66 (0)	0.049
	Individual intercept and trend	−1.07 (3)	0.142	−0.41 (0)	0.323

[a] Figures in parentheses represent lag length based on the Schwarz information criterion.

The results (Table 8.2) show that according to GDP, the null hypothesis is confirmed for the level values and it is rejected for the first differences, both for the model with intercept only and for the model with intercept and trend. This means that the GDP time series is non-stationary; however, the time series of the first differences is stationary. According to the number of the passengers and the model with intercept only, the null hypothesis is confirmed for the level values and it is rejected for the first differences. This means that the number of passengers is non-stationary; however, the time series of the first differences is stationary. Regarding the number of the passengers and the model with intercept and trend, the null hypothesis is confirmed both for the level values and for the first differences. This means that the number of passengers is non-stationary; however, the time series of the first differences is also non-stationary. These results led us to use the cointegration test based on the individual intercept.

Cointegration test

The results (Table 8.3) indicate that the GDP and PAX series have one cointegrating equation, thereby demonstrating a long-run relationship between GDP and PAX across Bulgarian regions. The results show that the null hypothesis is rejected – both time series are cointegrated.

Causality tests

Since both time series are cointegrated, the next step of the derived algorithm is to model causality by the vector error correction model (VECM) in the form:

$$\Delta X_t = \alpha_1 + \beta_1 ECT_{t-1} + \sum_{i=1}^{m} a_j \Delta X_{t-j} + \sum_{i=1}^{m} b_j \Delta Y_{t-j} + \varepsilon_t$$

$$\Delta Y_t = \alpha_2 + \beta_2 ECT_{t-1} + \sum_{i=1}^{m} c_j \Delta X_{t-j} + \sum_{i=1}^{m} d_j \Delta Y_{t-j} + \eta_t$$

Where X_t and Y_t are the time series, Δ is notation for the first-difference, ECT_{t-1} is the error correction term.

156 *Stela Todorova and Kaloyan Haralampiev*

Table 8.3 Johansen Fisher panel cointegration test statistics (based on the individual intercept)

Variable series	Hypothesised no. of CE(s)	Fisher statistics (from trace test)	Probability	Fisher statistics (from Max-Eigen test)	Probability
GDP and	None	25.12	0.000	22.59	0.001
Passengers	At most 1	13.09	0.042	13.09	0.042

Table 8.4 Results of vector error correction model for all airports

Explanatory factors	Model 1: growth in GDP (ΔGDP)				Model 2: growth in passengers (ΔPassengers)			
	Coefficient	S.E.	t-value	Probability	Coefficient	S.E.	t-value	Probability
Constant	212.30	192.45	1.10	0.273	71.42	28.29	2.52	0.013
1-year lag of ΔGDP	0.65	0.18	3.74	0.000	−0.02	0.03	−0.68	0.499
2-year lag of ΔGDP	−0.28	0.16	−1.78	0.079	−0.03	0.02	−1.41	0.162
3-year lag of ΔGDP	0.15	0.13	1.12	0.266	−0.00	0.02	−0.13	0.894
1-year lag of ΔPassengers	1.57	1.14	1.38	0.171	0.67	0.17	4.01	0.000
2-year lag of ΔPassengers	−1.05	1.19	−0.88	0.381	−0.08	0.17	−0.49	0.628
3-year lag of ΔPassengers	2.07	1.08	1.93	0.057	0.31	0.16	1.98	0.051
Long-run causality	0.04	0.03	1.40	0.166	−1.89	0.06	−3.42	0.001
R-squared	0.581				0.473			
Adjusted R-squared	0.513				0.387			
Log likelihood	−413.75				−315.96			
F-statistic	8.53				5.51			

Table 8.5 A summary of the causal relationships and direction between the two series

Null hypothesis	Short-run χ^2-statistics	Long-run t statistics	Long-run χ^2-statistics (strong Granger causality)
ΔPassengers does not cause ΔGDP	5,22	1.40	5,67
ΔGDP does not cause ΔPassengers	6,42	−3.42★	13,90★

★ Coefficients are significant at the 0.05 level.

The results (Table 8.4) indicate that there is long-run causality in Model 2, i.e. the growth in GDP causes the growth in the number of the passengers. There is no evidence for long-run causality in the opposite direction – the growth of the number of the passengers does not cause the growth of the GDP in the selected regions. There is no evidence for short-run causality in both directions. According to Baker et al. (2015), we can perform statistical tests for short-run causality, long-run causality and strong long-run Granger causality.

Table 8.5 displays a summary of the three types of causality tests based on the two models we ran: (1) short-run causality; (2) long-run causality; and

(3) strong Granger causality. The results show that there is no short-run causality. Our results clearly demonstrate that the long run causalities between air transport and the local economy in only one direction – the growth in GDP causes the growth in the number of the passengers.

Conclusion

This chapter has aimed to establish the first empirical evidence for determining causal relationships between regional aviation/airports and economic growth in Bulgaria. The results suggest that these causal relationships matter and should be considered more when discussing the role of the airport within regional communities (including their planning and funding). The local economic development strategies should ensure a strong focus on air transport – which will then boost local industries. The causality between economic growth and air traffic indicates that a subsidy reduction for the airports may be sensible when the economy is strong. During strong economic growth periods, subsidies can be delayed and saved up for weaker economic times, as regional economies often fluctuate. However, during economic downturns, subsidies should be in place to ensure that the level of air service to communities is maintained over time. It is difficult to develop a subsidy policy that is sensitive to economic growth; however, it is important to recognise the complexity of the airport context. Future research needs to determine the types of subsidies that will work within this context in Bulgaria. The local councils need to be supported to maintain and develop airport infrastructure, and this type of support may constitute part of the subsidy arrangement. In 2010, the municipalities from the Plovdiv region established a 'Development Fund for Plovdiv Airport – South Gate of Bulgaria'. In 2015, a second fund was set up – the non-profit association 'Development Fund for the South-East Region – Phoenix Fund'.

The results clearly demonstrate the long-run causalities between air transport and the local economy only in one direction – the growth in GDP causes the growth in the number of the passengers. This research provides evidence of the Granger causality between air transport and economic growth in one direction. Further studies should seek to incorporate such variables in bidirectional analysis and improve upon the model presented here. Additional research could further explore why airports do not affect economic growth, as measured in our case with GDP, despite their strong increase in passengers. The results are original in terms of the applied methodology for Bulgaria and deliver the first evidence for the government to justify the support of regional/remote aviation. Further research should aim at focusing attention on developing a more detailed understanding of air transport's effects on the economic growth of regions.

Notes

1 Country population as of 31 December 2017, NSI, Sofia, 2017, https://infostat.nsi.bg/infostat/pages/reports/query.jsf?x_2 = 1085

2 According to statistical data for international airports in Bulgaria for 2017, Directorate General Civil Aviation Administration at the Ministry of Transport, Information Technology and Communications, www.caa.bg/en/category/602/statistics
3 https://data.worldbank.org/indicator?tab=all

References

Allroggen, F. and Malina, R. (2014). Do the regional growth effects of air transport differ among airports? *Journal of Air Transport Management*, 37, 1–4.

Anagnostou, A., Kallioras, D. and Petrakos, G. (2013). *Integrating the neighbors: A dynamic panel analysis of EU-ENP trade relations*. SEARCH Working Paper, 2–11. Available at: http://www.ub.edu/searchproject/wp-content/uploads/2013/09/SEARCH_Working-Paper_2.11.pdf.

Baker, D., Merkert, R. and Kamruzzaman, M. (2015). Regional aviation and economic growth: Cointegration and causality analysis in Australia. *Journal of Transport Geography*, 43, 140–150.

Barbieri, L. (2006a). *Panel unit root tests: A review*. Serie Rossa: Economia – Quaderno N. 43. Piacenza, Università cattolica del sacro cuore, 1–53.

Barbieri, L. (2006b). *Panel cointegration tests: A review*. Serie Rossa: Economia – Quaderno N. 44. Piacenza, Università cattolica del sacro cuore, 1–33.

Bel, G. and Fageda, X. (2008). Getting there fast: Globalization, intercontinental flights and location of headquarters. *Journal of Economic Geography*, 8(4), 471–495.

Bidirici, M. and Bohur, E. (2015). Design and economic growth: Panel cointegration and causality analysis. *Procedia – Social and Behavioral Sciences*, 210, 193–202.

Blonigen, B. and Cristea, A. (2012). *Airports and urban growth: Evidence from a Quasi-natural policy experiment*. Working Paper No. 18278. Cambridge, MA, National Bureau of Economic Research (NBER).

Bowen, J. (2002). Network change, deregulation, and access in the global airline industry. *Economic Geography*, 78(4), 425–439.

Brueckner, J. (2003). Airline traffic and urban economic development. *Urban Studies*, 40(8), 1455–1469.

CAA (2019). *Statistic information about international airports in Republic of Bulgaria*. Available at: www.caa.bg/en/category/602/statistics (accessed 2 May 2019).

EUROSTAT (2019). *Your key to European statistics: Regional gross domestic product*. Available at: www.ec.europa.eu/eurostat/data/database (accessed 29 April 2019).

Feldhoff, T. (2002). Japan's regional airports: Conflicting national, regional and local interests. *Journal of Transport Geography*, 10, 165–175.

Granger, C. (1969). Investigating causal relations by econometric models and cross-spectral methods. *Econometrica*, 37(3), 424–438.

Granger, C. (2003). Time series analysis, cointegration, and applications. *Nobel Lecture*, 360–366, 8 December.

Green, R. (2007). Airports and economic development. *Real Estate Economics*, 35, 91–112.

Hakim, M. and Merkert, R. (2016). The causal relationship between air transport and economic growth: Empirical evidence from South Asia. *Journal of Transport Geography*, 56, 120–127.

Hlouskova, J. and Vagner, M. (2005). *The performance of panel unit root and stationarity tests: Results from a large-scale simulation study*. EUI Working Paper ECO No. 2005/5. Available at: https://EconPapers.repec.org/RePEc:eui:euiwps:eco2005/05.

Kasarda, J. and Lindsay, G. (2011). *Aerotropolis: The way we'll live next*, 1st edition. New York, Farrar, Straus and Giroux.

Lovely, M. E., Rosenthal, S. S. and Sharma S. (2005). Information, agglomeration, and the headquarters of U.S. exporters. *Regional Science and Urban Economics*, 35(2), 167–191. doi:10.1016/j.regsciurbeco.2003.09.002.

NSI (2019). *Gross domestic product (GDP)*. Available at: www.nsi.bg/en/content/5437/gross-domestic-product-gdp (accessed 25 April 2019).

OECD (2019). *Glossary of statistical terms: Gross domestic products (GDP)*. Available at: https://stats.oecd.org/glossary/detail.asp?ID=1163 (accessed 4 May 2019).

Oxford Economic Forecasting (2006). *The economic contribution of the aviation industry in the UK*. Oxford, Oxford Economic Forecasting.

Oxford Economics and Air Transport Action Group (2014). *Aviation benefits beyond borders*. Geneva, April.

Percoco, M. (2010). Airport activity and local development: Evidence from Italy. *Urban Studies*, 47, 2427–2443.

Petkov, P. (2007). Cointegration analysis of Bulgarian imports and exports. *Вісник донецького університету, Сер. В: Економіка і право, Вип*, 2, 63–75.

Petkov, T., Stanulov, S. and Yotsev, Y. (2015). Current review of Bulgarian aviation industry. *Journal of Mechanics, Transport and Communications*, 13(1–3), 71–73.

Rosenthal, S. and Strange, W. (2004). Evidence on the nature and sources of agglomeration economies. In: Thisse, J.-F. and Henderson, J. V. (eds) *Handbook of Urban and Regional Economics*, vol. 4. North Holland, Amsterdam, 2119–2171.

Stoyanov, M. (2014). Challenges of low-cost air carriers, scientific conference 'transport in a changing world – challenges and solutions'. *Sofia*, 226–236, October.

Zhang, A. and Zhang, Y. (2001). Airport charges, economic growth, and cost recovery: Transportation research part E: logistics. *Transport Review*, 37, 25–33.

9 The effects of air traffic on the economic development of Bosnia and Herzegovina

Rahman Nurković

Introduction

The air transport market in Bosnia and Herzegovina is undergoing significant changes, which are taking place on both the demand and supply sides. In Bosnia and Herzegovina, some airports have experienced unprecedented growth in air traffic. However, the increase in the number of airline connections benefiting the airports, passengers, the aviation industry and, indirectly, the whole of society, at the same time has resulted in a rise in social costs, which is reflected in the intensification of noise and environmental pollution (Večernji list, 2019; Borel, 2012). Air transport liberalisation has directly contributed to the increase in air traffic services, reducing the price of airline tickets, which has had a significant impact on the number of passengers. Moreover, demand has been stimulated by economic changes, such as an increase in average household income and the growing need for transport to open up the labour market.

Several studies in Bosnia and Herzegovina have focused on examining the relationship between air traffic and economic development (Mostar Airport, 2019). However, the existing literature generally reveals a knowledge gap in relation to the impact of air traffic in countries in transition such as Bosnia and Herzegovina. Therefore, the purpose of this chapter is to identify the economic importance of airports in Bosnia and Herzegovina, through exploring the economic benefits of air traffic. The complex development of air traffic in Bosnia and Herzegovina has been reflected in many economic factors, which are special and significant for the country's transformation. As an example, due to economic interests, Germany, Austria, Turkey, and Saudi Arabia have all invested in the development of airports in Bosnia and Herzegovina.

Given the scarce statistics on air traffic from official publications, a challenge with this research was to collect original statistics from all airports in Bosnia and Herzegovina that are used as a basis for the analysis. The number of passengers and freight tonnes at airports in Sarajevo, Tuzla, Banja Luka, and Mostar will mainly be used to show the impact of air traffic. Also, information will be used on the routes served that has been collected through a review of airport flight schedules. Specific economic development data is not available. When it comes to international traffic flows, tourist traffic is very significant at some airports. In addition, an important issue is the transport connection, via Bosnia and

Development of Bosnia and Herzegovina 161

Herzegovina, which with the European Union in certain parts, and in certain directions, is a geo-transport entity (Peneda et al., 2010).

This chapter reviews the growth of air transport in Bosnia and Herzegovina, and considers how this is related to economic development. It begins by exploring the factors affecting air transport development, and then examines air traffic patterns in Bosnia and Herzegovina. This leads on to a discussion of the opportunities and challenges that have emerged, with some brief concluding comments.

Factors influencing air transport development

There are numerous factors that affect the development of air transport. These factors may be classified into four groups of critical factors, namely connectivity, the economic potential of the hinterland, the commercial policies of the airport operators, and the sustainable development context. The factors having an impact on air transport development in Bosnia and Herzegovina are presented in Table 9.1.

Table 9.1 Critical factors influencing the development of air transport in Bosnia and Herzegovina

Connectivity	*Economic potential of hinterland*
• Excellent land traffic connectivity • Good air connectivity with main industrial centres • Central geographic position • Central position considering airline networks • Significant air cargo traffic • Good inter-modular connectivity of cargo traffic • Good air connectivity with main world metropolitans	• Strong local and regional economy providing a solid base for traffic development • Specialised suppliers and strong local market • Adequate economic structure to contribute to air traffic expansion and the development of non-aeronautical activities • Availability of educated work force
Commercial policies of airport operators	*Sustainable development context*
• Active role of airport operators (aggressive marketing, proactive land purchases) • Creation of company development (real estate sector in the air operator organisational structure) with air operator representatives and public administration offices	• Introduction of sustainable development into the regional and national development plans • Area planning and investment stimulation politics, planning of locations for the development of airport industries and activities • Existence of all-inclusive plans for connecting transport infrastructure and the development of the land area, within and outside of the airport area • Possibility of the development of the airspace • Inclusion of the community and acceptance by the community • Mutual coordinated development of operations in the airspace and real estate in the surrounding areas • Consensus between various levels and regional governments on strategy

Source: Devised by author

When planning air transport development in Bosnia and Herzegovina, it is not necessary to wait for the realisation of all the factors discussed in the table. Some of them, for various reasons, will never be realised at the optimal level. The creation of these and air transport development are parallel processes that are inter-related; they are intertwined, and they affect each other (Niemeier, 2001). The main reasons for planning, creating, and developing air transport is to improve the quality positioning of airports in the international market of air transport services through an increase of competitiveness, and also to contribute to the development of the economy at a local, regional and national levels.

Therefore, air transport in Bosnia and Herzegovina is considered as a development concept for the following reasons,

- It enables change in the income structure of airports where the share of the non-aeronautical income increases, which enables lower aeronautical prices and higher volumes of aircraft and passengers.
- It assumes the purchasing of land from the surrounding population which influences their material status, as well as the material status of the local community.
- It is an investment in the construction of needed infrastructure.
- It increases the income of the local community through utility fees and taxes.
- It employs construction workers, which decreases the level of unemployment.
- It creates a new investment cycle, and it improves the investment climate.
- It creates new job opportunities, which increases social stability of the local community.
- It encourages the establishment of the headquarters of a certain number of companies.
- It increases the competitiveness of airports and higher quality positioning in the market.

In relation to this, when specifically considering the development of airports, the complex nature of their operations must be assessed. There are numerous activities that should to be taken into account, as detailed in Figure 9.1.

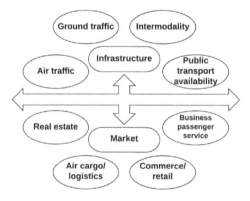

Figure 9.1 Different activities at airports

Source: Devised by author

Traffic growth at airports in Bosnia and Herzegovina

Overall, the main airports of Sarajevo and Tuzla have experienced a dynamic development of passenger air traffic in the recent years, while Banja Luka and Mostar airports have experienced less traffic growth (Nurković, 2016). This growth has been supported with the European Union allocating significant funds for the modernisation of airports in Bosnia and Herzegovina. In 2017, the total number of air passengers in Bosnia and Herzegovina amounted to 1,556,896 passengers, increasing by 133 per cent since 2012 (Table 9.2). Sarajevo airport handled 957,969 passengers, or 61.5 per cent of the total number of passengers in 2017, followed by Tuzla airport with 535,596 passengers and 34.4 per cent share, Mostar Airport with 42,512 passengers and 2.7 per cent share, and Banja Luka airport with 20,819 and 1.3 per cent share. The market share of Tuzla increased very significantly, while it dropped dramatically at Mostar. Figure 9.2 also shows the international air routes operated from airports in Bosnia and Herzegovina in 2017.

Freight traffic trends have been significantly more irregular, with the four airports overall experiencing a lower overall growth rate than passengers of 78 per cent. Sarajevo airport had the highest number of freight tonnes handled (2,551) and an overall market share of 88.3 per cent. with Tuzla handling 334 tonnes, having a market share of 12 per cent. There was none or very little freight traffic at the other two airports.

Air transport opportunities and challenges

Considering the long-term projection of the development of passenger and cargo traffic, it is necessary to create a business model as a precondition for positioning Bosnia and Herzegovina in the air market (Nurković, 2007). The new business model needs to be viewed in the context of a number of factors. The fundamental premise of building and operating a new business model is the competence of the management system. Since each management system is inherently integrated, to a greater or lesser extent, the competence of an integrated management system is needed, which is defined as a set of characteristics that make it a human process and a business capable of accomplishing the complex mission of an integrated system on a continuous basis (Rietveld and Bruinsma, 1998).

It needs to be noted that there have been reform processes in the air traffic management (ATM) system in Bosnia and Herzegovina, focused on the integration of European airspace through comprehensive dynamic compliance programmes. Strategic programmes for the development of European air traffic have been related to solving the problems of airspace in Bosnia and Herzegovina through ATM regionalisation, with the aim of effectively increasing the capacity of airspace, managing forecast traffic growth and increasing air traffic efficiency (Eurocontrol, 2016).

Nevertheless, air congestion over Europe, especially over Southeastern Europe to which includes Bosnia and Herzegovina, is increasing. Such a

Table 9.2 Airport passengers in Bosnia and Herzegovina, 2012–2017

Airport	2012	% share	2013	% share	2014	% share	2015	% share	2016	% share	2017	% share
Sarajevo	580,058	86.7	665,638	82.7	709,901	74.2	772,940	68.4	838,966	68.4	957,969	61.5
Mostar	78,207	11.7	68,939	8.6	67,974	7.1	75,244	6.7	53,618	4.4	42,512	2.7
Tuzla	4,191	0.6	61,564	7.6	151,353	15.8	259,094	22.9	311,398	25.4	535,596	34.4
Banja Luka	6,420	1.0	8,837	1.1	27,636	2.9	22,800	2.0	21,694	1.8	20,819	0.0
Total	668,876	100.0	80,4978	100.0	956,864	100.0	1,130,042	100.0	1,225,676	100.0	1,556,896	100.0

Source: State Agency for Statistics of Bosnia and Herzegovina (2012–2017)

Development of Bosnia and Herzegovina 165

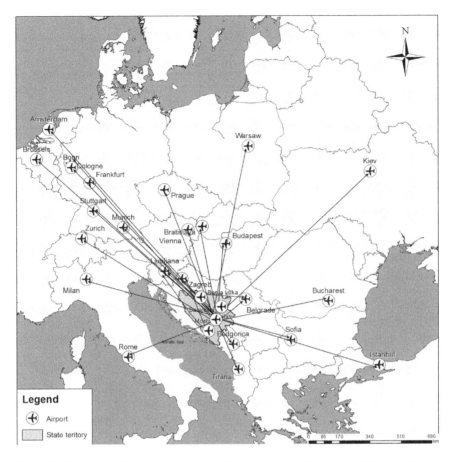

Figure 9.2 International air routes operated from airports in Bosnia and Herzegovina in 2017
Source: Devised by author

density of air traffic has a significant impact. As a result, restrictions on air traffic controls are increasing for airlines, whereby before they are even delayed, passengers become nervous, especially if they are transferring flights. So it is understandable that new radical measures are necessary to save the European air industry as a whole. Sarajevo's flight control is one of the most modern in Europe, as it has an airspace monitoring system like other countries in Europe (Rietveld and Bruinsma,1998). The new economic and political conditions that determine the development of Bosnia and Herzegovina and the changes in air traffic in this country, Europe, and the world require profound changes in the structure and organisation of air traffic in order for it to successfully

166 *Rahman Nurković*

Table 9.3 Airport freight tonnes in Bosnia and Herzegovina, 2012–2017

Airport	2012	% share	2013	% share	2014	% share	2015	% share	2016	% share	2017	% share
Sarajevo	1,526	94.0	1,603	99.6	2,060	79.0	4,238	43.5	2,470	28.9	2,551	88.3
Mostar	29	1.8	0	0.0	2	0.1	150	1.5	0	0.0	0	0.0
Tuzla	69	4.2	6	0.4	109	4.2	237	2.4	6,066	71.0	334	11.6
Banja Luka	0	0.0	0	0.0	436	16.7	5,109	52.5	5	0.1	3	0.1
Total	1,624	100.0	1,609	100.0	2,607	100.0	9,734	100.0	8,541	100.0	2,888	100.0

Source: State Agency for Statistics of Bosnia and Herzegovina (2012–2017)

integrate into the international air transport system with the most favourable effects on overall social and economic progress (Niemeier, 2001).

The impact of the substantial traffic growth at Sarajevo airport on the surrounding environment has both a positive and a negative dimension. Many of the effects created by airport operations are difficult to measure. The benefits of airport operations are reflected in the creation of employment and income. Sarajevo airport operations contributed to the direct, indirect and induced methods of creating about 450 jobs and achieved one million passengers in 2019. However, direct employment per million passengers is well above the European average. One of the reasons for the size of the workforce of state-owned companies operating at the Sarajevo airport rests with central economic planning. The size of production at the airport is expressed by the number of aircraft operations, and the number of passengers and goods serviced is positively related to the level of economic performance. Limiting the development of an airport, which is reflected in the inability to meet the transport needs expressed by society, can reduce the negative effects of airport operations, but can also create economic opportunities.

Environmental and spatial constraints may jeopardise the further development of Sarajevo airport. Given the immaturity of the air transport market in Bosnia and Herzegovina, and its prospects for growth, it may be justified to intensify work on expanding the airport. New facilities at Tuzla, Mostar, and Banja Luka would take some of the air traffic in Bosnia and Herzegovina. Given the potential social costs and benefits, if air travel were to move beyond the city limits of Sarajevo, the social costs associated with the loss of property caused by aircraft noise emissions would be eliminated while maintaining or increasing positive social benefits. The environmental effects associated with air, soil, and water pollution are largely independent of the location of the airport.

Bosnia and Herzegovina lags behind other countries on the path to EU membership. Air traffic of passengers and goods is increasing, as previously discussed. The increase in traffic of all airlines, and especially the low-cost ones, caused the need for more infrastructure. The first important step was made when a Civil Aviation Agency was established to be responsible for establishing functional airspace blocks and certifying air traffic control service providers.

Another important agreement signed by Bosnia and Herzegovina is the European Common Aviation Area. This is an agreement that will make air carriers more competitive, simplify procedures in the preparation of international flights and air traffic control, and greatly assist Bosnia and Herzegovina in the process of amending and adapting EU regulations. By signing this agreement, Bosnia and Herzegovina has fully aligned its legislation with that of the other signatories in the process of alignment with the provisions of the European Union. There are already several airport master plans and the European Union has recently been awarded the project to reconstruct the development of the main airport in Bosnia and Herzegovina. At the moment, such a large project is not necessarily needed at Sarajevo airport, but when Bosnia and Herzegovina joins the European Union, when the free movement of goods, people, goods and capital is realised, it may become one of the larger regional exchange centres. Then the airports in Sarajevo, Tuzla, Banja Luka, and Mostar will require newer and much larger passenger terminals. There is undoubtedly a huge potential for air traffic in this area, and governments, airlines, and airports should jointly find the best models to promote tourism and travel. An under-developed air network within the region is a fact – and it should be a challenge for everyone.

Conclusion

This chapter has analysed air transport growth in Bosnia and Herzegovina, and considered the likely economic impacts. It has been observed that the air transport market is undergoing significant changes which are taking place on both the demand and supply side. The main airport at Sarajevo has experienced significant growth in both the passenger and freight markets. Passenger numbers at Tuzla airport have also seen a dramatic increase, making it the second largest airport in Bosnia and Herzegovina, although at the same time, there has been a fall in passenger numbers at Mostar. These traffic developments have created many challenges which can create both opportunities and obstacles for economic development, especially as regards the country's relationship with the European Union.

References

Borel, G. (2012). *Airports – evolving business models and social and economic impact*. Air Traffic Workshop Importance of Air Transport Sector in Economic and Social Development of the South Fast Europe. Energy and Infrastructure Unit Regional Cooperation Council. SEETO Comprehensive Network Multi-Annual Plan (MAP), Sarajevo.

Eurocontrol (2016). *Market segments in European air traffic 2015*. Brussels, Eurocontrol.

Mostar Airport (2019). *Mostar airport*. Available at: www.mostar-airport.ba/onama.php.2015 (accessed 13 June 2019).

Niemeier, H. M. (2001). On the use and abuse of impact analysis for airports: A critical view from the perspective of regional policy. In Pfähler, W. (ed) *Regional input-output analysis*. Baden-Baden, Nomos Verlagsgesellschaft.

Nurković, R. (2007). *Contemporary bases of classification of the roads and their influence on regional development of Bosnia and Herzegovina*. Proceedings, University of Tuzla, Faculty of Natural Sciences, Bosnia and Herzegovina, 19–31.

Nurković, R. (2016). Geographical aspects of contemporary aviation in Bosnia and Herzegovina. *Geographical Review*, 37, 35–50.

Peneda, M. J. A., Reis, V. D. and Macário, M. R. (2010). *Critical factors for the development of airport cities*. Masters Dissertation on Complex Transport Infrastructure Systems, Instituto Superior Técnico, Portugal.

Rietveld, P. and Bruinsma, F. (1998). *Is transport infrastructure effective? Transport infrastructure and accessibility: Impacts on the space economy*. Berlin, Springer-Verlag.

State Agency for Statistics of Bosnia and Herzegovina (2012–2017). *Air transport first release data*. Sarajevo, State Agency for Statistics of Bosnia and Herzegovina.

Večernji List (2019). *Air transport news*. Available at: www.vecernji-list.hr/newsroom/news/bih/326759/index.do) (accessed 12 September 2019).

10 Expenditure of inbound passengers at Wroclaw airport and the significance for the regional economy

Łukasz Olipra

Introduction

As discussed elsewhere in this book, in studies of economic impact and the importance of air transport on the regional economy, four areas of impact are often identified and differentiated: direct, indirect, induced, and catalytic effects. Direct, indirect, and induced effects define the importance of air transport for the region as one of the sectors of the economy. Catalytic effects are described inter alia as transport benefits resulting from the operation of the airport in the region, which include, among others, stimulation of economic activity and access to markets through national and international transport links, which are considered crucial for decisions with respect to the location of companies. One of the other main areas of catalytic impact, in addition to the impact on investment location decisions and economic activity, is considered to be tourism.

According to research conducted by the Transportation Research Board (TRB, 2008), the main reason for conducting an economic impact study is to measure the airport's significance to its local community, most commonly to justify airport investment or expansion. The most frequently measured variables include employment, wages, local and regional spending, tourism, and air traffic levels. The impact of tourism on the regional economy is measured mainly through the estimation of expenditure made by tourists arriving to the region (Button and Taylor, 2000; Francis et al., 2003). In the next step, tourism multipliers are used to indicate the total increase in output, labour earnings, and employment through inter-industry linkages in a region as a result of tourism expenditure. Amongst other aspects, tourism expenditure is an essential factor in measuring the gross added value in tourism destinations (Button and Taylor, 2000). The expenditure of visitors generates additional demand for goods and services in the region, influencing the growth of GDP (Eugenio-Martin and Inchausti-Sintes 2016). In most studies on the impact and importance of air transport for regional economies, expenditure by tourists is the category taken into consideration when estimating the input to a regional economy of visitors arriving by air transport.

The aim of this chapter is to analyse the structure of the expenditure of inbound air transport passengers in a visited region according to the purpose of the visit (business, leisure tourism, visiting friends and relatives [VFR], others). To analyse the structure of total expenditure, it is necessary to estimate the

170 *Łukasz Olipra*

amount of expenditure of particular groups of passengers and then calculate the total amount of expenditure, which is also the aim of this chapter. In undertaking this research, the purpose is to assess the significance of leisure tourists brought by air transport, and their expenditure, for the regional economy of Wroclaw and Lower Silesia in Poland, compared with other types of passengers. It is important to note that this study focuses only on a part of the 'benefit-side' of the economic catalytic impact of air transport, which is defined as 'net economic effects' (Cooper and Smith, 2005). Cooper and Smith (2005) include in the 'benefit-side' of tourism expenditure both inbound and outbound tourists, but this study focuses only on expenditure of inbound visitors. The expenditure of incoming air transport passengers then creates demand-side effects in the regional economy in the tourism sector.

The data necessary to carry out the analysis were obtained through a survey conducted at Wroclaw airport in 2014, with the use of the CAPI method (computer-assisted personal interview). Statistical methods were used for calculations and the analysis of the obtained data.

Background to the research

Classification of tourism and air transport passengers

According to the glossary of the World Tourism Organisation,

> tourism is a social, cultural and economic phenomenon which entails the movement of people to countries or places outside their *usual environment* for *personal* or *business/professional purposes*. These people are called *visitors* (which may be either *tourists* or *excursionists*; residents or non-residents) and tourism has to do with their activities, some of which involve *tourism expenditure.*
>
> (UNWTO, 2014, Emphasis in original)

A tourism trip can be classified by the visitor's socio-economic characteristics or by specific features of the trip. One of attributes characterising tourism trips is the 'main purpose' of a trip, defined as the purpose in the absence of which the trip would not have taken place (UNWTO, 2010). The main purpose of a trip helps to determine whether it qualifies as a tourism trip and the traveller qualifies as a visitor. For instance, as long as it is incidental to the trip, a visitor might earn some income during his/her stay (for example, youth backpacking). Nevertheless, if the main purpose is to be employed and earn an income, then the trip is not a 'tourism' and the visitor is deemed to be a traveller for other purposes (UNWTO, 2010). The classification of a trip according to its main purpose should be related to the main activities undertaken during the traveller's stay. In case of travel, during which individuals may have more than one purpose, the main purpose of the trip should be the one that is central to the decision to take the trip (UNWTO, 2010).

Classification of tourism trips according to the main purpose distinguish two main categories as well as eight sub-categories (UNWTO, 2010):

- Personal

  - Holidays, leisure, and recreation
  - Visiting friends and relatives
  - Education and training
  - Health and medical care
  - Religion/pilgrimages
  - Shopping
  - Transit
  - Other

- Business and professional

Information on the purpose of a tourism trip, as detailed by the UNWTO, is useful for characterising tourism expenditure patterns. It is also important in identifying key segments of tourism demand for planning, marketing, and promotion purposes (UNWTO, 2010).

Classification of tourists according to the purpose of the tourism trip overlaps with classification of air transport passengers. Three main categories of air transport passengers are: business passengers, leisure tourism passengers, and VFR passengers. However, in most studies on impacts and the importance of air transport for regional economies, when expenditure of air passengers is taken into consideration as an input of visitors arriving by air transport to the regional economy, expenditure of leisure tourists is mainly, and sometimes solely, estimated and analysed as a visitor's spending impact. However, leisure tourists are not the only group of passengers flying to regions and spending money there, and leisure tourism destinations are not the only destinations where there is an inflow of air transport passengers.

Passenger expenditure in studies concerned with the economic impact of air transport on regions

The research on the economic impact of airports on regional economies was initiated in the 1980s in the United States. One of the earliest publications on the subject was a report produced by Wilbur Smith Associates on the economic impact of Los Angeles International Airport (Wilbur Smith Associates, 1988). In 1986, shortly before the release of this report, the Federal Aviation Administration (FAA) prepared a report on the research methodology and instruments for measuring the significance of airports for the surrounding communities, presenting different approaches to the research (Butler and Kiernan, 1986). The FAA report contains standardised definitions, illustrations of the most useful analytical techniques, and a description of the conditions which must be met in order to apply the various methodologies.

Since 1988, there have been many studies evaluating the impact of air transport on regional economies published by airports, consulting companies, and various national and international organisations. These include ACI-Europe (ACI-Europe, 1998; ACI-Europe and York Consulting, 2000; ACI-Europe and York Aviation, 2004; ACI-Europe and InterVISTAS, 2015), ACI-North America (2002), the Federal Aviation Administration (FAA, 2009), Eurocontrol (Cooper and Smith, 2005), and Oxford Economic Forecasting (OEF, 1999), as well as academics such as Robertson (1995), Braathen et al. (2006), Rekowski et al. (2006), Halpern and Bråthen (2010), Huderek-Glapska (2011), Pancer-Cybulska et al. (2014).

Particular studies on the economic impact of air transport may differ significantly, due to variations in terminology and methods, as well as with the use of models of varied computational complexity. This is evident with respect to American studies which employ a wide assortment of methodologies, despite the existing FAA recommendations on the identification and economic quantification of air transport impacts. Individual studies employ different definitions of multipliers and various approaches for the interpretation of direct and indirect effects. For example, the economic effects of airports that are manifested outside the airport facilities (off-site effects) are categorised as indirect effects, regardless of their true connection to the airport's operations. Such an approach makes it difficult to cross-examine the individual multiplier values. Another potential problem is the classification of economic activities performed on site, but unrelated to air transport operations. Often, the classification of activities into on-site and off-site reference groups depends on the physical delineation of an airport's facilities (or lack thereof) (Graham, 2018). Therefore, economists have not yet determined the most suitable method for evaluation of the economic impact of air transport (see the book ATARD methodologies for a more detailed discussion of the different methodologies).

One example regarding the various approaches to categorising effects of airports is an analysis of the expenditure of visitors. The FAA reports (Butler and Kiernan, 1986, 1992) include expenditure within the category of indirect effects. However, including expenditure of tourists and other visitors in the category of indirect impacts is not a widely accepted approach. Controversies in this respect are also made clear in Graham (2018). Some US airports, in line with the recommendations published in the FAA reports, classify the tourist sector workplaces under the indirect impacts subgroup. This methodology greatly enhances the volume of reported expenditures. Other studies use a separate category of *visitor impact*, identified as a self-contained category of impacts, and employing a more qualitative approach to the evaluation of these effects. Similar discrepancies in the evaluation of regional economic impact apply to studies of other sectors, such as construction and investments. In some cases, part-time and seasonal construction workers are classified under airport-derived economic impacts; in others, they are disregarded altogether (Graham, 2018). Scientific diligence dictates that the impact evaluation procedures recommended by the FAA be presented in this study (with respect to the classification of visitor impacts as indirect impacts), but it must be noted that, for the purpose of this study, the visitors impact is considered as a separate category and we are inclined to categorise the visitor impact measured by visitor expenditure as a catalytic effect. Nevertheless, we can find some advice in the FAA reports with regards to accurately measuring and estimating the visitor impact on regional economy.

With respect to the measurement of indirect effects, the FAA reports recommend that data be collected directly from businesses, either by mailed questionnaires or interviews of proprietors or employees of such businesses. If the region has a large number of travel agencies, a sample survey may be considered. The kind of information to be obtained is essentially the same as that collected from economic entities categorised under the direct impact subset, i.e. data on employment, wages, and expenditure. It is important that the respondents estimate the percentage of their business that is related to the use of the airport under study. Data on local expenditure of tourists and other visitors who come to the region by air may be estimated by a survey of hotels and travel agencies or a survey of air passengers.

Statistical information to be collected from these sources includes:

- The main purpose of visiting the region (business, leisure, VFR, convention, etc.).
- The number of trips to the airport over the past 12 months.
- The number of days spent in the region.
- The approximate amount of money spent locally (lodging, food, gifts, entertainment, transport, etc.).

This sample data may then be used as a basis for extrapolating total expenditure by tourists and other visitors to the region. The final output of the survey should be a set of estimates of such measures such as employment, wages, and local (and airport-related) expenditure of travel agencies, as well as annual expenditure of tourists and other visitors to the region (for lodging, food, entertainment, etc.) (Graham, 2018). These guidelines were used in this study; however, some modifications have been introduced to this procedure that will be described in the methodology section as follows.

Visitor expenditure, tourism development, and air transport

It can be observed that the issue of air transport passenger expenditure and its impact on regional economy has received only minimal attention from researchers. Very few papers devoted particularly to this topic can be found. However, there are some Spanish studies regarding visitor expenditure and its impact on the economy in reports prepared for particular airports and regions. Martí Selva et al. (2012) in their analysis identify and analyse two groups of inbound tourists by air and their expenditure: passengers of traditional carriers and those using low-cost carriers (LCCs). They focus on the differences in patterns and structure of expenditures of these two passenger groups. Using the input-output method, an analysis is also made of how the injection of money into the Spanish

174 *Łukasz Olipra*

economy, as a result of tourist spending, contributes to public income, job crea-tion, and new business opportunities, depending on the particular form of air transport that the tourists choose. The input–output table was created on the basis of the Tourism Satellite Account (TSA), which provides information about the relationships within the tourism industry (Martí Selva et al., 2012).

Eugenio-Martin and Inchausti-Sintes (2016), on the other hand, focus just on expenditure and the behaviour of LCCs passengers. In their research, they test the hypothesis that low-cost travel savings from the tourists' place of origin are transferred at least partially to higher tourism expenditure at the tourist des-tination. As far as the method is concerned, a system of simultaneous equations is estimated using the three-stage least squares (3SLS) method, distinguishing between tourism expenditure at the origin and at the destination. This study develops a methodology that allows for determining expenditure differences among different tourist profiles. It can be applied to multiple analyses such as understanding expenditure differences by nationality, the purpose of the visit, activities undertaken, or any type of variable that can describe tourist profiles of interest. The tourist profiles are defined as LCC tourists vs. non-LCC tourists, and categorised by the types of tourist packages and the categories of accom-modation (Eugenio-Martin and Inchausti-Sintes, 2016).

According to DeSalvo (2002), economic impact studies overestimate the direct impact of an airport on traveller expenditure. He provides two reasons. First, impact studies assume that the number of visitors to the local area via the airport would fall to zero in the absence of the airport. Second, impact studies implicitly assume that local residents would continue to travel outside the local area in the same numbers as when the local airport is available. So, it is assumed that the demand for travel into the local area by visitors is perfectly elastic with respect to the time and money costs of travel, while the demand for travel by local residents is perfectly inelastic with respect to these variables. DeSalvo develops a methodology that avoids both of these sources of error by explicitly incorporating air travel demand into the analysis. DeSalvo's analysis supports the conclusion of Butler and Kiernan (1992, 16) that

> it would be desirable to distinguish between tourists (and other visitors) who would not have travelled to the region if there were no airport and those who would not have come anyway by some other form of transportation. Only the former are really relevant for the estimation of indirect impacts.

When it comes to analysing the three main groups of passengers, it may be assumed that leisure passengers are those who do not have any other particular reason to visit the region other than their personal desire to travel, and in this case that no local airport exists to serve the region. Such tourists are more likely to choose another destination than VFR and business passengers, who probably would come (and sometimes would have to come) by other means of transport. Results of the survey carried out (discussed following) at Wroclaw airport, however, confirmed this assumption only partially. Around 23 per cent and 20 per cent of the overall number of passengers going back home declared that they would not have come to Wroclaw if there were no flight connections in the winter/spring and summer rounds of surveying, respectively. In both surveys in the group of leisure tourist passengers, the percentage of those who declared that they would not come was higher than average for all passengers: in the winter/spring round, it amounted to 39.9 per cent, whereas in the summer round, the difference was very small, namely 22.3 per cent.

Other studies of the relationship between aviation, tourism, and regional economies focus only on leisure tourism and leisure tourism destinations. In several, the significance of low-cost carriers is analysed. Donzelli (2010), for example, using evidence from southern Italy, analyses the effect of low-cost air transport on the local Italian economies. Other research focuses on Malta and the impact of low-cost airline operations on the development of cultural heritage tourism and the tourism market in general (Graham and Dennis, 2010; Smith, 2009), the impact of low-cost carriers on Korean Island tourism (Chung and Whang, 2011), the effect of low-cost tourism in Spain (Rey et al., 2011), and booming leisure air travel to Norway (Lian and Denstadli, 2010).

However, leisure tourists are not the only group of passengers visiting regions and spending money there, and leisure tourism destinations are not the only destinations where there is an inflow of air transport passengers. Migratory movements after the enlargement of the European Union in 2004 has substantially influenced the development of east-west routes of low-cost airlines in Europe and increased the number of passengers flying either to work abroad and/or later to visit their families.

> Waves of migration by European workers gave rise to new post-migration mobility of the 'visit to friends and relatives' (VFR) type. . . . The use of low-cost airlines has become the classic mode of travel and enables people to increase the frequency of their visits.
>
> (Dobruszkes, 2009, 427)

As far as low-cost airlines are concerned, Dobruszkes (2013, 77) also noted that 'visits to friends and relatives (VFRs) are largely associated with low-cost air travel, even more than travelling for holidays, while airfares are often a main reason to choose LCAs'. Data obtained in the surveys at Wroclaw airport showed, that on certain routes (for example: Wroclaw-Ireland and Wroclaw-UK), VFR passengers are in fact the largest group of passengers and so must be significantly contributing to inbound visitor spending money in Wroclaw and the surrounding region.

Characteristics of the City of Wroclaw and Wroclaw airport

The City of Wroclaw is located in the southwest Poland, close to borders with Germany (about 150 km away) and Czech Republic (about 100 km away). Wroclaw is the capital of Lower Silesia region – the second-best developed region in Poland after the Warsaw capital region, with GDP per capita in 2017 at the level of 110 per cent of the country's average (Statistics Poland, 2019a). When it comes to the City of Wroclaw, according to the Polish Statistical

176 Łukasz Olipra

Office, the level of this indicator reaches 160 per cent of the country's average (Statistics Poland, 2019b).

The heritage of Wroclaw includes multiculturalism – in its history it was a German, Czech, and a Polish city with a meaningful Jewish community. There are 640,000 inhabitants living in Wroclaw (December 2018). The city is also a strong academic centre with several universities and about 120,000 students. Since 2014, there has been considerable immigration of workers from the Ukraine to Wroclaw. The number of Ukrainians employed in Wroclaw reached 60,000 in 2016 and has remained at this level since then. Wroclaw attracts investments of companies in business process outsourcing (BPO) and shared services sectors, and the office space in the city reached 771,000 square metres in 2016. There are also many production plants of recognised international corporations based in Wroclaw or in the surrounding area.

Wroclaw is not a very popular tourist destination in Europe, but does manage to attract almost five million tourists per year. The strategy of tourism development in Wroclaw sets as its main objectives the promotion of business and conference-congress tourism in Wroclaw but also the promotion of the city as a destination for the city-break trips, with particular emphasis on cultural tourism. In 2016, Wroclaw held the title of the European Capital of Culture, in 2012 was one of host cities for UEFA European Football Championship Euro 2012, and in 2017 hosted the World Games. All these events aimed to increase recognition of the city as an attractive and interesting European tourist destination.

Wrocław Nicolaus Copernicus Airport is located in the western part of Wrocław. Since 2003, the airport has recorded a rapid increase in passenger traffic. Within five years, the number of passengers increased five times and this dynamic trend also lasted into the following years (Figure 10.1). The airport

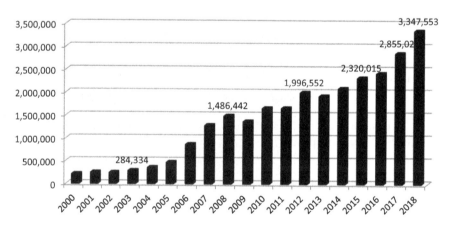

Figure 10.1 Number of passengers at Wroclaw airport in the period 2000–2018

Source: Devised by author from www.airport.wroclaw.pl

is served by network carriers which offer flights to the major hubs in Europe; low-cost carriers like Ryanair and Wizz Air, which have their operational bases at the Wrocław Airport; and also charter airlines hired by tour operators in providing part of package deals. In March 2012, a new passenger terminal was opened. Its capacity is almost four million passengers per year and in the future it will reach as much as seven million.

Methodology

The basic method of the research was a survey carried out among passengers departing from Wrocław Airport which was the source of data necessary for the estimation of expenditure of different category passengers, as well as for the total amount of the visitor spending. Butler and Kiernan (1992) stated that data necessary for an estimation of the visitor expenditures should be collected on the basis of a mail survey or direct interviews with owners or employees of travel agencies. This would be justified and suitable if the research concerned the structure of total visitor expenditure according to the mode of transport used to come to the region. However, in this case, the survey carried out only among passengers at the airport provides all data necessary for estimation and analysis.

The survey was undertaken in two rounds: first in the winter/spring period (17 March–6 April 2014), and second in the summer period (17 July–3 August 2014). The sample in the first round amounted 4,050 respondents, that is 9.1 per cent of the passengers, and in the second round 11,616 respondents, 14.5 per cent of the passengers. Such a large sample was dictated by the Board of Directors of the airport with the wish to build passenger profiles at the level of particular destinations. Thus, the size of sample also allowed for the estimation of total expenditure according to the purpose of visit. The procedure of estimation consisted of five stages, which were presented and described in Figure 10.2.

The expenditure was calculated separately for 16 different categories (Figure 10.3). Charter airlines were not taken into consideration, because there was no inflow of charter passengers to the analysed region.[1] The question regarding the amount of expenditure in the region during stay was only asked to passengers stating that they were going back to their place of residence, so only these were taken into consideration in the study.

It should be noted that the calculation and estimation of expenditure was made separately for the summer period (June–September) and the rest of the year. This distinction was due to the differences in the characteristics of air traffic and trips between these periods. The seasonal variations highlight first the changing nature of the structure of passenger traffic according to the purpose of travel (less business and more leisure trips in summer), and second the different features of summer trips, mainly in terms of length of stay.

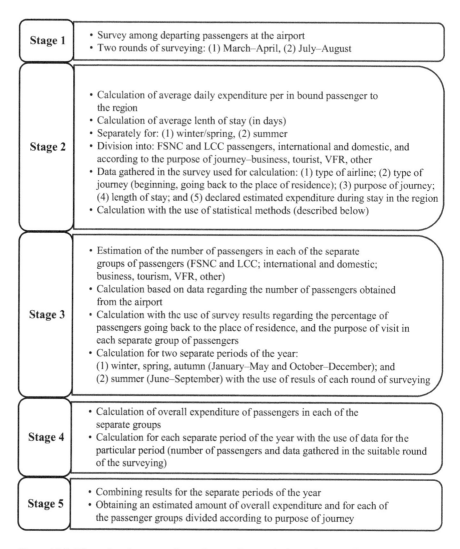

Figure 10.2 The estimation procedure of expenditure of inbound visitors by air to the region
Source: Devised by author

Research results

The most important information at the initial stage of the analysis concerns the type of the trip, i.e. whether the passenger is at the beginning or start of their trip, whether they are returning to their place of residence, whether they are transferring at Wroclaw airport, or maybe staying in the region as part of a longer trip (see Table 10.1). In all cases except one, the share of passengers

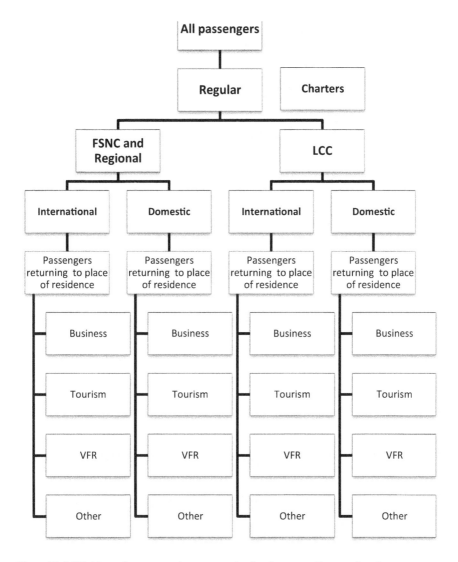

Figure 10.3 Division of passengers into categories for the expenditure estimation
Source: Devised by author

beginning the trip at Wroclaw airport exceeds the percentage of those going back home. It may therefore be concluded that most passengers using Wroclaw airport are inhabitants of the region, who do not generate additional demand-side effects in the region. For further calculations, data obtained from passengers returning to their place of residence or other types (for example, undertaking a longer trip) were taken into consideration. In Table 10.2, the structure of

Table 10.1 Structure of surveyed passengers according to the type of journey (beginning, return, others)

Measure	Survey carried in March–April 2014						Survey carried in July–August 2014					
	FSC			LCC			FSC			LCC		
	All	Intl	Domestic	All	Intl	Domestic	All	Intl	Domestic	All	Intl	Domestic
Beginning of journey	58.59%	58.71%	58.23%	62.80%	62.65%	52.72%	49.54%	52.37%	41.43%	58.43%	59.19%	53.48%
Going back to place of residence	38.84%	38.98%	38.42%	36.45%	36.61%	45.07%	47.87%	45.44%	54.82%	40.07%	39.63%	42.91%
Transfer at Wroclaw airport	1.02%	0.96%	1.19%	0.22%	0.23%	0.80%	0.74%	0.69%	0.89%	0.59%	0.42%	1.74%
Other. e.g. stage of a longer journey	1.56%	1.36%	2.15%	0.53%	0.51%	1.41%	1.85%	1.50%	2.86%	0.91%	0.76%	1.87%
Total	100.0%	100.0%	100.0%	100.0%	100.0%	100.0%	100.0%	100.0%	100.0%	100.0%	100.0%	100.0%
The percentage taken to further calculations (Passenger going back and others)	40.39%	40.34%	40.57%	36.98%	37.12%	46.48%	49.72%	46.94%	57.68%	40.98%	40.39%	44.78%

Source: Devised by author based on survey results

Table 10.2 Structure of surveyed passengers according to the purpose of journey

No.	Measure	Survey carried in March–April 2014						Survey carried in July–August 2014					
		FSC			LCC			FSC			LCC		
		All	Intl	Domestic	All	Intl	Domestic	All	Intl	Domestic	All	Intl	Domestic
1	Business trip	69.78%	66.14%	80.59%	13.23%	11.11%	32.47%	47.44%	38.96%	67.18%	7.88%	7.33%	12.50%
2	Tourism	7.26%	7.92%	5.29%	12.99%	12.86%	32.47%	11.16%	12.23%	8.67%	24.09%	22.09%	40.91%
3	VFR	14.96%	17.03%	8.82%	56.62%	59.18%	27.27%	30.23%	36.30%	16.10%	58.06%	60.82%	34.85%
4	Other	8.00%	8.91%	5.30%	17.16%	16.85%	7.79%	11.16%	12.50%	8.05%	9.97%	9.76%	11.74%
5	Total	100.00%	100.00%	100.00%	100.00%	100.00%	100.00%	100.00%	100.00%	100.00%	100.00%	100.00%	100.00%

Source: Devised by author based on survey results

182   *Łukasz Olipra*

passengers according to the purpose of journey is presented. A considerable amount of regularity can be observed, in that the leading group of passengers for full-service carriers (FSCs) are business travellers, while with low-cost airlines, this is VFR passengers. The share of leisure tourists within the total number of passengers is also noticeably higher for LCCs than for FSCs.

To estimate the amount of expenditure, it is necessary to calculate the average daily expenditure per passenger, as well as the average length of stay in Wroclaw or Lower Silesia. These measures estimated for each category separately for both analysed periods (winter/spring and summer rounds of surveying) are presented in the Table 10.3. The average weighted length of visit was achieved by dividing the estimated overall number of days spent in the region (a sum of number of days declared to be spent) by the number of respondents in a particular category of passengers. The daily expenditure per passenger was obtained by the division of the sum of all expenditures declared by respondents in the survey by the sum of declared number of days spent by them in the region. Analysis of the basic statistical measures shows that distribution of declared expenditure is highly asymmetrical. There are several very high amounts declared in each category, which significantly influences the mean calculation of expenditures. But these high amounts of declared expenditures can also be related to the length of stay. The longer the stay, the higher amount of money is usually spent. So to make data on expenditure comparable and useful for further calculations, there was a need to calculate average daily expenditure per passenger in each of the categories, as well as the average length of stay.

Analysing the data in Table 10.3, it can be noted that for all categories of passengers, average length of stay in the summer period is longer than in the winter time. Similarly, average stays of FSC passengers are longer than average stays of LCC passengers for all groups except business travellers. When it comes to the estimated average daily expenditure, clear regularity does not occur.

Table 10.3 includes estimated total expenditure of each group of passengers together for both periods: (1) winter, spring, and autumn; and (2) summer. The basis for the estimates was information given by the airport authority regarding the number of departing passengers in each group of passengers (FSC vs. LCC and international vs. domestic) in both analysed periods. Then, data obtained in the survey were taken for estimation (percentage of passengers going back to the place of residence and the structure of passengers according to the purpose of the trip), as well as measures calculated at the previous stage: average weighted length of visit (in days) and estimated average expenditure per day. As a result, we receive estimated overall expenditure of passengers in a particular period and particular category of passengers. The total amount of expenditure for passengers divided according to the type of carrier and character of the traffic (international or domestic) is the sum of total overall expenditures in each category. Estimated amounts of expenditure in each category were gathered together in Table 10.4, where they were summed, giving the final estimated total amount of expenditures.

Table 10.3 Average weighted length of visit and estimated average expenditure per day for different categories of passengers

No.	Measure	FSC international passengers					FSC domestic passengers					FSC in total
		In total	Division according to a purpose of trip				In total	Division according to a purpose of trip				
			Business	Leisure	VFR	Other		Business	Leisure	VFR	Other	
1	**March–April 2014**											
2	Average weighted length of visit (in days)	6.61	4.65	11.14	10.48	10.6	2.17	2.03	2.83	3	2.3	5.66
3	Estimated average expenditures per day (in PLN)	295.84	334.03	326.50	248.39	239.97	315.29	350.79	288.24	135.71	213.91	297.43
4	**July–August 2014**											
5	Average weighted length of visit (in days)	11.2	5.86	17.31	14.68	14.33	2.7	2.02	4.07	4.06	2.93	8.61
6	Estimated average expenditures per day (in PLN)	299.43	375.44	317.33	276.4	235.84	245.32	269.2	163.16	136.99	304.39	294.3

No.		LCC international passengers					LCC domestic passengers					LCC in total
7												
8	**March–April 2014**											
9	Average weighted length of visit (in days)	7.25	5.28	7.16	7.48	7.7	4.14	2.5	3.68	3	–	7.24
10	Estimated average expenditures per day (in PLN)	285.30	322.68	270.76	275.75	313.85	133.20	173.33	203.70	147.67	–	284.48
11	**July–August 2014**											
12	Average weighted length of visit (in days)	11.03	7.16	12.88	10.29	13.38	3.88	2.65	3.44	3.77	6.41	10
13	Estimated average expenditures per day (in PLN)	298.6	432.57	293.72	295.37	289.79	162.24	175.36	192.91	156.87	122.44	291.01

Source: Devised by author based on survey results

Table 10.4 Estimated amount of incoming air transport passengers' expenditures in Wroclaw and Lower Silesia region in 2014 (in PLN)

No.		FSC			LCC			FSC + LCC
		International	*Domestic*	*All*	*International*	*Domestic*	*All*	
1	Business trip	90,584,430	17,461,749	108,046,178	42,978,689	2,242,520	45,221,209	153,267,387
2	Tourism	41,711,868	1,797,419	43,509,287	101,402,681	5,281,691	106,684,371	150,193,658
3	VFR	80,769,645	2,165,923	82,935,568	309,198,635	3,206,655	312,405,291	395,340,859
4	Other	28,802,244	1,681,790	30,484,034	83,274,260	1,295,039	84,569,299	115,053,333
5	Total	241,868,186	23,106,881	264,975,067	536,854,265	12,025,905	548,880,170	813,855,237

Source: Devised by author

Table 10.5 Structure of the estimated expenditures according to the purpose of journey in each of distinguished groups of passengers

No.		FSC			LCC			FSC + LCC
		International	*Domestic*	*All*	*International*	*Domestic*	*All*	
1	Business trip	37.45%	75.57%	40.78%	8.01%	18.65%	8.24%	18.83%
2	Tourism	17.25%	7.78%	16.42%	18.89%	43.92%	19.44%	18.45%
3	VFR	33.39%	9.37%	31.30%	57.59%	26.66%	56.92%	48.58%
4	Other	11.91%	7.28%	11.50%	15.51%	10.77%	15.41%	14.14%
5	Total	100%	100%	100%	100.00%	100%	100%	100%

Source: Devised by author

The total volume of expenditure of inbound passengers in the Wroclaw and Lower Silesia region in 2014 has been estimated at the level of PLN813.9 million, which amounts approximately to €194.7 million. This sum is equal to 0.56 per cent of Lower Silesian GDP, 1.75 per cent of the GDP of the City of Wroclaw and 4.14 per cent of total expenditure of foreign tourists in Poland in 2014, which amounted to €4.7 billion. Moreover, the budget of the region of Lower Silesia amounted to about PLN2.17 billion in 2014. So, the estimated total amount of expenditure equals 37 per cent of the regional budget. Thus, the demand-side effect of inbound passengers by air generated by their expenditure during their stay in the City of Wroclaw and Lower Silesia region can be regarded as significant for the regional economy. Table 10.5 and Figures 10.4 and 10.5 present the structure of estimated total expenditure according to the purpose of visit.

Analysing the structure of passenger expenditure according to the destination (Table 10.5), it is important to note that the level of visitor spending impact generated by domestic passengers is very modest and amounts to less than 3 per cent of overall expenditures in the case of FSCs and approximately 1.5 per cent in the case of LCCs.

When it comes to international passengers, there is a significant difference between the spending impact generated by LCCs passengers (65 per cent of overall expenditure) and FSCs passengers (30 per cent). In the case of FSC passengers, a slightly higher impact is generated by business passengers than the second-placed VFR segment. Expenditure generated by leisure tourists flying with FSCs amounted to only 5 per cent of estimated total expenditure. The situation is the reverse when it comes to the LCC visitor spending impact generated by business passengers amounting to 5 per cent and leisure tourists to 12 per cent.

The largest share in total expenditure is generated by VFR passengers travelling with LCCs (38 per cent). Altogether, VFR passengers generate almost half of the spending impact in Lower Silesia of air passengers, while leisure tourists as well as business travellers generate only approximately 18 per cent.

186　Łukasz Olipra

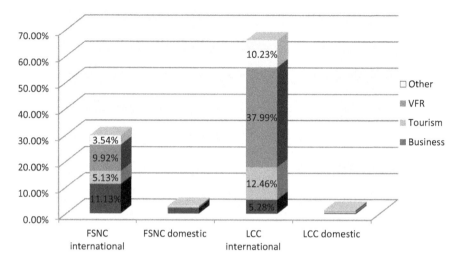

Figure 10.4 The structure of total expenditure according to the purpose of journey, type of carrier, and destination

Source: Devised by author

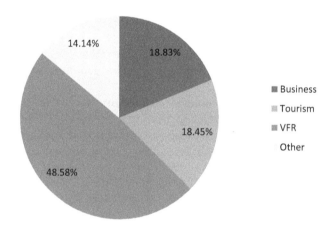

Figure 10.5 The structure of the estimated total expenditure according to the purpose of journey

Source: Devised by author

Conclusion

The aim of this chapter was to estimate the amount of total expenditure made by air passengers arriving at Copernicus Airport in the City of Wroclaw and the region of Lower Silesia. This chapter has analysed the structure of expenditure according to the purpose of visit. The total amount of inbound passenger expenditure has been estimated to be PLN813.9 million, which is approximately €194.7 million. This sum is equal to 0.56 per cent of Lower Silesian GDP and 1.75 per cent of the City of Wroclaw's GDP. This expenditure generates additional demand for goods and services in the regional economy of Wroclaw and Lower Silesia, contributing inter alia to the creation of jobs and GDP. Taking into account that the overall estimated amount of expenditure is equal to 37 per cent of the regional budget in 2014, this demand-side effect on the regional economy can be considered as significant.

Estimation of the amount of expenditure of particular categories of passengers, and the analysis of the structure according to the purpose of the trip, revealed that the biggest share (approximately 50 per cent) of the total amount of passengers' expenditure is generated by VFR passengers. Leisure passengers, as well as business travellers, generate approximately 18 per cent of the visitors' spending impact. Taking into account the assumption that leisure tourists are those who do not have any other reason to come except for visiting the city and region, they can be treated as the main contributors to the impact of air transport on the regional economy in the tourism sector area. The possibility that these passengers would come to the region if there were no air connections is lower in this group than with groups of VFR and business passengers who have more ties with the city and regions, and are much more likely to come anyway even if there were no flights to Wroclaw. Thus, to increase the visitors' spending impact and impact of air transport on the economy of the city and region, particular attention should be paid to leisure tourists and their share in the structure of passenger expenditure.

To increase the number of leisure tourists, and thus the amount of their expenditure, various actions and initiatives can be introduced. The promotion of the region should be focused on foreign markets, as the vast majority of estimated total expenditure is generated by international passengers. The use of LCC marketing channels should also be taken into consideration, as the share of leisure tourist expenditure in the overall amount generated by LCCs passengers is higher than in the case of FSCs passengers. Low-cost carriers have more power as well to generate new demand for travel to particular destination. In addition. it can be concluded that the structure of visitor spending impact depends on the character of the region, i.e. whether it is a traditional leisure tourist destination, as well as the level of economic development of the region in relation to other EU regions (regions of immigration versus emigration). In the presented case of Wroclaw airport, it is also important to take action and try to even up the number of passengers going back home after visiting the region with the number of those beginning their trip in Wroclaw. The existing imbalance between these two groups of passengers can be treated as lowering the net impact of air transport on the regional economy, as there are more inhabitants of the region leaving by air transport and possibly spending money out of the region, than there are visitors spending money in the

188 *Łukasz Olipra*

analysed region. However, this issue is not the main topic of this study and can be the subject of further analysis.

Note

1 Charter airlines are used almost always by outbound travellers from the region, mainly leisure tourists going from Wroclaw airport to holiday destinations. There is no reverse tourist traffic carried by charter airlines.

References

ACI-Europe (1998). *Creating employment and prosperity in Europe: A study of the social and economic impacts of airports*. Brussels, ACI-Europe.

ACI-Europe and InterVISTAS (2015). *Economic impact of European airports: A critical catalyst to economic growth*. Brussels, ACI-Europe.

ACI-Europe and York Aviation (2004). *The social and economic impact of airports in Europe*. Brussels, ACI-Europe.

ACI-Europe and York Consulting (2000). *Creating employment and prosperity in Europe: An economic impact study kit*. Brussels, ACI-Europe.

ACI-North America (2002). *The economic impact of US airports*. Washington, ACI-North America.

Braathen, S., Johansen, S. and Lian, J. I. (2006). *An inquiry into the link between air transport and employment in Norway*. Association for European Transport and Contributors. Available at: http://web.mit.edu (accessed 11 March 2018).

Butler, S. E. and Kiernan, L. J. (1986). *Measuring the regional economic significance of airports*. US Department of Transportation. Report No. DOT/FAA/PP/87-1. Washington, FAA.

Butler, S. E. and Kiernan, L. J. (1992). *Estimating the regional economic significance of airports*. US Department of Transportation. Washington, FAA.

Button, K. and Taylor, S. (2000). International air transportation and economic development. *Journal of Air Transport Management*, 6(4), 209–222.

Chung, J. Y. and Whang, T. (2011). The impact of low cost carriers on Korean Island tourism. *Journal of Transport Geography*, 19, 1335–1340.

Cooper, A. and Smith, P. (2005). *The economic catalytic effects of air transport in Europe*. EEC/SEE/2005/004. Brussels, EUROControl Experimental Centre.

DeSalvo, J. S. (2002). Direct impact of an airport on travelers' expenditures: Methodology and application. *Growth and Change*, 34(1), 130.

Dobruszkes, F. (2009). New Europe: New low-cost air services. *Journal of Transport Geography*, 17, 423–432.

Dobruszkes, F. (2013). The geography of European low-cost airline networks: A contemporary analysis. *Journal of Transport Geography*, 28, 75–88.

Donzelli, M. (2010). The effect of low-cost air transportation on the local economy: Evidence from Southern Italy. *Journal of Air Transport Management*, 16, 121–126.

Eugenio-Martin, J. L. and Inchausti-Sintes, F. (2016). Low-cost travel and tourism expenditures. *Annals of Tourism Research*, 57, 140–159.

FAA (2009). *The economic impact of civil aviation on the US economy*. Washington, FAA.

Francis, G., Fidato, A. and Humpreys, I. (2003). Airport – airline interaction: The impact of low-cost carriers on two European airports. *Journal of Air Transport Management*, 9(4), 267–273.

Graham, A. (2018). *Managing airports: An international perspective*, 5th edition. Abingdon, Routledge.

Graham, A. and Dennis, N. (2010). The impact of low cost airline operations to Malta. *Journal of Air Transport Management*, 16, 127–136.

Halpern, N. and Bråthen, S. (2010). *Catalytic impact of airports in Norway*. Report 1008. Molde, Møreforsking Molde.

Huderek-Glapska, S. (2011). Wpływ portu lotniczego na gospodarkę regionu. In Rekowski, M. (ed) *Regionalne porty lotnicze w Polsce: Charakterystyka i tendencje rozwojowe*. Poznań, Poland, Wydawnictwo Uniwersytetu Ekonomicznego w Poznaniu.

Lian, J. I. and Denstadli, J. M. (2010). Booming leisure air travel to Norway – the role of airline competition. *Scandinavian Journal of Hospitality and Tourism*, 10(1), 1–15.

Martí Selva, M. L., Calafat Marzal, C. and Puertas Medina, R. (2012). Tourism expenditure of airline users: Impact on the Spanish economy. In Gil-Lafuente, A., Gil-Lafuente, J. and Merigó-Lindahl, J. (eds) *Soft computing in management and business economics*. Berlin, Springer.

Oxford Economic Forecasting (1999). *The contribution of the aviation industry to the UK economy: Final report*. Oxford, Oxford Economic Forecasting.

Pancer-Cybulska, E. et al. (2014). *The impact of air transport on regional labour markets in Poland*. Wrocław, Publishing House of the Wroclaw University of Economics.

Rekowski, M. et al. (2006). *Ekonomiczny wpływ Portu Lotniczego im: Mikołaja Kopernika we Wrocławiu na rozwój miasta i region: A final report*. Wrocław, Wroclaw University of Economics.

Rey, A., Myro, R. L. and Galera, A. (2011). Effect of low-cost airlines on tourism in Spain: A dynamic panel data model. *Journal of Air Transport Management*, 17, 163–167.

Robertson, J. A. (1995). Airports and economic regeneration. *Journal of Air Transport Management*, 2(2), 81–88.

Smith, A. (2009). Effects of low cost airlines on efforts to develop cultural heritage tourism. *An International Journal of Tourism and Hospitability Research*, 20(2), 289–306.

Statistics Poland (2019a). *Gross domestic product and gross value added in the regions' breakdown in 2017*. Available at: https://stat.gov.pl (accessed 10 October 2019).

Statistics Poland (2019b). *Gross domestic product – regional accounts in the years 2015–2017*. Available at: https://stat.gov.pl (accessed 10 October 2019).

TRB (2008). *Airport economic impact: Methods and models*. Airport Cooperative Research Program Synthesis 7. Washington, Transportation Research Board.

UNWTO (2010). *International recommendations for tourism statistics 2008*. Available at: https://unstats.un.org/unsd/publication/Seriesm/SeriesM_83rev1e.pdf (accessed 30 May 2018).

UNWTO (2014). *Glossary of tourism terms*. Madrid, World Tourism Organisation.

Wilbur Smith Associates (1988). *The economic impact of Los Angeles international airport: Final report*. Los Angeles, City of Los Angeles Department of Airports.

11 Intangible effects of regional airports in the aviation system

The case of Switzerland

Andreas Wittmer and Claudio Noto

Introduction

Swiss regional airports provide numerous benefits to the aviation system and the Swiss economy as a whole. Some of these benefits can be measured as positive, monetised macroeconomic effects, whereas others are identified as intangible economic effects which cannot directly be related to revenues or employment numbers. These intangible effects can be broken down into network, competence, structural, and image effects; they are often cited as *wider economic benefits*. By contrast, as in many countries, the regional airports also face high infrastructure costs that are difficult to be borne by each airport alone. Thus, despite the macroeconomic benefits, the economic sustainability of regional airports remains a challenge.

Consequently, as an essential complement to any monetary evaluation of an airport's sustainability, it is necessary to identify and address the intangible effects of the regional airports to help justify the high infrastructure costs. However, although intangible effects are frequently cited implicitly and explicitly both in theory and in practice, for example in economic airport studies, by airport representatives, or by politicians, they often lack a concise definition and identification and thus are rarely assessed concisely.

Therefore, this chapter addresses this gap in the literature by providing the following conceptional and empirical contributions. First, we subsume the methodology of tangible and intangible effects based on a focused review of Wittmer and Bieger (2011); moreover, we present a conceptional framework for the location choice of firms according to different location theories from the literature. Subsequently, to illustrate the application of the above concepts, we summarise the conclusions of Wittmer et al. (2009) results concerning the intangible effects of the six Swiss regional airports – St. Gallen-Altenrhein, Bern-Belp, Sion, Lugano-Agno, Samedan, and Grenchen – which are based on qualitative empirical data from in-depth interviews with experts and exponents of the Swiss aviation system.[1]

Background and literature

The Swiss aviation system consists of several layers. The three national airports of Zurich, Geneva, and Basel-Mulhouse[2] represent the superior level, whose

considerable economic importance mainly rests on international and intercontinental connectivity. At a lesser level, several regional airports also provide interregional and international connectivity; moreover, together with several small
airfields, they enable activities such as flight training, aeromedical supply, and leisure
and tourism ventures, which are all essential economic contributors for the regions.

Based on these activities and their effects on location attractivity, the regional
airports are involved in various regional and national networks. In this respect,
they may affect the location choice of industries, businesses, and service facilities such as hotels and restaurants, which are attracted to the airport directly or
to its vicinity. Moreover, their beneficial effects in terms of the international
and interregional connectivity, the associated leisure and business activities, the
corresponding mutual customer-supplier partnerships, and the potential for
vertical or horizontal integration of the industry, or industry clustering, support various interactions among the concerned business entities. In turn, these
benefits again foster the importance of the regional airfields for the regional
and national economies. As a result, the Swiss regional airfields may arguably
be referred to as profoundly nested within Switzerland's aviation system.

A vast number of studies investigate the economic effects of airports and their
regional importance, for example: Hume and Mason (2000), Spengler (2000),
Sager et al. (2000), Niemeier (2001), Maibach et al. (2003), ACI-Europe (2004),
Baum (2005), Heymann (2005), Heuer et al. (2005), Koch et al. (2005), Air Transport Action Group (ATAG) (2005), Heuer and Klophaus (2006), Klophaus (2006),
Maibach et al. (2006a, 2006b), Wittmer and Laesser (2006), Peltzer et al. (2007),
Gantenbein (2008), Harsche et al. (2008), Malina et al. (2008), Button et al. (2010),
Bilotkach (2015), Florida et al. (2015) and Mosbah and Ryerson (2016). In this
respect, Zak and Getzner (2014) provide a meta-analysis of the various studies that
assess the different economic effects related to air transport facilities in a regional
economic context. They also confirm the difficulty of evaluating catalytic effects
due to identification, measurement, and their separation from other factors.

Typology

As Wittmer and Bieger (2011) delineate, many recent studies that investigate
the economic effects of airports apply the methodological approach of the
Airport Council International (ACI) (ACI, 2000, 2004). As Figure 11.1 shows,
this approach categorises the economic effects into direct, indirect, catalytic or
location, and induced effects;[3] from a resource-based perspective, the catalytic
effects are divided into tangible and intangible effects.

The tangible effects are monetary effects that arise from incoming passengers,
tourists, and attracted companies. By contrast, the intangible effects cannot
directly be captured by numbers like employment or monetary equivalents but
have an impact on the attractiveness of a region. As indicated in Figure 11.1, the
intangible effects can be further decomposed into structural, competence, network, and image effects. This distinction is delineated in Table 11.1, which is
discussed in the following subsections. In addition, the last subsection describes
a further differentiation of intangible effects into hard and soft factors.

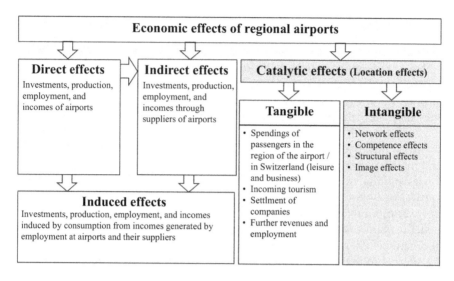

Figure 11.1 Economic effects of regional airports, according to ACI
Source: Adapted from Wittmer et al. (2009)

Table 11.1 Intangible catalytic effects of regional airports

Effects	Examples
Network effects	Horizontal and vertical integration with other companies
	Industry cluster creation (industries move close to airports)
Competence effects	Aviation industry
	Maintenance, repair and overhaul centres (MRO)
	Flight training organisations (ATO)
	Leisure facility (recreational flying, aviation competitions)
	Hosting premium events
	Fostering aviation in the social context
Structural effects	International and interregional accessibility and travel time savings
	Location attractiveness for new companies (location decision)
	Infrastructure for flight training and recreational flying
	Load relief for national airports (secondary airport function)
	Aeromedical supply
	Business opportunities based on connectivity, network effects, and clustering
Image effects	Attractiveness for business and leisure travel, private individuals (residence), and businesses
	Benefits for destination management (marketing)

Source: Adapted from Wittmer et al. (2009)

Network effects

From a theoretical systems perspective, the participating institutions, organisations, business entities, and consumers are conceived as the main components of the air traffic network – this includes airlines, infrastructure, and service providers (i.e. airports and handling agents), aircraft manufacturers and maintenance organisations, and private organisations and interest groups, financial institutions, as well as national and international aviation (Pompl, 2007). Hence, the network effects generally delineate the direct, indirect, bilateral, and multilateral relationships that arise from the interaction of the entities within that network (see Döring, 1999). Typically, they include the horizontal and vertical integration of the regional airports with their suppliers or other companies in the vicinity, or the creation of industry clusters, which delineates the tendency of industries to move and cluster close to airports. Network effects can be assessed, for example, based on a network analysis that evaluates the connections between all participants, such as in Freeman (1979).

Competence effects

By contrast, a competence effect is a purely qualitative effect that indicates the development of specific service skills or technologies based on the proximity or existence of industries, infrastructures, or companies (e.g. Wittmer et al., 2009; Strauf and Behrendt, 2006 or Strauf, 2007). In the case of regional airports, competence effects evolve from the related aviation industry in a general sense, as well as in terms of aviation-particular institutions such as flight training organisations (ATO) and maintenance, repair, and overhaul (MRO) facilities. In addition, the airports as leisure facilities for recreational flying and aviation competitions, as well as facilities that help to foster the integration of aviation into the social context, represent competence effects. Finally, the hosting of premium events also requires specific competencies that may be supplied by regional airports.

Structural effects

Structural effects are related to the benefits that arise from the infrastructure provision of aeronautical facilities (Wittmer et al., 2009). Primarily, the structural effects of a regional airport consist of fostering the accessibility of the region, which includes the attraction of new companies and businesses, and providing the necessary infrastructure for flight training and recreational flying. Moreover, regional airports may incorporate a load relief for national airports that operate at their capacity limits. In Switzerland, this concerns secondary airports for low-cost or legacy airlines to a lesser extent; more significantly, it applies to general and business aviation, and for charter flights of regional airlines for local passengers. Another structural effect of a regional airport consists of the contribution of the infrastructure for aeromedical care and rescue services, which may include helicopter landing sites.

Image effects

Image effects relate to the image of a region in the perception of various stakeholders, such as inhabitants, employees, industries, or tourists. For example, the international flair of an airport may affect the attractiveness of its location as a business or leisure destination. In this respect, particular tourist or business travellers may be attracted by the availability of commercial or private air transport into that region even if they choose a different actual mode of transport. As a result, the image effect may be used in tourism destination management: For example, the Swiss capital's regional airport, Bern-Belp, only provides limited connectivity but is also home to the federal air transport services and is used by the federal government for the reception of state guests and diplomats. Thus, despite its limited role for international tourism, the airport provides the capital city with the image of international connectivity.

Soft and hard intangible factors

Furthermore, intangible effects can also be divided into soft and hard intangible factors that influence the attractiveness of the location. Hard intangible factors represent elements that are located within the scope of action of the regional airport management. By contrast, soft intangible factors represent societal, political, and economic environmental conditions that surround the regional airport that can hardly be influenced by the management of the regional airport (Klophaus, 2006). Hence, in the analysis of the wider economic benefits of regional airports, it is crucial to make a connection between different tangible and intangible catalytic effects, as well as the soft and hard factors within the intangible catalytic effects.

Location choice

Location theories

Location theories are fundamental in explaining the attractiveness of a specific location for society and industry development. In regional economics, questions of location development and of empirical factors that lead to regional upturns are prominent. Hence, several theories exist that relate to regional development. As Figure 11.2 shows, they focus on two main perspectives: a regional economic perspective and a microeconomic or company perspective.

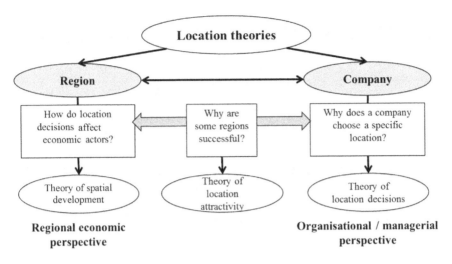

Figure 11.2 Location theories
Source: Adapted from Wittmer et al. (2009)

The regional economic perspective differentiates between theories of spatial development and location attractiveness; both these theories aim at explaining how locations develop and identifying the key factors that are responsible for the development. By contrast, the microeconomic perspective focuses on the companies, where location decision theories aim at explaining why companies choose certain locations for their production facilities or administrative headquarters. The analysis of the intangible catalytic effects of the Swiss regional airports requires an adoption of both of these perspectives and their associated theories.

Location choice criteria

In addition, based on an inclusive content analysis across several studies about the location choice of production companies in the United States, Jungthirapanich and Benjamin (1995) provide an indication of the importance of accessibility and transport on location choice. As indicated in Table 11.2, they identify transport as one of the critical concerns in company location choice.

Similarly, Walter and Suzuki (2002) investigate the location choice of production companies in the US Midwest, thereby showing that access to transport facilities and opportunities are essential. Based on further progress of societal mobility and globalisation, it can be assumed that the issue of transport as a location choice criterion has not lost its primary importance.

196 Andreas Wittmer and Claudio Noto

Table 11.2 Ranking of location choice criteria of production companies in the United States

Factor	Metrics
1 Market	Proximity to markets, purchasing power of local consumers
2 Transport	Land, water, and air transport
3 Labour	General workforce availability, availability of specialised employees (e.g. science and engineering), labour unions
4 Site consideration	Price of land, cost of plant construction
5 Raw materials and services	Availability of raw materials and business services
6 Utilities	Capability and capacity of energy generation, energy costs, availability of fuel and water
7 Government concerns	Federal aid to local government, government debt, taxes, governmental employee training
8 Community environment	Housing availability, education, health, and medical considerations, human services, security, environmental conditions, cost of living, business climate, physical climate

Source: Adapted from Jungthirapanich and Benjamin (1995)

Qualitative analysis

The goal of the subsequent qualitative evaluation is to gain insights into the specific location effects that arise at the Swiss regional airports (Table 11.3). In this respect, we assume that the different regional airports exhibit distinct functions, both in their respective region and as crucial parts of the Swiss aviation system. Therefore, the assessment of the network, structural and competence effects of the Swiss regional airports focuses on several concise vital aspects from the perspectives of different stakeholders in the aviation systems.[4]

The empirical data stem from a focus group workshop and qualitative interviews with government officials, regional and national airport directors, business entities, and attracted companies, hotels in the airport vicinity, and key companies of the Swiss aviation industry. Based on the research goal, the qualitative data gathering process follows an exploratory rather than a confirmative approach.

As Table 11.4 shows, the regional and national airport directors, the air operators at regional airports, air traffic control, the company managers in the vicinity of the regional airports, and the regional tourism managers state a wide variety of soft and hard factors that represent intangible effects. These effects are summarised in the subsequent subsections.

Regional airports

In particular, the agents at the regional airports favour the network effects in terms of personal relationships, the capability of the regional airport as a concentrator that bundles the services from different network partners, thereby providing a sole source/single point of contact, the flexibility toward the stakeholders, and short distances for fast and efficient travel.

Intangible effects of regional airports 197

Table 11.3 Swiss regional airports – perspectives, stakeholders, and key aspects

Perspective	Stakeholder	Key aspects
Strategic	• Regional airports	• The importance of the airport in the Swiss aviation system
Strategic	• National airports	• The general importance of regional airfields, and the links between regional and national airports based on the differing nature of distinct flight operators, such as network, regional, and charter airlines, business and general aviation, or low-cost carriers
Operational	• Airline and business aviation operators	• The benefits of the regional airport infrastructure from an operational point of view
Operational	• Air traffic control	• The challenge of air traffic management at various Swiss airports with their individual distinct nature of operations
Economic and location choice	• Regional companies	• Business perspectives and their dependence on the airport for companies who consider the regional airport as a vital location choice argument, or frequently utilise the regional airport
Economic	• Tourism	• Perspectives of the airport for regional tourism

Source: Devised by authors, based on Wittmer et al. (2009)

Table 11.4 Intangible effects of the Swiss regional airports

Stakeholder	Network effects	Structural effects	Competence effects
Regional airports	• Personal relationships • Concentration of services from different network partners to sole source/single point of contact • Flexibility toward the stakeholders • Short distances, fast check-in, efficient travel	• International connectivity • Leisure/charter flights for local passengers • Promotion platform for events, public leisure time facility	• Personnel with multi-role capabilities efficiently and flexibly perform distinct tasks (e.g., passenger handling, fire services, snow removal) • Safety and security knowledge at all levels/ by all employees • Business aviation handling, customer care • Flight training (operational and organisational)
National airports	• Feeder function	• Relief/alternative for national airports for general and business aviation, charter and leisure flights, and low-cost carriers	• Flight training • Promotion of the image of aviation in the society

(*Continued*)

198 *Andreas Wittmer and Claudio Noto*

Table 11.4 (Continued)

Stakeholder	Network effects	Structural effects	Competence effects
Airline and business aviation operators	• Connectivity for business travellers/ proximity to final destinations • Expeditious air traffic flows, higher operational flexibility, and lower costs • Personal relationships with responsible parties	• Regional economic development • Relief of national airports due to scarce airport capacity and congested airspace	• Flight training • Promotion and recruitment of young talents through local flying clubs • Promotion of tourism, reputation, and attractiveness of the region
Air traffic control	• Multiple airports in proximity may constitute a single virtual airport	• Relief function for seasonal demand fluctuations (particularly business aviation) • Focus on core competencies (with public subsidies)	• Flight training • Swiss Air Force and police training and operations (e.g. disaster management/ emergency aid)
Regional companies	• International connectivity for international firms (business, events, guests) • Travel time savings for business travel, air transport, freight	• Aeromedical care (in general and for events) • Location choice: airport is one location factor among others, has little influence on-site selection	• Customer care for business travellers and premium events
Tourism	• Direct regional access for upscale tourism (especially during winter)	• Tourism jobs/ employment • Social benefits from upscale tourism • Tourism and flight training camps increase occupancy rates	• Public understanding of aviation • Aeromedical care for sports injuries and direct international medical return transport • Competency transfer of safety and security to tourism

Source: Devised by authors, based on Wittmer et al. (2009)

Regional airports

With structural effects, they mention international connectivity, which includes leisure flights for passengers in the region, and the airport as a promotion platform for events and a public leisure time facility. With competence effects, they stress the multi-role capabilities of their personnel, which enables them to perform efficiently and flexibly switch between distinct tasks such as passenger handling, fire services, or snow removal. Moreover, they report a thorough knowledge concerning safety and security at all levels/by all employees, competencies in business aviation handling, and customer care, as well as in the operational and organisational aspects of flight training provision.

National airports

By contrast, the national airports mainly delineate the regional airport's feeder function[5] and its significance as a relief or alternative airport for business and general aviation activities, charter flights, or low-cost carriers, but confirm the flight training competencies; besides, they mention that regional airports may promote the image of aviation in the society.

Airline and business aviation operators

The aviation operators stress the connectivity that arises from regional airports, not least due to their proximity to the final destinations of business travellers, although they also indicate that regional airports may lack essential customer services that are required in this segment. Also, they appreciate the higher flexibility, more expeditious traffic flows, and lower costs, and as well confirm the benefits of personal relationships. As structural effects, they confirm the relief function but also mention the airport's importance for the economic development of the region. From a competence view, next to flight training, they mention the promotion and recruitment of young aviation talents through the local flying clubs and the promotion of tourism and the reputation and the attractiveness of the region.

Air traffic control

The air traffic control agency delineates that multiple airports in proximity may constitute a single virtual airport, which was particularly important in terms of the regional airport's potential relief function, particularly for seasonal demand fluctuations in the business aviation. Furthermore, it stresses the regional airport's importance in Swiss Air Force and police flight training and operations, which includes disaster relief or emergency aid, and appreciates the bottom-up airspace planning as opposed to the top-down approach that prevailed in the EU.

Regional companies

For the regional companies, the international connectivity for business travel, events, and guests and customers constitutes a significant network effect of regional airports, thereby providing substantial travel time savings for business travel, air transport, and freight. In addition, they mention the structural infrastructure provision for aeromedical care and the customer care competencies for business travel and guests at premium events. However, they severely limit the significance of the regional airport's existence regarding the firm's location choice by stating that regional airports represent only one factor among many, therefore having little influence on the companies' site selections.

Tourism representatives

Finally, the tourism representatives appreciate the regional airports as job providers in their industry, as drivers of occupancy rates, and as general contributors of social benefits from upscale tourism. Moreover, they find that airports increase the public understanding of aviation, provide the competencies for the aeromedical care of sports injuries and international medical repatriations, and attribute to competency transfers of safety and security to tourism.

Conclusion

Based on qualitative empirical data, this study evaluates the intangible catalytic effects that arise from Swiss regional airports. As a result, the analysis reveals a multitude of intangible effects that accrue in the context of the Swiss aviation system: first, the connectivity of the regional airports with their personal, single point of contact relationships, the flexibility toward stakeholders, regional and international connectivity, and service bundles as network effects; second, flight training, leisure and competitive aviation activities, technological knowledge, and multi-role employees as competence effects; third, the accessibility of regions, the relief function in terms of business and charter aviation for the national airports, aeromedical supply and air rescue services, and aviation infrastructure provision as structural effects. Finally, image effects are formally excluded from the analysis. Nonetheless, an image effect that attracts international business and leisure travel is mentioned.

These intangible effects are beneficial for the surrounding regions, thereby representing a positive externality of the regional airport. Thus, the corresponding hard and soft factors represent specific, significant economic and societal arguments in terms of regional airport subsidisation and infrastructure development. As an exception, the role of regional airports in the location choice of attracted companies may be overstated, as airport access is reported to be only one reason among many others.

In the discussion about distributional effects and sustainable airport development, these described benefits provide grounds for the evaluation of the positive externalities to the benefit of the economy against the negative externalities of airport operations that arise to the resident population in the vicinity of the airport. In addition, these results lead us to suggest that business aviation and its ancillary activities may represent a promising area of business model development for regional airports. This may be crucial for those regional airports which aim at economic sustainability by developing innovative, customer-oriented services. Moreover, further research should address the

Intangible effects of regional airports 201

potential synergies from centralised management, support functions, and back-office activities across multiple regional airports.

Notes

1 The content that draws on Wittmer and Bieger (2011) and Wittmer et al. (2009) is not further referenced.
2 Euroairport Basel-Mulhouse is a joint public airport of Switzerland and France.
3 Also, refer to Klophaus (2006) and Maibach et al. (2006).
4 The analysis draws on Wittmer et al. (2009) and abstracts from image effects.
5 This specifically concerns Lugano-Agno airport as the only regional airport that provides a domestic feed.

References

ACI (2000). *Airports council international world report 2000*. Geneva, ACI.
ACI (2004). *Airports council international world report 2004*. Geneva, ACI.
ACI-Europe (2004). *The social and economic impact of airports in Europe*. Brussels, ACI-Europe.
ATAG (2005). *The economic and social benefits of air transport*. Geneva, Air Transport Action Group.
Baum, H. (2005). The impact of airports on economic welfare. In Albers, S., Baum, H., Auerbach, S. and Delfmann, W. (eds) *Strategic management in the aviation industry*. London, Routledge.
Bilotkach, V. (2015). Are airports engines of economic development? A dynamic panel data approach. *Urban Studies*, 52(9), 1577–1593.
Button, K., Doh, S. and Yuan, J. (2010). The role of small airports in economic development. *Journal of Airport Management*, 4(2), 125–136.
Döring, T. (1999). *Airline-Netzwerkmanagement aus kybernetischer Perspektive – Ein Gestaltungsmodell*. Bern, Haupt Verlag.
Florida, R., Mellander, C. and Holgersson, T. (2015). Up in the air: The role of airports for regional economic development. *The Annals of Regional Science*, 54(1), 197–214.
Freeman, L. C. (1979). Centrality in social networks: Conceptual clarification. *Social Networks*, 1(3), 215–239.
Gantenbein, M. (2008). *Die volkswirtschaftliche Bedeutung von Flughäfen – Wirtschaftliche Effekte am Fallbeispiel Bern-Belp*. Bern-Belp, Schneider AG.
Harsche, M., Arndt, A., Braun, T., Eichinger, A., Pansch, H. and Wagner, C. (2008). *Katalytische volks- und regionalwirtschaftliche Effekte des Luftverkehrs in Deutschland*. Darmstadt, ECAD.
Heuer, K. and Klophaus, R. (2006). *Regionalökonomische Bedeutung und Perspektiven des Flugplatzes Zweibrücken*. Research Study, Centre for Aviation Law and Business, Trier, University of Applied Sciences.
Heuer, K., Klophaus, R. and Schaper, T. (2005). *Regionalökonomische Auswirkungen des Flughafens Frankfurt-Hahn für den Betrachtungsraum 2003–2015*. Research Study, Centre for Aviation Law and Business, Trier, University of Applied Sciences.
Heymann, E. (2005). *Expansion of regional airports: Misallocation of resources*. Frankfurt am Main, Deutsche Bank Research.
Hume, J. and Mason, N. (2000). *Creating employment and prosperity in Europe: An economic impact study kit*. Geneva, ACI Europe and York Consulting Ltd.
Jungthirapanich, C. and Benjamin, C. O. (1995). A knowledge-based decision support system for locating a manufacturing facility. *IIE Transactions*, 27(6), 789–799.

Klophaus, R. (2006). *Volkswirtschaftliche Bedeutung von Regionalflughäfen und Verkehrslandeplätzen – Wichtige Ergebnisse im Überblick.* Research Study, Centre for Aviation Law and Business, Trier, University of Applied Sciences.

Koch, A., Spehl, H., Osterbach, Z. and Benson, L. (2005). *Evaluierung regionalwirtschaftlicher Wirkungsanalysen.* Düsseldorf, Hans-Böckler-Stiftung.

Maibach, M., Müller, A. and Güller, M. (2003). *Volkswirtschaftliche Bedeutung der schweizerischen Landesflughäfen.* Zürich, INFRAS.

Maibach, M. et al. (2006a). *Volkswirtschaftliche Bedeutung der Luftfahrt in der Schweiz.* Zürich, INFRAS.

Maibach, M. et al. (2006b). *Luftfahrt und Nachhaltigkeit: Bestandesaufnahme – Perspektiven – Handlungsspielraum.* Zürich, INFRAS.

Malina, R., Wollersheim, C. and Schwab, M. (2008). *Die regionalwirtschaftliche Bedeutung des Flughafens Münster/Osnabrück.* Münster and Osnabrück, Institut für Verkehrswirtschaft.

Mosbah, S. and Ryerson, M. S. (2016). Can US metropolitan areas use large commercial airports as tools to bolster regional economic growth? *Journal of Planning Literature*, 31(3), 317–333.

Niemeier, H. M. (2001). *On the use and abuse of impact analysis of airports: A critical view from the perspective of regional policy.* Baden-Baden, Nomos Verlag.

Peltzer, S., Wollersheim, C. and Malina, R. (2007). *Die regionalwirtschaftliche Bedeutung des Dortmund airport.* Dortmund, Industrie und Handelskammer.

Pompl, W. (2007). *Luftverkehr – eine ökonomische und politische Einführung.* Berlin, Springer Verlag.

Sager, D., Graf, S. and Weiss Sampietro, T. (2000). *Volkswirtschaftliche Auswirkungen des Flughafens Zürich.* Research Study, Winterthur, Zürcher Hochschule.

Spengler, U. (2000). *Regionalwirtschaftliche Effekte des Flughafens Kassel-Calden.* Kassel, Industrie- und Handelskammer.

Strauf, S. (2007). *Regionalwirtschaftliche Effekte des Einsiedler Welttheaters 2007.* St. Gallen, IMP-HSG, Universität St. Gallen.

Strauf, S. and Behrendt, H. (2006). *Regionalwirtschaftliche Effekte der Hochschulen im Kanton Luzern.* St. Gallen, IMP-HSG, Universität St. Gallen.

Walter, C. K. and Suzuki, Y. (2002). Perceived high airfares: Effects on location and business travel decisions. *Transportation Journal*, 42(1), 42–50.

Wittmer, A. and Bieger, T. (2011). Intangible regional effects of regional airports: A system analysis of Switzerland. *Journal of Airport Management*, 5(4), 340–350.

Wittmer, A. and Laesser, C. (2006). *Die Bedeutung des Flughafens Zürich und dessen Flugangebot für die Standortattraktivität.* Research Study. St. Gallen, Center for Aviation Competence (CFAC-HSG), University of St. Gallen.

Wittmer, A. et al. (2009). *Regionalflugplätze und deren Wirkung auf das Luftfahrtsystem der Schweiz – Analyse der intangiblen regionalwirtschaftlichen Effekte.* Research Study. St. Gallen, Center for Aviation Competence (CFAC-HSG), University of St. Gallen.

Zak, D. and Getzner, M. (2014). Economic effects of airports in Central Europe: A critical review of empirical studies and their methodological assumptions. *Advances in Economics and Business*, 2(2), 100–111.

12 Swiss international and regional airports

An efficiency benchmarking

Claudio Noto and Carolina Kansikas

Introduction

Airports are important parts of a country's infrastructure. They benefit the local economies directly by connecting remote regions and enabling the transmission of goods, services, and information, as well as indirectly by generating investment opportunities and the agglomeration of economies (Button and Taylor, 2000). However, while efficiently functioning airports ensure connectivity, their capital-intensive operational requirements may be difficult to sustain (Adler et al., 2013a). Moreover, the room for capacity expansion at most airports operating near capacity is usually limited due to geographical, environmental, and political constraints. Therefore, input-output efficiency is key in airport operations.

Regional airports often face low demand and missing scale economies, which makes their economic sustainability a challenge, so that many regional airports are publicly subsidised. The economic rationale for these subsidies is the positive externalities arising from connectivity, and other indirect and direct economic effects of airports. However, while connectivity and airport services may be underprovided without public funding, the subsidies may deter airports from improving the efficiency in their operations, so that they are not allocated efficiently. In this respect, certain costs, such as runway maintenance, are independent from demand for airport services and airport management; by contrast, other costs depend on airport management, such as an efficient utilisation of inputs or an optimal operational organisation. As a result, there may be opportunities for efficiency improvements within the scope of the airport management that optimise the input resource allocation without decreasing operational output. Moreover, for airports without expansion opportunities, the development of the aviation infrastructure may focus on the optimisation of the existing facilities, which is achieved by increasing the efficiency of processes and resource utilisation (Federal Office of Civil Aviation (FOCA), 2016). In this case, management oversees the efficiency and optimisation of the existing infrastructure through its choice of a successful revenue strategy and its selection of inputs for efficient airport production (Adler and Liebert, 2014).

For these reasons, a broad field of studies has emerged that investigates airport efficiency. However, while many previous benchmarking papers have focused on comparisons between international airports in Europe, which may include the data of the Swiss international airports of Zurich, Geneva, and Basel, or on comparisons of national airports within various European countries, Swiss regional airports efficiency has not been investigated yet. At the same time, many studies stress that the relevance of different efficiency drivers may depend on the national context. These arguments motivate an international case study that investigates the relative efficiency of both the international and regional airports in Switzerland.[1]

Thus, this study provides a technical efficiency benchmarking of the three international and two of the four main regional Swiss airports against a representative set of 112 European airports based on a stochastic frontier analysis (SFA). We investigate the international airports Zurich, Geneva, and Basel-Mulhouse, as well as the regional airports Lugano-Agno and Bern-Belp. For the analysis, we choose an input-oriented, multi-output distance function that includes country and time effects, and controls for the institutional conditions of slot coordination and airport ownership (i.e. the degree of privatisation). The inputs are labour, capital, and other inputs, where capital is either approximated by physical runway length or financial depreciation. In this respect, the input orientation best suits the problems for airport managers who face exogenous airport demand and passenger traffic, thereby optimising airport operations through an optimal allocation of their inputs.

For the international airports, the measured outputs are air transport movements (ATM), passenger and cargo volumes, and non-aviation revenues. However, although we provide one estimation with runway length and one with depreciation as a capital proxy, we fail to estimate a significant production function with all three outputs simultaneously. Nonetheless, within the runway length model, we find that efficiency is higher with privatisation and with slot constraints, which is in line with the literature. For the regional airports, output is limited to air transport movements, and passenger and cargo volumes, due to data availability. As a result, we find that depreciation represents a suitable capital proxy while physical runway length does not yield a valid model. In addition, the absence of non-aviation revenues and airport ownership information may underestimate the efficiency of airports that exploit non-aviation activities and airport privatisation. These results illustrate that the efficiency measurement hinges on the availability and choice of input and output data, the model specification, and the choice of the capital proxy. Moreover, due to the parametric nature of the production function, the efficiency evaluation also relies on the functional form for airport technology and the orientation of the stochastic frontier.

Hence, the benchmarking here contributes to the literature by investigating the technical efficiency of the Swiss international and regional airports in a European context, and by illustrating the issues of applying different capital proxies and input prices. Nonetheless, when complemented with background information on sources of inefficiency, its results may be of interest to policymakers, airport managers, and researchers who are interested in benchmarking

Swiss international and regional airports   205

or ameliorating the economic sustainability and performance of international or regional airports. In addition, the data treatments applied illustrate how cross-country comparability is achieved in real terms, and how nominal input costs can be transferred into proxies for real input quantities.

Background

In Switzerland, there are three international airports, 11 regional airports, and many other small regional airports and airfields. The national airports ensure connectivity with global services and supply chains, whereas the larger regional airports cater to a smaller amount of scheduled passenger traffic and business jets. Finally, the many small regional airports and airfields are used for medical flights, maintenance, and flight training activities (Wittmer and Bieger, 2011). As a result of Swiss topography, these airports are mainly located in the western and northern parts of the country, as well as south of the Alps. As domestic point-to-point transport mainly relies on land-based transport modes, air travel within the country is quite sparse. Regional airports mainly provide a few direct international flights, serve as hub gateways, and provide for local holiday charters and business and general aviation.

The three international airports of Switzerland are Zurich-Kloten (ZRH), Geneva-Cointrin (GVA), and Basel-Mulhouse (BSL).[2] Zurich airport serves as the main hub for Swiss International Airlines, the national carrier of Switzerland, while Geneva provides a gateway for Swiss and the Star Alliance to the western part of the country and near France. Basel and Geneva also provide hubs for the low-cost carrier easyJet, which holds a market share of 57 per cent and 40 per cent at the two airports (easyJet, 2017), respectively, and both serve as cargo hubs. By contrast, the 11 regional airports are dispersed across the nation. Only four of them provide scheduled or regular charter air services: Bern-Belp (BRN), Lugano-Agno (LUG), St. Gallen-Altenrhein (STG), and Sion (SIO). Bern and Lugano represent hub gateways to Munich and Zurich, respectively, and serve business and the general aviation; in addition, Bern hosts the federal government's flight services. St. Gallen is a private airport that offers scheduled flight services to Vienna and seasonal holiday charter flights for eastern Switzerland and the northwestern region of Austria. Sion is a mixed military and civil aviation airport, providing charter flights, a competence centre for business aviation maintenance, repair and overhaul (MRO), and sparsely scheduled local air traffic. The remaining seven small regional airports, which are located mostly in the northwestern part of Switzerland, are for recreational and private use.[3]

As Table 12.1 shows, the international as well as the small regional airports feature both private and public ownership forms, while independent organisational units manage all airports. However, as the cases of Geneva, Basel, Lugano, and Sion indicate, public ownership is still prevalent. Moreover, Table 12.1 indicates the relative importance of the seven main airports that host scheduled air traffic: international airports account for nearly all passenger traffic, with

Table 12.1 Characteristics of Swiss international and regional airports, 2015

Airport	Ownership	Passengers (1,000s)	% of Switzerland	ATM	% of Switzerland
International Airports					
ZRH	private	26,281	52.6%	265,100	18.4%
GVA	public	15,771	31.5%	188,829	13.1%
BSL	public	7,061	14.1%	94,359	6.6%
Subtotal			**98.2%**		**38.1%**
Regional Airports					
BRN	private	189	0.4%	50,794	3.5%
LUG	public	167	0.3%	21,262	1.5%
STG	private	101	0.2%	27,301	1.9%
SIO	public	32	0.1%	41,016	2.8%
Subtotal			**1.0%**		**9.8%**
Total			**99.2%**		**47.9%**

Zurich airport accounting for the main share. By contrast, air transport movements (ATM), which include commercial and non-commercial movements and thus include also non-passenger traffic, are distributed more evenly. The seven main airports cover about half of the traffic volume. The importance of the international airports increases when only commercial ATMs are evaluated, as most regional airports mainly cater for private air traffic (see FOCA, 2017).

Previous studies

As Adler et al. (2013a) delineate, three prominent methodologies exist for the assessment of efficiency: data envelopment analysis (DEA), total factor productivity (TFP), and stochastic frontier analysis (SFA). DEA models explain inefficiencies in relation to a data envelope, which is based on minimal extrapolation (Bogetoft, 2012); TFP constructs an index to compare the outputs achieved with a specific set of inputs to capture airport specific production in economic terms. By contrast, SFA models relate observed outputs to a production function that extends the deterministic physical input specification by adding stochastic noise and inefficiency (see Martin et al., 2009).

Thus, DEA and TFP represent approaches to benchmarking in a nonparametric framework that do not require any specific functional form assumptions, whereas the SFA approach relies on a parametric production function, which requires structural assumptions about the distribution of the parameters to be estimated, on the structure of the production possibility set, and the data generation process. As a result, DEA and TFP exclude structural presuppositions and are deterministic, while SFA requires parametric assumptions and allows us to separate deterministic inefficiency from stochastic error terms, if the assumed structure is realistic (Bogetoft, 2012). Consequently, SFA is applied to disentangle factors related to airport management from environmental and fixed factors outside the scope of airport managers. Compared to the other efficiency evaluation techniques, this method allows us to distinguish between exogenous and endogenous efficiency constraints, thereby providing a ranking of airport performance based on improvements that could be achieved through improvements of the use of inputs. Overall, most airport benchmarking studies apply either the SFA or the DEA approach, while the estimation of TFP rarely occurs due to its high requirements on input and output price information (Adler et al., 2013a).

The recent literature has produced a solid body of empirical airport efficiency benchmarking studies based on SFA and DEA, both in national and international contexts. For example, Adler et al. (2013a) benchmark a balanced panel of 85 EU airports from 2002–2009 based on a DEA approach using the total number of passengers and cargo volume, air traffic movements, and non-aeronautical revenues as outputs and labour costs, other input costs, and runway length as inputs. Apart from applying financial depreciation, we draw on their input and output choice in the study here. By applying variable returns to scale and by separating discretionary from non-discretionary inputs, their analysis identifies inefficiencies ranging from 25–50 per cent compared to the optimum, based on excess cost increases over time. In addition, their second-stage regression reveals that own ground-handling and fuelling services increase airport inefficiency, along with weak commercial activities and belonging to an airport group.

Similarly, Bubalo (2012) investigates a 2002–2010 panel of 139 European airports from ten countries, where he relates depreciation and originating and inbound transfer passengers and costs as input variables to the airports' earnings before interest and tax (EBIT), revenues, and departing and terminating passengers; his main contribution is methodological, as he defines a new profitability-based specification which eliminates the need to classify airports based on other characteristics related to their size. Oum et al. (2008) provide one of the first studies evaluating the effect of ownership on a set of worldwide airports. In similar fashion, Adler and Liebert (2014) investigate the efficiency of 43 airports from 13 European countries in a time period from 1998–2007, thereby finding that the ownership form yields different effects as a function of an airport's competitive environment: if competition is low, private airports operate more efficiently than public airports. In all competitive settings, mixed private-public airports are less cost efficient than all other airports. Martin et al. (2009) investigate the Spanish airport system and find important inefficiencies and economies of scale in airport operations. Scotti et al. (2010) evaluate the impact of competition on the technical efficiency of Italian airports. They find that the intensity of competition yields a negative impact on the airport's exploitation of available inputs because passengers are easily diverted to nearby airports of substitution, and that publicly owned airports are more efficient than privately owned airports in their country. For a comprehensive survey of airport benchmarking studies, see Tovar and Martin-Cejas (2010), Liebert and Niemeier (2013), and Iyer and Jain (2019).

We prefer the SFA approach for our analysis due to its error decomposition, whereby the stochastic error term captures random deviations from optimal production while an inefficiency term denotes the inefficiency of the production unit concerned (see Bogetoft, 2012). However, although we apply generic prices to construct internationally comparable real costs and input quantity proxies, we do not dispose of accurate market prices for the productive inputs. Therefore, we concentrate on the evaluation of technical efficiency, which denotes the relation of input quantities to the production outputs but abstracts them from cost considerations and, hence, from productive, allocative, and cost efficiency (Bogetoft, 2012) considerations.

As noted, the SFA framework requires the choice of a parametric production function that represents the technology used by all observation units in the set (Kumbhakar et al., 2015). The two most popular production functions are the Cobb-Douglas (CD) and the Translog (TL) forms. While the former is known for its simple structure and its ability to track efficiency changes well, its functional form is nested in the Translog form and, therefore, is rather restrictive (Bogetoft, 2012). By contrast, the latter provides more flexibility to fit the data but may yield insensible results in an economic sense (Davis and Garcés, 2009). For its characteristics just described, we chose the Cobb-Douglas function.

Parmeter and Kumbhakar (2014) suggest complementing the estimation with an overview of the exogenous sources of inefficiency in the setting of interest to distinguish those inefficiency-inducing factors that can be influenced by airport management from those constraints that are exogenous. Exogenous factors may be based on the institutional structure in which the airport operates, whereas other exogenous constraints may be environmental, geographical, or political. In this respect, the literature highlights two key institutional variables that influence efficiency: the ownership structure of airports and the degree of competition. For instance, Oum et al. (2008) find that airports which are fully privately or fully publicly owned are more efficient compared to mixed-ownership airports. Similarly, Adler and Liebert (2014) argue that a uniform ownership structure might provide better incentives for airport management to achieve efficiency. However, these factors do not seem to yield univocal independent effects but, rather, may be country dependent.

Finally, technical efficiency can be viewed from an input- or output-oriented perspective. While the former denotes the problem of minimising inputs for a given output, the latter delineates maximising output with a given number of inputs. Thus, when firms have more control over inputs than outputs, an input-oriented perspective is suitable (Coelli et al., 2005). In an airport setting, a large part of the airport infrastructure is fixed-size capital goods that cannot be altered in the short run. Moreover, output in terms of air traffic movements, passenger and cargo volume is generally exogenous to the airport, as it is mainly determined by demand for flight services, so that input minimisation seems to be the main managerial problem. For these reasons, the input-oriented perspective is appropriate to assess the efficiency of an airport in making use of its resources (Oum et al., 2008).

Model

As usual in the literature, we start with a deterministic Cobb-Douglas production function that specifies a single output y_{nt} of airport $n \in \{1,...,N\}$ at time t in log-linear form as a function

$$\ln y_{nt} = \beta_0 + \sum_i \beta_i \ln x_{nit} + \sum_k \delta_k \ln z_{nkt}$$

of $i \in \{1,...,I\}$ distinct productive inputs x_{nit}, a variety of $k \in \{1,...,k\}$ institutional variables z_{nkt}, β_i, δ_k as the respective coefficients, and intercept β_0. From the various inefficiency specifications, we choose Battese and Coelli (1992), which suggests that the single output y_{nt} of firm n at time t is determined by

$$y_{nt} = f(x_{nt}, z_{nt}; \beta) e^{v_{nt} - u_{nt}}$$

where $v_{nt} \sim N(0, \sigma_v^2)$ delineates a random error term with normal distribution and $f(x_{nt}, z_{nt}; \beta)$ represents the generic form of the production function based on input vector x_{nt}, institutional variables z_{nt}, and coefficients β. Consequently, $u_{nt} \sim N^+(\mu, \sigma)$ represents the inefficiency of firm n at time t based on the truncated normal distribution N^+. Thus, inefficiency u_{nt} describes non-random output deviations from optimal production given the inputs x_{nt}, z_{nt}, whereas error term v captures positive and negative random noise. Based on its distributional assumptions, this specification is referred to as the *normal-half normal* model (e.g., see Kumbhakar and Lovell 2000). Finally, due to $e^{-u} \le 1$ by definition, technical efficiency TE is defined as

$$TE_{nt} = e^{-u_{nt}},$$

which is used to express the *relative output loss due to inefficiency* (Bogetoft and Otto, 2011).[4] Battese and Coelli (1992) decompose the time-variant inefficiency into

$$u_{nt} = \exp[\eta(t - T)] \cdot u_n,$$

where $\exp[\eta(t-T)] \ge 0$ and $u_{nT} = u_n$, so that parameter η captures the impact of cross-sectional technological change which increases ($\eta > 0$) or decreases ($\eta < 0$) over time. As a result, the output variations due to technological changes enter the density function of u_{nt} rather than the deterministic part of the frontier, which allows us to separate technological change from the time-variance of inefficiency (see Coelli et al., 2005, 278).[5] Finally, inefficiency is estimated by parameter

$$\gamma = \frac{\sigma_u^2}{\sigma^2} \in [0,1],$$

which delineates the variance caused by inefficiency as a share of total variance.

The input-oriented view is adopted by converting the production function into an input-oriented distance function, which, at the same time, solves the problem that a production function only accommodates a single output.[6] For this purpose, single output production function is expanded by introducing $j \in \{1,...,J\}$ distinct productive outputs y_{njt} for each airport n at time t and its inputs are normalised by productive input I.[7] This yields the multi-output, input-oriented stochastic distance function

$$-\ln x_{nIt} = \beta_0 + \sum_i \beta_i \frac{\ln x_{nit}}{\ln x_{nIt}} + \sum_j \alpha_j \ln y_{njt} + \sum_k \delta_k \ln z_{nkt} + v_{nt} - u_{nt},$$

where u_{nt} denotes the distance to the efficient frontier (i.e., inefficiency) that is estimated along with α_j, β_i, and δ_k.[8]

Ultimately, this model represents a *multiplicative, stochastic* framework, as it separates the random errors from inefficiency, and because the two stochastic terms are *multiplied* with the production function. Thus, in contrast with additive fixed-effects settings, this setting expresses the inefficiency of each firm relative to the efficient frontier (i.e. to the feasible output, given all inputs), rather than to the most efficient firm in the set. As a result, technical efficiency represents an absolute indicator with respect to the production technology rather than a purely comparative measure across firms (see Bogetoft and Otto, 2011).

Data

Our dataset is based on the German Airport Project (GAP) database and our own Swiss airports dataset, which we updated and complemented with public financial statements, Eurostat, and Swiss Federal Office of Statistics (BFS) data, and slot information from the European Airport Coordinators Association (EUACA). Thus, the consolidated dataset provides an unbalanced panel of 2000–2016 data for many German, Italian, French, and UK national and regional airports, the five Swiss airports under investigation, and some airports from other European countries. The data consist of total labour costs, overall input costs,[9] depreciation, physical runway capital, and airport outputs in terms of passenger and cargo volumes, air traffic movements, and revenues in annual terms. Moreover, the institutional data includes airport slot and ownership information. Based on the MCAR (missing completely at random)[10] assumptions, the imbalance does not affect the estimation.

We classify the airports into international airports that generate more than two million passengers per year and regional airports that generate fewer than two million passengers per year.[11] This classification is based on two arguments. First, we suggest that the two types of airports differ in terms of their production functions, and second, it enables us to include non-aviation revenues and ownership data, which are available for the international airports but not for the regional airports. Additionally, the airports with fewer than ten million passengers are sub-grouped by a dummy variable, whereas, based on plausibility considerations, exceedingly small airports with fewer than 50,000 annual passengers are excluded as potential outliers. Similarly, exceptionally large hub airports are discarded for the surmise that their production function may substantially differ from that of the large international and smaller regional airports. The imbalanced dataset spans 16 time periods between 2000 and 2015. For the international airports, we have 701 observations from 53 cross-sections; thus, the share of missing data is 18.9 per cent. For the regional airports, we have 628 observations from 64 cross-sections. with a missing data share of 38.6 per cent.

Tovar and Martin-Cejas (2010) mention three problems with data in the airport efficiency context: the input choice, the output choice, and international data comparability. For the input and output choice, we are oriented toward the most recent studies in the literature but bound by data availability. Ideally, we would account for aviation and non-aviation–related profits and costs, as especially large airports diversify their revenues with non-aviation activities (e.g. Tovar and Martin-Cejas, 2009 or Adler et al., 2013b). Therefore, for the international airports, we measure aviation output in terms of total passenger and cargo volumes[12] and the total number of air transport movements (ATM), as well as non-aviation revenues. For the regional airports, we measure aviation output only, as non-aviation revenues are only available for a few airports. Although this may induce unwarranted efficiency downgrades for the regional airports that diversify their business with non-aviation activities, we expect this distortion to be much less prominent than at large international airports – so we accept this limitation.

On the one hand, the international comparability of nominal costs obligates us to account for differences in the purchasing power across nations or regions. On the other hand, the evaluation of technical efficiency requires input *quantities*.[13] Therefore, we are obliged to perform some data treatment; first, to provide international comparability of costs and revenues, and second, to convert the costs into quantity proxies. For this purpose, the domestic labour costs C_L are transferred into labour work hours by applying the average hourly labour cost for production and services per country, as provided by Eurostat and BFS, as shown in Table 12.2.[14] Moreover, we convert input costs C_I and revenues R from domestic nominal expenses into real EU28 expenses based on Eurostat's Purchasing Power Parities for the Gross Domestic Product (PPP_{GDP}).

Table 12.2 Input data treatment

Input cost	Generic price	Input proxy*
Labour L	W_L^{DOM}: avg labour unit costs per hour	$x_L = C_L^{DOM} / W_L^{DOM}$
Inputs I	PPP_{GDP}: PPP for gross domestic product	$x_I^{EU28} = C_I^{DOM} / PPP_{GDP}$
Depreciation D	PPP for capital goods and construction**	$D^{EU28} = D^{DOM} / PPP_{CAP}$
Revenues R	PPP_{GDP}: PPP for gross domestic product	$R^{EU28} = R^{DOM} / PPP_{GDP}$

Notes: PPP stands for Purchase Power Parity; *EU28: Eurostat EU28 currency; DOM: domestic currency; **PPP_{GDP} for 2000–2003 due availability

212   *Claudio Noto and Carolina Kansikas*

Thus, presuming that, in real EU28 terms, the input prices are identical for all airports within both groups, these real EU28 expenses may also be interpreted as approximating input quantities. Finally, as the airports' capital stocks are not readily available, we follow the usual practice in airport benchmarking by applying capital proxies. In this respect, we convert financial depreciation D by the PPP for Capital Goods and Construction (PPP_{CAP}) into a theoretical quasi-quantity for capital.[15] Moreover, as also usual in the literature, we approximate all airports' physical capital by their total runway length. As Tovar and Martin-Cejas (2010) mention, data treatment introduces potential scaling errors. However, in our case, it is required for international comparability.

As Table 12.3 shows, labour, other inputs, outputs in terms of WLUs and ATMs, and non-aviation revenues (NAR) reasonably correlate. By contrast, for the international airports, runway length and depreciation highly correlate with the outputs, and with labour and other inputs, but only moderately correlate against each other. Although this indicates that a significant production function should be estimable, it also shows that the two capital proxies do not include the same information. For the regional airports, the runway length does not indicate a sensible correlation with any of the input and output data; this suggests that runway capital does not represent a reasonable proxy for the regional airports. In this respect, Adler et al. (2013b) note that financial depreciation may not represent an ideal capital proxy due to differences in accounting standards across countries and investment cycles across airports. Therefore, we estimate two distinct distance functions for each group of airports: one with depreciation and one with physical runway capital as a capital proxy.

Table 12.3 Correlations across input and output data for international and regional airports

	International airports						
	L	D	RL	I	WLU	ATM	NAR
Labour (L)	1.000	0.647	0.437	0.636	0.696	0.619	0.685
Depreciation (D)	0.647	1.000	0.577	0.806	0.782	0.759	0.808
Runway length (RL)	0.437	0.577	1.000	0.516	0.559	0.481	0.477
Other inputs (I)	0.636	0.806	0.516	1.000	0.865	0.773	0.845
Output (WLU)	0.696	0.782	0.559	0.865	1.000	0.859	0.867
Output (ATM)	0.619	0.759	0.481	0.773	0.859	1.000	0.864
Non-aviation revenues (NAR)	0.780	0.842	0.552	0.921	0.904	0.853	1.000

	Regional airports						
	L	D	RL	I	WLU	ATM	NAR
Labour (L)	1.000	0.626	0.004	0.763	0.798	0.397	–
Depreciation (D)	0.626	1.000	0.043	0.648	0.635	0.342	–
Runway length (RL)	0.004	0.043	1.000	0.074	0.226	−0.187	–
Other inputs (I)	0.763	0.648	0.074	1.000	0.809	0.366	–
Output (WLU)	0.798	0.635	0.226	0.809	1.000	0.355	–
Output (ATM)	0.397	0.342	−0.187	0.366	0.355	1.000	–

To control for exogenous sources of inefficiency, we introduce two institutional variables: airport ownership and slot coordination. *Airport ownership* refers to the degree of privatisation by distinguishing full public ownership from a minority private share of less than 50 per cent and a majority private share of more than 50 per cent; again, unfortunately, the privatisation data are only available for the international airports. *Slot coordination* denotes whether an airport is slot-coordinated and may take three values: slot constraints during all operating hours, during peak-period hours only, or a seasonal constraint during the summer or winter only. As slot information is available for the latest three seasons only, we extrapolate this information to all years. In addition, a dummy year controls for generalised annual shocks, whereas a dummy country accounts for national differences.

Results

Our airport grouping signifies that we assume similar technologies *within* but heterogenous technologies *across* the two sets of airports; this leads us to estimate two separate stochastic frontiers rather than a joint one. Hence, the two international airport and the regional airport models are estimated based on Maximum Likelihood (ML) in a random effects setting (Coelli et al., 2005).[16] In terms of outputs, the international airport models include passenger and cargo volumes in terms of WLUs, air traffic volume (ATM), and non-aviation revenues (NAR), whereas the regional airport models are constrained to aviation outputs only (WLUs and ATMs). In terms of inputs, all models include labour and other inputs, while we evaluate the production function with each of the two capital proxies for each group of airports.

The parameter estimates are shown in Appendix 12.1, where the ML estimation yields z-values with the corresponding p-values. The significances are indicated by $\star\star\star$ for $p < 0.001$, $\star\star$ for $p < 0.01$, and $\star$ for $p < 0.05$. In the distance functions, the coefficients represent elasticities rather than absolute values. Moreover, positive coefficients indicate a positive correlation between the variable at stake and the distance of the observation from the efficient frontier and, thus, inefficiency. By contrast, negative coefficients denote that inefficiency decreases (or efficiency increases) when the corresponding variable increases (see Fernandez et al., 2018). Therefore, in a valid specification, inputs need to have positive coefficients and output negative coefficients. Similarly, institutional variables indicate inefficiency decreases if their sign is negative because they denote vertical shifts.

The estimation results confirm intuition in terms of the capital proxy and the heterogenous technologies – for the international airports, depreciation as a proxy renders the ATM output insignificant. Hence, we estimate model D.NAR based on depreciation and non-aviation revenues (NAR) only. By contrast, with runway length as a proxy, the non-aviation revenues become insignificant. Consequently, we estimate model RL.ATM based on physical runway capital and ATMs but without the NAR. As a result, we find one valid production function for each of the capital proxies but fail to estimate a model that jointly includes all three outputs. For the regional airports, the non-aviation revenues are not available. Moreover, physical runway length as a capital proxy fails to represent a significant productive input. As a result, only financial depreciation as a capital proxy yields an empirically valid model for the regional airports. As the correlation coefficients suggest, this result indicates that the characteristics of the capital stock may vary between the two groups of airports, which justifies the ex-ante assumption of heterogenous technologies.

As the results show, in all three valid models, we obtain the correct signs for the input and output coefficients, which means that higher inputs increase inefficiency, whereas higher outputs decrease inefficiency. For the international airports, the input-labour elasticity in model D.NAR is both higher than depreciation as well as higher than in model RL.ATM. This shows that with depreciation as a capital proxy (in D.NAR), the input-labour elasticity represents the main determinant of inefficiency, whereas runway length dominates in the opposing case (RL.ATM). At the same time, the WLUs and the non-aeronautical revenues seem to both affect inefficiency in model D.NAR while, in model RL.ATM, both outputs seem relatively unimportant. In the regional airports model, both input elasticities are much lower, whereas the passenger and cargo output returns a high importance as compared to the ATMs; moreover, as stated, physical runway length does not yield a significant production function at all. These insights illustrate the impact of the capital proxy choice on the efficiency measurement. Nonetheless, the likelihood ratios indicate that all SFA models exceed their OLS counterparts.

In addition, the institutional variables vary along with the different production functions – for the international airports in the RL.ATM model, all institutional variables are highly significant. They imply that inefficiency decreases at the same magnitude with both minor or major private ownership. In addition, all three types of slot coordination decrease inefficiency, and they do so to a higher degree than privatisation. By contrast, in the D.NAR model, all significances are lost but for minority privatisation and full-time slot coordination at the 5 per cent level, whereas the sub-class of airports with less than ten million passengers are more efficient in the RL.ATM model but less efficient in the D.NAR model. For the regional airports, only full-time slot constraints are significant, while the variations in all other institutional variables indicate that the model specification affects the estimation of the production technology to a large degree. The country variables show mixed significance throughout the set, whereas the annual shocks are less important for the regional airports than for the international airports. These results may indicate that international airports face a higher exposure to international competition than regional airports. However, as the year and country dummies capture a multitude of generalised effects, they are difficult to interpret correctly.

In terms of inefficiency, the gamma values are extremely high for the regional airports and the RL.ATM model, whereas random output variations are not observed. By contrast, in the D.NAR model, they are lower, thereby indicating that four-fifths of the variance stems from inefficiency and one-fifth from random errors. Although Bogetoft (2012) comments that small residuals indicate a strong model fit, we suggest that this result is extreme and might indicate that the D.NAR model for the international airports, which includes non-aviation revenues, provides a more realistic approximation of airport production than the regional airport and the RL.ATM models, both of which include outputs from aviation operations only. Concerning the time trends of inefficiency, for the regional airports, we observe a shallow but significant efficiency *increment* over time due to technology. By contrast, in both models of the international airports, the time trend indicates a minor but significant *decrement* of efficiency.

Although both international airport models are based on a rich set of output and institutional variables, we observe widespread rank changes between the two models, which result in a low Spearman's rank coefficient of 0.45. These rank reversions confirm that the efficiency scores largely depend on the input-output specifications, which includes the delicate choice of a suitable capital proxy. Thereby, we refer to Barros (2008), who also encounters widespread changes in his results with different model specifications. Since the two model outputs differ substantially, and since we cannot find a valid production function that accounts for all three kinds of outputs (passenger and cargo volumes, ATMs, and NAR), we refrain from publishing the efficiency scores.

Nonetheless, concerning the Swiss international airports, our SFA reports that Geneva yields constant high scores in both models, whereas both Zurich and Basel seem to fare better in the non-aviation revenues model. In the runway length model (RL.ATM), Geneva's advantage might relate to its highly frequented single runway as compared to Basel's two and Zurich's three runways, where both airports exhibit a cross runway configuration. This explanation also supports the latter two airports' relative efficiency increase in the depreciation and non-aviation revenues model (D.NAR), as both possess highly commercialised landside areas. In addition, Geneva airport's location might result in a substantial share of cross-border commuting labour, so that we are likely to underestimate the labour input quantity and overestimate the technical efficiency when applying the Swiss national wage levels. As an opposite case, Basel airport is located on French territory but near Germany and Switzerland. While we compute its units of labour with French wages, the salaries of cross-border employees might instead be determined by Swiss or German standards.

For the regional airports, we find that higher efficiency scores involve most larger airports and some small airports, whereas lower efficiency scores mainly accommodate small airports. Tentatively, these results are likely to illustrate the problem of low airport demand for small regional airports. By contrast, the airports with difficult operational conditions due to topography – such as Bern, Lugano, Bolzano, Florence, and Salzburg – are dispersed across the set, although this precondition is not included as an institutional variable.[17] As the regional airport model contains aviation outputs but excludes non-aviation revenues, as well as ownership information, we also refrain from publishing the regional airport efficiency ranking.

Conclusion

We benchmark the three international and two of the four main regional Swiss airports against a representative set of 112 European airports based on a stochastic frontier analysis with an input-oriented, multi-output distance function. For the regional airports, the estimation yields a significant Cobb-Douglas production function with depreciation as a capital proxy and aviation outputs in terms of passenger and cargo volumes and air traffic movements. For the international airports, the production function is significant either with runway length and aviation outputs but without non-aviation revenues, or with financial depreciation and non-aviation revenues but without air traffic movements. Hence, we fail to estimate a single production function whereby capital (either in terms of physical runways or depreciation), air traffic movements, and non-aviation revenues are simultaneously significant.

Concerning the technical efficiency scores, the non-availability of non-aviation revenues and ownership information may underestimate the efficiency of regional airports who diversify their business models based on non-aviation activities and services, and who increase their efficiency by privatisation. In the two international models, to some degree, the efficiency results may be explained by distinct physical capital bases, runway utilisation, and cross-border effects within the labour force. However, many airports encounter substantial rank reversions across the two models, which results in a low Spearman rank correlation. This indicates that the model specification – which includes the delicate choice of a suitable capital proxy – may substantially affect the efficiency scores. As a result, the explanatory power of our efficiency ranking remains severely limited.

Regarding the exogenous efficiency determinants, we investigate the impact of the institutional environment by accounting for the ownership of the airport and the degree of airport slot coordination. In this respect, the estimation indicates that efficiency is higher with privatisation and with slot constraints. These results most closely relate to those of Adler et al. (2013b) and Oum et al. (2008); however, they are not significant throughout all our three model specifications. In addition, the required data treatment for cross-country comparability, the unavailability of specific input prices, and the restrictive functional form of the production function limit the scope of the above efficiency results. First, the applied country-level purchasing power parities might induce deviations from effective input prices. Second, the use of national wages does not account for domestic wage differentials between urban regions with high labour costs and non-urban regions with lower labour costs; similarly, airports in a multi-country catchment area might employ a significant share of their workforce at foreign rather than domestic wage levels. Moreover, the fact that several important institutional variables do not prove significant in all settings may indicate that other sources of inefficiency might remain hidden. For instance, the geographical or topographical location of an airport may create operational limitations that severely limit its potential output. Finally, the chosen orientation of the distance function also affects the efficiency scores, as input-inefficient airports might become more efficient from an output maximisation perspective.

With due consideration of these stated limitations and background information on the various sources of inefficiency, the study here might be of interest to policymakers, airport managers, and researchers who are interested in benchmarking operational infrastructures for the purpose of ameliorating their economic sustainability and operational performance. Nevertheless, subsequent studies may explore the partial insignificance of the institutional variables by evaluating different functional forms and by distinguishing discretionary from non-discretionary inputs, such as in Adler and Liebert (2014).[18] Moreover, an empirical estimation of appropriate factor prices would allow researchers to more precisely approximate input quantities, and evaluate cost and profit efficiency. However, such undertaking would require a rich dataset with detailed airside and landside financial data that may be difficult to obtain.

Acknowledgements

We are extremely grateful to Nicola Volta, formerly from Cranfield University, for his invaluable, substantial methodological support, and to the organisers of the GAP database, Frank Fichert and Hans-Martin Niemeier, as well as all its previous contributors, for the access to their invaluable airport and ownership data. Moreover, we appreciate the many helpful comments at the GARS Amsterdam Workshop 2017 and the COST ATARD Dublin Workshop 2017, the essential feedback from Nicole Adler, and the constructive inputs from Tolga Ülkü, who also helped us with obtaining and understanding the GAP database. Finally, we thank the COST ATARD project chair for the STSM grant, which allowed us to finalise the empirical part of this study; Andreas Wittmer of the University of St. Gallen, who encouraged the data collection and a preliminary case study analysis within Carolina's CEMS programme; and an anonymous reviewer for their critical feedback.

Notes

1 This study is preceded by Kansikas (2017) which investigates the Swiss airport system in a descriptive manner.
2 Basel is a joint public airport owned by Switzerland and France.
3 Data availability for this study restricts the analysis to the three international airports, and to Bern and Lugano.
4 E.g., see Bogetoft and Otto (2011, 199, 218); for the formal derivation of estimate $\widehat{TE} = e^{-\hat{u}}$, refer to Bogetoft and Otto (2011, 217).
5 In this setting, the efficiency *ranking* across firms cannot change over time, whereas $\eta = 0$ yields an estimation of time invariant inefficiency (Battese and Coelli 1992, 154).
6 See Bogetoft (2012, 126) or Bogetoft and Otto (2011, 236); for a single output, the output distance function is equivalent to the production function.
7 Normalizing imposes the required homogeneity of degree 1 (e.g. Coelli and Perelman, 1996, 9).

8 In this respect, the institutional variables z do not change the properties of the error structure (see Coelli et al. 2005, 285).

9 In contrast with the EU28 cost data, which exclude ground handling, the Swiss regional airports provide fuelling services on their own grounds; therefore, the fuel purchases are deducted from the overall input costs for these airports.

10 MCAR means no attrition and no correlation with unobserved effects; see Baltagi (2013, 189) or Kumbhakar and Lovell (2000, 97).

11 Generally, the critical passenger numbers are taken as the averages across all years.

12 As usual in the literature, we accommodate the passenger and the cargo volumes into a single aggregate output whereby one work-load unit (WLU) corresponds to one passenger or 100 kg of cargo.

13 However, among many, Battese and Coelli (1992) mix input costs and *quantities*.

14 Hourly labour costs account for wages, salaries, and employers' social contributions and taxes; see Eurostat's NACE2 definition. For 2000–2008, production and services correspond to sectors C–K, which excludes public administration, whereas for 2009–2016, they are referred to as the business economy (Eurostat B–N). The missing years are linearly interpolated.

15 Due to unavailability of PPP_{CAP} before 2004, we apply PPP_{GDP} for 2000–2003; as financial depreciation is not disclosed into air- and ground-side values, our depreciation measure includes both the operational airside capital and the groundside facilities.

16 We apply the statistical program 'R' and the software package 'Frontier' due to Coelli and Henningsen (2017) for the estimation.

17 All these airports only feature instrument approaches in one runway direction due to topography; depending on the cloud ceiling, visibility, and wind, this may induce severe operational constraints.

18 For this purpose, Bogetoft (2012, 29) proposes a sub-vector efficiency approach.

References

Adler, N. and Liebert, V. (2014). Joint impact of competition, ownership form and economic regulation on airport performance and pricing. *Transportation Research Part A: Policy and Practice*, 64, 92–109.

Adler, N., Liebert, V. and Yazhemsky, E. (2013a). Benchmarking airports from a managerial perspective. *Omega*, 41(2), 442–458.

Adler, N., Ülkü, T. and Yazhemsky, E. (2013b). Small regional airport sustainability: Lessons from benchmarking. *Journal of Air Transport Management*, 33, 22–31.

Baltagi, B. (2013). *Econometric analysis of panel data*, 5th edition. Chichester, John Wiley and Sons.

Barros, C. P. (2008). Technical efficiency of UK airports. *Journal of Air Transport Management*, 14, 175–178.

Battese, G. and Coelli, T. (1992). Frontier production functions, technical efficiency and panel data: An application to paddy farmers in India. *The Journal of Productivity Analysis*, 3(1–2), 153–169.

Bogetoft, P. (2012). *Performance benchmarking – measuring and managing performance*. New York, Springer.

Bogetoft, P. and Otto, L. (2011). *Benchmarking with DEA, SFA, and R*. Berlin, Springer.

Bubalo, B. (2012). Benchmarking European airports based on a profitability envelope: A break-even analysis. In Hao, H., Shi, X., Stahlbock, R. and Voss, S. (eds) *Computational Logistics*. Berlin, Springer.

Button, K. and Taylor, S. (2000). International air transportation and economic development. *Journal of Air Transport Management*, 6(4), 209–222.

Coelli, T. and Henningsen, A. (2017). *Frontier: Stochastic frontier analysis*. Software Package for the Statistical Program 'R'. Cambridge, Cambridge University Press.

Coelli, T. and Perelman, S. (1996). *Efficiency measurement, multiple-output technologies and distance functions: With application to European railways*. Belgium, CREPP, University of Liège, CEPA, University of New England.

Coelli, T., Rao, P., O'Donnell, C. and Battese, G. (2005). *An introduction to efficiency and productivity analysis*. New York, Springer.

Davis, P. and Garcés, E. (2009). *Quantitative techniques for competition and antitrust analysis*. Princeton, Princeton University Press.

easyJet (2017). *Results for the year ending 30 September 2017*. Available at: http://Corporate.easyjet.com/Investors/Reports-and-Presentations/2017.

Fernandez, X. L., Coto-Millan, P. and Diaz-Medina, B. (2018). The impact of tourism on airport efficiency: The Spanish case. *Utilities Policy*, 55, 52–58.

FOCA (2016). *Rapporto Sulla Politica Aeronautica Della Svizzera 2016*. Neuchâtel, Swiss Federal Office of Civil Aviation.

FOCA (2017). *Swiss civil aviation 2016*. Neuchâtel, Swiss Federal Office of Civil Aviation.

Iyer, K. C. and Jain, S. (2019). Performance measurement of airports using data envelopment analysis: A review of methods and findings. *Journal of Air Transport Management*, 81, 101707.

Kansikas, C. (2017). *Swiss airports – characteristics, prospects, and efficiency*. Paper for the GARS Aviation. Student Research Workshop, Amsterdam.

Kumbhakar, S. C. and Lovell, C. A. K. (2000). *Stochastic frontier analysis*. Cambridge, Cambridge University Press.

Kumbhakar, S. C., Wang, H. J. and Horncastle, A. P. (2015). *A practitioner's guide to stochastic frontier analysis using stata*. Cambridge, Cambridge University Press.

Liebert, V. and Niemeier, H. M. (2013). A survey of empirical research on the productivity and efficiency measurement of airports. *Journal of Transport Economics and Policy*, 47(2), 157–189.

Martin, J. C., Roman, C. and Voltes-Dorta, A. (2009). A stochastic frontier analysis to estimate the relative efficiency of Spanish airports. *Journal of Productive Analysis*, 31, 163–176.

Oum, T. H., Yan, J. and Yua, C. (2008). Ownership forms matter for airport efficiency: A stochastic frontier investigation of worldwide airports. *Journal of Urban Economics*, 64, 422–435.

Parmeter, C. F. and Kumbhakar, S. C. (2014). Efficiency analysis: A primer on recent advances. *Foundations and Trends in Econometrics*, 7(3–4), 191–385.

Scotti, D., Malighetti, P., Martini, G. and Volta, N. (2010). *The impact of airport competition on technical efficiency: A stochastic frontier analysis applied to Italian airports*. Bergamo, Italy, Department of Economics, Technology Management, University of Bergamo.

Tovar, B. and Martin-Cejas, R. R. (2009). Are outsourcing and non-aeronautical revenues important drivers in the efficiency of Spanish airports? *Journal of Air Transport Management*, 15(5), 217–220.

Tovar, B. and Martin-Cejas, R. R. (2010). Technical efficiency and productivity changes in Spanish airports: A parametric distance functions approach. *Transportation Research Part E*, 46, 249–260.

Wittmer, A. and Bieger, T. (2011). Intangible regional effects of regional airports: A system analysis of Switzerland. *Journal of Airport Management*, 5(4), 340–350.

Appendix 12.1

Stochastic Frontier Estimates

International Airports	Model RL.ATM					Model D.NAR				
Parameter (factor = fac)	Coeff	SE	z-Val	p-Val	Sig	Coeff	SE	z-Val	p-Val	Sig
(Intercept)	−7.738	0.319	−24.250	0.000	★★★	−7.607	0.553	−13.765	0.000	★★★
LN IL	0.102	0.011	9.037	0.000	★★★	0.695	0.021	33.694	0.000	★★★
LN CL	−	−	−	−		0.104	0.016	6.695	0.000	★★★
LN RLL	0.859	0.013	66.034	0.000	★★★	−	−	−	−	
LN PAX&Cargo	−0.058	0.016	−3.673	0.000	★★★	−0.379	0.035	−10.728	0.000	★★★
LN ATM	−0.043	0.016	−2.681	0.007	★★	−	−	−	−	
LN NAR	−	−	−	−		−0.154	0.024	−6.489	0.000	★★★
fac(Belgium)	−0.130	0.501	−0.260	0.795		0.489	0.201	2.435	0.015	★
fac(Switzerl)	0.515	0.268	1.917	0.055	.	0.493	0.127	3.889	0.000	★★★
fac(CzechRp)	−0.240	0.286	−0.838	0.402		−0.095	0.240	−0.396	0.692	
fac(Denmark)	0.827	0.268	3.087	0.002	★★	0.981	0.158	6.205	0.000	★★★
fac(Estonia)	0.071	0.263	0.271	0.786		0.580	0.306	1.894	0.058	.
fac(France)	0.379	0.255	1.486	0.137		0.367	0.223	1.644	0.100	
fac(Germany)	1.258	0.281	4.474	0.000	★★★	0.512	0.145	3.528	0.000	★★★
fac(Greece)	−0.628	0.404	−1.556	0.120		0.507	0.305	1.664	0.096	.
fac(Hungary)	0.869	0.344	2.529	0.011	★	−1.443	0.208	−6.926	0.000	★★★
fac(Italy)	1.036	0.274	3.789	0.000	★★★	0.621	0.142	4.356	0.000	★★★
fac(Latvia)	0.124	0.273	0.454	0.650		1.296	0.361	3.592	0.000	★★★
fac(Malta)	0.509	0.395	1.288	0.198		0.503	0.146	3.446	0.001	★★★

fac(UK)	1.436	0.269	5.330	0.000	★★★	0.594	0.133	4.460	0.000	★★★
fac(2001)	−0.005	0.012	−0.412	0.680		−0.059	0.034	−1.772	0.076	.
fac(2002)	0.004	0.013	0.298	0.766		−0.074	0.034	−2.175	0.030	★
fac(2003)	−0.001	0.012	−0.068	0.946		−0.119	0.035	−3.342	0.001	★★★
fac(2004)	−0.004	0.013	−0.321	0.748		−0.182	0.038	−4.775	0.000	★★★
fac(2005)	−0.021	0.014	−1.552	0.121		−0.249	0.040	−6.196	0.000	★★★
fac(2006)	−0.020	0.014	−1.444	0.149		−0.248	0.042	−5.921	0.000	★★★
fac(2007)	−0.026	0.015	−1.719	0.086	.	−0.300	0.045	−6.694	0.000	★★★
fac(2008)	−0.033	0.016	−2.003	0.045	★	−0.370	0.048	−7.752	0.000	★★★
fac(2009)	−0.042	0.016	−2.594	0.009	★★	−0.422	0.049	−8.680	0.000	★★★
fac(2010)	−0.051	0.017	−2.933	0.003	★★	−0.495	0.052	−9.523	0.000	★★★
fac(2011)	−0.065	0.019	−3.474	0.001	★★★	−0.563	0.055	−10.311	0.000	★★★
fac(2012)	−0.064	0.019	−3.348	0.001	★★★	−0.609	0.058	−10.536	0.000	★★★
fac(2013)	−0.071	0.020	−3.596	0.000	★★★	−0.645	0.058	−11.100	0.000	★★★
fac(2014)	−0.057	0.021	−2.715	0.007	★★	−0.644	0.060	−10.822	0.000	★★★
fac(2015)	−0.011	0.024	−0.452	0.651		−0.686	0.069	−9.980	0.000	★★★
fac(Priv<50)	−0.068	0.017	−3.896	0.000	★★★	−0.102	0.045	−2.273	0.023	★
fac(Priv>50)	−0.060	0.016	−3.728	0.000	★★★	−0.049	0.037	−1.330	0.184	
fac(SlotSeas)	−0.622	0.178	−3.501	0.000	★★★	−0.031	0.217	−0.145	0.885	
fac(SlotPeak)	−0.778	0.083	−9.389	0.000	★★★	−0.201	0.198	−1.013	0.311	
fac(SlotPerm)	−0.725	0.069	−10.434	0.000	★★★	−0.422	0.192	−2.201	0.028	★
fac(Pax10m)	−0.092	0.031	−2.969	0.003	★★	0.225	0.064	3.507	0.000	★★★
sigmaSq	0.319	0.057	5.605	0.000	★★★	0.110	0.028	3.875	0.000	★★★
gamma	0.990	0.002	537.541	0.000	★★★	0.812	0.053	15.242	0.000	★★★
time	0.005	0.001	3.428	0.001	★★★	0.060	0.007	8.469	0.000	★★★

LR-Test	Df	LgLk	χ^2	p-Val	Sig	Df	LgLk	χ^2	p-Val	Sig
OLS	40	145.4	−	−		40	73.7	−	−	
SFA	42	879.8	1468.8	0.000	★★★	42	248.3	349.2	0.000	★★★

Regional Airports

Parameter	Coeff	SE	z-Val	p-Val	Sig	Parameter	Coeff	SE	z-Val	p-Val	Sig
(Intercept)	−6.931	0.530	−13.079	0.000	★★★	fac(2008)	−0.133	0.048	−2.793	0.005	★★
LN_IL	0.189	0.021	9.153	0.000	★★★	fac(2009)	−0.105	0.050	−2.104	0.035	★
LN_CL	0.049	0.013	3.926	0.000	★★★	fac(2010)	−0.081	0.059	−1.376	0.169	
LN_Y	−0.401	0.020	−19.571	0.000	★★★	fac(2011)	−0.046	0.061	−0.764	0.445	
LN_ATM	−0.089	0.019	−4.771	0.000	★★★	fac(2012)	−0.022	0.064	−0.351	0.726	
fac(France)	1.696	0.431	3.933	0.000	★★★	fac(2013)	−0.075	0.066	−1.124	0.261	
fac(Germany)	0.028	0.418	0.068	0.946		fac(2014)	−0.056	0.069	−0.808	0.419	
fac(Italy)	1.300	0.435	2.989	0.003	★★	fac(2015)	−0.036	0.115	−0.309	0.757	
fac(Slovenia)	−0.538	0.423	−1.271	0.204		fac(SlotSeas)	0.073	0.093	0.782	0.434	
fac(Switzerl)	1.571	0.545	2.885	0.004	★★	fac(SlotPeak)	0.072	0.131	0.546	0.585	
fac(UK)	0.855	0.432	1.977	0.048	★	fac(SlotPerm)	−1.275	0.293	−4.353	0.000	★★★
fac(2001)	−0.036	0.041	−0.890	0.373		sigmaSq	0.788	0.184	4.288	0.000	★★★
fac(2002)	−0.042	0.037	−1.117	0.264		gamma	0.971	0.007	133.609	0.000	★★★
fac(2003)	−0.049	0.038	−1.267	0.205		time	−0.022	0.006	−3.774	0.000	★★★
fac(2004)	−0.059	0.040	−1.483	0.138							
fac(2005)	−0.104	0.041	−2.527	0.012	★	**LR-Test**	**Df**	**LogL**	χ^2	**p-Val**	**Sig**
fac(2006)	−0.104	0.043	−2.395	0.017	★	OLS	30	127.58	−	−	
fac(2007)	−0.120	0.046	−2.629	0.009	★★	SFA	32	163.39	581.9	0.000	★★★

13 A Belgian case study of the economic importance of air transport and airport activities

Sven Buyle, Franziska Kupfer, and Evy Onghena

Introduction

Thanks to its location, logistics activities have long since played an important role in the economy of Belgium. Not only logistics service providers, but also the activities in Belgian ports and airports have been driving the economy. At first sight, the six Belgian airports do not seem to play a crucial role in the European aviation context with Brussels, Belgium's biggest airport, placed 26th in the European top passenger airports in 2017 and Liège placed ninth for cargo (ACI-Europe, 2018; IATA, 2018). However, they are not only vital for the Belgian economy and connections to Brussels, the 'Capital of Europe', but the presence of international institutions also reinforces the otherwise small Belgian aviation market (Burghouwt and Dobruszkes, 2014).

The National Bank of Belgium (NBB) has been studying the economic importance of the Belgian ports for more than 15 years, focusing on the employment, added value, and investment that the sector brings to the economy. While at first, only Flemish ports and the Liège Port Complex were considered, an analysis of the Port of Brussels has been included since 2008. Furthermore, the original studies focused solely on the direct economic impact. The indirect importance of the sector was introduced in 2004 (Lagneaux, 2004). By conducting the analysis every year, a complete dataset on the evolution of the economic importance of the Belgian port sector has been collected. This means that not only the direct effects but also indirect effects generated by the Belgian ports can be analysed over time.

In 2008, the NBB decided to expand its analysis to the air transport sector. This decision was based, among other reasons, on demand from the Belgian aviation sector. The new study had two aims: first, it was meant to provide a stable time series of the economic importance of the air transport sector in Belgium. Second, although before 2008 studies were carried out with regard to the economic importance of Brussels Airport (see studies from the NBB Louvain [1996] and Sleuwaegen and De Backer [2003]), the new study by the NBB was meant to provide an overview of the economic impact of all six Belgian airports and the air transport sector in Belgium in general. Therefore, up until 2019, four working papers on the economic effects of air transport in Belgium have been published.

This chapter aims to summarise and analyse the studies of the National Bank. Case studies such as this provide insight into how countries apply methodologies to measure economic impact of aviation and hence might be used as inputs for similar studies in other countries. The remainder of this chapter is structured as follows. In the next section, the airports of Belgium are introduced. Here, we focus on the traffic development of the airports, but also sketch the respective ownership structure of the airports. The methodology used by the National Bank is then explained. It is necessary to understand that there are two clusters affecting the economic impact of the air transport sector in Belgium. First, there is the air transport sector, which incorporates all companies that directly fall under the definition of the air transport sector. However, we also incorporate other airport-related activities, as they affect economic activity due to their location at the airport. The method to derive the direct and indirect effects of the airports is also explained here. Then in the next section, the direct and indirect effects of the airports and their evolution are shown and analysed. This is followed by a comparison of the economic impact of air transport in Belgium with other European countries and also an examination of noise pollution at Brussels Airport as part of the external effects which are often overlooked in economic impact studies. Finally, conclusions are drawn.

The airports in Belgium

There are six international airports situated in Belgium (Figure 13.1). Brussels Airport, as the largest airport, is considered the main airport of the country. The other airports have a more regional character or are more specialised than Brussels Airport. Liège Airport, for example, focuses mainly on cargo traffic and charter flights, while Brussels South Charleroi Airport (Charleroi Airport) is a preferred airport for low-cost traffic. Furthermore, there are three smaller airports in Flanders: Antwerp International Airport (Antwerp airport), focusing on business and charter traffic; Ostend-Bruges International Airport (Ostend airport), focusing on cargo and charter traffic; and Kortrijk Wevelgem International Airport (Kortrijk Wevelgem airport), focusing on non-scheduled business and helicopter traffic. Figure 13.1 shows the location of all six Belgian airports.

Airport ownership

Most airports in Belgium are partially or fully privatised. Brussels Airport Company, the company that owns and manages Brussels Airport, is 25 per cent owned by the Belgian government and 39 per cent owned by Ontario Teachers' Pension Plan which was acquired in 2011. While Macquarie Airports was involved in the ownership of the airport from 2004–2019, owning a 36 per cent share, the sale of its participation – to the Australian investor QIC (Queensland Investment Corporation), the Dutch pension fund APG Asset Management, and the insurer Swiss Life – was announced in 2019.

A Belgian case study 225

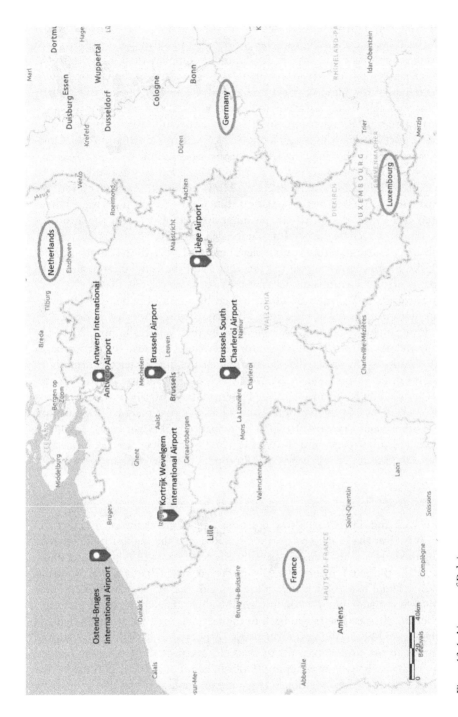

Figure 13.1 Airports of Belgium
Source: Devised by authors using arcGIS

226 *Sven Buyle, Franziska Kupfer, Evy Onghena*

The airports of Antwerp and Ostend are currently run by a private company. Until 2014, both airports were owned and operated by the Flemish government. In 2008, the Flemish government decided to split up the airports into two different entities: the airport development company (luchthaven ontwikkelingsmaatschappij, LOM), which owns the basic assets of the airports and is in the hands of the Flemish government; and the airport operation company (luchthaven exploitatie maatschappij, LEM), which is responsible for the commercial operation of the airport. In 2014, the concession for the management of the airport for 25 years was given to the LEM Antwerpen and LEM Oostende, which are both owned by EGIS Airport operations.

Originally, the small airport of Kortrijk Wevelgem was also meant to be restructured in the LEM-LOM structure. However, due to the high costs of the restructuring and a number of practical difficulties, the changes were implemented at a lower speed than at the other airports. Currently, the airport is owned and managed by the NV Internationale Luchthaven Kortrijk-Wevelgem, which is in the hands of three public shareholders: POM West-Flanders (57 per cent), the Flemish government (33 per cent), and the Intercommunal Leiedal (10 per cent) (Internationale Luchthaven Kortrijk Wevelgem, 2018).

The airports in Wallonia are characterised by a mix of public-private ownership, with a majority of public stakeholders. Brussels South Charleroi Airport, for example, is owned 27.65 per cent by the Wallonia region, 27.64 per cent by Belgian Airports (a joint-venture between the Italian airport manager SAVE Group S.p.A. and a Belgian communal holding which is currently in liquidation), 22.56 per cent by SOWAER (Société Wallonne des Aéroports), 19.16 per cent by Sambrinvest, 2.32 per cent IGRETEC and 0.67 per cent by SABCA – i.e. 52.53 per cent public and 47.47 per cent private. Liège airport, on the other hand, is owned by TEB Participations (50.4 per cent), Aéroports de Paris (25.5 per cent) and SOWAER (24.1 per cent) – i.e. 74.5 per cent public and 25.5 per cent private (ACI-Europe, 2016; Belgian Airports, 2019).

Passenger traffic

Figure 13.2 and Table 13.1 show the passenger traffic at the six Belgian airports. It is clear that Charleroi Airport has achieved the highest traffic growth during the last 15 years. This is especially due to the growth in passenger traffic of Ryanair, the main airline flying from the airport. Charleroi was Ryanair's first continental base, which the airline opened in 2001. Furthermore, a new terminal was inaugurated at the airport in 2008. The decrease in passenger numbers in 2014 can be traced back to the fact that in 2013, Ryanair changed its strategy and began flying from Brussels Airport, as well. While Ryanair did not move routes from Charleroi to Brussels, seven of the ten newly opened routes in Brussels were overlapping (Dobruszkes et al., 2017). Ultimately, the impact of this decision was not as large as expected, as it was partly offset by the expansion of other airlines such as Wizz Air and the start of new airlines from the airport.

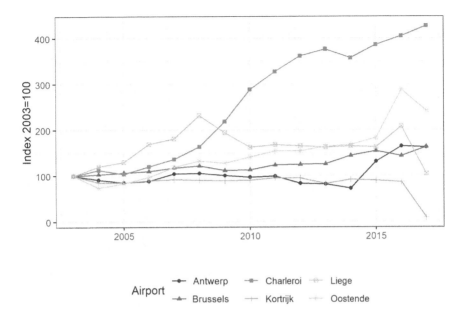

Figure 13.2 Passenger numbers at Belgian airports
Source: Federal Public Service Mobility and Transport (2019)

In addition, at Brussels Airport during the last few years, a steady growth in passenger numbers can be observed. The airport grew from 17.8 million passengers in 2007 to 24.8 million passengers in 2017. Only in 2016 was there a fall in passenger numbers due to the terrorist attacks on 22 March. After the attacks, the airport was forced to close for 12 consecutive days and only opened gradually afterwards. Some of the flights in the aftermath of the attacks were diverted to the Belgian regional airports. This is also clearly illustrated by the passenger numbers where a peak can be observed in 2016 at Ostend, Liège, and Antwerp. Furthermore, the effect of the new management at Ostend airport and Antwerp airport becomes clear in the traffic evolution: both airports achieved a significant passenger growth since 2014. This growth can mainly be attributed to TUI: in Antwerp due to the start of operations of this airline, in Ostend due to the addition of new destinations.

With the traffic development of Liège and Kortrijk Wevelgem airports, a strong drop in 2017 is notable. In the case of Liège Airport, the traffic decrease can mainly be attributed to the discontinuation of some charter flights to China. For Kortrijk Wevelgem, the development is due to a decrease in light aviation and training. However, for Antwerp and Ostend airports, a decrease in passenger numbers from 2016–2017 is also apparent, but for a different reason: the increased passenger numbers due to the diversion of flights after the

Table 13.1 Passenger numbers at Belgian airports

	2013	2014	2015	2016	2017	Growth 2007–2017	Growth 2013–2017	Growth 2016–2017
Antwerpen	137,015	121,357	221,155	276,311	273,130	56.07%	99.34%	−1.15%
Brussel	19,133,222	21,933,190	23,460,018	21,818,418	24,783,911	38.93%	29.53%	13.59%
Charleroi	6,786,163	6,439,957	6,957,596	7,304,800	7,702,099	213.35%	13.5%	5.44%
Kortrijk	60,506	67,013	65,400	63,122	6,512	−90.28%	−89.24%	−89.68%
Liège	299,263	302,667	299,427	382,619	192,381	−42.23%	−35.72%	−49.72%
Oostende	247,669	253,044	276,027	434,970	365,555	103.09%	47.6%	−15.96%

Sources: Federal Public Service Mobility and Transport (2019)

terrorist attacks in March 2016 led to a natural decrease in flights in 2017 in comparison with 2016.

Cargo traffic

Not all six Belgian airports handle air cargo. The airport through which most of the cargo is shipped in Belgium is Liège Airport, which overtook Brussels Airport as the main airport for cargo in 2009 (Figure 13.3 and Table 13.2). Liège Airport benefits from the extended opportunity for night-time flights and is mainly served by cargo aircraft. Furthermore, it served as the main hub of TNT Express, which was acquired by FedEx in 2016. In addition, in December 2018, Alibaba announced its plan to establish a smart logistics hub at Liège Airport, which will boost the airport's cargo traffic even more.

Brussels Airport also saw a growth of air cargo during recent years. The growth came after a decrease in cargo traffic due to DHL moving its European hub from Brussels Airport to Leipzig in 2008, even though DHL never moved its operations entirely. However, after its move, the airport could attract other cargo airlines, and also DHL traffic to Brussels increased again. The growth in recent years can mainly be attributed to the new focus of the airport towards perishables, pharmaceutical products, and, recently, e-commerce (Van Asch et al., 2019).

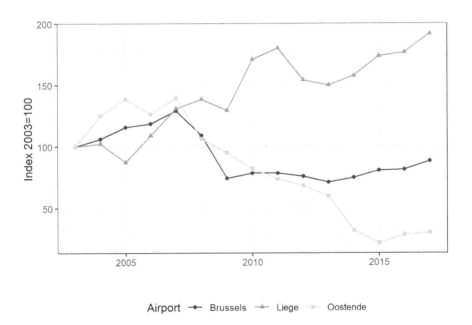

Figure 13.3 Cargo traffic (in tonnes) at Belgian airports

Sources: Department of Mobility and Public Works, Flemish Civil Services (2020)

230 *Sven Buyle, Franziska Kupfer, Evy Onghena*

Table 13.2 Cargo traffic (in tonnes) at Belgian airports

	2013	2014	2015	2016	2017	Growth 2007–2017	Growth 2013–2017	Growth 2016–2017
Brussels	429,938	453,953	489,303	494,637	535,634	−31.66%	24.58%	8.29%
Liège	561,159	590,579	649,829	660,830	717,706	46.49%	27.90%	8.61%
Ostend	46,485	24,885	16,843	22,224	23,369	−78.55%	−49.73%	5.15%

Sources: Department of Mobility and Public Works, Flemish Civil Services (2020)

The airport with the largest decrease in cargo traffic is Ostend airport. From 2007–2017, the airport reported a negative growth of 78 per cent. During the observed period, many cargo airlines decided to leave Ostend Airport or went bankrupt (e.g. MK airlines in 2010). Also, the departure of ANA Aviation in 2014 is apparent in the traffic numbers. The airline decided to move its operations to Liège due to its location closer to the market and other factors such as high fuel costs at Ostend airport. Moreover, Ethiopian Airlines was once a customer at the airport but moved its business to other airports. In February 2019, only EgyptAir still operated cargo flights from Ostend.

Methodology

The purpose of the study of the NBB was to analyse the economic effects of the air transport and airport activities in Belgium. To this aim, two categories of economic activities have been defined. First, activities that have a direct link with air transport and are defined as the air transport cluster. These activities include, for example, airlines, air traffic control, and airport authorities. In the earlier versions of the study, a distinction has been made between air transport activities inside the airport and outside the airport. This was done in order to see the economic influence of the airport itself in contrast to activities related to air transport outside the airport. The second type of activities that were defined were other airport-related activities, which incorporate activities by companies not directly related to air transport but located within the airport zone such as shops, restaurants, and hotels at the airport. The selection of the companies included in the study was based on the standard European NACE (Nomenclature of Economic Activities) codes, as well as geographic location for the airport-related activities. However, some of the considered NACE branches include activities which fall outside of the scope of the NBB studies. For these branches, the NBB made estimates as to how much turnover is attributable to air transport activities. These percentages were then multiplied with the values of the firms located outside of the airports. Figure 13.4 shows the original scope of the economic influence study.

In the most recent version of the study by the NBB, the difference between the air transport cluster inside airports and the air transport cluster outside

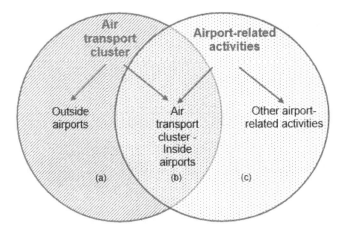

Figure 13.4 Categories of activities
Source: Adapted by authors from Kupfer and Lagneaux (2009)

airports was not maintained. Therefore, only the distinction between the air transport cluster and other airport-related activities has been used. For the economic effect of companies operating inside as well as outside of the airport or at different airports, an allocation key based on the employment at the respective locations was used. All data concerning employment was provided by the airport authorities or the companies in question.

Economic effect studies often focus on four different levels: direct impacts, indirect impacts, induced impacts, and catalytic impacts (see Figure 13.5). While the direct effects quantify the impacts of the economic activity directly generated by the air transport sector (e.g. airlines, air traffic control, ground handling) or activities at the airport (e.g. food and beverage, hotels), the indirect effects relate to upstream activities at suppliers such as catering companies supplying airlines. Induced and catalytic effects, on the other hand, relate to the downstream impact of air transport/airport activities. Expenditures of direct or indirect employment incomes are the basis of the induced effects. Catalytic effects incorporate the economic activity that is created as a result of the accessibility and attractiveness of the region due to the existence of the airport.

All effects are usually calculated with regards to value added and/or employment. However, while direct and indirect effects are relatively easy to be quantified, the calculation of induced and catalytic effects is not without difficulty and criticism, amongst others, due to possible double counting. (Sleuwaegen and De Backer, 2003; Kupfer and Lagneaux, 2009). This is why the studies of the NBB, as well as this chapter, concentrate on the direct and indirect effect of air transport activities in Belgium.

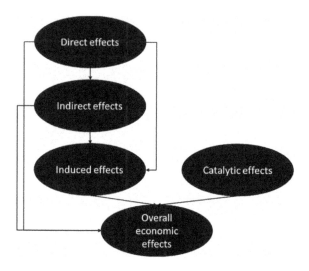

Figure 13.5 Classification of economic impacts
Source: Devised by authors

The following variables were calculated with regard to the direct economic impact:

- Employment in full-time equivalents (FTEs).

   Data on FTEs is supplied by the airport authorities and relevant companies. It includes the employees on the payroll, as well as some self-employed workers.

- Value added at current prices, including operating grants that the airport operators may receive from the government.

   The value added at current prices is calculated as the sum of staff costs, depreciation, and value adjustments, provisions for liabilities and charges, other operating expenses, and the operating profit or loss, less the operating costs capitalised as restructuring expenses and non-product-related operating subsidies. The value added includes operating grants that the airport operators may receive from the government, as they are seen as product-related subsidies which reduce market prices. For the Belgian companies, most of this data is gained from the company annual accounts which are filed to the NBB. However, for foreign companies there is no obligation to file annual accounts and hence the NBB has to rely on estimates.

- Investment at current prices (not included in the discussion of this paper, as this is outside of the chapter's scope).

For the analysis of the indirect effects, an input-output analysis was carried out. The methodology of input-output analysis is often critically perceived due to its lack of incorporating cost and the absence of welfare measurement. Therefore, it is argued that it should not be used for investment or policy analysis. For that kind of analysis, the methods of cost-benefit analysis and the computable general equilibrium (CGE) model are preferred (Forsyth et al., 2014). However, for a general view on the socio-economic impact of airports, input-output models are often used (Dimitriou and Sartzetaki, 2018). The advantage of these models is that, due to their relative simplicity compared with other methods, it becomes possible for a government institution such as the NBB to repeat the analysis periodically. However, there are drawbacks with the input-output method and there needs to be care with the interpretation and use of the results as detailed in what follows:

- There might be difficulties in the data collection stage, as for most countries, the input-output tables are not provided at a regional level by the national statistical office. For the NBB studies, the national figures are applied in a top-down approach to the more local level.
- Traditional input-output models are static, meaning that the choice of the year to be analysed has an impact on the conclusions. Peak years might lead to overestimation of the economic impact, while studies conducted during a recession might lead to an underestimation. While the NBB studies are not dynamic, they are conducted periodically and for multiple years, which makes it possible to analyse the evolution of the economic impact of air transport over time. This should overcome possible bias coming from the selection of the analysed year.
- Input-output models do not take into account efficient resource allocation. It cannot be assumed that, in the absence of the airport, the employment and added value generated by that airport would be fully lost. It is quite likely that those resources will be used by other sectors of the economy. Moreover, input-output models favour those airports that use (labour) resources more inefficiently as they generate more employment. Therefore, economic impact studies based on input-output models should not be used as a motivation for investment projects, as they always present a positive picture and neglect the wider socio-economic impact. The only purpose of the NBB studies is to provide a general overview of the impact of Belgian airports on the Belgian economy, not to evaluate transport infrastructure projects.
- As already mentioned, input-output models entail the possibility of double-counting economic impacts when calculating induced and catalytic effects. To prevent this issue, the NBB studies only look at direct and indirect effects.

For the studies of the NBB, the indirect effects for the employment and value added were calculated based on input-output tables. In the earlier studies, data

234   *Sven Buyle, Franziska Kupfer, Evy Onghena*

for the input-output tables were gathered from the Central Balance Sheet Office based on the annual accounts of companies. However, the problem with this data was that foreign companies, public entities, and authorities, as well as self-employed operators, were disregarded. To address this shortcoming, in the report from 2017, data from the National Accounts Institute was used. This led to a break in the methodology used and therefore lower indirect effects, but to a more accurate calculation of the indirect effects.

Direct and indirect effects

In this part of the chapter, the different economic effects of the air transport and airport industry are analysed. Table 13.3 presents the direct and indirect value added generated by the air transport cluster and other airport-related activities in Belgium between 2013 and 2015. In 2015, total value added by air transport and airport activities in Belgium amounted to more than €6 billion. From 2013–2015, total value added grew at an annual average rate of 7.4 per cent, which is much higher than the 1.8 per cent annual average growth rate of GDP during this period. The air transport cluster and airport activities in Belgium represented 1.5 per cent of national GDP in 2015 (Vennix, 2017).

The air transport cluster was responsible for 75 per cent of direct value added created, of which more than 25 per cent in this cluster was generated by building and repairing of aircraft. The latter sector enjoyed the strongest annual average growth rate between 2013 and 2015, which was due to the strong performance of three main players in this sector, namely Safran Aero Boosters, SONACA, and Asco. The second strongest growing sector between 2013 and 2015 was the air transport sector, which accounts for 16 per cent of the air transport cluster. The strong performance of this sector mainly resulted from Brussels Airlines, which nearly doubled its value added in two years. The value added generated by airport operators experienced an average annual growth of 7 per cent, which was to the largest extent caused by Brussels Airport Company. Travel agencies and tour operators saw a decrease of value added generated between 2013 and 2015, which was mainly due to tour operator TUI Belgium (Vennix, 2017).

Focusing on the other airport-related activities, the annual average growth between 2013 and 2015 was positive but smaller than that of the air transport cluster. The strongest growing sector was cargo handling and storage, while courier and post activities accounted for the largest share in value added in 2015 (Vennix, 2017).

Figure 13.6 shows the evolution of direct, indirect and total value added during the 2006–2015 period. Remarkable is the strong increase in 2007, followed by the significant decrease in 2009 due to the economic downturn, especially for indirect and total value added. Between 2010 and 2012, total value added experienced a moderate growth. However, in 2013, total and indirect value added decreased by 7 per cent and 15 per cent, respectively, compared to 2012, due to the previously described adjustment in methodology, while direct value

Table 13.3 Value added of air transport cluster and other airport-related activities, 2013–2015 (in € million, current prices)

Cluster and sector	2013	2014	2015	Share 2015 (%)	Change from 2014–2015 (%)	Change from 2013–2015 (%)	Annual average change from 2013–2015 (%)
1 Direct effects	**2,879.4**	**3,050.3**	**3,317.3**	**100**	**8.8**	**15.2**	**7.3**
Air transport cluster	**2,127.9**	**2,271.1**	**2,489.9**	**75.1**	**9.6**	**17.0**	**8.2**
Air transport	442.1	461.6	538.7	16.2	16.7	21.9	10.6
Travel agencies and tour operators	330.7	338.4	323.8	9.8	–4.3	–2.1	–1.0
Airport operator	388.9	417.4	445.3	13.4	6.7	14.5	7.0
Airport handling	110.4	108.7	113.2	3.4	4.1	2.5	1.3
Building and repairing of aircraft	652.1	738.0	843.6	25.4	14.3	29.4	13.7
Other air transport supporting activities	203.7	207.0	225.3	6.8	8.8	10.6	5.2
Other airport-related activities	**751.5**	**779.2**	**827.4**	**24.9**	**6.2**	**10.1**	**4.9**
Passenger transport over land	20.0	18.6	19.5	0.6	4.8	–2.5	–1.1
Freight transport over land	13.4	11.6	12.4	0.4	6.9	–7.5	–3.3
Cargo handling and storage	156.0	175.9	190.4	5.7	8.2	22.1	10.5
Courier and post activities	207.0	221.2	230.5	7.0	4.2	11.4	5.5
Security and industrial cleaning	66.0	70.6	76.3	2.3	8.1	15.6	7.5
Trade	49.5	48.7	50.2	1.5	3.1	1.4	0.7
Hotels, restaurants, and catering	69.9	62.6	66.1	2.0	5.6	–5.4	–2.4
Other services	44.3	45.0	47.5	1.4	5.6	7.2	3.6
Other industries	18.4	18.3	19.9	0.6	8.7	8.2	4.1
Public services	107.0	106.7	114.6	3.5	7.4	7.1	3.6
2 Indirect effects	**2,328.9**	**2,423.9**	**2,693.9**		**11.1**	**15.7**	**7.6**
Total	**5,208.3**	**5,474.2**	**6,011.2**		**9.8**	**15.4**	**7.4**

Source: Vennix (2017)

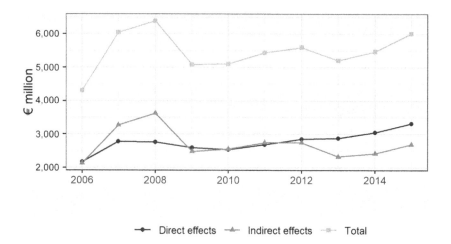

Figure 13.6 Direct, indirect, and total value added of air transport cluster and other airport-related activities, 2006–2015 (in € million, current prices)

Sources: Kupfer and Lagneaux (2009), Deville and Vennix (2011), Van Nieuwenhove (2014), Vennix (2017)

added grew very slightly by 1 per cent. Between 2013 and 2015, both direct and indirect value added grew at a comparable rate of more than 7 per cent. The multiplier for value added equals 1.81, implying that €1 of value added generated directly by companies operating in air transport or airport activities generates €1.81 via the intersectoral links between these companies and companies upstream and downstream in the air transport value chain. Figure 13.7 looks more in detail at the evolution of the direct value added generated by the air transport cluster and other airport activities. The graph illustrates that the growth in direct value added is mainly driven by the air transport cluster, especially in the years after the economic crisis. The share of the air transport cluster increased from 69 per cent in 2006 to 75 per cent in 2015.

Figure 13.8 focuses on the air transport cluster, depicting the evolution of the direct value added generated by the different sectors comprising this cluster between 2006 and 2015. Building and repairing of aircraft experienced the strongest increase, especially between 2011 and 2016, when the annual average growth rate amounted to 153 per cent. The share of this sector in the direct value added grew from 18 per cent in 2006 to 25 per cent in 2015. Three major construction companies, Techspace Aero, ASCO Industries and SONACA, were driving this growth. The drop in 2008 was due to a decrease in the value added generated by this sector outside the airports. Value added generated by the six airport operators also showed an increasing trend with an annual average growth rate of 5 per cent and a share in the direct value added growing from 11 per cent in 2006 to 13 per cent in 2015. Brussels Airport

A Belgian case study 237

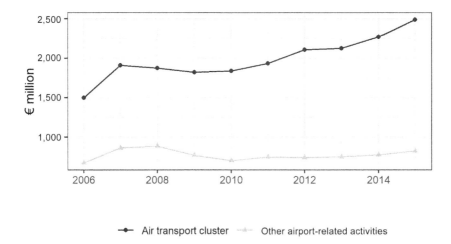

Figure 13.7 Direct value added of air transport cluster and other airport-related activities, 2006–2015 (in € million, current prices)

Sources: Kupfer and Lagneaux (2009), Deville and Vennix (2011), Van Nieuwenhove (2014), Vennix (2017)

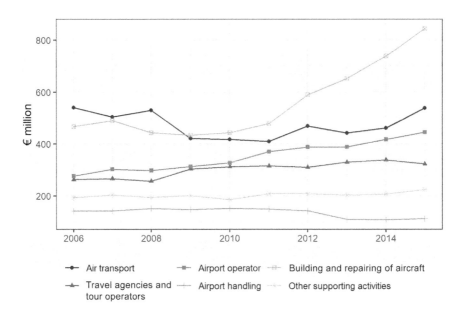

Figure 13.8 Direct value added of air transport cluster 2006–2015 (in € million, current prices)

Sources: Kupfer and Lagneaux (2009), Deville and Vennix (2011), Van Nieuwenhove (2014), Vennix (2017)

238 *Sven Buyle, Franziska Kupfer, Evy Onghena*

Company accounts for the major part of this growth. The air transport sector, consisting of airlines, exhibits the largest volatility, with only in 2015 generating a direct value added comparable to the level of 2006. It is the second largest sector generating 16 per cent of direct value added, with Brussels Airlines and, to a lesser extent TUI Airlines Belgium, the main engines behind the growth in 2014 and 2015.

Table 13.4 presents the direct and indirect employment generated by the air transport cluster and other airport-related activities in Belgium between 2013 and 2015. In 2015, total employment amounted to 62,530 FTEs or 1.5 per cent of domestic employment (including the self-employed). Looking at the growth between 2013 and 2015, indirect employment increased stronger than direct employment. It increased by 6.2 per cent in 2015 compared to the level of 2013, while direct employment only grew by 3.8 per cent. The reason for the stronger growth of indirect compared to direct employment is that some sectors which generate relatively high indirect employment, such as cargo handling and storage, and other services, have gained more weight in the last two years. The employment multiplier equals 1.89, which means that 1 FTE generated directly by companies operating in air transport or airport activities generates approximately 1.89 FTEs via the intersectoral links between these companies, their suppliers, the firms supplying the latter, etc. This multiplier effect is slightly more than in the case of value added (1.81). Focusing on direct employment, the growth between 2013 and 2015 was mainly concentrated in the other airport-related activities. Cargo handling and storage was the best performing sector within other airport-related activities, with an annual average growth of 10 per cent. This is mainly the result of a reorganisation within AviaPartner Belgium by which AviaPartner Cargo, a separate entity for its cargo division, was created. This led to a shift of employees from the airport handling sector, which belongs to the air transport cluster, to cargo handling and storage, part of other airport-related activities. Building and repairing of aircraft, the largest sector within the air transport cluster, achieved the strongest increase in direct employment. Courier and post activities were the largest sector within other airport-related activities in terms of employment in 2015 (Vennix, 2017).

Figure 13.9 depicts the evolution of direct, indirect, and total employment between 2006 and 2015. Indirect employment increased in 2008, followed by a significant decrease in 2009. Indirect employment decreased also in 2013 (due to methodological changes), after which it started to increase at an annual average rate of 3.1 per cent between 2013 and 2015. However, as mentioned previously, the indirect effects are an estimate and need to be interpreted with caution. Figure 13.10 focuses on direct employment generated by the air transport cluster and other airport-related activities between 2006 and 2015. The graph clearly shows that direct employment only increased slightly over the observed period at an annual average growth rate of 0.5 per cent. Other airport-related activities contributed to the majority of this growth, especially since 2012. Its annual average growth over the 2006–2015 period amounted

Table 13.4 Employment of air transport cluster and other airport-related activities, 2013–2015 (in FTEs)

Cluster and sector	2013	2014	2015	Share 2015 (%)	Change from 2014–2015 (%)	Change from 2013–2015 (%)	Annual average change from 2013–2015 (%)
1 Direct effects	**31,961**	**32,470**	**33,181**	**100.0**	**2.2**	**3.8**	**1.9**
Air transport cluster	**20,446**	**20,502**	**20,704**	**62.4**	**1.0**	**1.3**	**0.6**
Air transport	5,037	4,967	5,183	15.6	4.3	2.9	1.5
Travel agencies and tour operators	4,530	4,521	4,470	13.5	−1.1	−1.3	−0.7
Airport operator	1,577	1,566	1,591	4.8	1.6	0.9	0.4
Airport handling	2,212	2,264	2,108	6.4	−6.9	−4.7	−2.3
Building and repairing of aircraft	5,855	6,006	6,173	18.6	2.8	5.4	2.7
Other air transport supporting activities	1,235	1,178	1,179	3.6	0.1	−4.5	−2.3
Other airport-related activities	**11,515**	**11,968**	**12,477**	**37.6**	**4.3**	**8.4**	**4.1**
Passenger transport over land	407	418	434	1.3	3.8	6.6	3.3
Freight transport over land	226	218	220	0.7	0.9	−2.7	−1.3
Cargo handling and storage	2,041	2,252	2,471	7.4	9.7	21.1	10.0
Courier and post activities	2,988	3,045	3,097	9.3	1.7	3.6	1.8
Security and industrial cleaning	1,538	1,617	1,782	5.4	10.2	15.9	7.7
Trade	596	619	640	1.9	3.4	7.4	3.6
Hotels, restaurants, and catering	1,362	1,388	1,363	4.1	−1.8	0.1	0.1
Other services	385	417	435	1.3	4.3	13.0	6.3
Other industries	233	234	271	0.8	15.8	16.3	8.1
Public services	1,739	1,760	1,764	5.3	0.2	1.4	0.7
2 Indirect effects	**27,633**	**28,251**	**29,349**		**3.9**	**6.2**	**3.1**
Total	**59,594**	**60,721**	**62,530**		**3.0**	**4.9**	**2.4**

Source: Vennix (2017)

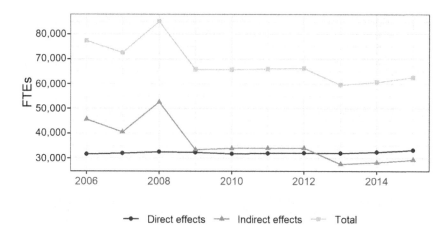

Figure 13.9 Direct, indirect, and total employment of air transport cluster and other airport-related activities, 2006–2015 (in FTEs)

Sources: Kupfer and Lagneaux (2009), Deville and Vennix (2011), Van Nieuwenhove (2014), Vennix (2017)

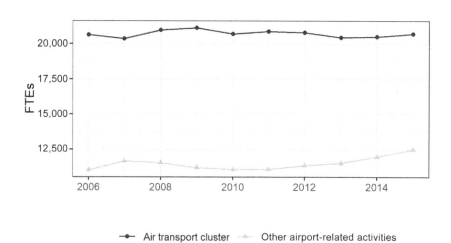

Figure 13.10 Direct employment of air transport cluster and other airport-related activities, 2006–2015 (in FTEs)

Sources: Kupfer and Lagneaux (2009), Deville and Vennix (2011), Van Nieuwenhove (2014), Vennix (2017)

to 1.4 per cent. As indicated previously, this is mainly the result of the strong growth in direct employment generated by cargo handling and storage. The evolution of the air transport cluster's direct employment between 2006 and 2015 is shown in Figure 13.11. This cluster only grew at an annual average rate of 0.05 per cent in terms of employment. The figure illustrates that building

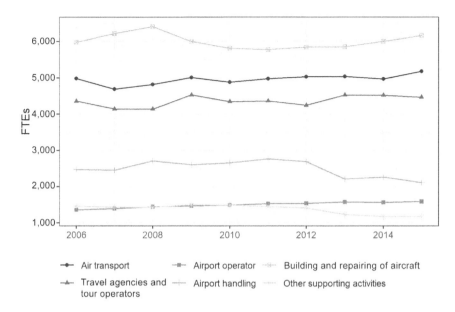

Figure 13.11 Direct employment of air transport cluster, 2006–2015 (in FTEs)

Sources: Kupfer and Lagneaux (2009), Deville and Vennix (2011), Van Nieuwenhove (2014), Vennix (2017)

and repairing of aircraft and air transport were the best performing sectors in terms of direct employment generation. Airport handling, as well as other airport supporting activities, showed a decrease since 2013. The reorganisation at AviaPartner Belgium was responsible for the decline in airport handling, while other airport supporting activities were to a large extent impacted by decreasing staff levels at Belgocontrol (now Skeyes). The air transport sector benefitted in 2015 from expanding business at TUI Airlines Belgium and a helicopter company (Noordzee Helikopters Vlaanderen).

The economic importance of Belgian airports within an international comparison

In order to put the figures on employment and added value of aviation in Belgium into perspective, it is interesting to compare them with those of other European countries. However, comparing results of different economic impact studies is difficult because of differences in methodology. Therefore, Tables 13.5 and 13.6 present estimates on employment and value added, both direct and indirect, taken from a study executed by Oxford Economics for the Air Transport Action Group, and the NBB studies are not used. To estimate the indirect effects, they rely on national input-output tables sourced from the OECD and official national statistical offices. Other data is taken from a variety

242 Sven Buyle, Franziska Kupfer, Evy Onghena

Table 13.5 Aviation direct and indirect employment in Europe, 2017 (in FTEs)

	Direct	Indirect	Aviation Total	Country Population	% Aviation
Austria	35,000	28,000	63,000	8,772,865	0.718
Belgium	40,000	34,000	74,000	11,351,727	0.652
Cyprus	10,000	3,000	13,000	854,802	1.521
Czech Republic	25,000	20,000	45,000	10,578,820	0.425
Denmark	34,000	21,000	55,000	5,748,769	0.957
Finland	25,000	17,000	42,000	5,503,297	0.763
France	273,000	431,000	704,000	66,804,121	1.054
Germany	315,000	337,000	652,000	82,521,653	0.790
Greece	41,000	19,000	60,000	10,768,193	0.557
Hungary	13,000	23,000	36,000	9,797,561	0.367
Iceland	11,000	14,000	25,000	338,349	7.389
Ireland	39,000	25,000	64,000	4,784,383	1.338
Italy	204,000	185,000	389,000	60,589,445	0.642
Latvia	7,000	6,000	13,000	1,950,116	0.667
Luxembourg	9,000	1,100	10,100	590,667	1.710
Malta	4,000	3,000	7,000	460,297	1.521
Netherlands	85,000	59,000	144,000	17,081,507	0.843
Norway	52,000	38,000	90,000	5,258,317	1.712
Poland	44,000	47,000	91,000	37,972,964	0.240
Portugal	53,000	46,000	99,000	10,309,573	0.960
Romania	25,000	30,000	55,000	19,644,350	0.280
Spain	269,000	163,000	432,000	46,528,024	0.928
Sweden	49,000	39,000	88,000	9,995,153	0.880
Switzerland	67,000	49 000	116,000	8,419,550	1.378
Turkey	154,000	117 000	271,000	79,814,871	0.340
UK	353,000	419 000	772,000	65,844,142	1.172

Sources: Air Transport Action Group (2018), Eurostat (2018a)

of sources (e.g. Airport Council International, Civil Air Navigation Services Organisation, International Air Transport Association, Eurostat, and national statistical offices). Six key sub-sectors are considered: airlines, airport operators, providers of goods and services on-site airports, civil aircraft manufacturers, air navigation service providers, and tourism activity that air travel makes possible.

Based on the methodology of Oxford Economics, the air transport sector in Belgium creates employment for around 0.652 per cent of the Belgian population, which puts Belgium at the beginning of the second quantile together with countries such as e.g. Latvia (0.667 per cent) and Austria (0.718 per cent). Lower relative contributions to employment are found, for example, in Poland (0.240 per cent), Romania (0.280 per cent), and Turkey (0.340 per cent), while Luxembourg (1.71 per cent), Norway (1.712 per cent), and especially Iceland (7.389 per cent) are much more dependent on air transport as a driver for employment. The high dependence on air transport in Luxembourg might be explained by its relatively small size, while Norway and Iceland are remote European regions where air transport is crucial in terms of accessibility.

Table 13.6 Aviation direct and indirect value added in Europe, 2017 (in million €)

	Direct	Indirect	Aviation Total	Country GDP	% Aviation
Austria	3,000	2,500	5,500	369,899	1.487
Belgium	3,800	3,400	7,200	439,175	1.639
Cyprus	374	139	513	19,649	2.612
Czech Republic	908	790	1,697	191,722	0.885
Denmark	359	344	703	292,806	0.240
Finland	1,900	1,500	3,400	223,918	1.518
France	30,200	38,400	68,600	2,295,063	2.989
Germany	25,900	26,700	52,600	3,244,990	1.621
Greece	2,000	993	2,993	180,218	1.661
Hungary	1,100	682	1,782	124,050	1.437
Iceland	1,400	1,400	2,800	21,709	12.898
Ireland	5,300	3,500	8,800	297,131	2.962
Italy	11,700	15,000	26,700	1,727,382	1.546
Latvia	198	188	385	27,033	1.426
Luxembourg	1,000	269	1,269	55,299	2.294
Malta	205	161	366	11,305	3.239
Netherlands	7,800	5,800	13,600	738,146	1.842
Norway	4,800	5,300	10,100	354,287	2.851
Poland	1,700	1,300	3,000	467,304	0.642
Portugal	2,900	2,000	4,900	194,614	2.518
Romania	748	679	1,427	187,517	0.761
Spain	17,500	10,900	28,400	1,166,319	2.435
Sweden	5,400	4,000	9,400	475,224	1.978
Switzerland	9,900	6,600	16,500	601,396	2.744
Turkey	5,800	3,700	9,500	753,904	1.260
UK	30,800	32,200	63,000	2,337,971	2.695

Sources: Air Transport Action Group (2018), Eurostat (2018b).

With regard to direct and indirect value added, similar conclusions can be drawn. The air transport sector in Belgium directly and indirectly adds 1.639 per cent to GDP, which puts Belgium again in the second quantile together with Germany (1.621 per cent) and Greece (1.661 per cent). Countries where aviation has a relatively low contribution to GDP are Denmark (0.240 per cent), Poland (0.642 per cent), and Romania (0.761 per cent), whereas the direct and indirect contribution of aviation to GDP in France (2.989 per cent), Malta (3.239 per cent), and Iceland (12.898 per cent) is relatively high. It is remarkable that Belgium has a similar share of GDP coming from the aviation sector as Germany, which is home to one of Europe's largest hub airports.

Bringing the economic importance into perspective: noise development around Brussels Airport

Economic impact studies such as those developed by the NBB usually only look at the positive effects of the air transport sector, while neglecting the negative externalities. Research done by Schipper (2004) suggests that the environmental costs of aviation accounts for 2.5 per cent of the average ticket price, of which noise pollution has the highest share (75 per cent). Therefore, in order to put the studies by the NBB in perspective, this section will focus on analysing the noise impact of the largest airport in Belgium, Brussels Airport. Unfortunately, the data used was not available for the other Belgian airports.

Since 1996, Brussels Airport is obliged by law to measure the number of inhabitants impacted by the noise generated by the airport. From 1996–2014, these studies were conducted by the Acoustics Laboratory of the KU Leuven and since 2015 by the WAVES research group of the University of Ghent. These studies only report on the findings as required by the legislation, but do not provide any policy advice. As required by Flemish law, the noise contours are estimated by use of the most recent version of the Integrated Noise Model developed by the US Federal Aviation Administration (FAA) (Dekoninck et al., 2019).

The studies measure noise pollution by reporting on the area within so-called L_{den} contours, as well as on the population living in those areas. The L_{den} noise measure captures the exposure of noise over a longer time period. It is a weighted energetic sum of the noise exposure during three time periods: day (7–19 hours), evening (19–23 hours) and night (23–7 hours), in which a correction of 5 dB(A) is made for noise during the evening period and 10 dB(A) for the noise in the night period (Dekoninck et al., 2019).

Figure 13.12 compares the evolution of commercial aircraft movements at Brussels Airport over the period 2000–2018 with the area and population

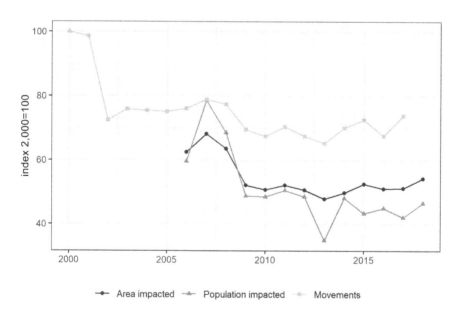

Figure 13.12 Evolution of movements, area, and population impacted by >55 dB(A) L_{den} contours (index 2000)

Sources: Dekoninck et al. (2019), Eurostat (2018c)

impacted by the L_{den} contours above 55 dB(A). After the bankruptcy of the national flag carrier Sabena in 2001, the commercial aircraft movements at Brussels Airport have been fluctuating between 70 per cent and 80 per cent of the level in 2000. However, the area and population impacted by L_{den} contours above 55 dB(A) dropped dramatically to a level not higher than 54 per cent and 46 per cent, respectively, of the level in 2000. The largest improvement in noise pollution has been achieved in the period 2007–2009, when DHL moved its hub operations to Leipzig. This led to a small reduction of the number of late evening and night movements. Nevertheless, the impact on noise emissions was much larger as full freighter operations often use older and more noise polluting aircraft. The area and population impacted have been more stable since then. While the area impacted has been fluctuating around 50 per cent of the 2000 level, the population impacted continued to drop slightly more.

Table 13.7 shows the evolution of the area (in hectares) within the L_{den} contours from 2000–2018 for different dB levels, while Table 13.6 shows the population living in these areas. It seems that the largest impact reductions are seen in the higher noise contours. While the area within the >75 dB(A) and 70–75 dB(A) contours was reduced by 55 per cent from 2000–2018, the population living within these contours reduced with more than 90 per cent. In 2017 and 2018, no people were living within these noise contours. For the lower noise contours, the reductions in area and population impacted have been more aligned between 45 per cent and 50 per cent of the 2000 level.

There are two main reasons explaining the reduction in noise pollution of Brussels Airport from 2000–2018. First, there has been a shift in fleet composition to more modern aircraft with fewer noise emissions due to technological progress. Second, there have been changes over time in the preferential use of the runway system of the airport, as well as in departure and landing route procedures towards less densely populated areas (Dekoninck et al., 2019).

Table 13.7 Evolution of the area within the L_{den} contours of Brussels Airport (ha)

Year	55–60 dB	60–65 dB	65–70 dB	70–75 dB	>75 dB	Total
2000	10,664	4,063	1,626	745	497	17,595
2006	6,963	2,448	957	373	251	10,992
2007	7,632	2,640	1,036	416	271	11,995
2008	7,118	2,483	953	379	246	11,179
2009	5,771	2,077	797	316	203	9,164
2010	5,576	2,052	782	308	199	8,917
2011	5,767	2,076	800	316	208	9,167
2012	5,623	1,998	771	308	205	8,905
2013	5,152	1,981	767	299	216	8,415
2014	5,429	2,066	800	325	136	8,756
2015	5,695	2,159	825	332	224	9,235
2016	5,554	2,085	797	326	213	8,975
2017	5,579	2,088	795	325	213	9,000
2018	5,957	2,186	832	336	228	9,539

Source: Dekoninck et al. (2019)

Table 13.8 Evolution of the population within the L_{den} contours of Brussels Airport

Year	55–60 dB	60–65 dB	65–70 dB	70–75 dB	>75 dB	Total
2000	166,767	36,797	14,091	3 952	264	221,871
2006	107,514	18,697	5,365	560	63	132,199
2007	147,349	19,498	6,565	946	82	174,440
2008	125,927	19,319	5,938	717	24	151,925
2009	87,766	15,105	4,921	404	9	108,205
2010	87,083	15,619	4,506	337	11	107,556
2011	90,988	15,941	4,664	362	13	111,968
2012	86,519	16,220	4,617	319	6	107,681
2013	56,516	16,517	3,994	197	5	77,229
2014	84,747	16,525	5,076	368	9	106,725
2015	72,628	17,721	5,244	428	55	96,076
2016	77,229	16,694	5,284	450	23	99,680
2017	70,139	17,645	5,264	257	0	93,305
2018	77,812	19,476	5,413	413	0	103,114

Source: Dekoninck et al. (2019)

Tables 13.7 and 13.8, and Figure 13.10 give a useful overview of the evolution of the noise impact of Brussels Airport. However, to be able to compare noise externalities with the value added of aviation to the Belgian economy, they should be expressed in monetary terms. Schipper (2004) has presented estimates for the compensation required by impacted households for each dB(A) of noise pollution above certain levels, but these figures are debatable. When comparing the evolution of noise pollution with the evolution in value added and employment, it can be concluded that there has been a decrease in the burden of air transport without compromising the added value to the Belgian economy.

Conclusion

In this chapter, the economic impact of the air transport and airport sector in Belgium was analysed based on four working papers published by the National Bank of Belgium (NBB). First, the background and history of the studies was presented. While studies on the economic effects of the Belgian ports have already been carried out by the NBB for more than 15 years, the first study on the economic effects of airports and the air transport sector was published only in 2009. The main reason to start investigating the impact of the aviation sector was the demand from industry stakeholders who requested more information on the effects of the air transport sector in Belgium.

In the second part of the chapter, the six Belgian airports were described. An analysis of the passenger traffic showed that most of the airports were able to grow their traffic since 2003. Charleroi Airport in particular, due to the arrival of Ryanair, has experienced a large increase in passenger numbers. It is also notable that since the privatisation of Antwerp and Ostend airports, a significant growth at these airports has been observed. With regard to the evolution of cargo traffic, the airport of Liège almost doubled its cargo volumes between 2003 and 2017.

While not without flaws, the input-output method was used to determine the economic effects of the air transport and airport sector in Belgium. For direct as well as indirect effects, the sector was divided into the air transport cluster and other airport-related activities. In 2015, total employment amounted to 62,530 FTEs, or 1.5 per cent of domestic employment (including the self-employed). Looking at the growth between 2013 and 2015, indirect employment increased more strongly than direct employment. Furthermore, one FTE generated directly by companies operating in air transport or airport activities generates approximately 1.89 FTEs via the intersectoral links between these companies and companies upstream and downstream in the air transport value chain. With regard to value added, this multiplier effect is slightly smaller: €1 of value added generated directly by companies operating in air transport or airport activities generates €1.81 via the intersectoral links. Total value added by air transport and airport activities in Belgium amounted to more than €6 billion in 2015, growing at an annual average rate of 7.5 per cent between 2013 and 2015.

The last section briefly covered the impact of noise pollution at Brussels Airport. There have been large reductions in both the area and the number of inhabitants impacted by airport noise from 2000–2018. While the value added and employment generated by the Belgium aviation sector grew over time, the burden of air transport in terms of noise decreased gradually.

In conclusion, it can be said that the research of the NBB as a case study adds to the knowledge of the economic effects of the air transport and airport sector. Furthermore, it may be one of the few studies that is carried out regularly and therefore provides a time series analysis that can serve as an inspiration for other governments. However, when analysing investment projects, and not just the economic impact, the negative externalities should also be taken into consideration.

References

ACI-Europe (2016). *The ownership of Europe's airports 2016*. Available at: www.aci-europe.org/component/downloads/downloads/5095.html (accessed 9 October 2019).

ACI-Europe (2018). *Top 30 European airports 2017*. Available at: www.aci-europe.org/component/downloads/downloads/5401.html (accessed 9 October 2019).

Air Transport Action Group (2018). *Aviation benefits beyond borders*. Available at: www.aviation-benefits.org/media/166344/abbb18_full-report_web.pdf (accessed 22 October 2019).

Belgian Airports (2019). *Comptes annuels et autres documents à déposer en vertu du code des sociétés*. Available at: https://cri.nbb.be/bc9/web/catalog;jsessionid=7EA9BBCECBC36462F A3454F856230774?execution=e1s2# (accessed 18 November 2019).

Burghouwt, G. and Dobruszkes, F. (2014). The (mis)fortunes of exceeding a small local air market: Comparing Amsterdam and Brussels. *Tijdschrift Voor Economische en Sociale Geografie*, 105, 604–621.

248 Sven Buyle, Franziska Kupfer, Evy Onghena

Dekoninck, L., Van Renterghem, T. and Botteldooren, D. (2019). *Geluidscontouren rond Brussels Airport voor het jaar 2018.* Available at: https://media.brusselsairport.be/bru-web/default/0001/24/6ad9ef94025ef6a9cb2f11a413e0a96fdc03312a.pdf (accessed 22 November 2019).

Department of Mobility and Public Works, Flemish Civil Services (2020). *Statistics on Belgian airports* (data collected through personal communication).

Deville, X. and Vennix, S. (2011). *Economic importance of air transport and airport activities in Belgium.* Report 2009, NBB Working Paper No. 218. Brussels, National Bank of Belgium, December.

Dimitriou, D. and Sartzetaki, M. (2018). Assessing air transport socio-economic footprint. *International Journal of Transportation Science and Technology*, 7(4), 283–290.

Dobruszkes, F., Givoni, M. and Vowles, T. (2017). Hello major airports, goodbye regional airports? Recent changes in European and US low-cost airline airport choice. *Journal of Air Transport Management*, 59, 50–62.

Eurostat (2018a). *Population.* Available at: https://appsso.eurostat.ec.europa.eu/nui/show.do?dataset=demo_pjan&lang=en (accessed 16 August 2019).

Eurostat (2018b). *GDP.* Available at: https://appsso.eurostat.ec.europa.eu/nui/show.do?dataset=nama_10_gdp&lang=en (accessed 16 August 2019).

Eurostat (2018c). *Airline traffic data by main airport.* Available at: https://appsso.eurostat.ec.europa.eu/nui/show.do?dataset=avia_paoa&lang=en (accessed 20 November 2019).

Federal Public Service Mobility and Transport (2019). *Statistical data of airports.* Available at: https://mobilit.belgium.be/nl/luchtvaart/luchthavens_en_luchtvaartterreinen/statistieken (accessed 20 November 2019).

Forsyth, P., Njoya, E. and Niemeier, H. M. (2014). *Economic assessment of airports- a survey.* Melbourne, Monash University, Mimeo.

IATA (2018). *World air transport statistics 2018.* Geneva, IATA.

Internationale Luchthaven Kortrijk Wevelgem (2018). *Nieuwe beheerstructuur voor de luchthaven Kortrijk-Wevelgem formeel geactiveerd – de luchthaven eist haar plaats op als volwaardige Vlaamse regionale luchthaven.* Available at: www.kortrijkairport.be/index.php?id=62&tx_ttnews%5Btt_news%5D=66&tx_ttnews%5BbackPid%5D=4&cHash=c0d9a0f11bb6006626c07e5c2d328908 (accessed 9 October 2019).

Kupfer, F. and Lagneaux, F. (2009). Economic importance of air transport and airport activities in Belgium. NBB Working Paper No. 158. Brussels, National Bank of Belgium, March.

Lagneaux, F. (2004). *Economic importance of the Flemish maritime ports – report 2002.* NBB Working Paper No. 56. Brussels, National Bank of Belgium.

NBB Louvain (1996). *Het Economisch Belang van de Luchthaven Zaventem.* Louvain, NBB Louvain.

Schipper, Y. (2004). Environmental costs in European aviation. *Transport Policy*, 11, 141–154.

Sleuwaegen, L. and De Backer, K. (2003). De luchthaven Brussel Nationaal: Nieuwe uitdagingen – Economische impact voor de Belgische economie. *Over Werk Tijdschrift van het Steunpunt WAV*, 13(4), 190–194.

Van Asch, T., Dewulf, W., Kupfer, F., Cárdenas, I. and Van de Voorde, E. (2019). Cross-border e-commerce logistics – strategic success factors for airports. *Research in Transportation Economics*, 79, 100761.

Van Nieuwenhove, F. (2014). *Economic importance of air transport and airport activities in Belgium.* Report 2012, NBB Working Paper No. 273. Brussels, National Bank of Belgium, November.

Vennix, S. (2017). *Economic importance of air transport and airport activities in Belgium.* Report 2015, NBB Working Paper No. 324. Brussels, National Bank of Belgium, July.

14 The impact of Oporto Airport on the development of the Norte Region of Portugal

An econometric study

Susana Freiria and António Pais Antunes

Introduction

On 6 February 2016, the Portuguese legacy airline TAP – at presenta 50/50 per cent public/private company – announced major changes in its Oporto-based network. The flights to Barcelona, Brussels, Milan, and Rome were to be discontinued, and the number of daily flights to Geneva, London, and Madrid were to be decreased. By contrast, the number of daily flights to Lisbon were to be substantially increased.

The decision of TAP was rightly seen as a downgrade of Oporto Airport's position in TAP's network, motivating harsh public reaction from several businessmen and politicians, including the mayors of Oporto and of several municipalities of the Norte Region. One of the major business associations of Portugal, AEP – Associação Empresarial de Portugal, with headquarters in Oporto – expressed concerns about the implications of the changes for the large export-oriented manufacturing industry and the growing tourism sector of the area. From the political side, the most impressive statement was made after a meeting held on 25 February 2016 by the Norte Regional Council, the entity that officially represents all the 86 municipalities of the region. In the final part of the communication issued on that occasion, the council summarised the reasons why it was asking TAP (and the government) to revert the decisions (CCDRN, 2016):

> Reaffirm the strategic importance of Oporto Airport as a fundamental platform for the internationalization of the regional economy, in the support of tourism activity and regional exports, within the development process of the Norte Region and the promotion of territorial cohesion in Portugal.

In this context, some figures were provided on social media to underline the importance of Oporto Airport for the economic activities of the Norte Region. However, the fact is that the information then available did not properly capture the impact of air transport (thus of the airport) on these activities.

The main objective of the study described in this chapter was to assess comprehensively and accurately the magnitude and geographic extent of that impact, thus providing regional authorities and other stakeholders with precise and in-depth information on how air transport has been supporting the region's economy.

Despite the focus of our study being on a specific situation, we believe to have contributed more broadly to an area of research – air transport and regional development – that is attracting increasing interest from the scientific community. Within this area, the impacts of air transport on regional development have been essentially dealt with through cost-benefit analysis (CBA) and econometric approaches. In our study, we use an econometric approach (we could not use CBA because the more detailed data and tools required to apply this method were not available). The novelty brought by our study is that we investigate how those impacts spread across a vast region.

To our best knowledge, the first journal papers where econometric approaches were used in the research area under consideration date back to the early 1990s, with Goetz (1992) and Benell and Prentice (1993). Both papers used regression analysis and the ordinary least-squared (OLS) method to analyse, respectively, the relationship between air passenger growth and population growth (in both directions) in the 50 main urban (metropolitan) areas of the United States for the period 1950–1987 and the relationship between enplaned and deplaned passengers in 38 airports of Canada and 'direct employment' (and revenues) using data from 1988. One of the best-known papers in this literature stream is Brueckner (2003), which examined the link between airline traffic and employment in 91 US metropolitan areas based on data from 1996. The two-stage least square estimation method was used to properly address endogeneity issues (more specifically, causality issues: is air transport causing economic development, or is it the reverse?). The conclusion was that airline traffic is clearly correlated with service employment ('a 10 percent increase in passenger enplanements in a metro area leads approximately to a 1 percent increase in employment in service', 1467), but the same effect was not found for manufacturing and other goods-related employment.

Later, Green (2007), in similar work, found that passenger boardings per capita and passenger originations per capita are powerful predictors of population growth and employment growth in the United States. In the last ten years, many authors have examined the same relationship also using econometric approaches for other geographic contexts and/or economic activity variables. Among these many authors, we highlight the following: Percoco (2010), who focused on the 103 provinces of Italy concluding, in particular, that the impact of air transport on service employment was approximately half of that in the United States; Mukkala and Tervo (2013), who analysed 86 regions of 13 European Union countries using variables expressing growth in employment and growth in purchasing power to find that air transport was contributing to regional development in remote regions, but this was not so clear in core regions; Allroggen and Malina (2014), who concentrated on the 'affected areas' of the 19 main airports in Germany and on regional output to conclude that the impact of airports were significantly dependent on the characteristics of the airports and of air traffic connectivity; Bilotkach (2015), who considered the regions of the (almost 400) primary airports of the United States and concluded that the impact of the number of destinations served with non-stop flights on the level of employment, number of business establishments, and average wage in the region is much clearer and more robust than those of traffic volume; Blonigen and Cristea (2015) analysed the effect of air passenger service on regional growth and economic development for the 263 American metropolitan statistical areas, and found evidence of positive effects of air transport in regional development such as services and retail industries experience growth effects; lastly, Brugnoli et al. (2018) estimated the impact of civil aviation on international trade between Lombardy and 30 European countries and identified a positive impact of air transport on international trade. None of these works, or others that we are aware of, have addressed the distribution of the economic impacts of air transport within a given region, as we have in our study.

The remainder of this chapter is organised as follows. In the next section, we provide information on the economic evolution of the Norte Region over the period 2000–2016, and on the three areas into which the region was divided for the purposes of our study. We then show how Oporto Airport infrastructure and activity have grown over the same period. The econometric model we used in our study and the method we employed to estimate it are presented afterward. This is followed by the presentation and discussion of the application of the model to Oporto Airport and the Norte Region. Finally, in the last section, we summarise the chapter and indicate directions for further study.

Norte Region

Mainland Portugal is divided into five 'coordination and development' regions (NUTS 2). The Norte Region is one of them. It occupies an area of approximately 21,300 km² and, according to the latest census is home to a population of 3.69 million, being the most populated in the country (INE, 2011).

For this study, the Norte Region was divided into three sub-regional areas: Greater Oporto, Oporto Periphery, and Remote Norte (Figure 14.1). This division resulted from the aggregation of NUTS 3 considering their distance to Oporto Airport. Greater Oporto is the NUTS 3 region where the airport is located and Oporto Periphery is composed of all NUTS 3 regions adjacent to Greater Oporto. The rest of the region is called (here) Remote Norte. In Figure 14.1, we include information on the distance between the airport and the main cities of the Norte Region. The distance to the furthest of these cities, Bragança, is 213 km. In contrast, Braga and Guimarães are located at just 49 km and 54 km, respectively, from Oporto Airport.

252 *Susana Freiria and António Pais Antunes*

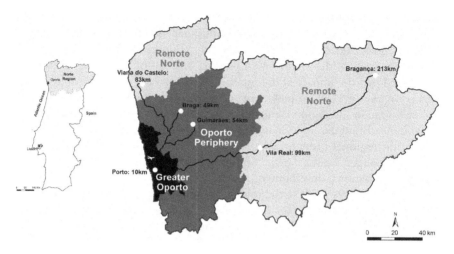

Figure 14.1 Norte Region and its sub-regional areas
Source: Devised by the authors

Greater Oporto consists of the municipality of Oporto and of the five neighbouring municipalities: Gaia, Gondomar, Maia, Matosinhos, and Valongo. Oporto Airport is located in Matosinhos, approximately 10 km northwest of the historic city centre of Oporto. The city of Oporto is the region's largest city and the second largest of Portugal, after the capital city of Lisbon. A total of 1.29 million people live in Greater Oporto, where the GDP per capita is €13,970 (the equivalent figures for Greater Lisbon are 2.81 million and €22,761) (INE, 2011).

The total gross value added (GVA) for Greater Oporto is much higher than that of the other two areas of the Norte Region (Figure 14.2). This is also true for the GVA of the service sector. However, Oporto Periphery is the area where total GVA has increased more significantly between 2000 and 2016 – around 60 per cent. This increase relied especially on the service sector, which has grown by 84 per cent in the same period. Regarding the GVA of the industry sector, Greater Oporto and Oporto Periphery are now practically at the same level, as growth in the latter area (39 per cent) has been faster and steadier than in the former (8 per cent). The Remote Norte area clearly lags behind the other two. However, it should be noted that this is where the industry GVA has increased more in the period under analysis (57 per cent).

Oporto Airport

The inauguration of Oporto Airport took place in 1945, but it was only in 1960 when it started receiving regular international flights. In 1990, the initial small terminal was replaced by a larger one. Between 2003 and 2006, major

The impact of Oporto Airport 253

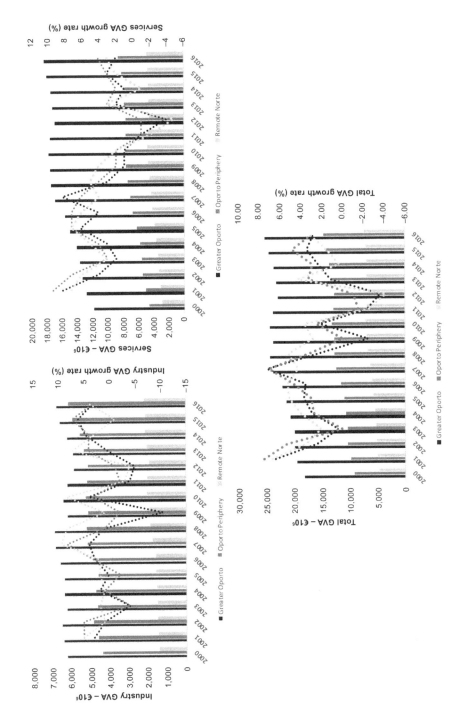

Figure 14.2 Evolution of GVA in the Norte Region between 2000 and 2016: industry (top left), services (top right), and total (bottom)

expansion and upgrading works were carried out in the airport, transforming it into one of the best in Europe (since 2006, it has been consistently ranked among the top three in ACI's Airport Service Quality Awards). At present, the catchment area of Oporto Airport is the largest one amongst the Portuguese airports. Besides the Norte Region, it encompasses large parts of the Centro Region (in Portugal) and of Galicia (in Spain). The population living in this area is approximately 4 million (INE, 2011).

The number of yearly flights (movements) using Oporto Airport increased from 22,500–73,800 between 2000 and 2016, i.e. it more than tripled (Figure 14.3). In the early 2000s, most flights were operated by TAP, the Portuguese legacy carrier. Since then, the share of low-cost carriers in the airport has grown considerably, being currently of the order of 80 per cent. In the same period, the number of annual passengers increased even more sharply, from 2.7 million to 9.3 million passengers. This number is estimated to have reached 11.9 million in 2018, putting Oporto Airport into the top 50 in Europe. In line with these figures, the aeronautical revenues (landing fees plus passenger service charges) generated by the airport rose from around €160 million to almost €400 million in the period under analysis.

In the year 2016, there were 56 different routes operated from/to Oporto Airport (Figure 14.4). The vast majority of these routes served European destinations (the only exceptions were Rio de Janeiro, São Paulo, Newark, and Toronto). In many cases, the flight frequency for these routes was one or two daily flights (in each direction), but several cities were served more often, e.g. Madrid (6) and Paris (13). The city served most frequently was Lisbon, with 17 daily flights.

Econometric model

As mentioned before, the goal of our study was to assess the economic and geographic extent of the impact of Oporto Airport, both in the surrounding areas and in furthest areas. With this goal in mind, we built an econometric model to assess the impact of air transport on economic performance for the three areas into which we divided the Norte Region: Greater Oporto, Oporto Periphery, and Remote Norte. In our study, the variables used to measure air transport activity and economic performance were, respectively, the aeronautical revenues collected by Oporto Airport and the gross value added (GVA). In order to understand the impact of air transport on different economic activities, we also applied the model separately to the industry and service sectors of the three areas. Since economic activity might also impact on air transport, the specific estimation method we applied was two-stage least squares (2SLS), as this method is suitable to deal with endogeneity issues. One of the main challenges that 2SLS entails is the choice (and data availability) of suitable instrumental variables. In the remainder of this section, we first present our methodological approach then discuss and test for possible endogeneity issues.

The impact of Oporto Airport 255

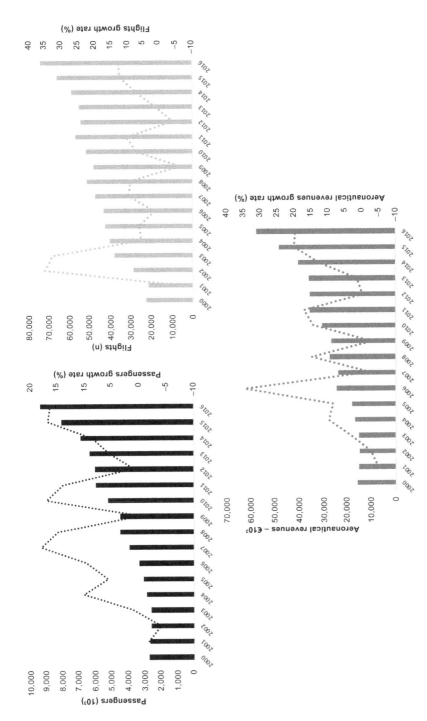

Figure 14.3 Evolution of Oporto Airport activity between 2000 and 2016: passengers (top left), flights (top right), and aeronautical revenues (bottom)

256 *Susana Freiria and António Pais Antunes*

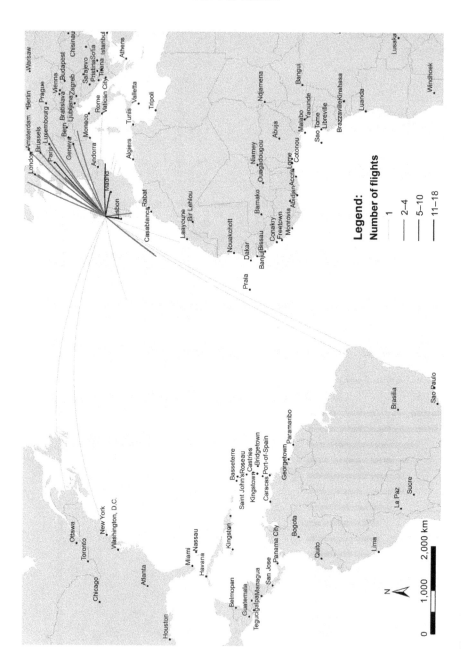

Figure 14.4 Routes and daily flights operated from/to Oporto Airport
Source: Devised by the authors using Skyscanner and Flights.com

Model formulation

The model we employed in our study is described in Equation (1). The dependent variable is the natural logarithm of GVA for each area or the Norte Region in each year of the period 2000–2016 (t = 2000, . . . , 2016), and the explanatory variables are the natural logarithms of aeronautical revenues and employment (number of employees). Aeronautical revenues are taken as a proxy of air transport activity. The number of employees is a control variable representing the labour resources available in each area and period but also the capital resources (indeed, in the regions of Southwest Europe, the data available show that employment and capital stock variables are often correlated).

$$lnGVA_{rt} = \alpha + \beta_1 \times lnAR_t + \beta_2 \times lnEmp_{rt} + \epsilon \tag{1}$$

where GVA_{rt} represents the gross value added in region r in year t, AR_t represents the aeronautical revenues collected by Oporto Airport in year t, Emp_{rt} represents the employment (number of employees) in region r in year t, $\in$ is an error term, and α, β_1, and β_2 are regression coefficients.

The variables were used in a log-linear functional form because this form typically describes well the kind of impact under analysis. Furthermore, the regression coefficients express response elasticities, i.e. in this case, the per cent variation of GVA consecutive to a 1 per cent variation of aeronautical revenues (β_1) and employment (β_2), which facilitates the interpretation of results.

Estimation method

A relevant issue in the estimation of Equation (1) is related to the possible endogeneity of GVA and aeronautical revenues, as well as of GVA and number of employees. A way to overcome this possible endogeneity is by applying the 2SLS method. The use of this method requires the consideration of a third set of variables in addition to the dependent and the explanatory variables. The number of these variables, called instrumental variables (or instruments), has to be chosen carefully because they must be correlated with the explanatory variables and should not be correlated with the error term. Finding variables with these properties can be quite challenging. In our study, after some research and performing some tests, we chose these two instrumental variables: number of passengers from outside the European Union and regional unemployment rate. The number of extra EU passengers was the instrument for the aeronautical revenues and the regional unemployment rate was the instrument for the employment.

The existence of endogeneity problems can be assessed by performing a Wu-Hausman test. Such problems are confirmed if the p-value associated with the test is smaller than 0.05 (in this case, the assumptions behind the OLS method are not verified). The validity of the instrumental variables also needs to be assessed. For this, the tests to use are the F-test if there is only one instrument,

258 *Susana Freiria and António Pais Antunes*

and the Cragg-Donald Wald *F*-test (hereafter designated simply as a Wald test) if there are more than one. In both cases, the hypothesis that instruments are weak is rejected if the test statistic exceeds a given value (the rule of thumb is that *F* should be greater than 10, but this is not exactly correct; see Staiger and Stock, 1997; Stock and Yogo, 2005).

Study results

Through the econometric model described in the previous section and using the data summarised in Table 14.1, we were able to answer the questions regarding the magnitude and geographic extent of the impact of Oporto Airport that we wanted to address through our study. All these data come from the National Statistics Institute of Portugal (INE, 2016, 2017), with the exception of those concerning aeronautical revenues and extra EU passengers, which we obtained from Eurostat (2018).

One of the questions we addressed was whether aeronautical revenues (i.e. air transport activity) have influenced GVA (i.e. economic performance), considering not only the total GVA but also, separately, industry and services GVA. At this stage, we also analysed whether the potential influence of aeronautical revenues on GVA has depended on the distance from/to Oporto Airport. Assuming that aeronautical revenues had influenced GVA, in addition we addressed the issue of the strength of the influence, not only by itself but also comparing with the control variable – employment. Another relevant question we addressed is whether there were endogeneity issues in the relationship between aeronautical revenues and GVA.

The coefficients on aeronautical revenues and number of employees can be interpreted as elasticities. These coefficients indicate that all else being equal, a 10 per cent increase in aeronautical revenues has led to an increase in total GVA of 1.2 per cent in Greater Oporto, 2.0 per cent in Oporto Periphery and 1.4 per cent in Remote Norte, as shown in Table 14.2. Employment presents coefficient values much higher than the aeronautical revenues, which means that the number of employees had a higher impact on total GVA than aeronautical revenues. In Greater Oporto and in Oporto Periphery, the aeronautical revenues are significant at the 1 per cent level and in the Remote Norte only at the 5 per cent level. In Oporto Periphery, the impact of the number of employees was not as significant as that of the aeronautical revenues.

Concerning the validity of the instruments, both the *F*-tests and the Wald test indicate they are strong. Moreover, the Wu-Haussmann test concerning the Oporto Periphery and the Remote Norte areas denote the existence of endogeneity and the need for instrument variables. However, the same test suggests that, in the case of Greater Oporto, the 2SLS method is as consistent as the OLS method, which means that the aeronautical revenues, as well as the number of employees, are not endogenous with respect to total GVA.

We will now focus on the impact of the aeronautical revenues on industry GVA (Table 14.3). Concerning the validity of the instruments, the *F*-tests

Table 14.1 Descriptive statistics of model variables

Statistics		Dependent variables			Explanatory variables		Instrumental variables	
		Total GVA (€10⁶)	Services GVA (€10⁶)	Industry GVA (€10⁶)	Aeronautical revenues (€ 10³)	Number of employees	Extra EU passengers	Regional unemployment (%)
Average	Oporto Airport				3.392		64.524	
	Norte Region							10
	Greater Oporto	22.499	15.902	6.388		45.888		
	Oporto Periphery	12.165	6.876	5.099		565.606		
	Remote Norte	6.263	4.132	1.793		135.232		
Standard deviation	Oporto Airport				17.191		344.103	
	Norte Region							4
	Greater Oporto	203	1.981	284		49.527		
	Oporto Periphery	1.559	115	452		65.396		
	Remote Norte	837	605	265		36.275		
Minimum	Oporto Airport				14.751		242.798	
	Norte Region							4
	Greater Oporto	18.318	11.849	5.884		366.498		
	Oporto Periphery	9.214	4.629	4.403		411.878		
	Remote Norte	4.671	2.922	1.394		61.094		
Maximum	Oporto Airport				76.576		1,404,181	
	Norte Region							17
	Greater Oporto	25.276	18.215	6.905		526.809		
	Oporto Periphery	14.765	8.519	6.124		634.653		
	Remote Norte	7.306	477	2.186		171.136		

260   Susana Freiria and António Pais Antunes

Table 14.2 Impact of aeronautical revenues on total GVA

Dependent variable: Total GVA

Explanatory variables	Greater Oporto		Oporto Periphery		Remote Norte	
	Coef.	*t-stat*	*Coef.*	*t-stat*	*Coef.*	*t-stat*
Constant	0.68	0.39	−1.07	−0.54	3.9 (★★★)	7.49
Aeronautical revenues	0.12 (★★★)	5.37	0.2 (★★★)	5.63	0.14 (★★)	3.41
Number of employees	0.63 (★★★)	4.36	0.63(★★)	3.86	0.28 (★★★)	4.66
Adj. R^2	0.87		0.85		0.86	
F-test weak instruments (aeronautical revenues)	27.2 (★★★)		27.2 (★★★)		27.2 (★★★)	
F-test weak instruments (number of employees)	4.1 (★)		7.6 (★★)		22.9 (★★★)	
Wu-Haussman test	3.71		8.8 (★★)		7.8 (★★)	
Wald test	47.2		48.8		52.3	

Notes: ★★★ significant at 1%; ★★ significant at 5%; ★ significant at 10%.
Instrumental variables
Regional unemployment
Extra EU air passengers

Table 14.3 Impact of aeronautical revenues on Industry GVA

Dependent variable: Industry GVA

Explanatory variables	Greater Oporto		Oporto Periphery		Remote Norte	
	Coef.	*t-stat*	*Coef.*	*t-stat*	*Coef.*	*t-stat*
Constant	11.22 (★★)	3.56	5.09(★★)	3.33	2.71(★★★)	4.71
Aeronautical revenues	0.001	0.05	0.16(★★★)	6.05	0.24(★★★)	5.15
Number of employees	−0.19	−0.74	0.13	1.05	0.19(★)	2.84
Adj. R^2	−0.81		0.81		0.85	
F-test weak instruments (aeronautical revenues)	27.2 (★★★)		27.2 (★★★)		27.2 (★★★)	
F-test weak instruments (number of employees)	4.1 (★)		7.6(★★)		22.9 (★★★)	
Wu-Haussman test	8.2 (★★)		0.91		12.5 (★★)	
Wald test	0.35		31.08		51.83	

★★★ significant at 1%; ★★ significant at 5%; ★ significant at 10%
Instrumental variables
Regional unemployment
Extra EU air passengers

indicate that the instruments are strong. However, in the case of Greater Oporto, the Wald test value is lower than the critical value, which means that according to this test the instruments are weak. Analysing the results presented in Table 14.3, neither the aeronautical revenue nor the number of employees has a significant impact on the industry GVA of Greater Oporto. Fageda and Gonzalez-Aregal (2017), who have analysed the impact of air transport on industrial employment, concluded that the effects of airports do not seem to have a large impact on their own regions. However, the aeronautical revenues have a significant impact on Oporto Periphery and even more on the Remote Norte areas. In both these areas, the aeronautical revenues present an influence more significant than the number of employees. In the case of the Remote Norte, an increase of 10 per cent in aeronautical revenues is associated with a 2.4 per cent increase in industry GVA. It is also interesting to observe that the constant coefficient values are significant in the three areas of the Norte Region, which means that there are other variables in addition to the aeronautical revenues and the number of employees that influence the industry GVA.

Results for the impact of aeronautical revenues on services GVA are reported in Table 14.4. According to these results, the model better explains the variation in data as we move away from the airport (as the adjusted R^2 decreases from 81 per cent to 86 per cent). Aeronautical revenues are significant at the 1 per cent level in Greater Oporto and Oporto Periphery, but only at the 10 per cent level in the Remote Norte. There is not a relationship between the distance from the Oporto Airport and the impact of aeronautical revenues on services GVA, as this impact, measured by the regression coefficient, first increases from Greater Oporto (0.18) to the Oporto Periphery (0.23) and then decreases for the Remote Norte (0.11).

Summing up, the results of our study indicate that Oporto Airport activity has influenced in a significant way the economic performance of the three areas of the Norte Region. This activity did not have a significant impact on the industry of Greater Oporto, but was significant to the industry of Oporto

Table 14.4 Impact of aeronautical revenues on services GVA

Dependent variable: Services GVA

Explanatory variables	Greater Oporto		Oporto periphery		Remote Norte	
	Coef.	*t-stat*	*Coef.*	*t-stat*	*Coef.*	*t-stat*
Constant	−5.02	−1.66	−7.74 (★)	−2.56	2.84(★★★)	4.87
Aeronautical revenues	0.18(★★★)	4.37	0.23(★★★)	4.32	0.11 (★)	2.48
Number of employees	0.98(★★)	4.01	1.07(★★★)	4.31	0.36 (★★★)	5.31
Adj. R²	0.81		0.82		0.86	
F-test weak instruments (aeronautical revenues)	27.2 (★★★)		27.2 (★★★)		27.2 (★★★)	
F-test weak instruments (number of employees)	4.1 (★)		7.6 (★★)		22.9 (★★★)	
Wu-Haussman test	11.8 (★★)		20.4 (★★★)		5.9 (★)	
Wald test	39.9		39.9		49.67	

★★★ significant at 1%; ★★ significant at 5%; ★ significant at 10%
Instrumental variables
Regional
  unemployment
Extra EU air passengers

262 *Susana Freiria and António Pais Antunes*

Periphery and Remote Norte areas. When we analysed service sector performance, it was observed that Oporto Airport activity was significant for all the three areas, being more significant for Greater Oporto and Oporto Periphery (level of confidence of 1 per cent in both cases) than for the Remote Norte (10 per cent). Results also indicate that, for the economy as a whole and for the service sector, there was not a direct relationship between the distance from/to the airport and the impact of Oporto Airport activity.

Conclusion

The study described in this chapter has analysed the impact of Oporto Airport on the economy of the Norte Region between 2000 and 2016, considering different sectors (industry and services) and how this impact was felt in three different areas of the region at different distances from the airport. The study was carried out in a context in which TAP, the Portuguese legacy airline, was cancelling some routes and decreasing the frequency of other routes connecting Oporto Airport and several European cities.

The results of our study provide evidence that Oporto Airport activity had a significant impact on the economic performance of the Norte Region in the period under analysis. Moreover, it showed that the impact can be stronger in the most distant areas from the airport than in closer ones. For instance, air transport activity had a significant impact on the industry of areas distant from the airport, and not in the vicinity of the airport, in the Greater Oporto area. It has also been shown the importance of considering different economic sectors separately. In fact, air transport activity may not be significant to the industry sectors of Greater Oporto, but is quite significant to the service sector of this area.

While we consider that our study provides useful insights into the relationship between air transport and economic performance of the Norte Region and its sub-regional areas, we must acknowledge that it suffers from one important limitation: the length of the period analysed is probably too short to allow strong conclusions. In the future, we plan to update our study in order to strengthen the conclusions as new data become available. Moreover, although our study has focused on Norte Region, the approach it used can be applied to other regions to assess how the impact of air transport spreads across a region. The comparison of the Norte Region with other regions, in Portugal and elsewhere, could also be an interesting direction to pursue in the future.

References

Allroggen, F. and Malina, R. (2014). Do the regional growth effects of air transport differ among airports? *Journal of Air Transport Management*, 37, 1–4.

Benell, D. W. and Prentice, B. E. (1993). A regression model for predicting the economic impacts of Canadian airports. *Logistics and Transportation Review*, 29(2), 139.

Bilotkach, V. (2015). Are airports engines of economic development? A dynamic panel data approach. *Urban Studies*, 52(9), 1577–1593.

The impact of Oporto Airport   263

Blonigen, B. A. and Cristea, A. D. (2015). Air service and urban growth: Evidence from a quasi-natural policy experiment. *Journal of Urban Economics*, 86, 128–146.

Brueckner, J. K. (2003). Airline traffic and urban economic development. *Urban Studies*, 40(8), 1455–1469.

Brugnoli, A., Dal Bianco, A., Martini, G. and Scotti, D. (2018). The impact of air transportation on trade flows: A natural experiment on causality applied to Italy. *Transportation Research Part A: Policy and Practice*, 112, 95–107.

CCDRN (2016). *Proposta de Tomada de Posição sobre o Aeroporto Francisco Sá Carneiro*. Available at: https://www.ccdr-n.pt/sites/default/files/cp_conselhoregional.pdf.

Eurostat (2018). *Database*. Available at: https://ec.europa.eu/eurostat/data/database.

Fageda, X. and Gonzalez-Aregall, M. (2017). Do all transport modes impact on industrial employment? Empirical evidence from the Spanish regions. *Transport Policy*, 55, 70–78.

Goetz, A. R. (1992). Air passenger transportation and growth in the US urban system, 1950–1987. *Growth and Change*, 23(2), 217–238.

Green, R. K. (2007). Airports and economic development. *Real Estate Economics*, 35(1), 91–112.

INE (2011). *XV Recenseamento Geral da População e V Recenseamento Geral da Habitação*. Instituto Nacional de Estatística, Lisboa, Portugal.

INE (2016). *Contas económicas regionais*. Instituto Nacional de Estatística, Lisboa, Portugal.

INE (2017). *Inquérito ao emprego*. Instituto Nacional de Estatística, Lisboa, Portugal.

Mukkala, K. and Tervo, H. (2013). Air transportation and regional growth: Which way does the causality run? *Environment and Planning A*, 45(6), 1508–1520.

Percoco, M. (2010). Airport activity and local development: Evidence from Italy. *Urban Studies*, 47(11), 2427–2443.

Staiger, D. and Stock, J. H. (1997). Instrumental variables regression with weak instruments. *Econometrica*, 65(3), 557–586.

Stock, J. and Yogo, M. (2005). Asymptotic distributions of instrumental variables statistics with many weak instruments. In Andrews, D. W. K. and Stock, J. H. (eds) *Identification and inference for econometric models: Essays in honor of Thomas Rothenberg*. Cambridge, Cambridge University Press.

15 Spanish Transport Accounts[1]

José Manuel Vasallo, Armando Ortuño,
and Ofelia Betancor

Introduction

In this chapter, we estimate the socio-economic accounts for the four main interurban transport modes in Spain: road, rail, air, and maritime. The aim is to determine if each mode bears its costs, which includes infrastructure and the external costs. In other words, we wish to examine to what extent the 'user pays' principle and the 'polluter pays' principle are currently being applied. Our analysis considers several transport modes, not only air transport, which may allow for a wider view of the transport policy options available with an intermodal perspective. This work was mostly inspired by the methodology used in the UNITE project (see Link et al., 2000), one of the few works available that conducted a European wide research on transport accounts.

With respect to transport external effects, the main issues are air quality, greenhouse gas emissions, noise, and congestion. About 90 per cent of all lead emissions, about 50 per cent of all nitrogen oxides (NOx) emissions and about 30 per cent of all volatile organic compound (VOC) emissions, can be attributable to the transport sector (Hensher and Button, 2003). As regards air transport, it is its impact on climate change that is currently being subject to special scrutiny, and although the aviation's share of overall greenhouse gas emissions may seem modest (about 3 per cent), what matters is the radiative warming effect, not only the volume of emissions (European Commission, 2019). Since January 2012, air transport in Europe was included under the European Emission Allowance Trading Scheme (ETS), and since October 2016, the International Civil Aviation Organisation (ICAO) has decided to adopt a global ETS that it is expected to start in 2021.

With a global perspective, the analysis of the transport accounts focuses on a comparison between the amount paid by users and operators for utilising the infrastructure versus the transport costs not directly borne by them – basically infrastructure, accidents, and environmental costs. Costs directly assumed by users and transport operators (travel time, energy consumption, vehicle depreciation, etc.) are excluded from the analysis since they are always internalised by them. The goal of this comparison is to have a top-down overview of the extent to which different transport modes cover the infrastructure and external costs they generate. When enough data is available, we estimate more disaggregated accounts according to the type of vehicle (i.e. passenger cars, buses and heavy-duty vehicles on the road), type of services (passenger versus freight in the rail sector), or individual infrastructure facilities (individual airports).

The estimation of costs takes into account three different items:

1   *Infrastructure costs.* This item includes construction, maintenance and operation of infrastructure assets. For the yearly allocation of the construction costs, the annuity method is the preferred option. When there is not enough data to apply that method, we employ the depreciation of the assets. For disaggregated accounts, we have set several hypotheses to share common costs between different types of operators.
2   *Accident costs.* This item includes material damages, administrative and medical costs, productivity loses, and the value of risk. We consider that part of these costs is internalised through, for instance, insurance payments or damages anticipated by the users. These internal costs are removed from the analysis in order that only external costs related to accidents appear in the accounts.
3   *Environmental costs.* These costs refer to health and environmental damages caused by air pollution and noise at the local level, and climate change at the global level. Upstream and downstream processes associated to the availability of vehicles, infrastructure, and energy should be incorporated, as well.

The estimation of revenues for the use of infrastructure includes the following items:

1   *Tolls and infrastructure fees.* These items reflect direct payments from users or transport operators to infrastructure managers. Road tolls, as well as rail, port, and airport fees, are included here.
2   *Special taxes.* These are charged in a discriminatory way to different transport modes. This item includes those taxes that are imposed to a certain transport mode in a discriminatory way compared to other mode. For instance, fuel taxes applied to road transport are much higher than the ones applied to other modes such as rail, air, and maritime transportation.
3   *Subsidies.* These are included with a negative sign in the analysis since, because of them, operators do not internalise part of the internal costs they should bear.

As previously mentioned, for the estimation of the accounts, we follow the methodology used in the UNITE project (see Link et al., 2000). In this approach, we have incorporated methodological improvements for the estimation of the different items, as well as some adjustments in order to deal with the lack of information in the estimation of some costs. The accounts were calculated for 2013, the last year when full information was available at the time of

266 *José Manuel Vasallo, et al.*

the analysis. The work focuses on interurban transport modes since a study at the urban level requires much more detailed information at the city level and a different methodological approach.

The structure is as follows. In the next section, we describe the methodological approach for the estimation of the different components of the accounts. We then present our estimates of the interurban transport accounts in Spain, and finally provide concluding comments.

Methodology, data, and estimates

Infrastructure costs

In this section, the methodology used to calculate the costs of infrastructure in Spain is described, including the sources and hypotheses used in their calculation. This methodology is based on the procedure established in the European project UNITE regarding transport accounts. Infrastructure costs are comprised of two categories: the cost of capital and the cost of maintenance. With respect to the former, the UNITE methodology establishes two possibilities for its calculation:

- *An estimate based on historical series of investments.* Using the annuity method – the calculation of the annualised investment which have not exceeded their useful lives – all the investments carried out within the useful life period are annualised, with the cost of capital being equal to the sum of all the annuities. This method is only applied for roads, as it is the only case in which the historical series of investment necessary for its calculation were available (Fundación BBVA, 2013; Yearbooks of the Ministry of Development, 1964–2013).
- *An estimate based on the direct valuation of assets.* This estimation is applied when the necessary information to calculate the cost of capital based on the annuity method is not available. In this case, the information contained in the yearly economic reports of the entities involved should be used as a reference. These reports should quantify the net value of tangible fixed assets and their depreciation for the year of reference. The cost of capital in the year of reference is obtained using the sum of the depreciation of tangible fixed assets – whose data is contained in the annual economic reports – and the interest, calculated by applying a real interest rate to the value of the material fixed assets. This rate has been established based on the interest of long-term Spanish debt, in this case 1.7 per cent. This method is then applied to rail, air, and maritime transport modes.

On the other hand, maintenance costs for the year of reference have been obtained from the reports of the Spanish government's Ministry of Development and the yearly economic reports of the public entities that undertake the maintenance.

In what follows, we show the hypotheses used for estimating the infrastructure costs for each mode of transport. Once the total costs for the year of reference have been obtained, they are disaggregated as much as possible according to different criteria.

Road

With respect to the cost of capital, which encompasses the cost of the construction of the whole network, it is important to emphasise that pavement costs represent on average 35 per cent of total construction costs (Dirección General de Tráfico, 2000), and that the selection of the surface – and therefore its total cost – is based on the flow of heavy vehicle traffic, given that it generates a much greater road wear than that generated by light vehicles. It is therefore appropriate to assign the whole of the proportion of the increase in pavement costs to heavy vehicles as they are the ultimate cause of this increase.

In order to quantify this aspect, the study carried out by Kraemer and Albelda (2004) has been analysed, which indicates that the cost of the sections of pavement with a low presence of heavy vehicles is approximately 48 per cent lower than those sections of pavement able to bear the average intensity of heavy vehicle traffic in Spain. In applying these percentages, the increase in costs attributable to the choice of road surface have been wholly assigned to heavy vehicles, and the rest of the construction costs to light and heavy vehicles proportionately in accordance with the traffic recorded.

With respect to maintenance costs, the procedure was very similar to the one used for the capital cost. Maintenance covers both road rehabilitation, which according to the General State Budget (Spanish Government, 2004–2009) accounts for an average of 75 per cent of the total cost, and ordinary road maintenance, which represents 25 per cent of the total. Given that pavement rehabilitation accounts for a larger proportion of the total figure dedicated to road rehabilitation, the majority of the amount of this extraordinary maintenance has been attributed to heavy vehicles, assigning the rest of the rehabilitation and ordinary maintenance amounts in proportion to the traffic recorded of light and heavy vehicles.

Rail

Based on the total capital and maintenance costs published in the annual reports of Adif, the Spanish Railway Infrastructure Administrator (Adif, 2014; Adif Alta Velocidad, 2014), the total figures for the rail infrastructure costs have been obtained.

In Spain, there are two types of railway networks: the high-speed network, exclusively devoted to passenger traffic and therefore, the costs of its capital and maintenance are attributed solely to this type of traffic; and the conventional network which transports both passengers and freight, therefore requiring a disaggregation of the costs. In order to assign the capital cost of the conventional network, a disaggregation has been made between passengers and freight in accordance to the use of the infrastructure based on the number of trains-kilometres in each case. Meanwhile, maintenance costs have been disaggregated based on the number of gross tonnes-kilometre hauled (GTKH), in this case, in order to reflect the deterioration of the infrastructure.

Air

The data referring to the capital and maintenance costs in this case has been obtained from the economic reports of the company that owns and operates the Spanish airports, Aena, and the public entity responsible for air navigation in Spain, Enaire.

Based on these data, the profit and loss statements of the ten airports with larger levels of passenger traffic in Spain have been drawn up. In each case, they include the capital costs and the infrastructure of both Aena, which is disaggregated by airport; and of Enaire, which is assigned in accordance with estimated traffic in passenger-kilometres.

Maritime

The data published in the annual reports of each of Spain's 28 port authorities has been used to obtain the capital costs using the direct valuation method of the assets and the maintenance and operating costs. In this case, given that the necessary information is unavailable, these infrastructure costs have not been split into passengers and freight.

Accident costs

The costs generated by accidents have been studied in depth in recent decades, and a consistent methodological basis has been established (Lindberg, 2006; CE Delft et al., 2011; RICARDO-AEA, 2014). In this methodology, three groups of costs are considered:

*   *Direct costs*: those directly assumed by the state after an accident (medical, police or fire service costs) and material damages.
*   *Indirect costs*: those that are borne by the state after the accident, such as the permanent or temporary loss of productive capacity.
*   *Value of risk*: monetary valuation that reflects the estimate of the pain and suffering caused by traffic accidents. This valuation is carried out through the 'willingness to pay' method.

When estimating the accident costs, it should be indicated that not all of these costs are external, but some of them may be internalised, either by the insurance system in the case of material damages, or by the users themselves who might internalise part of the value of risk being aware that they are exposed to a risk of an accident (Lindberg, 2001). This latter aspect has only been taken into account in the case of roads, as for the rest of the modes of transport the degree of internalisation to apply cannot be estimated due to lack of information (CE Delft et al., 2011).

In Spain, there are reliable studies in the case of roads that publish the direct and indirect unit costs and the value of risk (Lladó Gomà-Camps and Roig Solé, 2007; Abellán Perpiñán et al., 2011a, 2011b), so they have been used to estimate the total costs of road accidents. However, no relevant studies have been conducted at the national level for rail and air, so in these cases the unit costs established in CE Delft et al. (2011) are applied for Spain, based on the accident data in the European Union. Finally, in maritime transport, the accident costs are not calculated given that there is no data available in this respect for Spain.

Environmental costs

These are the costs borne by society as a consequence of emitting pollutants, generating noise etc., when developing transport activities. Nowadays, there are available quite a number of references providing estimates of these cost for European countries (INFRAS/IWW, 1995, 2000, 2004; CE-Delft et al., 2011). As well as other important studies conducted within European projects (NEEDS, UNITE, HEATCO, and GRACE), and the meta-analysis and recommendations of the IMPACT Project (Maibach et al., 2008). In turn, values provided by the IMPACT Project were updated in RICARDO-AEA (2014).

For the purpose of building the Spanish Transport Accounts, the main reference in the area of environmental costs is CE-Delft et al. (2011). This is due to the fact that it is the only study that provides estimates of environmental costs for Spain in average terms per mode of transport (except for maritime), type of vehicle and type of load (passengers or freight). This study also provides estimates of total, average, and marginal costs for the EU 27 countries, except Malta and Cyprus, but adding Norway and Switzerland. According to this reference, the main categories of environmental costs are:

1   *Air Pollution.* Pollutants with the largest impact are fine particles (PM10 and PM2.5). Other pollutants to consider are nitrogen oxides (NOx), sulphur dioxide (SO_2), volatile organic compounds (VOC), and ozone (O_3). In order to estimate these costs, the model usually applied is the *Impact Pathway Approach* (Bickel and Friedrich, 2005).
2   *Climate change.* Regarding transport, the main greenhouse gases are carbon dioxide (CO_2), nitrogen oxide (N_2O), and methane (CH_4). In aviation, other emissions should be considered, too, such water vapour, sulphates, and soot aerosols. These costs were approached based on avoidance. Nevertheless, a high degree of uncertainty is acknowledged, resulting in a range of values.

270 *José Manuel Vasallo, et al.*

3 *Noise.* There are two main negative impacts: annoyance and health damages. Such costs were estimated through the dose-response methodology.
4 *Upstream-downstream processes.* The processes should include environmental costs associated to production and distribution of energy, vehicles and infrastructure. CE-Delft et al. (2011) provides values only for energy due to lack of data, resulting in a range of values as well due to uncertainty.
5 *Other environmental costs.* Nature, landscape, and soil and water pollution.

Taxes, tolls, charges, and subsidies

In this section, it is explained how an estimation of the revenues of the four transport modes was obtained: road, rail, aviation, and maritime.

Road

Road transport in Spain is charged from two different sources: tolls and special taxes. Moreover, some services receive operation subsidies. Regarding special taxes, road users and operators are subject to three types of taxes that are not applied to other transport modes: fuel taxes (FT), vehicle ownership taxes (VOT), and car acquisition taxes (CAT).

Fuel taxes are levied on the volume of fuel (both diesel and gasoline) acquired for road transport purposes. Fuel tax rates applied to diesel and gasoline are slightly different, the gasoline rates being higher. As the valued-added tax (VAT) is calculated on the basis of the cost of fuel plus the fuel tax, we also consider as a special taxation the percentage of the VAT applied to the fuel tax. Fuel taxes are the main revenue sources for the road sector.

The vehicle ownership tax is charged to all the vehicles by the municipalities in which they are registered on a yearly basis. State law establishes a range for the calculation of the rates. Every municipality is free to set specific rates for the vehicles registered there.

Car acquisition taxes are charged to new cars purchased for private use the year they are bought. Commercial buses and trucks are exempt from this tax. The tax is calculated as a percentage of the price of acquisition. Rates depend on the size and power of the car, and the region where the vehicle is registered. Rates vary between 4.75 per cent and 16.90 per cent of the purchase price of the car.

Apart from special taxes, 23 per cent of the high capacity network of Spain is tolled. Toll stretches are all operated by private companies that use the tolls to finance the construction works, and maintain and operate the road facilities entrusted to them. Tolls have different rates according to the type of vehicle (cars, buses, and heavy vehicles).

Unlike other transport modes, the road sector in Spain receives few subsidies. Three different subsidy sources have been identified: subsidies to incentivise the modernisation of the fleet, subsidies to the acquisition of electric vehicles, and subsidies to bus companies that operate routes subject to public service obligations.

Rail

In the case of rail transport, the following revenue sources are included in the account: special tax on the purchase of electricity (STE), security fees (SF), infrastructure usage fees (IUF), and other services (OS).

Unlike what happens with road transport, fuels used by rail locomotives in Spain are exempt of the special tax applied to hydrocarbon fuels. Locomotives, wagons, and coaches are also exempt of the vehicle ownership tax. The only special tax applied to the rail sector, which is discriminatory compared to other modes, is the electricity tax. The rate applied to electricity is 5.11 per cent of the average price of a kilowatt-hour (KWh).

Rail passengers also pay the security fee (SF) intended to cover the surveillance and security services provided at the rail stations managed by Adif, the Spanish national rail infrastructure operator. The amount of this fee depends on the type of service and the trip distance.

Trains are also subject to a set of fees for using the tracks and stations. For the purpose of this analysis, we put all these fees within the group of infrastructure usage fees (IUF). Fees associated with the use of the tracks include: the access fee, the slot reservation fee, the rail circulation fee, and the high-speed traffic fee. Moreover, trains pay several fees associated with the usage of different spaces (track, platforms, etc.) at the stations.

The usage of available land and infrastructure facilities owned by the Spanish rail infrastructure manager for other services (OS) rather than moving freight and passengers also produces revenues that are also included within the accounts. Those services are: logistic services; rent of optical fibre, buildings, etc.; and other revenue (personnel allocated to third parties, computer services, etc.).

Finally, railway services also receive large subsidies addressed to the routes operated as public service obligations (PSO). Freight and long-distance passenger lines do not receive subsides from PSOs. However, some commuter and regional services receive important subsidies. It is worth noting that overall subsidies coming from PSOs are higher than all the revenue generated through special taxes, fees, and other revenue sources.

Air

Unlike the road and rail sector, the air sector is not subject to any special tax. The revenue sources of the airports come mostly from airport fees (AF) and air navigation fees (ANF). Moreover, airlines flying with origins and destinations in the EU have to pay for the carbon dioxide they emit.

Airport fees (AF) include security fees and airport infrastructure charges. Security fees have the aim of financing the surveillance and inspection costs incurred by AESA, the Spanish State Agency for Air Safety. The amount charged in 2013 was €0.37 per passenger. Airport infrastructure charges, in turn, intend to cover the infrastructure costs and services provided by the airports. Infrastructure revenues also include those from rents paid by private companies running commercial activities at the airports (restaurants, duty-free services, shops, advertisement, etc.) and outside the terminals (car parks, warehouses, cargo logistics centres, etc.).

Air navigation fees (ANF) are paid by the air companies to Enaire, the authority in charge of coordinating air navigation services in Spanish airspace. There are two air navigation fees: route fees and approximation fees.

From 2012 on, air transport markets in Europe were included within the greenhouse gas emissions trading programme of the European Union. This means that airlines have to pay for emitting CO_2 in routes within the European Union. We have estimated the amount paid by the airlines corresponding to the use of the Spanish airspace. In turn, the allocation to each airport has been conducted on the basis of the amount of passenger-kilometres of each airport for routes which have both origins and destinations in the EU.

Air transport in Spain also receives subsidies from different sources: subsidies to residents in remote regions, subsidies to members of large families, and subsidies to routes subject to public service obligations. Due to its complexity, subsidies to the specific airports have not been allocated.

Maritime

Like the air sector, the maritime sector is not subject to any special tax related to fuel or electricity. The revenue sources of the sector are mostly the fees paid by vessels for the use of port facilities. There are four types of port charges in Spain: land use fees, charged to port operators occupying land in the port; activity fees, charged to companies for conducting commercial activities in the port; usage fees, charged to ships for using the port and its facilities; and navigation aid fees, paid by the ships for assistance to enter and leave the port.

Maritime traffic in Spain, especially for passengers, receive subsidies through several concepts: subsidies to residents and freight in remote regions, members of large families, routes subject to PSOs, and short sea shipping promotion.

Spanish Transport Accounts

As already mentioned, the objective of the Transport Accounts is to establish whether each mode covers its infrastructure and external costs with the revenues produced. The results of the accounts provide important useful information for the discussion of applicable transport policies.

The estimates provided within the accounts are based on the available information, and hence, fit within the definition of the UNITE project of *Pilot Accounts* (Link et al., 2000). In order to build the accounts, they have been differentiated, in the first place, by mode of transport. In turn, for each mode, the most reasonable and feasible disaggregation – according to available information – is conducted. In the case of roads, this refers to type of

Spanish Transport Accounts   273

Table 15.1 The accounts general framework

Costs		*Revenues or contributions*
Infrastructure	Capital	Taxes
	Maintenance and operation	Tolls, charges, and canons
External costs	Direct costs	Environmental taxes
of accidents	Indirect costs	Subsidies for the purchase of
	Risk value	vehicles (with negative sign)
Environmental	Air pollution	
costs	Climate change: high-costs	
	scenario (1)	
	Climate change: low-costs	
	scenario (2)	
	Noise	
	Other: high-costs scenario (1)	
	Other: low-costs scenario (2)	

vehicle; for railways, a distinction between passengers and freight services, and type of business, is provided; for air, the disaggregation is done to the airport level by taking into account the routes with origin/destination at each airport.

The accounts framework corresponds to the structure shown in Table 15.1. The costs of infrastructure (capital and maintenance), jointly with accidents and environmental costs, appear on the left-hand side of the account. The uncertainty associated to the calculation of global warming environmental costs prompted us include a range of values in the account. This uncertainty is affecting the global warming item itself, as well as the *upstream-downstream* component. On the other hand, the right side of the account captures the mode revenues and contributions from special taxes, tolls, fee charges, and from payments directly linked to environmental impacts (only emission trading system in air transport). Subsidies that are not associated to infrastructure provision appear with a negative sign also on this right side of the account. Subsidies connected to the infrastructure are implicitly contained within the account (such subsidies result from deducing infrastructure costs from corresponding revenues). Subsidies for the operation of services are presented as complementary information to the main account. Finally, when there are transfers between infrastructure operators (e.g. Aena and Enaire) or when the operator acts as an intermediary (e.g. Adif, which buys and sells electricity for Renfe), this information is not incorporated in the account.

Road

The road account is provided in an aggregated and disaggregated manner (by type of vehicle). The results are shown in Tables 15.2 and 15.3. We regard the estimations of these accounts as robust, but for the fact that environmental

274 *José Manuel Vasallo, et al.*

Table 15.2 Road transport aggregate account for Spain, 2013

External costs and infrastructure			*Revenues*		
		Millions €			*Millions €*
Infrastructure	Capital	5,531.68	**Taxes**	Fuel taxes	6,348.36
	Maintenance, operation	2,148.81		VAT on fuel	1,333.15
	Total Infrastructure	**7,680.49**		Vehicle ownership taxes	1,675.15
Accidents	Direct costs	73.17		Car acquisition taxes	212.22
	Indirect costs	354.83			
	Value of risk	862.23			
	Total accidents	**1,290.23**		**Total taxes**	**9,568.88**
Environment	Air pollution	1,836.87	**Tolls**		**1,645.20**
	Climate change (1)	8,446.91	**Subsidies**		**−147**
	Climate change (2)	1,462.89			
	Noise	15.16			
	Other (1)	3,163.51			
	Other (2)	2,205.47			
	Total environment (1)	**13,462.45**			
	Total environment (2)	**5,520.39**			
Total costs (1)		**22,433.17**	**Total revenues**		**11,067.08**
Total costs (2)		**14,491.11**			

Notes: (1) high environmental costs scenario; (2) low environmental costs scenario.

costs are underestimated (do not incorporate all the costs linked to provision of energy, vehicles, and infrastructure). Considering this precaution, the coverage rate of total costs is in the range of 49–76 per cent

The revenues reach a figure slightly higher than €11,000 million. In turn, the largest revenues come from fuel taxes. For this mode of transport, the main problem appears to be the coverage of environmental costs.

Rail transport

The railways account is also provided as an aggregate and then disaggregated (see Tables 15.4, 15.5, and 15.6). The coverage rate of total costs is between 24 per cent and 25 per cent. The disaggregation is made, first, for passengers and freight services, and second, by type of business (HSR and conventional services). In this case, environmental costs seem to be small, though likely underestimated.

For the aggregated account, main revenues are given by fees, reaching a figure of €503 million. On the cost side, infrastructure costs are around €3,000 million. Interestingly, the amount of subsidy for the operation of services is quite large, (€880 million), and even larger than the amount of total revenues in the aggregated account.

Table 15.3 Road transport disaggregate account for Spain by type of vehicle, 2013

External costs and infrastructure

Million €		Passenger vehicles	Buses	Trucks LDV	Trucks HDV	TOTAL
Infrastructure	Capital	3,391.03	135.89	506.38	1,498.38	5,531.68
	Maintenance, operation	1,020.49	63.87	238.07	826.35	2,148.78
	Total Infra.	**4,411.52**	**199.76**	**744.45**	**2,324.73**	**7,680.46**
Accidents	Direct Cots	69.42	0.46	1.51	1.78	73.17
	Indirect Costs	331.95	2.53	9.32	11.03	354.83
	Value of risk	728.14	17.34	53.47	63.28	862.23
	Total accidents	**1,129.51**	**20.33**	**64.30**	**76.09**	**1,290.23**
Environment	Air pollution	1,098.73	55.57	231.81	450.76	1,836.87
	Climate change (1)	5,805.19	208.52	938.15	1,495.06	8,446.92
	Climate change (2)	1,006.65	36.66	160.22	259.35	1,462.88
	Noise	8.81	0.45	2.89	3.00	15.15
	Other (1)	2,082.00	95.13	316.24	670.13	3,163.50
	Other (2)	1,422.64	66.89	218.56	497.39	2,205.48
	Total envirom. (1)	**8,994.73**	**359.67**	**1,489.09**	**2,618.95**	**13,462.44**
	Total envirom. (2)	**3,536.83**	**159.57**	**613.48**	**1,210.50**	**5,520.38**
Total costs (1)		**14,535.76**	**579.76**	**2,297.84**	**5,019.77**	**22,433.13**
Total costs (2)		**9,077.86**	**379.66**	**1,422.23**	**3,611.32**	**14,491.07**

Revenues

Million €		Passenger vehicles	Buses	Trucks LDV	Trucks HDV	TOTAL
Taxes	Fuel taxes	3,746.92	190.86	679.48	1,731.10	6,348.36
	VAT on fuel	786.85	40.08	142.69	363.53	1,333.15
	Vehicle ownership taxes	1,501.96	16.83	59.91	96.46	1,675.16
	Car acquisition taxes	212.22				212.22
	Total taxes	**6,247.95**	**247.77**	**882.08**	**2,191.09**	**9,568.89**
Tolls		**1,469.30**	**17.66**	**62.88**	**95.36**	**1,645.20**
Subsidies		−147.00				−147.00
Total revenues		**7,570.25**	**265.43**	**944.96**	**2,286.45**	**11,067.09**

Notes: (1) high environmental costs scenario; (2) low environmental costs scenario.

276 *José Manuel Vasallo, et al.*

Table 15.4 Railway transport aggregate account for Spain, 2013

External costs and infrastructure			Revenues		
		Millions €			*Millions €*
Infrastructure	Capital	1,304.26	**Taxes**	Fuel taxes	0.00
	Maintenance, operation	1,738.68			
	Total infrastructure	**3,042.94**		Car acquisition taxes	0.00
Accidents	Total direct and indirect costs	13.15		Electricity	20.95
	Total accidents	**13.15**		**Total taxes**	**20.95**
Environment	Air pollution	52.79	**Canons**		**503.00**
			Security fees		**16.70**
	Climate change (1)	34.45	**Logistic services**		**42.8**
	Climate change (2)	7.15	**Rents and optical fibre**		**179.75**
	Noise	4.31	**Other**		**33.07**
	Other (1)	182.52	**Subsidies**		**–**
	Other (2)	101.52			
	Total environment (1)	**274.07**			
	Total environment (2)	**165.77**			
Total costs (1)		**3,330.16**	**Total revenues**		**796.27**
Total costs (2)		**3,221.86**			

Notes: (1) high environmental costs scenario; (2) low environmental costs scenario.

Air transport

The results for this mode are also provided in an aggregated and disaggregated way at the airport level (see Tables 15.7, 15.8, 15.9, and 15.10 for a sample of Spanish airports). Now there are two infrastructure providers, Aena (airport services) and Enaire (ATC services).

It is important to notice that even when the disaggregation takes place at the airport level, the figures in the account refer to the costs and revenues of the air transport mode (airports and airlines). They are allocated taking into account the transport activity conducted at each airport.

In this mode, most of the revenues come from airport charges (nearly €3,000 million). The impact on climate change appears as a very important component, reaching in the worst-case scenario values greater that €7,000 million. Moreover, although there is an emission trading system in place, the degree of internalisation of those costs seems insignificant. For this mode, the coverage rate is between 32 per cent and 72 per cent in aggregate terms.

Maritime transport

The aggregate account for maritime transport is presented in Table 15.11. The lack of data on accident and environmental costs results in an account with only infrastructure costs and revenues.

Table 15.5 Railway transport disaggregate account for Spain by freight and passenger services, 2013

External costs and infrastructure						Revenues				
Millions €		*Passengers*	*Freight*	*Total*		*Millions €*		*Passengers*	*Freight*	*Total*
Infrastructure	Capital	1,204.40	99.86	1,304.26		**Taxes**	Fuel taxes	0.00	0.00	0.00
	Maintenance, operation	1,198.31	540.37	1,738.68						
	Total infrastructure	**2,402.71**	**640.23**	**3,042.94**			Car acquisition taxes	0.00	0.00	0.00
Accidents	Total direct and indirect costs	11.28	1.87	13.15			Electricity	15.45	5.50	20.95
	Total accidents	**11.28**	**1.87**	**13.15**			**Total taxes**	**15.45**	**5.50**	**20.95**
Environment	Air pollution	42.36	10.43	52.79		**Canons**		**499.00**	**4.00**	**503.00**
	Climate change (1)	22.67	11.78	34.45		**Security fees**		**16.70**	**0.00**	**16.70**
	Climate change (2)	4.53	2.62	7.15		**Logistic services**		**0.00**	**42.80**	**42.80**
	Noise	2.58	1.73	4.31		**Rents and optical fibre**		**149.50**	**30.25**	**179.75**
	Other (1)	141.34	41.18	182.52		**Other**		**23.18**	**9.89**	**33.07**
	Other (2)	75.53	25.98	101.51		**Subsidies**		–	–	–
	Total envirom. (1)	**208.95**	**65.12**	**274.07**						
	Total envirom. (2)	**125.00**	**40.76**	**165.76**						
Total costs (1)		**2,622.94**	**707.22**	**3,330.16**						
Total costs (2)		**2,538.99**	**682.86**	**3,221.85**		**Total revenues**		**703.83**	**92.44**	**796.27**

Notes: (1) high environmental costs scenario; (2) low environmental costs scenario.

Table 15.6 Railway transport disaggregate account for Spain by type of business, 2013

External costs and infrastructure					Revenues				
Millions €		HSR	Conventional railways	TOTAL	Millions €		HSR	Conventional railways	TOTAL
Infrastructure	Capital	744.65	559.61	1,304.26	**Taxes**	Fuel taxes	0.00	0.00	0.00
	Maintenance, operation	418.08	1,320.60	1,738.68					
	Total infrastructure	**1,162.73**	**1,880.21**	**3,042.94**		Vehicle acquisition costs	0.00	0.00	0.00
Accidents	Total direct and indirect costs	4.82	8.33	13.15					
						Electricity	4.81	16.14	20.95
	Total accidents	**4.82**	**8.33**	**13.15**		**Total taxes**	**4.81**	**16.14**	**20.95**
Environment	Air pollution	18.11	34.68	52.79	**Canons**	Infrastructure	334.10	68.60	402.70
	Climate change (1)	9.69	24.76	34.45		Stations	62.10	33.10	95.20
	Climate change (2)	1.94	5.21	7.15		Metric width	0.00	5.10	5.10
	Noise	1.10	3.21	4.31		**Total canons**	**396.20**	**106.80**	**503.00**
	Other (1)	60.43	122.09	182.52	**Security fees**		**10.02**	**6.68**	**16.70**
	Other (2)	32.29	69.22	101.51	**Logistic services**		**0.00**	**42.80**	**42.80**
	Total envirom. (1)	**89.33**	**184.74**	**274.07**	**Rents and optical fibre**		**132.64**	**47.11**	**179.75**
	Total envirom. (2)	**53.44**	**112.32**	**165.76**	**Other**		**10.67**	**22.40**	**33.07**
Total costs (1)		**1,256.88**	**2,073.28**	**3,330.16**	**Subsidies**		–	–	–
Total costs (2)		**1,220.99**	**2,000.86**	**3,221.85**	**Total revenues**		**554.34**	**241.93**	**796.27**

Notes: (1) high environmental costs scenario; (2) low environmental costs scenario.

Table 15.7 Air transport aggregate account for Spain, 2013

External costs and infrastructure		Millions €	Revenues		Millions €
Infrastructure Aena	Capital	1,080.42	**Taxes**	Fuel taxes	0.00
	Maintenance, operation	1,162.55		Car acquisition taxes	0.00
				Other	0.00
Infrastructure Enaire	Capital	58.85		**Total taxes**	0.00
	Maintenance, operation	749.22	**Aena**	Security fees	39.57
	Total infrastructure	**3,051.04**		Airport charges	2,872.38
Accidents	Direct and indirect costs	76.14	**Enaire**	En-route charges	696.95
				Naviagtion charges	17.51
	Total accidents	**76.14**	**Emission permits for CO$_2$**		18.00
Environment	Air pollution	71.29	**Subsidies**		–
	Climate change (1)	7,336.26			
	Climate change (2)	1,251.39			
	Noise	39.66			
	Other (1)	988.11			
	Other (2)	577.47			
	Total environment (1)	**8,435.33**			
	Total environment (2)	**1,939.81**			
Total costs (1)		**11,562.51**			
Total costs (2)		**5,066.99**	**Total revenues**		**3,644.41**

Notes: (1) high environmental costs scenario; (2) low environmental costs scenario.

Table 15.8 Air transport account for Spain by route origin/destination at Madrid airport, 2013

External costs and infrastructure			Revenues		
		Millions €			*Millions €*
Infrastructure Aena	Capital	344.24	**Taxes**	Fuel taxes	0.00
	Maintenance, operation	328.79		Car acquisition taxes	0.00
				Other	0.00
Infrastructure	Capital	18.15		**Total taxes**	0.00
Enaire	Maintenance, operation	231.02	**Aena**	Security fees	8.39
	Total infrastructure	**922.20**		Airport charges	887.61
Accidents	Direct and indirect costs	23.48	**Enaire**	En-route charges	214.9
				Naviagtion charges	5.40
	Total accidents	**23.48**	**Emission permits for CO_2**		2.27
Environment	Air pollution	21.98	**subsidies**		–
	Climate change (1)	2,262.11			
	Climate change (2)	385.86			
	Noise	12.23			
	Other (1)	304.68			
	Other (2)	178.06			
	Total environment (1)	**2,601.00**			
	Total environment (2)	**598.13**			
Total costs (1)		**3,546.68**			
Total costs (2)		**1,543.81**	**Total revenues**		**1,118.57**

Notes: (1) high environmental costs scenario; (2) low environmental costs scenario.

Table 15.9 Air transport account for Spain by route origin/destination at Barcelona airport, 2013

External costs and infrastructure		Millions €	Revenues		Millions €
Infrastructure Aena	Capital	195.00	**Taxes**	Fuel taxes	0.00
	Maintenance, operation	204.08		Car acquisition taxes	0.00
				Other	0.00
Infrastructure Enaire	Capital	8.10		**Total taxes**	0.00
	Maintenance, operation	103.15	**Aena**	Security fees	7.44
	Total infrastructure	**510.33**		Airport charges	663.11
Accidents	Direct and indirect costs	10.48	**Enaire**	En-route charges	95.95
				Naviagtion charges	2.41
	Total accidents	**10.48**	**Emission permits for CO_2**		2.14
Environment	Air pollution	9.82	**Subsidies**		–
	Climate change (1)	1,010.03			
	Climate change (2)	172.29			
	Noise	5.46			
	Other (1)	136.04			
	Other (2)	79.50			
	Total environment (1)	**1,161.35**			
	Total environment (2)	**267.07**			
Total costs (1)		**1,682.16**			
Total costs (2)		**787.88**	**Total revenues**		**771.05**

Notes: (1) high environmental costs scenario; (2) low environmental costs scenario.

Table 15.10 Air transport account for Spain by route origin/destination at the smallest airports,★ 2013

External costs and infrastructure		Millions €	Revenues		Millions €
Infrastructure Aena	Capital	242.11	**Taxes**	Fuel taxes	0.00
	Maintenance, operation	273.26		Car acquisition taxes	0.00
				Other	0.00
Infrastructure Enaire	Capital	8.41		**Total taxes**	0.00
	Maintenance, operation	107.05	**Aena**	Security fees	6.96
	Total infrastructure	**630.83**		Airport charges	351.75
Accidents	Direct and indirect costs	10.88	**Enaire**	En-route charges	99.58
				Naviagtion charges	2.5
	Total accidents	**10.88**	**Emission permits for CO$_2$**		3.07
Environment	Air pollution	10.19	**Subsidies**		–
	Climate change (1)	1,048.21			
	Climate change (2)	178.80			
	Noise	5.67			
	Other (1)	141.18			
	Other (2)	82.51			
	Total environment (1)	**1,205.25**			
	Total environment (2)	**277.17**			
Total costs (1)		**1,846.96**			
Total costs (2)		**918.88**	**Total revenues**		**463.86**

Notes: (★) All Aena airports except Madrid, Barcelona, Palma de Mallorca, Málaga, Gran Canaria, Alicante, Tenerife Sur, Ibiza, Lanzarote, and Valencia; (1) high environmental costs scenario; (2) low environmental costs scenario.

Table 15.11 Maritime transport aggregate account for Spain, 2013

External costs and infrastructure		Millions €	Revenues		Millions €
Infrastructure	Capital	441.32	**Taxes**	Fuel taxes	0.00
	Maintenance, operation	576.49			
	Total infrastructure	**1,017.81**		Vehicle acquisition taxes	0.00
Accidents	Total direct and indirect costs			Other	0.00
				Total taxes	0.00
	Total accidents	**Not available**	**Charges**	Occupation charge	266.70
				Utilisation charge	536.80
Environment	Air pollution			Activity charge	115.90
	Climate change (1)			Navigation assistance charge	10.90
	Climate change (2)			**Total port charges**	930.30
	Noise		**Subsidies**		–
	Other (1)				
	Other (2)				
	Total environment (1)	**Not available**			
	Total environment (2)				
Total costs		**1,017.81**	**Total revenues**		**930.30**

Notes: (1) high environmental costs scenario; (2) low environmental costs scenario.

284 *José Manuel Vasallo, et al.*

Conclusion

In this chapter, we have estimated the transport accounts in Spain for interurban services (year 2013) from publicly available information. The objective of the accounts is to know to what extent each mode bears its infrastructure and external costs with the revenues and contributions produced.

The accounts provide data for an informed transport policy debate. For all transport modes, we have built an aggregate account that offers a global view. With the exception of the maritime transport mode, we have also provided disaggregated accounts for a more detailed analysis. In the case of roads, the disaggregation refers to type of vehicle; for railways to passengers and freight, and type of business; while in air transport, we differentiate by airport, taking into consideration the routes with origin/destination at each of them.

The estimation of the external costs of accidents in transport is an area that deserves more research. This is especially relevant in the case of roads, as the discussion about the degree of internalisation of these costs has been considered in a limited number of studies and the evidence is still scarce. In this work, recommendations from Lindberg (2006) and Link et al. (2007) have been applied. Furthermore, when interpreting the account, we should note that the climate change cost item is subject to a high degree of uncertainty. Following the recommendation from the original source that provides unit costs (CE-Delft et al., 2011), we report a range of environmental values that in turn, make us also provide a range of total costs and coverage rates. Environmental external costs regarding *upstream-downstream* processes are underestimated, too, as they do not incorporate the impact from provision of infrastructure and vehicles. This aspect can be potentially very important for railways, and to a lesser extent, also for the road (Kageson, 2009; Chester and Hovarth, 2009).

The main conclusions of this work are as follows:

1   The interpretation of the accounts results should be conducted with the stated precautions. No mode of transport has enough revenues and contributions allowing it to cover the total account of costs, though there are important differences among them. Table 15.12 shows different coverage rates for the aggregate accounts to facilitate the comparison.
2   The aggregate road account results in a total coverage rate between 49 per cent and 76 per cent, with passenger cars behaving better as they have a greater amount of special taxes. In addition, it can be seen that the account revenues allow for payment of infrastructure and accident costs. The main problem seems to be how to cover environmental costs, and this can be potentially very high due to the effect on climate change.
3   In the case of railways, even considering the fact that environmental costs may be underestimated, it seems that the main problem is paying for infrastructure costs. The total coverage rate in the global account is between 24 per cent and 25 per cent, though especially low for freight (13 per cent) and conventional services (12 per cent). The highest rate appears for HSR

Table 15.12 Summary of results for aggregate accounts: coverage rates, 2013

	Total revenues / Total costs (1)	Total revenues / Total costs (2)	Total revenues − subsidies / Total costs (1)	Total revenues − subsidies / Total costs (2)	Total revenues / Total costs of infrastructure	Total revenues − subsidies / Total costs of infrastructure	Total revenues / Total costs of infrastructure + accidents costs	Total revenues − subsidies / Total costs of infrastructure + accidents costs
Road	0.49	0.76	0.49	0.75	1.44	1.42	1.23	1.21
Railways	0.239	0.247	−0.025	−0.026	0.262	−0.027	0.261	−0.027
Air	0.32	0.72	0.29	0.67	1.19	1.10	1.17	1.08
Maritime	n.a.	n.a.	n.a.	n.a.	0.91	0.84	n.a.	n.a.

Notes: n.a.: not available; (1) high environmental costs scenario; (2) low environmental costs scenario.

services that pay bigger canons. Besides, as a difference from other railway services, HSR operations do not receive subsides linked to public services obligations. Nevertheless, the results for this mode are specially unbalanced if compared to other modes of transport. Furthermore, if we consider that some potentially high environmental costs are omitted, and that subsidies for the operation of services are larger than the account revenues, the situation could be even worse.

4   The air transport mode mirrors in some aspects the results obtained in the road account. Total revenues would also allow coverage of the infrastructure and the external costs of accidents. However, the environmental impact of climate change is really worrying, as it could reach as much as €7,000 million in the worst-case scenario, with a market of emission permits allowing to internalise just a very small amount. The coverage rate is between 32 per cent and 72 per cent. When interpreting these results, we have to bear in mind that airport charges are linked to aircraft movements or number of passengers, not to the distance of routes originating or arriving at a particular airport. On the other hand, external costs of accidents and the environment were allocated according to the level of activity measured in terms of passenger-kilometres, and hence airports with larger routes will show also larger external costs. This explains why Barcelona airport has better performance than Madrid. It can also be seen that the group of the smallest airports reach a coverage rate between 25 per cent and 50 per cent, not even exceeding the infrastructure costs.

5   The maritime transport account suffers from lack of data due to the international nature of services and the scarcity of research in this area. Therefore, it shows only revenues from port charges against infrastructure costs, that are covered by 91 per cent.

Note

1   This chapter is a summary of a larger work published by FEDEA. All the details of the analysis are available at: http://documentos.fedea.net/pubs/eee/eee2017-14.pdf

We are grateful to Jairo Casares, Laura López and Gloria Alemán for their assistance. The work has also benefitted from the comments and suggestions made by Ginés de Rus and Ángel de la Fuente. The usual disclaimer applies. This research was undertaken within the DIGITTA project, which is funded by the Spanish Ministry of Economics, Industry and Competitiveness, research grant ECO 2016-80268-R.

References

Abellán Perpiñán, J. M., Martínez Pérez, J. E., Méndez Martínez, I., Pinto Prades, J. L. and Robles Zurita, J. A. (2011a). *El valor monetario de una víctima no mortal y del año de vida ajustado por la calidad en España*. Murcia and Sevilla, Universidad de Murcia, Universidad Pablo Olavide de Sevilla.

Abellán Perpiñán, J. M., Martínez Pérez, J. E., Méndez Martínez, I., Pinto Prades, J. L. and Sánchez Martínez, F. I. (2011b). *El valor monetario de una vida estadística en España:*

Estimación en el contexto de los accidentes de tráfico. Murcia and Sevilla, Universidad de Murcia, Universidad Pablo Olavide de Sevilla.

Adif (2014). *Memoria económica 2013*. Madrid, Ministerio de Fomento.

Adif Alta Velocidad (2014). *Memoria económica 2013*. Madrid, Ministerio de Fomento.

Bickel, P. and Friedrich, R. (2005). *Externalities of energy, methodology 2005 update*. Brussels, European Commission.

CE-Delft, INFRAS and ISI (2011). *External costs of transport in Europe: Update study for 2008*. The International Union of Railways (UIC). Available at: https://ec.europa.eu/transport/sites/transport/files/studies/internalisation-handbook-isbn-978-92-79-96917-1.pdf.

Chester, M. and Horvath, A. (2009). Environmental assessment of passenger transportation should include infrastructure and supply chains. *Environmental Research Letters*, 8, 024008.

Dirección General de Tráfico (2000). *Kilómetros a precio de oro. Revista Tráfico noviembre-diciembre 2000*, 31–34.

European Commission (2019). *Air climate change*. Available at: https://ec.europa.eu/transport/modes/air/environment/climate_change_en.

Fundación BBVA (2013). *Series históricas de capital público en España y su distribución territorial (1900–2013)*. Fundación BBVA and Ivie. Available at: https://www.ivie.es/es_ES/ptproyecto/capital-publico-en-espana-evolucion-y-distribucion-territorial-1900-2012/.

Hensher, D. and Button, K. (2003). Introduction. In Hensher, D. and Button, K. (eds) *Handbook of transport and the environment*. Handbooks in Transport Volume 4. Boston, Elsevier.

INFRAS/IWW (1995). *External costs of transport*. Paris, The International Union of Railways (UIC).

INFRAS/IWW (2000). *External costs of transport: Accident, environmental and congestion costs of transport in Western Europe*. Paris, The International Union of Railways (UIC).

INFRAS/IWW (2004). *External costs of transport: Update study*. Paris, The International Union of Railways (UIC).

Kageson, P. (2009). *Environmental aspects of intercity passenger transport*. Discussion Paper No. 2009–28. Paris, International Transport Forum, OECD.

Kraemer, C. and Albelda, R. (2004). *Evaluación técnico-económica de las secciones de firme de la Norma 6.1-IC*. VI Congreso Nacional de Firmes. Madrid, Asociación Española de la Carretera.

Lindberg, G. (2001). Traffic insurance and accident externality charges. *Journal of Transport Economics and Policy*, 35(3), 399–416.

Lindberg, G. (2006). *D3 – marginal cost case studies for road and rail transport*. GRACE Project. Available at: https://trimis.ec.europa.eu/sites/default/files/project/documents/20130221_132738_90943_del3v124nov2006.pdf.

Link, H., Becker, A., Matthews, B., Wheat, P., Enei, R., Sessa, C., Meszaros, F., Suter, S., Bickel, P., Ohlau, K., de Jong, R., Bak, M. and Lindberg, G. (2007). *D-5 monitoring pricing policy using transport accounts*. GRACE Project. European Commission. Available at: http://www.isis-it.net/grace/public/D5%20Final%20080607.pdf.

Link, H., Stewart, L., Maibach, M., Sanson, T. and Nellthorp, J. (2000). *The accounts approach: Deliverable 2*. Leeds, Institute of Transport Studies, UNITE Project European Commission.

Lladó Gomà-Camps, A. and Roig Solé, R. (2007). *El coste de los accidentes de tráfico en España en 2004. Una consideración especial de la accidentalidad entre los jóvenes. Jóvenes y conducción: Un derecho y una responsabilidad. Comisión de Expertos para el estudio de la problemática de los jóvenes y la seguridad vial. Informe de ponencias*. Fundación RACC. Available at: http://oa.upm.es/7722/1/INVE_MEM_2010_78726.pdf.

Maibach, M., Schreyer, D., Sutter, D., van Essen, H. P., Boon, B. H., Smokers, R., Schroten, A., Doll, C., Pawlowska, B. and Bak, M. (2008). *Handbook on estimation of external costs in the transport sector*. IMPACT Project. European Commission. Available at: https://ec.europa.eu/transport/sites/transport/files/themes/sustainable/doc/2008_costs_handbook.pdf.

RICARDO-AEA (2014). *Update of the handbook on external costs of transport*. Brussels, European Commission.

Spanish Government (2004–2009). State's general budgets.

16 The spatial economic effects of airport de-hubbing

The Milan case

Marco Percoco

Introduction

Transport infrastructures are considered to be key policy tools for promoting local development, and in the age of increasing demand for moving people around the globe, aviation and airports are widely viewed as essential ingredients in driving the success and prosperity of cities and metropolises. According to Florida (2012), 'Airports are much more than places to catch planes, attend an in-transit business meeting, or do some duty-free shopping; they are among the largest investments a city and region make'.

The reasons for attributing a large emphasis on airports as crucial investments for local development are multifaceted, but can be reduced to two broad categories. First, airports are complex facilities characterised by a significant use of technologies, even the most advanced ones, and labour to produce services needed by the demand and the supply of air transport markets. Second, they 'play a considerable role in economic development, and the most important cargo they move is people' (Florida, 2012). From the production perspective, airports, through aviation, increase the international accessibility of places, which means that more locations can be reached at lower transport costs, possibly through a significant contraction in travel time.

Interestingly, the two aforementioned rationales for the focus on airports from a policy perspective also mimic the two types of economic impact of air transport terminals. From an aggregate demand perspective, airports generate direct, indirect, and induced effects produced by expenditure on construction and operations. From the perspective of the production sectors, mainly the manufacturing and the service sectors, airports and airline activities increase their market potential and, in a new economic geography framework, their productivity. According to this view, the presence of an airport may promote the attractiveness for firm location (Kasarda and Linday (2011).

This chapter deals with the impact of a specific category of airports, namely hubs that are global in their nature. Their impact is expected to be particularly large because of their size and because of the international connectivity they provide to surrounding areas. In particular, in the next section, we discuss the more recent literature on de-hubbing events as types of natural experiments

290 *Marco Percoco*

to study the relevance of airport hubs for local development. This is followed by a summary of empirical results of the case of Milan Malpensa as studied by Cattaneo et al. (2018) and Cifarelli and Percoco (2018). Then it is argued that de-hubbing can be considered as a productivity shock and that the results are consistent with the theory of the spatial equilibrium. The final section concludes with suggestions for future research.

Literature review

The impact of airports on local economies has been the subject to extensive scrutiny by transport economists and geographers over the past two decades. This move to new and mainly empirical studies came at a time when mainstream economics was still considering transport infrastructure as mere sums of public investment spending (through permanent inventory measures) and was investigating the possible impact of this expenditure on a variety of economic outcomes ranging from productivity to gross domestic product and employment (see e.g. Aschauer, 1989).

Early literature on the impact of airports took a different perspective, as the prior rationale for considering the impact of aviation on economic activities was assumed to be related to the operations; that is, on the level and quality of air transport services provided to local economies. Locating an airport in a given area implies a substantial increase in the accessibility of the surroundings, with a larger market potential at lower transport costs. This relationship, which is almost mechanical in nature, should result in positive economic outcomes for local economies, especially for those more specialised in the service sector, relying the most on social interactions to increase productivity (Brueckner, 2003; Percoco, 2010). This hypothesis comes from the fact that the service sector is more dependent on labour with respect to manufacturing, which has higher capital intensity. Most of freight is shipped by sea so that aviation is crucial for moving workers more than goods. In this vein, air transport increases the possibilities of face-to-face interactions so that the basic idea which the most recent literature is supporting with empirical evidence is the positive impact of social interactions on labour productivity.

In particular, Brueckner (2003) found a 0.1 elasticity of service sector employment to airport activity in US metropolitan areas. Percoco (2010) considered the relationship between airline traffic and local economic development in Italian provinces. In doing so, the Brueckner (2003) framework is adopted, but the approach differs not only because it considers a different country but also because, in dealing with endogeneity issues, it explicitly takes the possibility of self-selection into account. It finds that the elasticity of service sector employment to airline traffic is about 0.056; however, this value decreases to 0.045 when spillover effects, which amount to 0.017, are taken into account.

As previously stated, the more recent literature on airports and development assumes that aviation increases accessibility of the areas in which an airport is located. In this perspective, airport hubs are assumed to play a crucial role in increasing intercontinental accessibility as they provide higher levels of connectivity to local consumers through a higher frequency of flights and through international and intercontinental flights. These features imply an enlargement of the network scope of consumers with respect to a simple origin-destination system (Burghouwt and Redondi, 2013). In this vein, Bel and Fageda (2010) found that a 10 per cent increase in intercontinental routes increases the number of headquarters of multinationals in European metropolitan regions by 4 per cent.

A growing body of literature has recently analysed the consequences of de-hubbing for airport operations and consumer welfare, although the literature has provided mixed results, as de-hubbing itself cannot be generally considered as fatal (Rodríguez-Déniz et al., 2013). In some cases, a new mix of alternative carriers might emerge (Wei and Grubesic, 2015), and in others, service quality may increase because of a reduction in travel times and on-time performance (Rupp and Tan, 2016). Redondi et al. (2012) questioned the resilience of airports after a de-hubbing by considering 37 cases worldwide; in the vast majority, traffic did not recover after five years from the shock, unless low-cost carriers replaced the hub carrier.

The impact of de-hubbing on local development: the case of Malpensa airport

The literature on the impact of de-hubbing on local development is limited. In this section, we summarise empirical evidence on the de-hubbing of Malpensa airport as in Cattaneo et al. (2018) and Cifarelli and Percoco (2018). The de-hubbing of Malpensa airport took place after the decision of Alitalia to modify its network strategy. Between 2001 and 2007, the Italian flag carrier ran a dual-hub strategy at Rome Fiumicino and Malpensa airports, with a significant duplication of flights and routes at national and even international levels. In addition, the passenger attractiveness of Malpensa airport, which is about 50 kilometres from the centre of Milan, was severely limited by the competition of Milan Linate (the city airport) and Bergamo Orio al Serio, which specialised in low-cost carrier operations.

The combination of an unsustainable network strategy for Alitalia and the limited competitiveness of Malpensa airport lead to the de-hubbing decision. As a result, the number of intercontinental flights dropped by 36 per cent, while the number of served airports dropped by 19 per cent, from 58 to 47. The total number of annual passengers decreased from 23.8 million in 2007 to 17.5 million in 2009. When considering European and medium-haul connectivity, the decline was less pronounced, with a cumulative decrease in the number of flights equal to 18 per cent (Cattaneo et al., 2018).

The contraction in the supply of air services produced a decrease in the number of passengers between 2008 and 2010 (Figure 16.1), the year in which easyJet expanded significantly its supply of flights with origins or destinations at Malpensa airport. However, the (partial) absorption of the de-hubbing shock

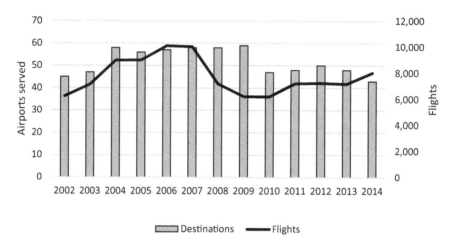

Figure 16.1 Annual supply from Malpensa airport toward non-EU destinations
Source: Devised by author from Cattaneo et al. (2018)

hides the fact that Alitalia cancelled almost entirely its supply of intercontinental flights and this was not substituted by the entry of easyJet.

Figure 16.2 shows an index of international air accessibility of Milan developed and maintained by the local Chamber of Commerce. It weights destinations served by all airports in the area by distance and country population at destination. Furthermore, it is standardised with the same indicator calculated for London. The figure shows a sharp and persisting contraction in air accessibility, indicating that the entry of low-cost carriers, as predicted in the literature, does not counterbalance the effect of de-hubbing in terms of types of services offered. In this chapter, we aim to discuss the literature on the effect of de-hubbing on the local economy, starting from the evidence that the de-hubbing of Malpensa airport has altered the possibilities of international interaction of the surrounding area.

Cifarelli and Percoco (2018) evaluated the impact of the de-hubbing of Malpensa airport on regional exports by making use of a three-dimensional panel containing information on trade flows between 28 European countries[1] in the period 2004–2011, with a further breakdown of 30 sectors.[2] In particular, they estimated the following regression equation:

$$\log(\text{trade})_{i,s,t} = \alpha_i + \alpha_s + \lambda \log(\text{trend}_t) + \beta \text{post}_t \times \log(c_s) \times \log(\text{dist}_i) \\ + \gamma_1 \text{post}_t \times \log(c_s) + \gamma_2 \log(c_s) \times \log(\text{dist}_i) + \gamma_3 \text{post}_t \\ \times \log(\text{dist}_i) + \delta \text{post}_t + s_{i,s,t} \quad (1)$$

The dependent variable indicates the value of trade (either exports or imports or their sum) from sector s in Lombardy to country i in year t. Post$_t$ is a dummy

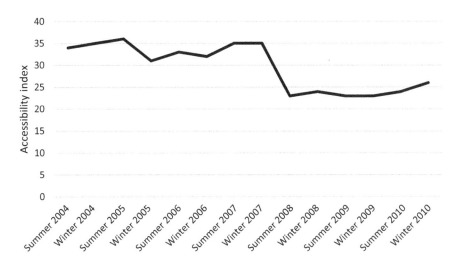

Figure 16.2 International accessibility of Milan area

Source: Devised by author using Milan Chamber of Commerce data (Osservatorio sull'accessibilità intercontinentale di Malpensa)

taking the value 1 if the de-hubbing decision has already occurred, i.e. from 2008 onward; cs is the technological coefficient for the use of air transport services by sector s, and disti is the distance in kilometres from country i to Malpensa airport. Distance is calculated as the Euclidean distance between Malpensa airport and the major airport in origin/destination country. The inclusion of this variable is meant to capture the role of spatial frictions in our trade equation. If we assume that they are a proxy or a component of transport costs, then dist × post is an indicator for a shift in accessibility and hence in transport cost. Pairwise interaction of these variables, as well as controls for countries and sectors, and time trends – indicated respectively as αi, αs, and trend – are included. All continuous variables are in logs, with standard errors clustered across sectors.

Estimates of Equation (1) are shown in Table 16.1. Columns 1, 2, and 3 show the coefficients for the regressions for 2007–2008 only, between 2006 and 2009, and between 2005 and 2010, respectively, while Column 4 shows the results from the baseline specification, taking into consideration the whole sample period from 2004–2011. It is evident that the largest impact occurred in the time interval in Column 2. Indeed, β is equal to −0.08 and significant at 1 per cent for the period 2007–2008, indicating that, as distance from Malpensa airport increases by 100 km, the average decrease in log(export) is equal to 2.36, which corresponds to −15.43 per cent or a loss of €13,053,780. Interestingly, estimates over longer time periods are smaller and less significant, possibly indicating that, from 2009, a gradual process of adjustment in the regional economy in response to the new connectivity took place.

294   *Marco Percoco*

Table 16.1 Exports: baseline regression and time intervals analysis

	Log(exports)			
	2007–2008	*2006–2009*	*2005–2010*	*2004–2011*
$post_t \times log(c_s) \times log(dist_i)$	−0.078★	−0.08★★★	−0.064★★	−0.051★
	(0.045)	(0.021)	(0.028)	(0.027)
$post_t \times log(c_s)$	0.535★	0.571★★★	0.465★★	0.377★
	(0.304)	(0.156)	(0.197)	(0.188)
$log(c_s) \times log(dist_i)$	0.116★	0.094	0.086	0.076
	(0.064)	(0.068)	(0.072)	(0.063)
$post_t \times log(dist_i)$	−0.465	−0.546★★★	−0.452★★★	−0.393★★
	(0.299)	(0.128)	(0.156)	(0.153)
$post_t$	3.158	3.872★★★	3.067★★	2.64★★
	(1.998)	(0.967)	(1.121)	(1.089)
Trend	–	−0.104★	0.0264	0.0584★★★
	–	(0.052)	(0.0226)	(0.0138)
Observations	1,432	2,904	4,381	5,813
Country	Yes	Yes	Yes	Yes
Sector	Yes	Yes	Yes	Yes

Source: Cifarelli and Percoco (2018)

Notes: ★★★ p < 0.01, ★★ p < 0.05, ★ p < 0.1; standard errors in parentheses, adjusted for 30 clusters in sectors.

These results are not completely in line with the framework proposed in the introduction, as the early literature has argued that the non-tradable sector is more affected by airline activities and hence we should not have expected an impact on the level of exports, especially for the sectors relying the most on air transport services.

Cattaneo et al. (2018) turn to the issue of the local effects of the de-hubbing by using a panel data model of Travel-to-Work Areas (TTWAs) around Malpensa airport with heterogeneous effects, depending on the distance from the airport. In particular, our baseline specification is as follows:

$$y_{it} = \alpha_i + \beta Post_t + \gamma Post_t \times distance_i + \delta trend_{i,t} + \phi X_{i,t} + \varepsilon_{it} \qquad (2)$$

where y_{it} indicates employment in TTWA i in year t, Postt is an indicator variable taking the value of 1 after de-hubbing (from 2008 onwards) and zero otherwise, $distance_i$ measures the distance between the core city of $TTWA_i$ and Malpensa airport, and $trend_{i,t}$ indicates TTWA-specific temporal trends. The specification includes TTWA-specific fixed effects (α_i). Thus, the effect of de-hubbing, according to Equation (1), is $\beta + \gamma distance_i$, meaning that it is a function of the spatial distance between $TTWA_i$ and Malpensa airport. Ideally, β should be negative (the effect in the immediate surroundings, that is, when the distance is zero) and γ should be positive, indicating an attenuation of the impact across the space. Importantly, controls for the number of aircraft movements in airports in the regions of Piedmont, Lombardy, Liguria, and

Emilia-Romagna are included as well as fixed effects. Variable trend$_{i,t}$ indicates local trends influencing employment, that is, they capture the cross-sectional and temporal variation of all TTWA-specific and time-varying unobserved variables, which can be approximated by a trend. Equation (2) is estimated in logs and through OLS, such that parameters β, γ are correctly identified under the assumption of the independence of Post$_t$ from variables, which are eventually omitted.

Table 16.2 reports estimates of Equation (2). Model (1) indicates an effect of de-hubbing on employment equal to -4.3 per cent on average (variable Post). In Models (2)–(4), the sample is split into urban TTWAs, TTWAs specialising in export-oriented activities, and TTWAs characterised by heavy industries. It is noteworthy that our coefficients of interest are only significant in Model (3), where $\beta = -7.3\%$ and $\gamma = 1.0$ per cent, indicating that de-hubbing produced a contraction in employment by 7 per cent in the TTWA where Malpensa is located and that this effect declines with a gradient of 1 per cent in (log) road distance.

By considering together results in Tables 16.1 and 16.2, we can conclude that this evidence points to a significant impact of de-hubbing on local economies through a contraction in exports. This result is consistent with those discussed in the literature review, but only partially. Brueckner (2003) and Percoco (2010), in fact, found a significant impact of air traffic on the service sector, whereas only limited evidence was found in the case of manufacturing employment. In relation to de-hubbing, a more significant effect was found in the case of TTWAs specialised in the export-oriented manufacturing industries.

Table 16.2 Baseline regressions (OLS estimates, dependent variable: total employment)

Variables	Whole sample	Urban	Export-oriented	Heavy industry
	(1)	(2)	(3)	(4)
Post*Distance	0.004	−0.013*	0.010***	0.003
	(0.003)	(0.007)	(0.003)	(0.005)
Post	−0.047***	0.035	−0.073***	−0.038
	(0.015)	(0.036)	(0.015)	(0.027)
Movements	0.0003	0.0003	0.001	−0.003
	(0.0003)	(0.0004)	(0.003)	(0.003)
Population	0.904***	0.951***	0.875***	0.902***
	(0.063)	(0.126)	(0.086)	(0.147)
Constant	−82.259***	−129.742***	−62.755***	−40.758*
	(11.969)	(23.949)	(16.269)	(23.029)
Observations	912	294	456	150
R-squared	0.421	0.441	0.465	0.419
	Yes	Yes	Yes	Yes
Fixed effects	Yes	Yes	Yes	Yes

Source: Cattaneo et al. (2018)

Note: Standard errors in parentheses; significance levels: ***: $p < 0.01$; **: $p < 0.05$; *: $p < 0.1$; all independent variables are lagged by one period.

Furthermore, the de-hubbing affected exclusively passenger services, so that the channel of transmission of such shock is not completely clear. A preliminary hypothesis could be that by mobbing workers, firms increase the probability to trade internationally, and a de-hubbing reduces such possibilities. However, a more compelling argument can be proposed and will be subject to critical scrutiny in the next section.

Speculating on the mechanisms behind the nexus between de-hubbing and local development

Contemporary cities are exposed to international markets in a variety of ways. Urban residents tend to be very mobile and are frequent flyers. Airport connectivity is often principally measured as the number of international destinations reached directly from the airport, and in this context, having an efficient and well-connected airport is essential to be part of international networks. In other words, having a hub airport in the territory is an important comparative advantage for firms located in the surroundings, as it provides a large variety of possible destinations.

A shock to air accessibility, as the one imposed by de-hubbing, negatively affects firm productivity in the surrounding area and this, in turn, affects employment, wages, and housing rents. A simple framework to describe these patterns may start from the assumption that there is a dual equilibrium in the labour and in the housing markets, as in Figure 16.3 and Figure 16.4. A shock to firm productivity implies a shift in the labour demand to D' with a subsequent decrease in employment and wages. Furthermore, there is a shift in the isocost of firms as it is more costly to move people internationally, which further reduces land and housing rents.

This conceptual model assumes that airport de-hubbing should be considered as a productivity shock and not as a change in the accessibility to a specific amenity to which workers attach given value. If airports are to be considered as amenities, in fact, a negative shock should result in an increase in wages to compensate workers for the reduction in the quality of life.

On a different point of view, airports can also be considered as disamenities since they generate considerable negative externalities in terms of noise and pollution. A contraction in their activities can hence be perceived as an

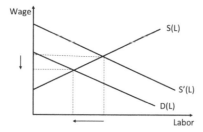

Figure 16.3 The labour market

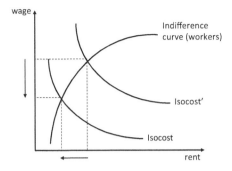

Figure 16.4 Wage-rent curves

event with positive repercussions for the territory. However, even though this event will generate a contraction in wages due to the improved quality of life, it will also result in an increase in housing rents. Our analysis centred on the employment and exports effect, but specifically what happened to wages and rents. Following are two estimated equations for export-oriented TTWAs in the spirit of Equation (2) for income and housing prices, hence they are only indicative of the impact of de-hubbing on wages and rents (standard errors in parentheses; significance levels: ★★★: $p < 0.01$; ★★: $p < 0.05$; ★: $p < 0.1$):

$$housing\ prices = 0.000 Post_t - 0.11 Post_t \times distance_i + controls$$
$$\qquad\qquad\qquad (0.000) \qquad (0.003)\text{★★★}$$

$$income = 0.000 Post_t - 0.008 Post_t \times distance_i + controls$$
$$\qquad\qquad (0.000)\text{★} \qquad (0.001)\text{★★★}$$

Interestingly, these two equations seem to confirm our intuition that de-hubbing can be considered as a shock to a local spatial equilibrium with contemporary contraction in employment, wages, and housing rents. Therefore, an airport, especially if a hub, can be considered as a large firm with substantial spatial spillovers, and its de-hubbing can be assimilated to a downsizing with cascade effect on the supply chain.

Conclusion

The literature on the impact of airports has expanded considerably in the past two decades, with an increasing focus on the international accessibility provided by air terminals to the surrounding area. In this chapter, we have reviewed and discussed the most recent developments in the empirical literature focusing on de-hubbing of airports. These contributions consider a de-hubbing event as a sort of natural experiment to estimate the effect of air accessibility on local economies. The rationale, in fact, is not to track the co-movement of air

298   *Marco Percoco*

transport and socio-economic variables, but rather to observe the likely contraction in employment after the contraction in air accessibility. Results from the case of Malpensa airport show that the effect of de-hubbing on local economies happens because of a contraction in exports, and that these estimated impacts are coherent with a simple spatial equilibrium model with a productivity shock.

Future research can be directed towards four issues. First, firm-level analysis is needed to confirm that our results are driven from supply-side factors. Second, as de-hubbing may also have demand-side effects through aircraft maintenance services and types of passengers using the airport, an analysis from this point of view may also prove to be useful. Third, a more general analysis of the impact of carrier strategies of network configuration on local development may shed new light on the geographical linkages behind the relationships between de-hubbing and local economies. Finally, de-hubbing implies a change in the types of aircraft utilised by the carriers, and this, in its turn, may modify the environmental quality in the surrounding area. Further research may hence explore the welfare implications of these changes.

Acknowledgements

I would like to thank seminar participants at JRC Ispra for useful comments, as well as my co-authors Mattia Cattaneo, Flavia Cifarelli, and Paolo Meleghetti for the joint work on which this chapter is based.

Notes

1 Countries include: Austria, Belgium, Bulgaria, Croatia, Czech Republic, Denmark, Estonia, Finland, France, Germany, Greece, Hungary, Iceland, Republic of Ireland, Latvia, Lithuania, Luxembourg, Netherlands, Norway, Poland, Portugal, Romania, Slovakia, Slovenia, Spain, Sweden, Switzerland, and the United Kingdom.
2 Sectors follow NACE 2 classification and include: crop and animal production, hunting and related service activities (01); forestry (02); fishing (03); mining and quarrying (05–08); food, beverage and tobacco (10–12); textile, clothing and fur (13–15); wood (16); paper (17); printing (18); manufacture of coke and refined petroleum products (19); manufacture of chemicals (20); manufacture of pharmaceutical products (21); manufacture of rubber and plastic products (22); manufacture of other non-metallic mineral products (23); metallurgy (24); manufacture of fabricated metal products (25); manufacture of computer, electronic, and optical products (26); manufacture of electrical equipment (27); manufacture of machinery and equipment not elsewhere classified (28); manufacture of motor vehicles, trailers and semi-trailers (29); other transports (30); manufacture of furniture and others (31–32); electricity, gas, steam and air conditioning supply (35); water supply, sewerage, waste management and remediation activities (37–38); publishing activities (58); media (59); software (62); other professional, scientific, and technical activities (74); arts, entertainment, and recreation (90–91); other personal service activities (96).

References

Aschauer, D. (1989). Is public expenditure productive?, *Journal of Monetary Economics*, 23(2), 177–200.

Bel, G. and Fageda, X. (2010). Privatization, regulation and airport pricing: An empirical analysis for Europe. *Journal of Regulatory Economics*, 37, 142–161.

Brueckner, J. K. (2003). Airline traffic and urban economic development. *Urban Studies*, 40, 1455–1469.

Burghouwt, G. and Redondi, R. (2013). Connectivity in air transport networks: An assessment of models and applications. *Journal of Transport Economics and Policy*, 47, 35–53.

Cattaneo, M., Percoco, M. and Malighetti, P. (2018). The impact of intercontinental air accessibility on local economies: Evidence from the de-hubbing of Malpensa. *Transport Policy*, 61, 96–105.

Cifarelli, F. and Percoco, M. (2018). *Airport de-hubbing and international trade: Evidence from Lombardy*, Milan, Italy, Università Bocconi, mimeo.

Florida, R. (2012). Airports and the wealth of cities. *CityLab*, 23 May. Available at: www.citylab.com/transportation/2012/05/airports-and-wealth-cities/855/.

Kasarda, J. D. and Linday, G. (2011). *Aerotropolis: The way we'll live next*. New York, Farrar, Strauss and Giroux.

Percoco, M. (2010). Airport activity and local development: Evidence from Italy. *Urban Studies*, 47(11), 2427–2443.

Redondi, R., Malighetti, P. and Paleari, S. (2012). De-hubbing of airports and their recovery patterns. *Journal of Air Transport Management*, 18(1), 1–4.

Rodríguez-Déniz, H., Suau-Sanchez, P. and Voltes-Dorta, A. (2013). Classifying airports according to their hub dimensions: An application to the US domestic network. *Journal of Transport Geography*, 33, 188–195.

Rupp, N. G. and Tan, K. M. (2016). *Mergers and product quality: A silver lining from de-hubbing in the U.S. airline industry*. Working Paper. Available at: https://editorialexpress.com/cgi-bin/conference/download.cgi?db_name=IIOC2017&paper_id=74.

Wei, F. and Grubesic, T. H. (2015). The de-hubbing of Cincinnati/Northern Kentucky international airport (CVG): A spatiotemporal panorama. *Journal of Transport Geography*, 49, 85–98.

Index

Note: Page numbers in *italic* indicate a figure and page numbers in **bold** indicate a table on the corresponding page.

accessibility *see* regional accessibility
accident costs 265, 268–269
Adler, Nicole xiii, 206–208, 211–212, 216–217
aeronautical revenues 74, 97, 207, 214, 254–255, 257–261, **259–261**
airlines 6–7; and Belgium 226–227, 229–231; and Bosnia and Herzegovina 165–167; and Bulgaria 145–148; and Central and Eastern Europe 122, 129–136, *131*, **131**; and Norway 28–29, 45–46; and Shannon Group 95–97, 102–106, 110–114; and Spain 271–272; and Switzerland 193–194, 199; and UK 64–65, 69–72, *69*, 74, 76, 78–81; and Wroclaw airport 175
air passengers *68*, *71*, *131*, *178–179*; Bosnia and Herzegovina **164**; Burgas Airport *153*; CEE countries **135**; classification of 170–171; data 149; expenditure 171–173, **183–185**; length of visit **183**; purpose of journey **181**; Sofia Airport *153*; type of journey **180**; Varna Airport *154*
airport activities *162*; Belgium 223–224, 230–231, 234–241, 247; categories of *231*; employment **239**, *240*; Oporto Airport *255*; value added **235**, *236–237*
airport de-hubbing 289–290, 297–298; literature review 290–291; impact on local development 291–297
airport freight **166**
airports *33*, *53*, *89*; activities at *162*, **235**, *236–237*, **239**, *240*; airport size and cost per passenger *73*; Belgium 224–230, *225*; in Bosnia and Herzegovina 163, *165*; Bulgaria 147–149; climate and the

environment 45–46; correlations across input and output data for **212**; destination cities and Business Connectivity Index **75**; direct jobs at **40**; economic effects and impacts 37–40, **39**, **109**, *192*; economic importance 241–243; and government policies 79–81; impacts in geographical peripheries 26, 28–29, 31–37, 41–47; intangible catalytic effects **192**; main airlines *70*; operating margin *69*; ownership of 64–68, **66–67**, 224–226; passenger numbers *68*, *71*, **90**, **135**; privatisation of 64–68; profitability 37–40; regional accessibility 31–37; regional connectivity 74–77; and regional economic development 41–42; and regional social development 43–45; stakeholders *111*; Swiss **197**, **206**; traffic and financial performance 68–74, **73**; traffic growth 163; travel time to *34*, **91**; UK 64–82; vector error correction model for **156**; *see also* airport activities; airport de-hubbing; international airports; London Heathrow Airport; national airports; ownership; regional airport business models; structures; *and specific airports*
Airports Council International 86–88, *192*
air routes 79, 92, 130, 136; international 163, *165*; Oporto Airport *256*
air sector: Spain 268, 271–272
air traffic: Bosnia and Herzegovina 160–167; data and historical considerations 51–54; in Finland 50–61; and Granger causality 59–61; statistical properties of the data 54–56; UK

Index   301

regional airports 68–74, **73**; and the vector error correction model 57–59

air traffic control 2, 166–167, 196, **197–198**, 199

air transport development 161–162

air transport markets: analysis of 137–139; CEE countries 121–141, **138**; and the process of transformation and integration 126–137

air travel 36–38, *37*, 174–175

algorithm 150–151, *151*, 155

Antunes, António Pais xiii, 4

aviation: employment **242**; importance of regional and national planning policies 108–110; Ireland 88–91; value added **243**

aviation connectivity measurement 9–10

Barcelona airport **281**, 286

bargaining power 102–103

Belgium 223–224, *225*, 246–247; airports in 224–230; cargo traffic **229**, **230**; economic effects of air transport and airport industry 234–241; economic importance of airports 241–246; methodology 230–234; passenger numbers *227*, **228**; *see also* Brussels Airport

Betancor, Ofelia xiii, 4

Bilotkach, Volodymyr xiii, 51, 251

Bosnia and Herzegovina 160–167, *165*; airport freight **166**; airport passengers in **164**; development of air transport in **161**; traffic growth 163

Brexit 100

Brussels Airport **245–246**; noise development 243–246

Bulgaria 145–147; data and methods 149–152; overview of airports in 147–149; results and discussion 152–157

Burgas Airport 148, 152, *153*

business aviation operators 199

Business Connectivity Index (BCI) 75–76, **75**

Business Model Canvas 95–98, *96*

business models *see* Business Model Canvas; regional airport business models

buyers 102

Buyle, Sven xiv, 4

Calderón, Enrique J. xiv

cargo traffic 229–230; Belgian airports *229*, **230**

causality analysis 145–147; data and methods 149–152; results and discussion 152–157

causality models 150

causality tests 155–157

causal relationships 3, 57, 156–157, **156**

causal two-variable model 150–151, *151*

CEE countries *see* Central and Eastern Europe

Central and Eastern Europe 121–124, 139–141; air passengers by airport **135**; air transport **128**; air transport markets 137–139; convergence path *125*; core regions **21**; economic performance 124–126, **125**; growth of air transport in *129*; LCCs in low-cost markets **132**; main airlines **131**; the process of transformation and integration of 126–137; SWOT analysis of air transport markets **138**

centrality index 31–32, *32*

central planned economies 127, **127**

charges 270–272

climate 45–46

cointegration test 155

competence effects 193

connectivity 6–7, *10*, *15*, 17–23; best-connected regions **22**; data and methods 9–12; empirical evidence 13–17; literature review 7–9; maps *18–19*; NUTS 2 **14**; and passenger numbers **36**; remote regions **20**; and seats **16**; *see also* regional connectivity

convergence path *125*

core regions 6–9, 13, 16–17, **21**, 22; identification of 10–12

cost: per passenger at airports 72–73, *73*

daily flights 249, 254; Oporto Airport *256*

data 51–54, 210–213, 266–272; airport passenger data 149; economic growth 149–150; statistical properties of 54–56

de-hubbing *see* airport de-hubbing

destination 75–76, **75**, 186–187, *186*

direct economic effects *192*, 203, 223, 231, 234–241

disaggregate accounts: Spain air transport **279**; Spain maritime transport **283**; Spain railway transport **277–278**; Spain road transport **275**

Dumitrescu and Hurlin 60, **60**

econometric model 254–258

econometric study 249–251; model for 254–258; and the Norte Region 251–252; and Oporto Airport 252–254; results 258–262

economic development: Bosnia and Herzegovina 160–167; regional 41–45

302   Index

economic effects 190–192, *192*; direct *192*, 203, 223, 231, 234–241; indirect 146, 172–172, *192*, 223–224, 233–241; *see also* spatial economic effects

economic growth: Bulgaria 146–147, 149–150, 157

economic impact assessment: Shannon Airport/Group 107–108

economic impacts: classification of *232*; Ireland **109**; Norway 37–40, **39**; and passenger expenditure 171–173; of Shannon Group **108**

economic importance: Belgium 223, 241–243; noise development 243–246

economic performance: CCE countries 124–126, **125**

efficiency benchmarking 203–205, 216–217; background 205–206; data 210–213; model 209–210; previous studies 206–208; results 213–21

Efthymiou, Marina xiv, 3, 86, 111

empirical evidence 13–17

empirical results 152–157

employment: Belgium 238–240, **239**, 241–242, *240–241*, **242**, 246–247; Milan 294–298, **295**; Portugal 250–251, 257–258; *see also* jobs

environment, the 45–46

environmental costs 265, 269–270

estimates 266–272

estimation method 257–258

expenditure 173–175, *179*, *186*; classification of tourism and air transport passengers 170–171; methodology 177–178; passenger **183–185**; and purpose of journey **185**; research results 178–186; in studies concerned with the economic impact of air transport 171–173; and tourism development 173–175; Wroclaw airport 170, 174–188

exports 282–285, **294**, 297–298

financial performance: UK regional airports 68–74, **73**

financial ratios: Shannon Group 97, **98**

Finavia 52–53, *53*, 88

Finland 50–51, *53*, 61; data and historical considerations 51–54; Granger causality 59–61; statistical properties of the data 54–56; vector error correction model 57–59

Fisher test 152, **156**

Five Forces model 100–105, *101*

freight service (railway transport) 271, 273–274, **277**, 284

Freiria, Susana xiv, 4

geographical peripheries 3, 26–28, 46–47; case study area in Norway 29–31; climate and the environment 45–46; impacts of airports in 28–29, 31–37; and profitability of airports 37–40; and regional economic development 41–42; and regional social development 43–45

Glasgow Prestwick 103–105; key characteristics **104**

government policies 79–81

Graham, Anne xiv, 50, 71, 74, 87

Google Maps 34

Granger causality 59–61, **60**

gross value added (GVA) 252–254, *253*, 257–261, **260–261**

Halpern, Nigel xiv–xv, 3, 35, 41, 51, 71, 74

Haralampiev, Kaloyan xv, 3

hard intangible factors 194

headwinds: Shannon Airport 105–107, **105**

Hiney, Noel xv, 3

historical considerations 51–54; Shannon airport 91–92

Huderek-Glapska, Sonia xv, 3

image effects 194

indirect economic effects 146, 172–172, *192*, 223–224, 233–241

industry rivalry 103

inefficiencies 206–210, 213–217; in central planned economies 127, **127**

infrastructure costs 265, 266–268

infrastructure fees 265

intangible catalytic effects **192**, 194–195, 200

intangible effects of regional airports 190, **197**, 200–201; background and literature 190–191; location choice 194–196; qualitative analysis 196–200; typology 191–194

integration: CEE countries 126–137

international accessibility 289, *293*, 297

international airports 204–206, 210–217

investments 50, 52, 55, 56, 58, **58**, 61

IPS (Im, Pesaran and Shin) test 150–152, 154–155, **155**

Ireland: aviation industry 88–91; economic impact assessments **109**; key airports *89*; passenger numbers **90**; travel time **91**

jobs 31, 39–40, **40**, 42

Kansikas, Carolina xv, 4
Kupfer, Franziska xv–xvi, 4

labour market 123, 160, *296*; *see also*
  employment; jobs
length of visit 182–183, **183**
literature review 7–9, 150, 152, 290–291, 295
local development: and airport de-hubbing
  291–297
location choice 194–196, **196**
location theories 194–195, *195*
London Heathrow Airport *78*; issues 78–79
low-cost carriers (LCCs) 7, 9, 13–17,
  16, 20–23, **20–21**; in CEE countries
  127–129, 132–135, **132**
low-cost markets 132, **132**
Lower Silesia region 170, 175, 182–187, **184**

Madrid airport **280**
Malpensa airport 291–296, *292*
maps 11–12, *12*, 17–19, *18–19*, 52–53,
  53; Google Maps 34
maritime transport 268, 272, 276, **283**
Martini, Gianmaria xvi, 2
measurement: aviation connectivity 9–10
methodologies 177–178, 230–234, 266–272
Milan 289–290, 297–298; international
  accessibility *293*; literature review
  290–291; and local development
  291–297
model formulation 257
Morgenroth, Edgar xvi, 3
movements 244–254, *244*

national airports 140, 190–193, 196–200,
  197–198, 204–205
national planning policies 108–110
network effects 193
new entrants 102
Niemeier, Hans-Martin xvi, 217
noise development 243–246
Norte Region 249–252, *252–253*, 262; and
  econometric model 254–258; Oporto
  Airport 252–254; study results 258–262
Norway 26, *37*, 46–47; airports and their
  impacts 28–29, 31–37, *33*; case study
  area 29–31; climate and the environment
  45–46; economic impact of airports **39**;
  geographical peripheries 26–27; jobs **40**;
  profitability and their economic impacts
  37–40; regional accessibility 31–37;
  regional economic development 41–42;
  regional social development 43–45
Noto, Claudio xvi, 4

Nurković, Rahman xvi–xvii, 4
NUTS 2 9–10, 13–15, **14**, *15*
NUTS 3 51–53, *53*, 59

Olipra, Łukasz xvii, 4
Onghena, Evy xvii, 4
operating margins 68–69, *69*, **73**
Oporto Airport 249, 252–254, *255*, 262;
  econometric model 254–258; and the
  Norte Region 251–252; study results
  258–262
ordinary least-squared (OLS) method
  257–258, 262, **295**
Ortuño, Armando xvii, 4
ownership 64–68, **66**, 87–88; Belgium
  224–226; group/fund **67**; Shannon
  Airport 92–93

panel cointegration testing 152, **156**
panel unit-root testing 150–152, 154–155
passenger numbers *68*, 70–78, *71*; Belgian
  airports 226–228, *227*, **228**; domestic
  connections **36**; Irish airports 86–92, **90**;
  Wroclaw airport *176*
passenger service (railway transport) 274,
  277, 284, 286
passenger traffic 55–61, **58–59**, 226–229
Pedroni cointegration 56, **56**, 59–60
Percoco, Marco xvii–xviii, 5, 51, 250, 290,
  292–295
peripherality 29–31; *see also* geographic
  peripheries
policies: government 79–81; impacts
  of 110; national planning 108–110;
  regional planning 108–110
population 244–246, *244*
Porta, Flavio xviii, 2
Portugal 249–251; econometric
  model 254–258; Norte Region
  251–252; Oporto Airport 252–254;
  study results 258–262
privatisation 64–68
production 56, 58–59, **59**, 61
production companies 195–196, **196**
profitability 37–40
purpose of journey 181–182, **181**, **185**, *186*

qualitative analysis 196–200

railway transport 267–268, 271, 273–276,
  276–278
regional accessibility 31–37
regional airport business models 86–87,
  113–115; airport industry 91–92;

304   *Index*

airport ownership and structures 87–88; aviation industry in Ireland 88–91; Business Model Canvas 95–98; Five Competitive Forces analysis 100–105; planning policies 108–110; Shannon Airport current focus 112–113; Shannon Airport economic impact assessment 107–108; Shannon Airport ownership 92–93; Shannon Airport policy impacts 110; Shannon Airport strategic position 94–107; Shannon Group structure 93–94; Shannon group summary and current performance 105–107; stakeholder engagement 111; SWOT analysis 98–100

regional airports: background and literature 190–191; intangible effects 190–201; location choice 194–196; qualitative analysis 196–200; Swiss 203–206, 210–216; typology 191–194; *see also* regional airport business models

regional air transport connectivity 6–7, **16**, 17–23, *18–19*; data and methods 9–12; empirical evidence 13–17; literature review 7–9

regional companies 199–200

regional connectivity 74–77; *see also* regional air transport connectivity

regional development 50–51; data and historical considerations 51–54; Granger causality 59–61; statistical properties of the data 54–56; the vector error correction model 57–59

regional economic development 41–42

regional economy 169–170, 186–188; classification of tourism and air transport passengers 170–171; development 41–42; methodology 177–178; passenger expenditure 171–173; research results 178–186; visitor expenditure and tourism development 173–175

regional planning policies 108–110

regions *see* core regions; geographical peripheries; regional air transport; remote regions

remote regions 6–9, *12*, 13, **14**, 15–17, **20**, 22–23; identification of 10–11

revenue *see* aeronautical revenues; revenue analysis

revenue analysis **98**

Ringbom, Staffan xviii, 3

road transport 267, 270, 273–274, **274–275**

Scotti, Davide xviii, 2

seats 13–17, **14**; evolution in the number of 20–22, **20–21**; FSCs **16**; LCCs **16**, **20–21**

Shannon Airport 91–94, *96*, *101*; broader issues 107–113; Business Model Canvas 95–98; current focus 112–113; Five Competitive forces analysis 100–105; headwinds and tailwinds **105**; history 91–92; ownership 92–93; policy impacts 110; strategic position 94–107; strategic summary and current position 105–107; SWOT analysis 98–100, **99**

Shannon Group 91–99, 106, 109–111, 114–115; economic impact assessment 107–108, **108**; key characteristics **104**; key financial ratios **98**; revenue analysis **98**; structure 93–94

Sofia Airport 147–148, 152–153, *153*

soft intangible factors 194

Spain 264–266, 284–286, **285**; accident costs 268–269; accounts general framework **273**; air transport accounts 276, **279–282**; environmental costs 269–270; infrastructure costs 266–268; maritime transport accounts 276–283, **283**; railway transport accounts 274–276, **276–277**; road transport accounts 273–274, **274–275**; taxes, tolls, charges, and subsidies 270–272; transport accounts 272–283

spatial economic effects 289–290, 297–298; impact on local development 291–297; literature review 290–291

special taxes 265

stakeholders *111*; engagement of 111; Swiss regional airports **197**

statistics 54–56, **55**, **154–156**, **259**

stochastic frontier analysis (SFA) 204, 206, 213, 220–222

strategic position of Shannon Airport 94–95; Business Model Canvas 95–98; Five Competitive Forces analysis 100–105; strategic summary and current performance 105–107; SWOT analysis 98–100

Strengths, Weaknesses, Opportunities, and Threats (SWOT) analysis 98–100; air transport markets in CEE countries **138**; Shannon airport **99**

structural effects 193–194

structures 87–88; Shannon Group 93–94

subsidies 265, 270–272

substitutes 102

Index   305

suppliers 102–103
Switzerland 190, 200–201, 203–205, 216–217; background 190–191, 205–206; data 210–213; international **206**; location choice 194–196; model 209–210; previous studies 206–208; qualitative analysis 196–200; regional airports **197**, **206**; results 213–215; typology 191–194
SWOT analysis *see* Strengths, Weaknesses, Opportunities, and Threats (SWOT) analysis

tailwinds **105**
taxes 265, 270–272
time intervals analysis 293–294, **294**
time saved *37*
time series 152–154
Todorova, Stela xviii, 3–4
tolls 265, 270–272
tourism: classification of 170–171; development of 173–175; representatives 200
transformation 126–137
transport accounts 272–283, **273**; air 276, **279–282**; maritime 276–283, **283**; railway 274–276, **276–277**; road 273–274, **274–275**
travel time 34–35, *34*, *37*, **91**
type of business (railway transport) 273, 274, **278**, 284
type of carrier 17, 182, *186*

type of journey *178*, **180**
type of vehicle (road transport) 265, 269–270, 273, **275**
typology 191–194

United Kingdom (UK) 64, 81–82; airports *68–71*, *73*, *78*; destination cities and Business Connectivity Index at regional airports **75**; government policies 79–81; group/fund ownership in **67**; London Heathrow issues 78–79; ownership and privatisation 64–68, **66**; regional connectivity 74–77; traffic and financial performance 68–74, **73**
United States 195–196, **196**
unit-root tests 55, **55**, 150–152, 154–155, **155**

value added 231–238, **235**, *236–237*, 241–243, **243**, 246–247
Varna Airport 147–149, 152–154, *154*
Vasallo, José Manuel xviii, 4
vector error correction model 57–59, **156**
visitor expenditure 173–175, 177

wage-rent curves *297*
Wittmer, Andreas xix, 4, 190–191
Wroclaw, City of 170, 175–177, 182, 185, 187
Wroclaw airport 170, 174, 178–179; characteristics of 175–177; passenger numbers *176*; passengers' expenditures **184**

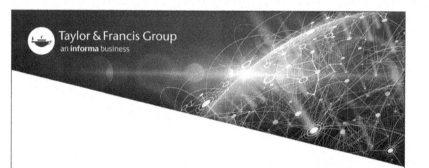